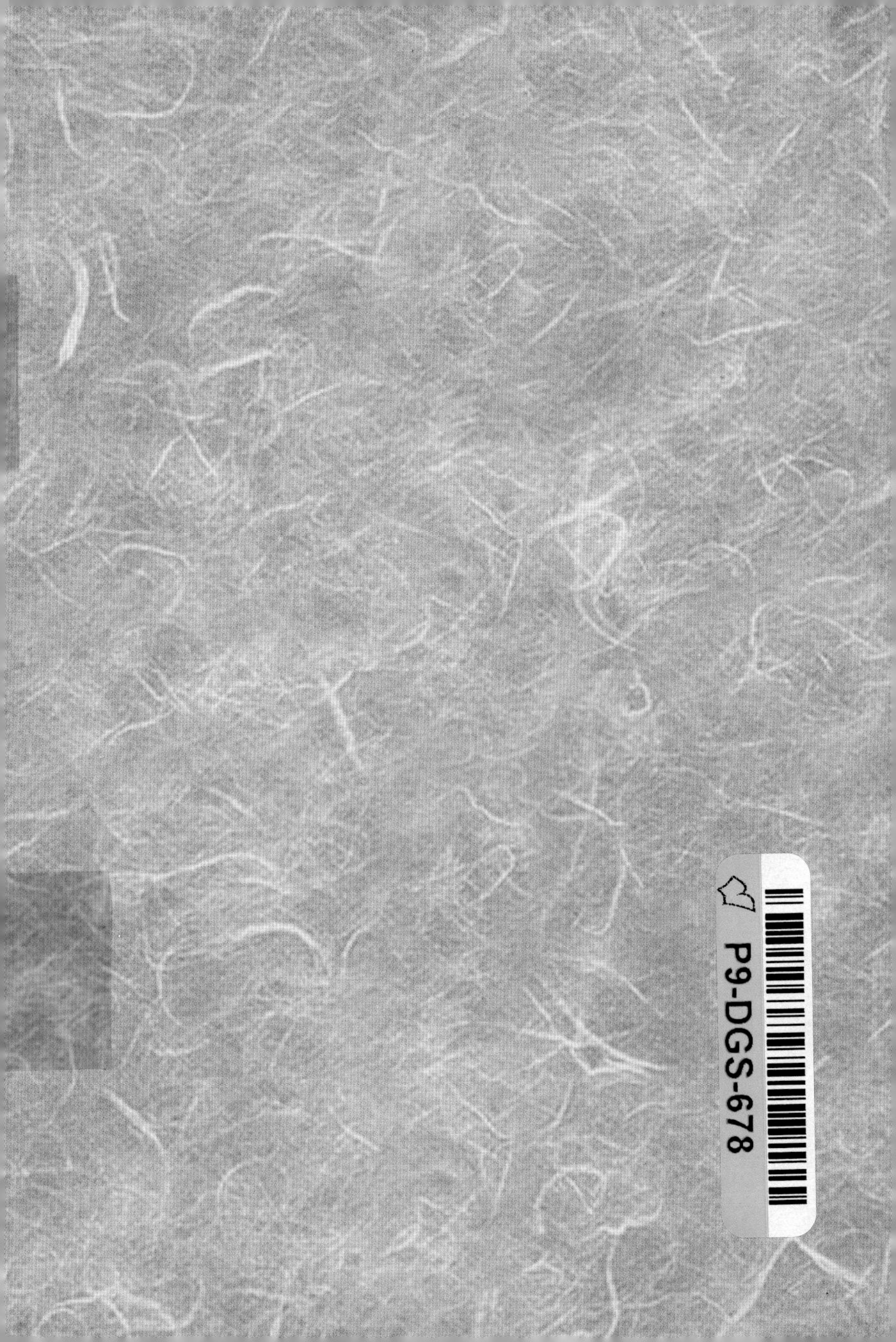
P9-DGS-678

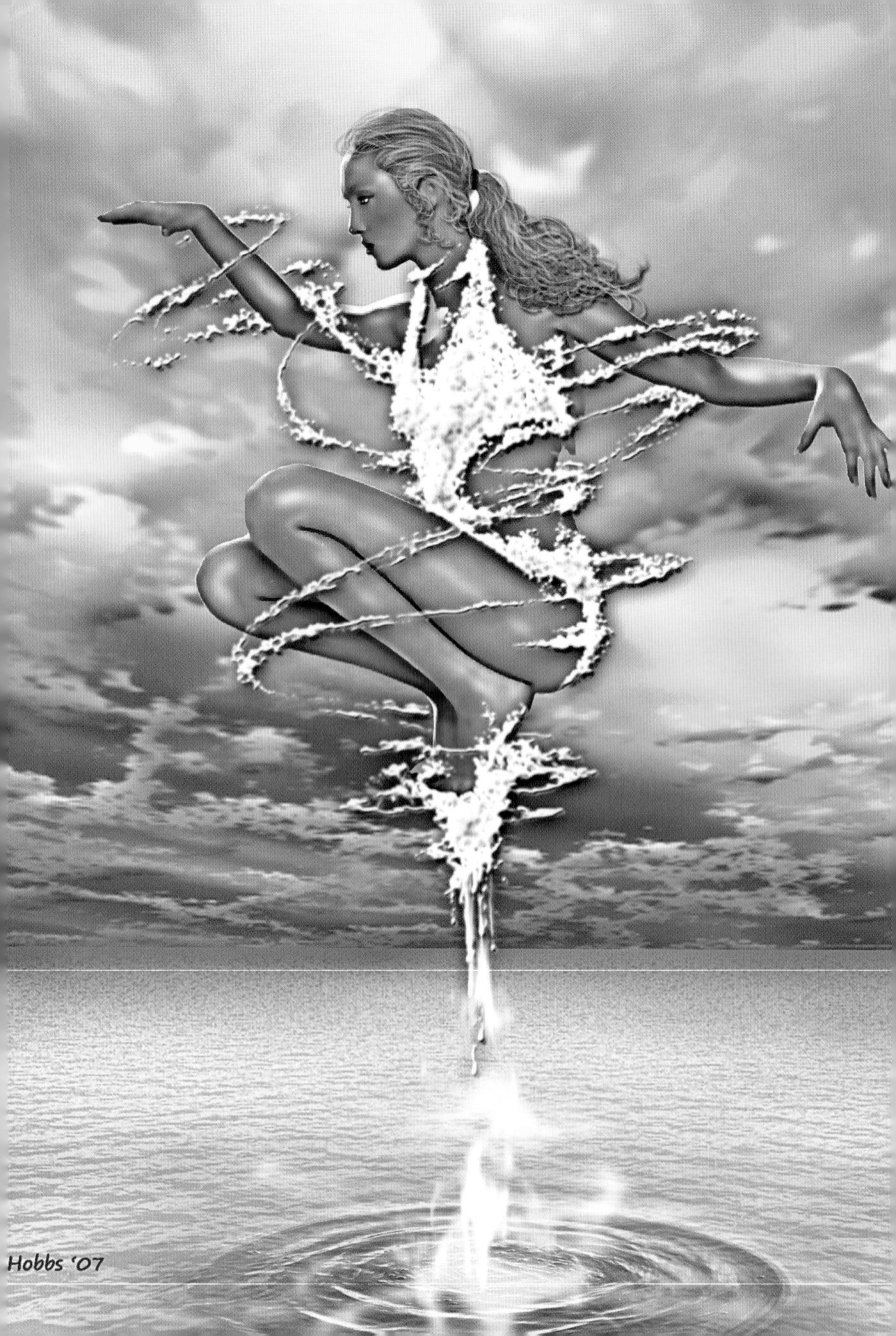
Hobbs '07

FANTASY ARTIST'S POCKET REFERENCE

phantastic faeries

BOB HOBBS

with Finlay Cowan, Artemis Kolakis, Julianna Kolakis, RK Post, Christopher Shy and Alain Viesca

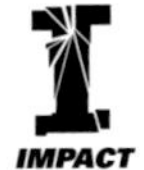

IMPACT

This book is dedicated to all those who believe in faeries. May the magic stay with you forever.

A DAVID & CHARLES BOOK

David & Charles is an F+W Publications Inc. company
4700 East Galbraith Road
Cincinnati, OH 45236

First published in the UK in 2008

A catalogue record for this book is available from the British Library.

ISBN-13: 978-1-60061-109-4 hardback
ISBN-10: 1-60061-109-5 hardback

Printed in China By Shenzhen Donnelley Printing Co Ltd for David & Charles
Brunel House, Newton Abbot, Devon

Senior Commissioning Editor: Freya Dangerfield
Editorial Manager: Emily Pitcher
Editor: Verity Muir
Project Editor: Ame Verso
Senior Designer: Jodie Lystor
Designer: Eleanor Stafford
Production Controller: Kelly Smith

Visit our website at www.davidandcharles.co.uk

David & Charles books are available from all good bookshops; alternatively you can contact our Orderline on 0870 9908222 or write to us at FREEPOST EX2 110, D&C Direct, Newton Abbot, TQ12 4ZZ (no stamp required UK only); US customers call 800-289-0963 and Canadian customers call 800-840-5220.

Contents

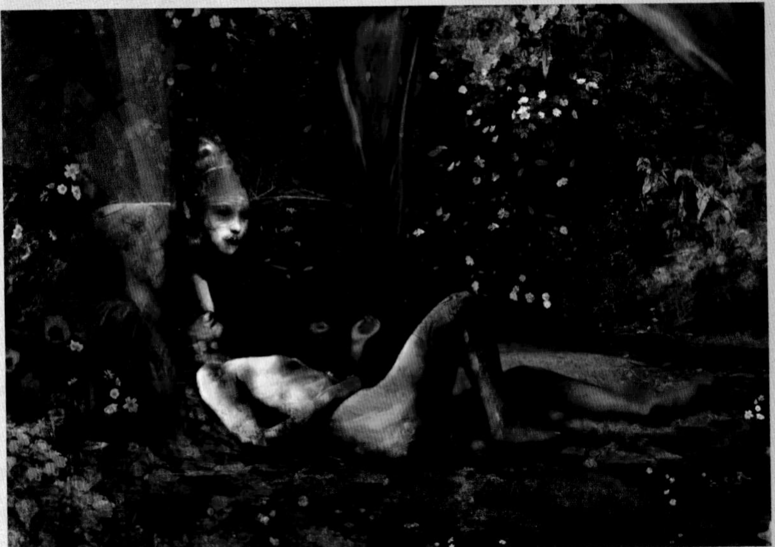

Introduction

There are no such things as faeries. They are figments of the imagination, the stuff of myths and legends, fanciful tales told to children or the visions of a delusional mind. Well, that's certainly one school of thought. However, for thousands of years mankind has lived side-by-side, whether knowingly or not, with the elusive beings that occupy the realm of Faerie, a place that lies somewhere between the heavens and Earth.

The book you hold in your hands exposes this mysterious world and showcases a collection of its colourful inhabitants. *Fantasy Artist's Pocket Reference: Phantastic Faeries* provides a basic understanding of faeries and serves as a gateway to further exploration by creatives who wish to incorporate the 'wee folk' into their artwork. In no way are the contents exhaustive, as the faerie world is inhabited by many thousands of creatures from nearly every culture on the planet. In fact, it was a very long and difficult task to select which few to include here.

This book looks at faeries of many kinds, from archetypal faerie creatures, to nature and domestic sprites, dark faeries, spirits from around the world, as well as modern-day faeries. Each spread includes a brief introduction to the faerie, its origin, type, physical characteristics, powers and personality. Included are developmental sketches to show how the image was created, pointers on its design, tips on media used and finally, several keywords that can be used for further research.

Realizing the unreal

Creating artwork from the imagination can be a difficult task. Most of the characters and locations that make up the fantasy domain do not exist in our physical world – at least not to the extent where you can just go and take photographs of them to use as reference. Fantasy artists therefore have to depend on the legends, myths and folk tales that were passed on orally, or occasionally written down, through the ages. As well as faerie tales there is also a wealth of illustrated material dating back centuries that can be used for inspiration.

Most of the faeries in this book have a history within their respective cultures, with fairly clear-cut descriptions of how they appear and behave. However, an artist does have some license to expand on what is already known; perhaps substituting colours, adjusting hairstyles, modifying clothing designs and so on. Like humans, faeries do not all look exactly alike so there is room for variation. The artists whose work appears in this book have let their imaginations guide them in the creation of their faerie characters; the aim of the book is to spark your creativity to produce weird and wonderful faerie artwork of your own.

Work ethic

Art is not generally something that one does on a whim or as a hobby merely to kill time. If you intend to be a professional artist, even in the fanciful world of fantasy and science fiction, time must be spent to create work that is the best you can possibly make it. Even enthusiastic amateurs want to see their work improve and develop. This means putting in long hours on minute details, redoing parts of an image to get it right or sometimes starting from scratch if the artwork is not satisfactory.

Many people do not see art as a skill that requires years of study and practice. As it's an enjoyable pursuit and most people can draw to some extent, art is often dismissed and not taken seriously. However, just because it's fun, doesn't mean that it's not hard work and anyone wanting to better their creations needs to have a strong work ethic, and be prepared to put the hours in.

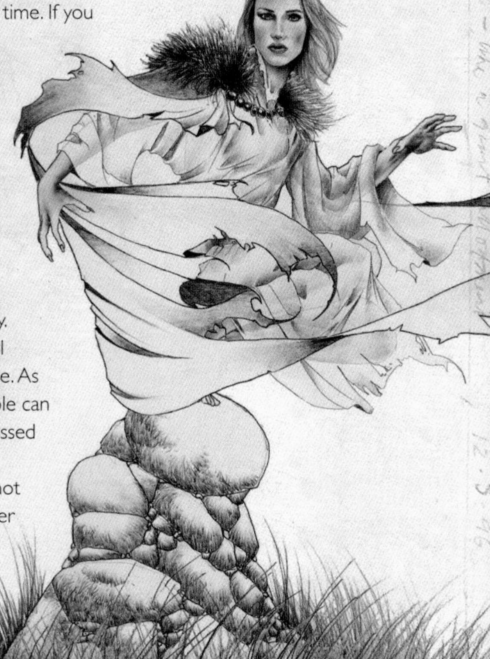

Stocking the shelves

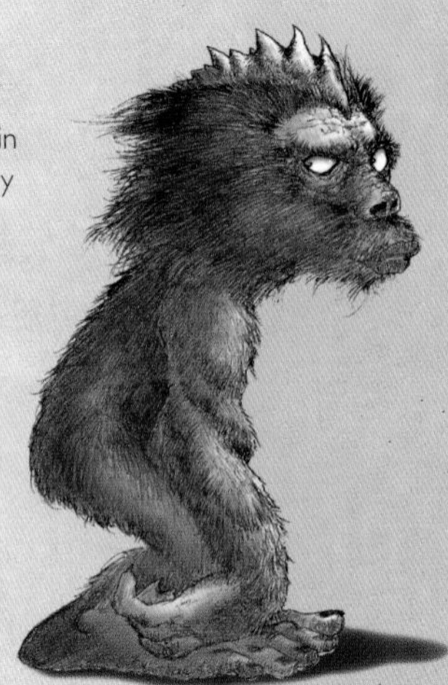

When creating any work of art, you should always begin with research. Look everywhere – from the local library to the bookshops to the Internet – for information that will aid you in your creative process. At first, your goal is only to find the data, collect it, organize it and store it. This should then be followed by a process of refinement where you weed out all the information that is redundant, unsubstantiated or just plain useless. Before long you will have a rich source of essential reference material that you can tap into as you create your artwork. Not only does this prevent you from making glaring mistakes that will be noticed by the viewing public, but it also feeds your imagination, stokes the fires of creativity and keeps you focused.

Personal experience

As an artist, you can't help but draw upon your own life experience to fuel your artistic vision. It's often done through your subconscious, as elements in your past, such as people you've known, places you've been and things you've done, will find their way into your work. If you look at the collected works of many well-known artists, you'll notice certain elements appear over and over again. Sometimes, such as in the case of Flemish painter Jan Vermeer, it seems that all of the paintings were done in the same room: the artist's studio. In the work of Pre-Raphaelite painter Lawrence Alma Tadema, you'll notice certain items of his personal furniture and décor appear repeatedly. Artist Alan Lee draws upon the lush forests that surround his home as inspiration for his fantasy worlds. Other artists might turn the pain of a past event into a work of art as a form of catharsis, as author James O'Barr did with his Gothic graphic novel *The Crow*. Using your own experiences in your work is what can turn technically proficient yet cold and lifeless records of information into moving, poignant and emotionally vibrant works of art.

The 'dead file'

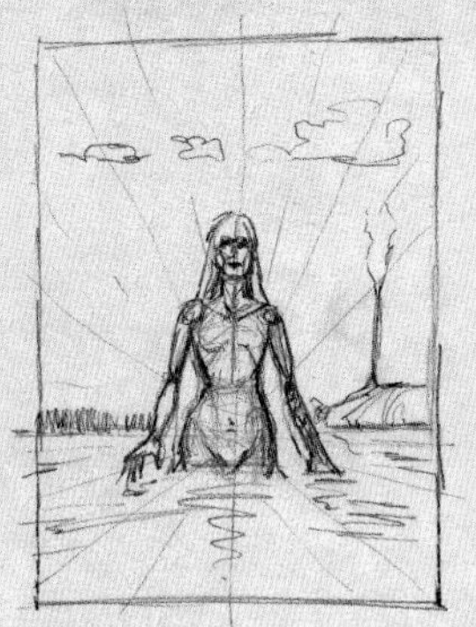

In art school, one of the first things students learn is how to create a dead file. This is a rather morbid name for what amounts to an ever-evolving reference file of images that an artist collects over the course of his or her career. Another term for it is a morgue file or clip art file. Organized in alphabetical or subject-matter order, these files contain photos, clippings and sketches of everything from apples to zebras. No artist, no matter how talented, can draw everything from memory. Sometimes you have to look something up in order to draw it accurately.

When it comes to fantasy art, your dead file should contain images of castles, forests, horses, birds, medieval clothing and tools, various types of dwellings and any other elements that you might find in a fantasy painting. There should be a heavy emphasis on historical items since most fantasy work, especially that which involves faeries, often comes from legends and myths from hundreds, if not thousands of years ago.

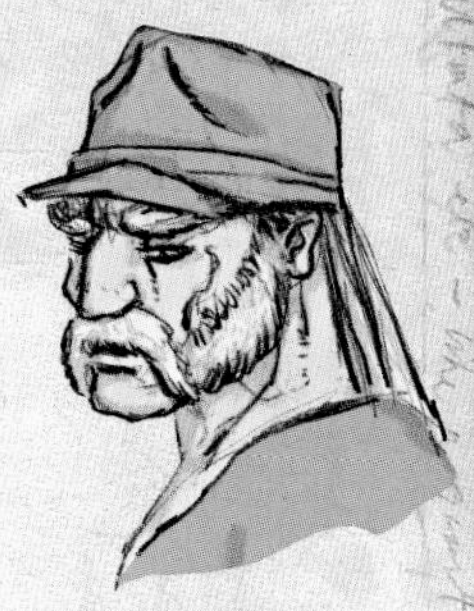

You can also use the work of other artists, both from the present and the past, as sources of reference for certain things, especially if the artists are well known for their accurate and detailed depictions. Many of the Pre-Raphaelite painters, for example, were meticulous in their highly realistic works of the old-world myths and legends.

Keeping your skills up

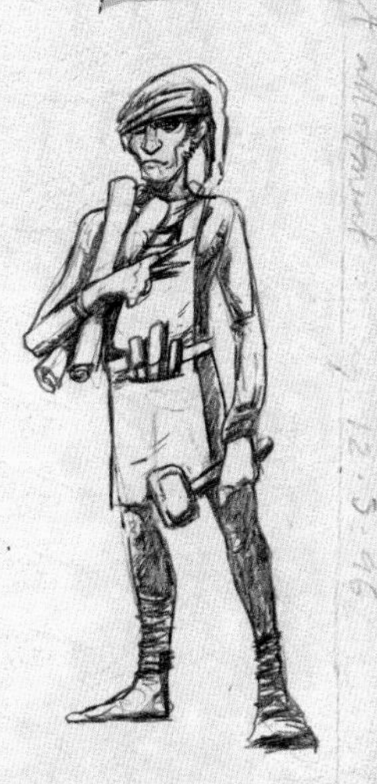

Being an artist is not a 9-to-5 job. It's a 24–7 commitment. You're always an artist even when you're not actively working on a piece. During the day, your mind is absorbing information, imagery and inspiration from the world around you, even though you're not aware of it all the time. You must keep your drawing and painting skills sharpened – don't think of it as a chore but rather as growth. The more you do it, the better you'll get, which is true of all things in life. Carry a small sketchpad and pencil around with you so you can jot down images and notes of whatever ideas come into your head as you go through your day. You can also use the sketchpad to practice your drawing skills and to keep your hands loose and your hand-eye coordination well oiled. If it's not practical for you to carry a sketchbook all the time, you should still try and draw something every day – even if it's just a little doodle. Ultimately your aim is for your art skills to become almost like breathing: completely fluid and effortless.

Equipment

There is a wide variety of equipment and tools available to the modern artist, but you don't need them all to create great work. You can produce amazing art with just a pencil and paper; or you can use an expensive custom-built graphics computer with the latest digital software. What you use is up to you, based on a combination of what works for you and what you can afford. Whatever tools you use, nothing can replace basic art skills. The important thing is to be able to create work both traditionally and digitally, making the best use of all the available tools.

Pencils, paper and ink

Quite possibly the cheapest art tools you can buy. Pencils are also the most basic, and are the tools that you should learn to draw with first. If you master them, you fulfil the basic foundation of being an artist. Every other tool you pick up builds upon what you learn at this stage. When it comes to choosing pencils, paper, pens and ink there's a virtual smorgasbord at your fingertips. You can order them from online sources, your local art supplier or even supermarkets that stock artists' supplies. If you've got the funds, you can spend quite a bit of money on high-quality tools, but it's really not necessary when first starting out. As you advance in your craft you may want to purchase the higher quality materials though.

Brushes and paints

Artists have been using brushes and paints for centuries. Most of the greatest works of art known to man are paintings. From Da Vinci's *Mona Lisa* to Waterhouse's *Lady of Shalott*, from Michelangelo's ceiling of the Sistine Chapel to Basquiat's graffiti-inspired canvases, paintings remain the mainstay of the fine arts and of the commercial arts too. The majority of fantasy artists today continue to work with brushes and paints despite the overwhelming popularity of computers. Painting does require a bit more training and discipline than pencils and pens, but don't let that intimidate you into not at least giving it a try.

Computers

I am a traditional artist by nature and training, and was at art school before the computer revolution invaded the world of art. At that time only a handful of artists were doing any sort of creative work with computers, and software such as Corel Draw and Adobe Photoshop wasn't even invented. However, I have since learned to use many of the graphics programs and now use them often in my work.

Today, there is a plethora of computer software on the market, which can help to create truly stunning artwork. Firstly, there are programs such as Corel Draw and Adobe Illustrator, which produce 'vector' art. This artwork is created using lines and coordinates, and is most useful for creating flat colour graphics that can be reproduced from the size of a postage stamp to the size of a football field with no loss of quality. Secondly, there are programs such as Adobe Photoshop and Paint Shop Pro, which create 'raster' art, made up of tiny dots called pixels. These programs are much more painterly and can help to create realistic digital paintings for print or the web. Thirdly, there is Corel Painter, a unique software package that can practically mimic the look

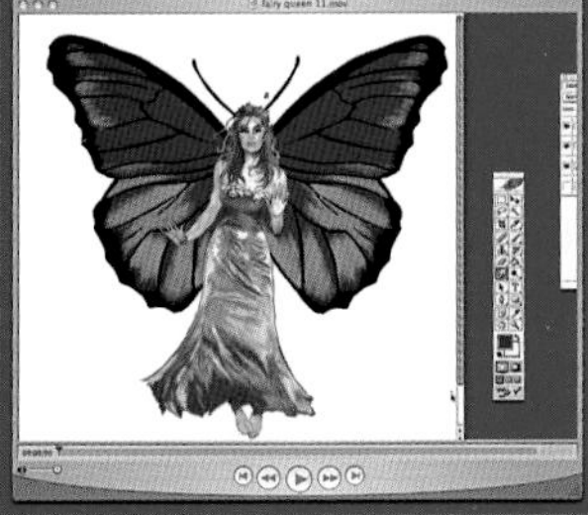

of real media when used with a high-end graphics tablet and pen, and can duplicate the textures of various media from pencil and ink to chalk and oil paint. And finally at the far upper end of the spectrum are the 3D programs such as 3D Studio Max, Maya, Cinema 4D and Lightwave. These programs produce the most realistic looking images and are the major tools used by movie studios to create the amazing special effects and animations you see on the big screen. These programs are also the most expensive, sometimes running into the thousands.

Despite the incredible things that a computer can do, the artist is ultimately in control of what comes out. Don't fall into the trap of letting the computer do all the work for you; it's simply another tool.

The artists and their media

Bob Hobbs

- *Traditional media*: pencils, crowquill pens and india ink, Rapidograph technical pens, Vidalon tracing vellum, Crescent hotpress illustration board.
- *Digital media*: Photoshop CS2, Poser 6, 3D Studio Max 8, Vue d'Esprit 4, Microtek flatbed scanner, Wacom Intuos 3 graphics tablet.

Finlay Cowan

- *Traditional media*: B and HB 0.9mm self-propelling pencils, rough and smooth 220gsm paper, Schminke watercolours, Muji propelling eraser.
- *Digital media*: Photoshop CS2, Sony Cybershot digital camera, Epson Perfection 1670 scanner, Wacom Intuos 3 graphics tablet.

Artemis Kolakis

- *Traditional media*: pencils.
- *Digital media*: Photoshop CS2, Painter X, Epson Stylus CX6000 scanner, Wacom Intuos 3 graphics tablet.

Julianna Kolakis

- *Digital media*: Photoshop CS2, Softimage XSI, Pixologic Zbrush, Autodesk Mudbox, Wacom Intuos 3 graphics tablet.

RK Post

- *Traditional media*: pencils, technical pens, oils, watercolour paper.
- *Digital media*: Photoshop CS2, Painter X, scanner, graphics tablet, printer, water-resistant archival inks.

Christopher Shy

- *Traditional media*: pencils, acrylic paints, inks, China markers, tempura, Canon AE-1 film camera.
- *Digital media*: Photoshop CS2, scanner, graphics tablet, printer.

Alain Viesca

- *Traditional media*: pencils, technical pens, brilliant white illustration paper.
- *Digital media*: Photoshop CS2, Zbrush 3, 3D Studio Max 9, Dell 968 multipurpose scanner, Wacom Cintiq 12WX.

What are Faeries?

Faerie (also Fairy, Fay, Fae or Fey) is the name given to a type of mythological supernatural being that occupies the limbo between Earth and heaven. There are those who believe that the faerie world exists totally apart from our world where they are the supreme rulers. Others subscribe to the belief that they exist in our world but are on a different astral plane, which explains why we can't see them unless we truly believe in them. According to legends, faeries have existed alongside mankind for thousands of years and often interacted with humans. But over the ages, mankind's fading belief in the hidden world has rendered faeries invisible to all but those who are most sensitive and perceptive to their presence.

Although most of what we Westerners know about faeries comes from European myths and folklore, tales of faerie-like beings are universal. From the Fylgiar of Iceland and the Peri of Persia to the Chin Chin Kobakama of Japan and the Abatwa of Africa, faeries have always been the stuff of fantastic tales told around the world.

Classes of faeries

Unknown to many, faeries include other creatures such as Gnomes, Brownies, Dwarves, Leprechauns, Banshees and many more that are often considered separate entities from faeries. In reality these other beings are simply names by which faeries are known in various countries. Brownies are English and Scottish, Elf is German, Dwarf is Teutonic, Troll is Norse and so on.

In general, faeries can be grouped into four classes:

1. Enchanters – creatures with supernatural powers.
2. Demons – dark creatures that have a connection to faeries or share similar characteristics.
3. Nature faeries – such as water sprites, tree spirits and flower faeries.
4. Faerie people – or 'True Faeries' are a race of human-like beings but not fully substantial or real, ordinarily invisible, moving silently, living underground in caves or mounds.

These categories can be broken down even further. For example, in the case of nature faeries, there are spirits associated with each of the four elements – air, water, Earth and fire – each with their own particular characteristics.

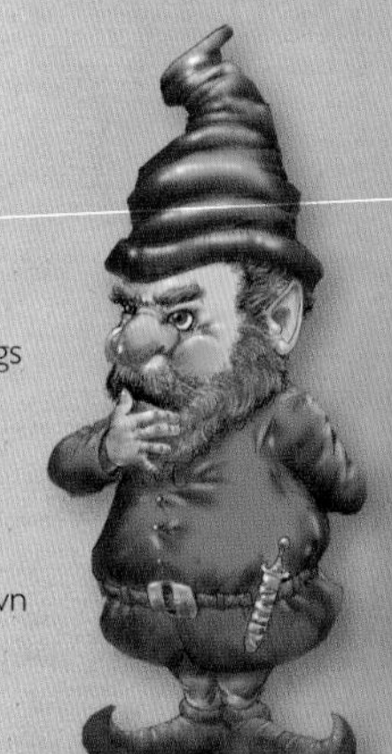

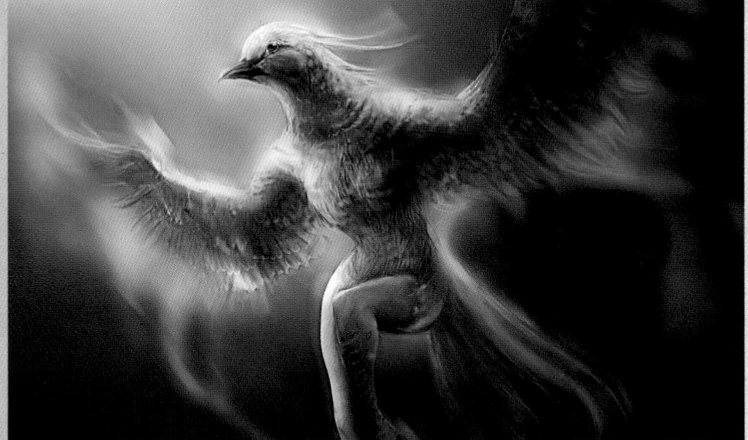

Appearance

Faeries have a very wide variety of physical characteristics from small, fragile beings with tiny gossamer wings, to large, lumbering ill-tempered brutes with shaggy hair. According to most ancient legends, faeries did not have wings. The notion of them being winged stems from Shakespeare's play *A Midsummer Night's Dream* and that concept lingers to this day. Some faeries don't appear very human-like, some shape-shift and some have no physical form at all. They can be male or female, beautiful or ugly, small enough to dance on the head of a pin or the size of giants in whose lap grown men would seem like infants.

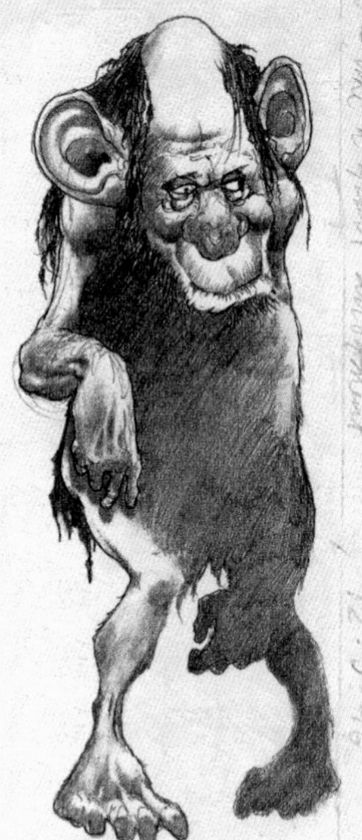

Characteristics

Most of the myths and folklore surrounding faeries suggests that mankind spent a good deal of time avoiding them and protecting themselves from their malice through a variety of charms: amulets, herbs, magic or simply staying away from places where faeries were known to frequent. Faeries were thought to kidnap babies and substitute them with changelings, steal things, play pranks and malicious tricks and abduct the elderly. Often easily offended, there were very specific prescribed methods of approaching them, communicating with them and appeasing them. But at other times faeries could be quite kind and helpful to humans.

Sources of faerie legends

Arthurian Legends – King Arthur's half-sister was Morgan Le Fay, whose connection to faeries is revealed in her name. Morgan was a faerie who changed into a human woman, learning magic and sorcery from Merlin, who was also half-human and half-incubus.

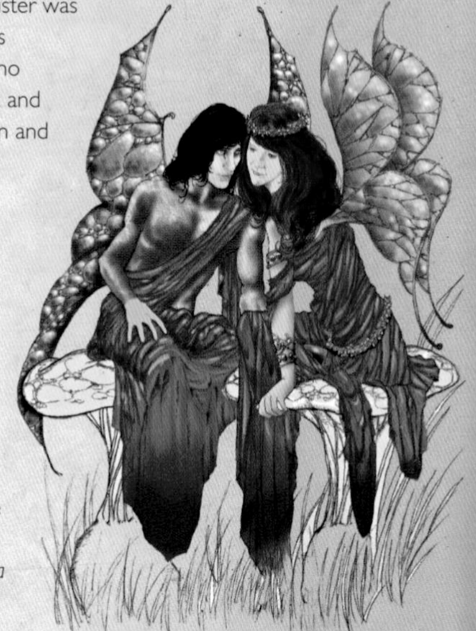

William Shakespeare

Faeries play a significant role in the comedy *A Midsummer Night's Dream*, in which we find Oberon, Titania and Puck, as well as other faeries such as Peaseblossom, Cobweb, Moth and Mustardseed. *The Tempest* also features an air spirit known as Ariel.

The Brothers Grimm

Over 240 traditional Germanic folktales were collated in the first edition of *Grimms' Fairie Tales*, which included stories such as *Cinderella* featuring a Faerie Godmother, *Rumpelstiltskin* and *Snow White and the Seven Dwarves.*

Faerie origins

There are several theories on how faeries came into being:

- They are the dead or a subclass of the dead
- They are the inhabitants of purgatory
- They are an intelligent species distinct from humans and angels
- They are a class of demoted angels
- They are a class of devils or demons
- They are actual humans but of very small stature with supernatural powers
- They are a class of gods and goddesses

Whatever their true origins, you can see from this that there is much scope for interpretation and it is up to you as the artist to decide on the specific nature of every faerie you illustrate.

JRR Tolkien

The Lord of the Rings trilogy, *The Hobbit* and other works included faeries as major characters, such as Legolas the Elf.

JM Barrie

The famous story of *Peter Pan* the magical boy who never grows up and his adventures in Neverland with his tiny female winged companion, Tinkerbell.

Greek mythology

Replete with spirit beings, gods, goddesses and other creatures who have many of the same characteristics as faeries.

Faeries in popular culture

Faeries appear in many children's cartoons, films, video games, role-playing games and books. Two of the most enduring faeries were brought to life by Walt Disney: Tinkerbell and the Blue Fairy, who changed the puppet Pinocchio into a real boy.

Also worth looking at are:

- The children's show *Winx Club*
- The motion picture *Pans Labyrinth*
- The horror film *Darkness Falls*
- Games such as *Everquest*, *Legend of Zelda*, *Dungeons and Dragons*, and *Magic: The Gathering*

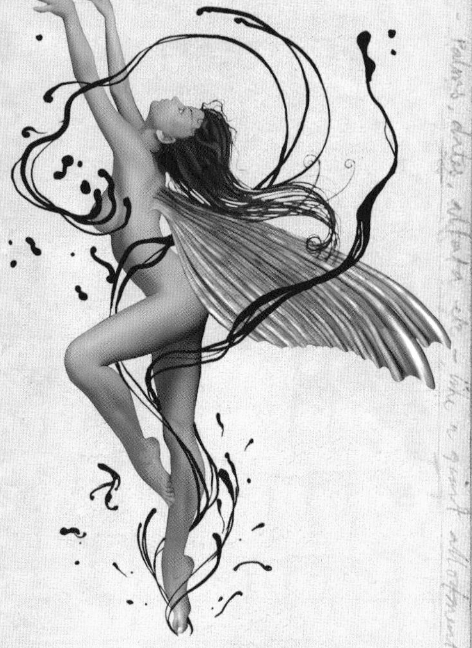

Faeries in art

There are numerous artists who are well known for their depictions of faeries. They include:

- Cicely Mary Barker
- Jasmine Becket-Griffith
- Amy Brown
- David Delamare
- Brian Froud
- Warwick Goble
- Anders Hansen
- Kylie InGold
- Alan Lee
- Arthur Rackham

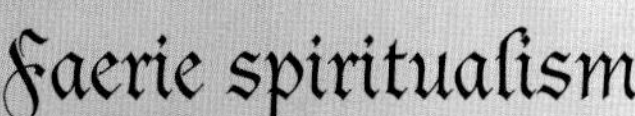

Faerie spiritualism

In modern times, the New Age movement and the rise in popularity of Pagan religions such as Wicca, have incorporated the belief in faeries into their traditions. The branch of Wicca known as Faerie Wicca is based on the first religious tradition of Ireland, which was of the Tuatha Dé Danaan, a Pagan oral tradition with the goddess Dana as the matron deity.

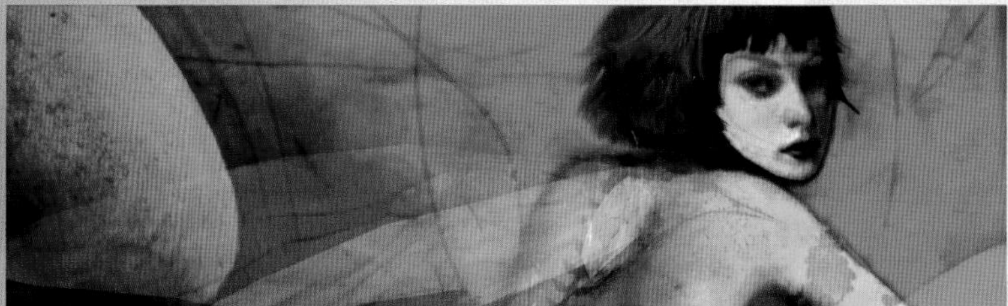

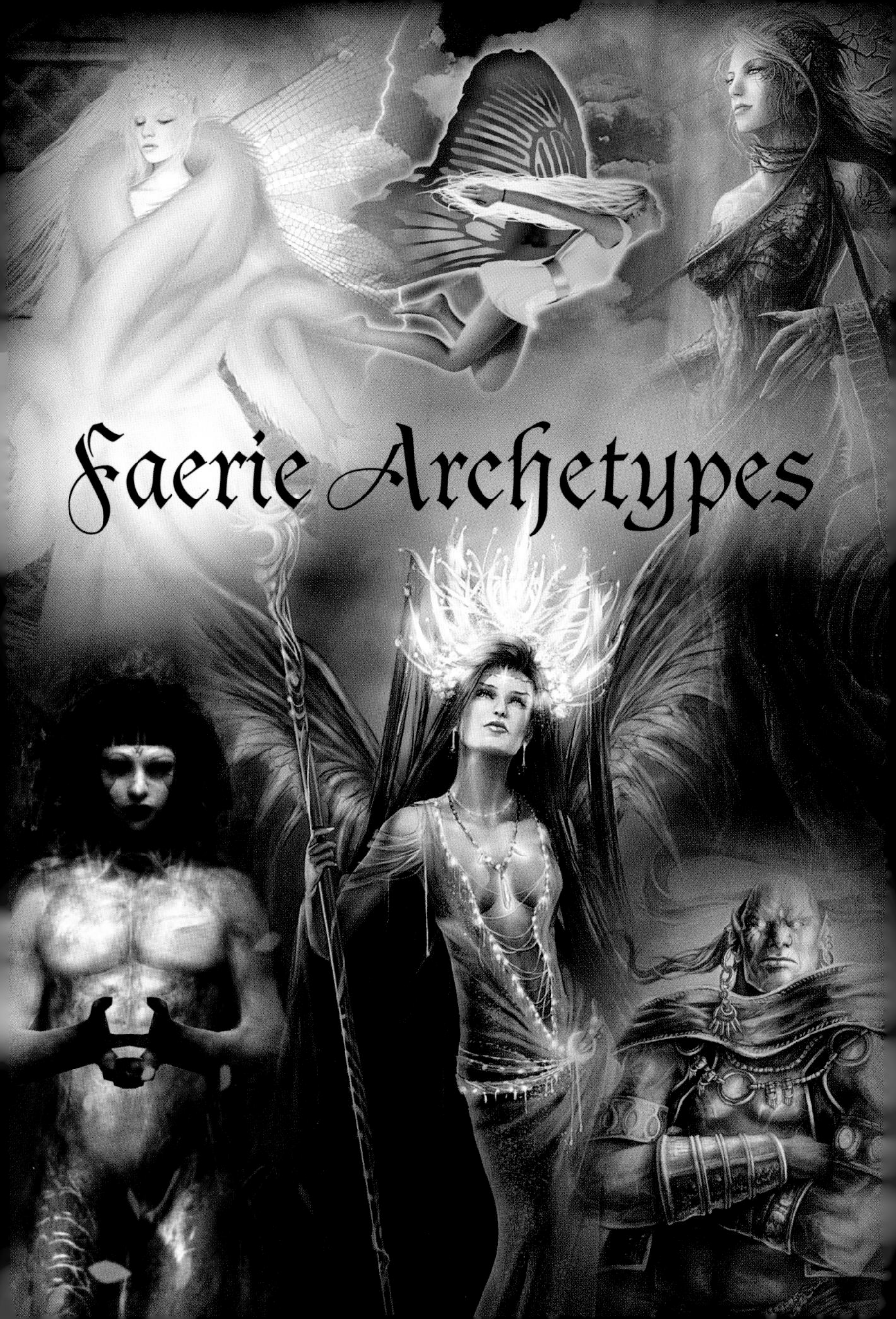
Faerie Archetypes

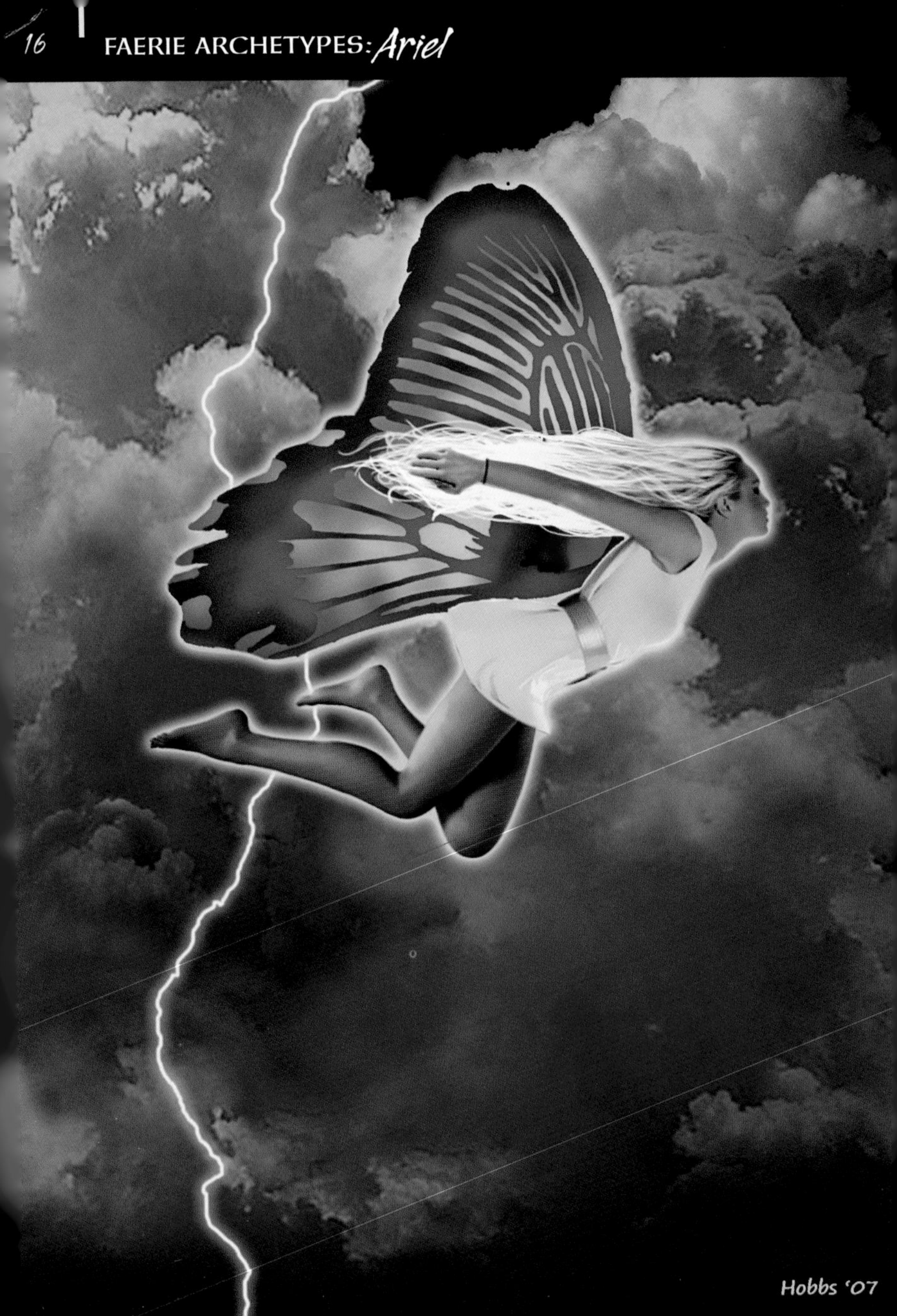
Hobbs '07

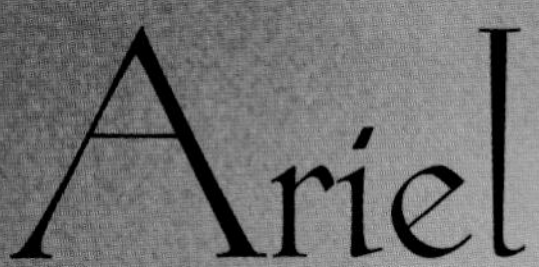

THE AIR SPIRIT KNOWN AS ARIEL FIRST APPEARED IN THE PLAY *THE TEMPEST* BY WILLIAM SHAKESPEARE. ARIEL IS FOREVER BOUND TO SERVE PROSPERO THE MAGICIAN AFTER BEING RESCUED BY HIM FROM A SPELL CAST BY SYCORAX THE WITCH. AMONG ARIEL'S POWERS IS THE ABILITY TO CONTROL THE WIND AND CREATE VIOLENT STORMS. SHAKESPEARE'S SOURCE FOR ARIEL IS UNKNOWN BUT SOME SPECULATE IT MAY BE FROM THE BOOK OF ISAIAH IN THE BIBLE. THE NAME MEANS 'LION OF THE LORD' IN HEBREW. ARIEL'S GENDER HAS NEVER TRULY BEEN DETERMINED ALTHOUGH THE PRONOUN 'HE' IS USED TWICE IN THE PLAY. HOWEVER, THE STAGE ROLE OF ARIEL WAS TRADITIONALLY PLAYED BY YOUNG BOYS, AND IS PERFORMED BY WOMEN IN MOST MODERN PRODUCTIONS.

Development

- Air spirits can usually fly so make sure you choose a pose that reflects this. Obviously you can't get a photograph of a live model flying, so you will need to use Poser software.
- Place your character on an appropriate background – as Ariel is able to control storms, a cloudy background was used with a streak of lightning for dramatic effect.
- Butterfly-like wings give a delicate feel, perfect for an air spirit.

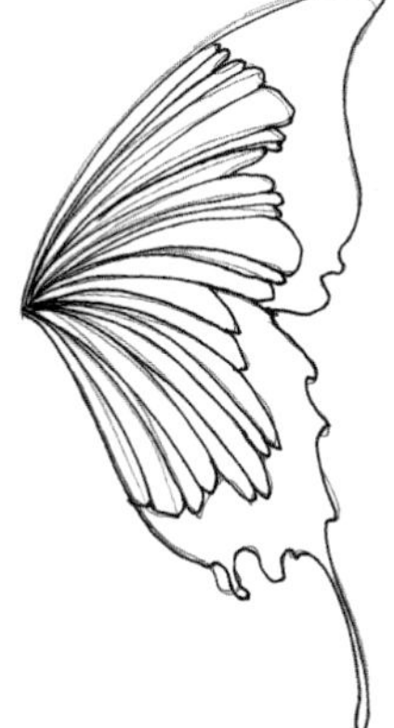

Media and Execution

- Photograph, pen and ink, Poser, Photoshop
- The pose was created in Poser and then merged with a photograph of a live model for the face, hair and clothing.
- An ink drawing of the wing was scanned into Photoshop, cleaned up and put in place.
- A stormy sky image was dropped on to the background layer. The lightning flash was drawn in and given a glow effect.
- Photoshop tools and effects were used to finalize the colourization.

FURTHER STUDY
William Shakespeare (playwright)
The Tempest, nature sprites, air spirits.

ART BOB HOBBS
MODEL KRISTEN PEOTTER

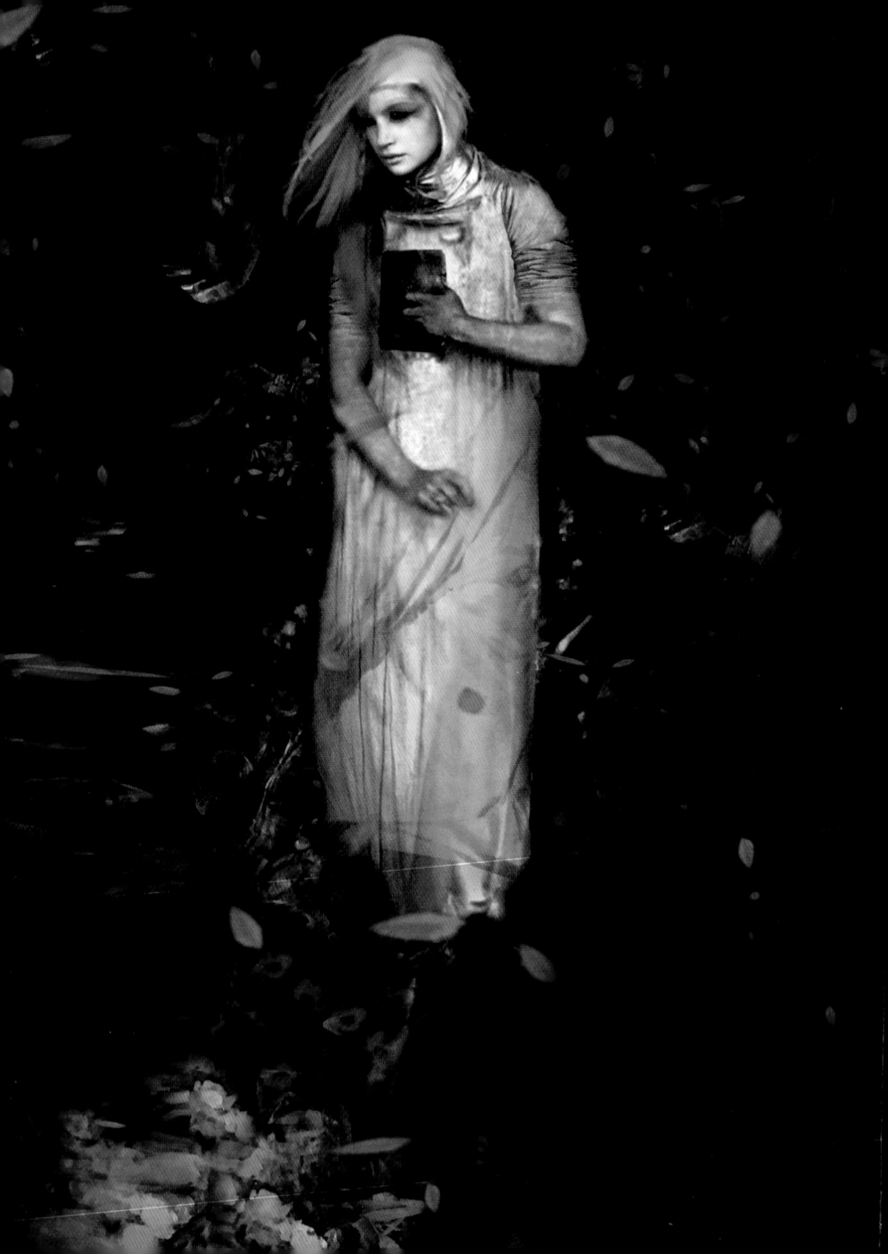

Banshee

THE WORD BANSHEE COMES FROM THE GAELIC *BEAN SIDE*, MEANING 'WOMAN OF THE FAERIE MOUND', OR 'WOMAN OF PEACE'. OFTEN CITED AS A MESSENGER FROM THE AFTERLIFE, AN ENCOUNTER WITH HER IS USUALLY SEEN AS AN OMEN OF DEATH. A BANSHEE IS SAID TO WAIL A SAD AND HAUNTING SOUND WHEN SOMEONE IN THE VICINITY IS CLOSE TO DEATH. THE BANSHEE'S ORIGINS GO BACK TO THE PRE-CHRISTIAN CELTIC DEITIES AND NATURE SPIRITS. SOME FAMILIES REPORTED HAVING A BANSHEE ATTACHED TO THEM, AS SHE COULD BE HEARD WAILING MOURNFULLY BEFORE EVERY DEATH IN THE FAMILY. IF NUMEROUS BANSHEES APPEAR TOGETHER, IT IS SAID TO SIGNIFY THE DEATH OF SOMEONE OF VERY HIGH STATUS.

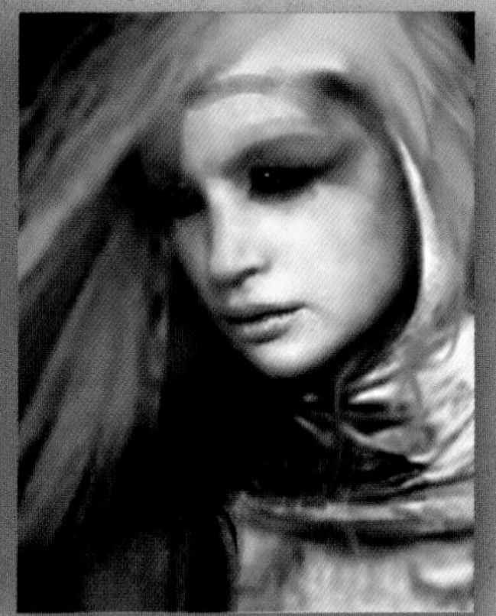

Development

• Using a very different palette and lighting scheme for your character than your background makes the faerie stand out and suggests they are more supernatural than natural. Here the Banshee is light and almost monochromatic, set against a dark, richly coloured background.

• Use unusual tones to create a feeling of unease in the viewer. The greenish hue of this Banshee's face creates a slightly disturbing air, and taps in to the sense of death and decay so crucial to this archetype.

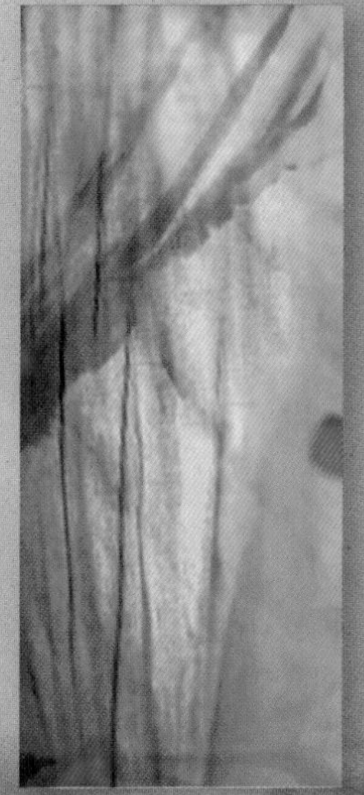

FURTHER STUDY
Bean Side, Bean Nighe, Gaelic folklore, Morrigan, keeners.

Media and Execution

• Pencil, Photoshop, acrylic paints
• A rough pencil sketch was scanned and opened in Photoshop.
• The painting was finished quickly in one sitting to avoid losing the feeling.
• The image was printed out and then painted over using acrylic paint to create the folds and creases in the fabric of her dress.
• It was then scanned back in to Photoshop be softened and colour corrected.

ART CHRISTOPHER SHY

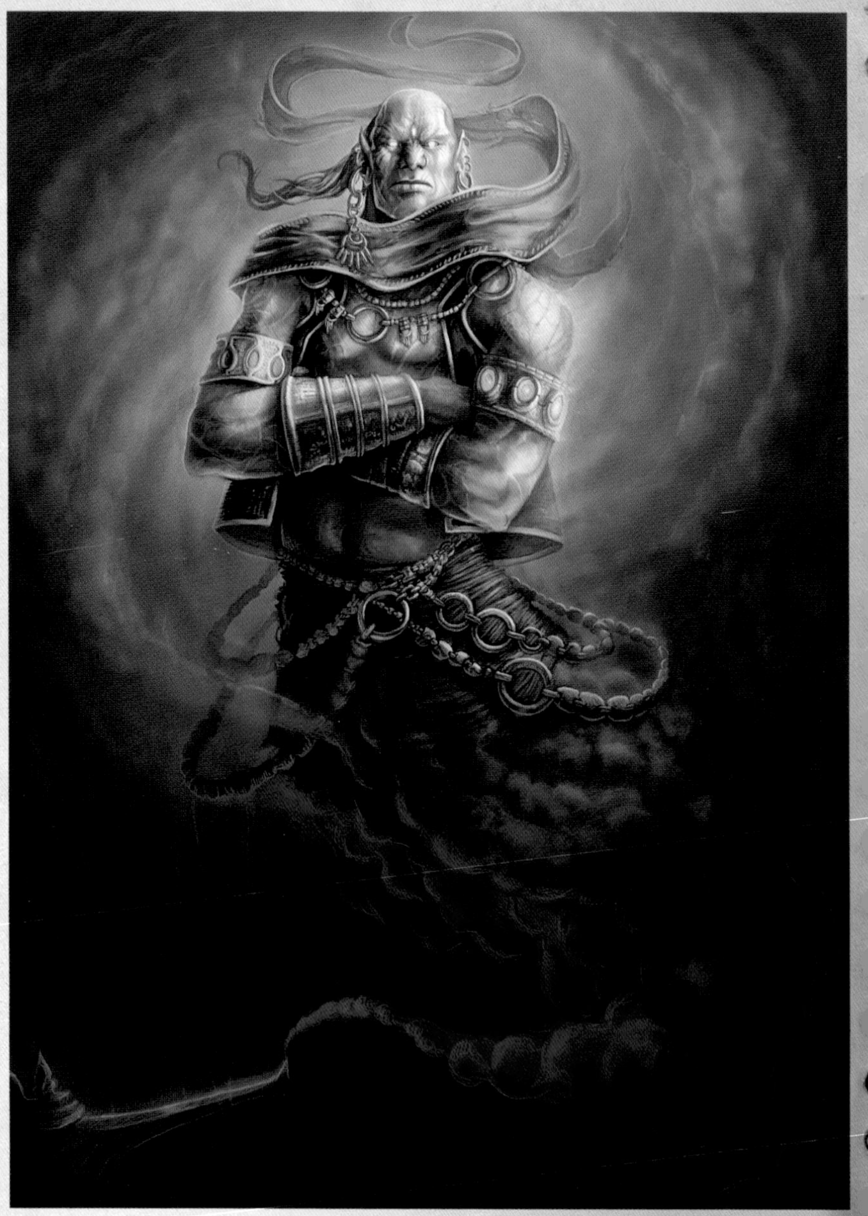

Djinn

APPEARING IN ISLAMIC MYTHOLOGY, DJINN ARE SHAPE-SHIFTING SPIRITS MADE OF SMOKELESS FIRE. THE NAME 'GENIE' IS A CORRUPTION OF DJINN. THEY SHUN DAYLIGHT AND MAKE THEIR HOME IS SMALL DARK PLACES SUCH AS OIL LAMPS. THEY AVOID SALT AND STEEL AND ARE AFRAID OF THE SOUND OF SINGING. DJINN ARE GENERALLY CONSIDERED TO BE MISCHIEVOUS AND DISRUPTIVE, AND WERE BELIEVED TO BRING ON DISEASE AND INSANITY. HOWEVER, THEY CAN SOMETIMES BE OF SERVICE TO HUMANS AND ARE SAID TO BE ABLE TO GRANT WISHES TO ANYONE CLEVER ENOUGH TO FIND THEM.

Development

- Designing a figure that materializes out of smoke is a careful balancing act; getting the right blend between solid and vapour should be the focus of your attention.
- Use facial expressions and powerful posturing to indicate a stern, immovable being, that is capable of bringing your deepest desires true, or twisting them into your worst nightmare.

FURTHER STUDY
Islamic texts, Ifrit, Marid, Genie, *The Book of One Thousand and One Nights.*

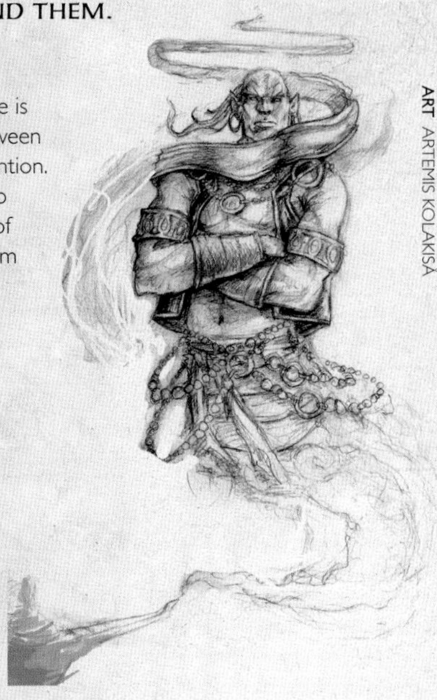

ART ARTEMIS KOLAKISÅ

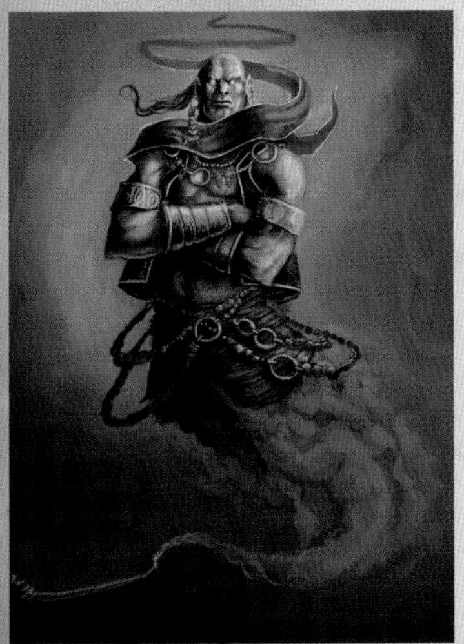

Media and Execution

- Pencil, Photoshop
- The Djinn was sketched in pencil and then scanned and opened in Photoshop.
- Colours were added and the Liquify filter was used to distort some of the shapes.
- Filter effects were used to accentuate the smoke effect and finally the image was colour corrected.

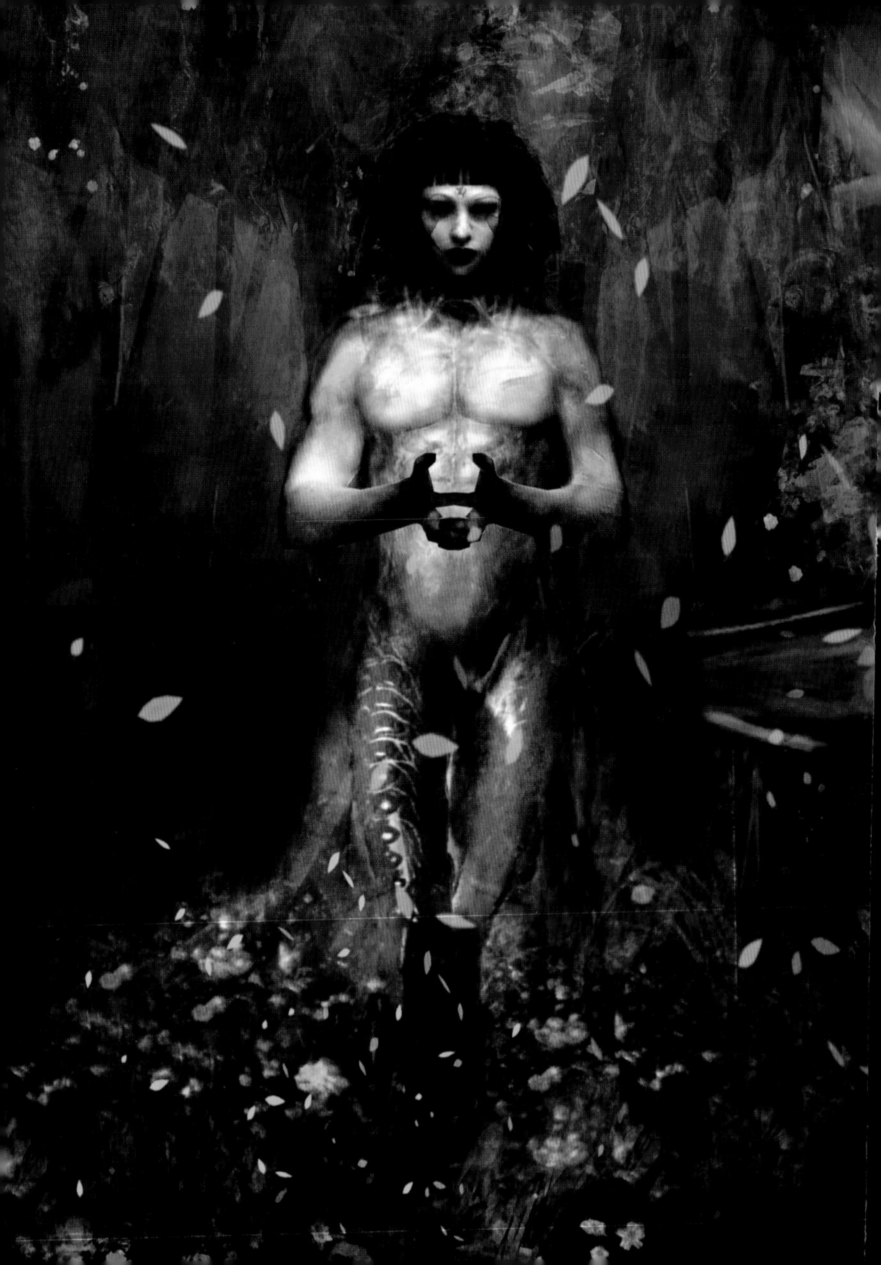

Dockalfar

DARK ELVES ORIGINATING FROM NORSE MYTHOLOGY, DOCKALFAR ARE THE COUNTERPARTS TO THE LIGHT ELVES, LJOSALFAR. ALTHOUGH THEY HAVE A RATHER INTIMIDATING APPEARANCE, THEY ARE GENERALLY BELIEVED TO BE THE PROTECTORS OF MANKIND, BUT CAN BECOME EXTREMELY MENACING UNDER THREAT. THEY SHARE MANY SIMILARITIES WITH DWARVES AND TROLLS, LIVING UNDERGROUND AND SHUNNING DAYLIGHT, WHICH IS SAID TO TURN THEM INTO STONE. THEIR SKIN IS BELIEVED TO BE DISCOLOURED FROM MANY HOURS OF TOIL AT THE FORGE. THEY ARE LED BY THEIR CHIEF ELF, VOLUND, WHO IS A VERY POWERFUL SPIRIT, CAPABLE OF WREAKING HAVOC AND CAUSING TERRIFYING NIGHTMARES. IT WAS COMMONLY HELD BELIEF THAT A HUMAN COULD BE ELEVATED TO THE RANK OF A DARK ELF AFTER DEATH.

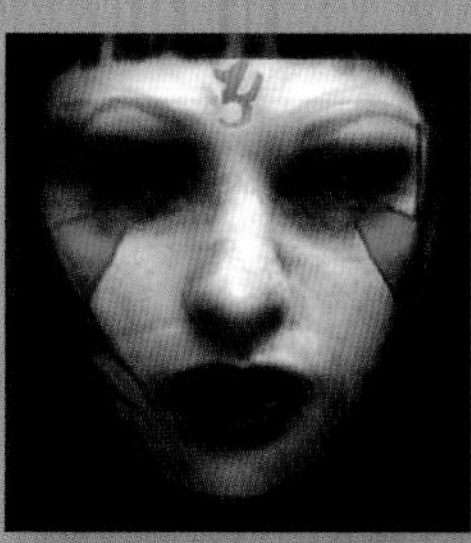

Development

- Dark elves are a staple of the fantasy realm, so seek out inspiration in stories and role-play games.
- There is a powerful dichotomy between beauty and danger to be explored in any portrayal of a dark elf.
- Use hand gestures and facial markings to suggest a race with a rich and complex culture.

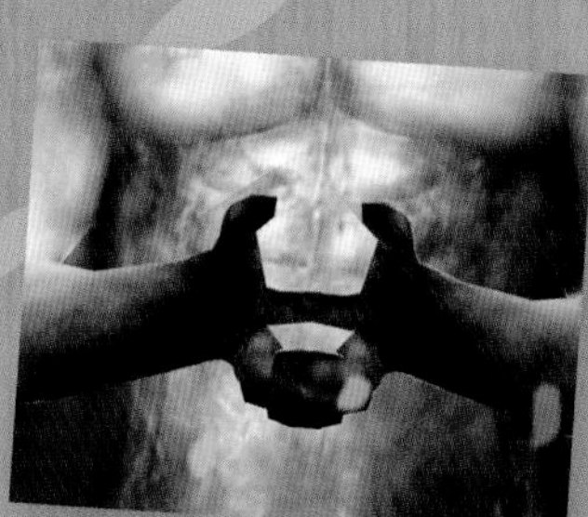

Media and Execution

- Photograph, Photoshop
- A model photograph was used as the starting point, with layers of colour built up on top.
- The flowers in the foreground were painted in a loose, impress-ionistic style.
- The Colour Balance dialog was used to bring out the red and magenta shades.

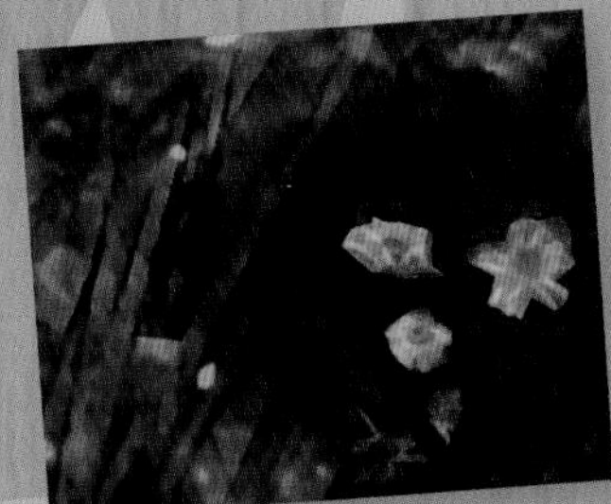

FURTHER STUDY

JRR Tolkien (author) *The Lord of the Rings*, black elves, Svartalfar, Dungeons and Dragons, Drow, Trow.

ART CHRISTOPHER SHY

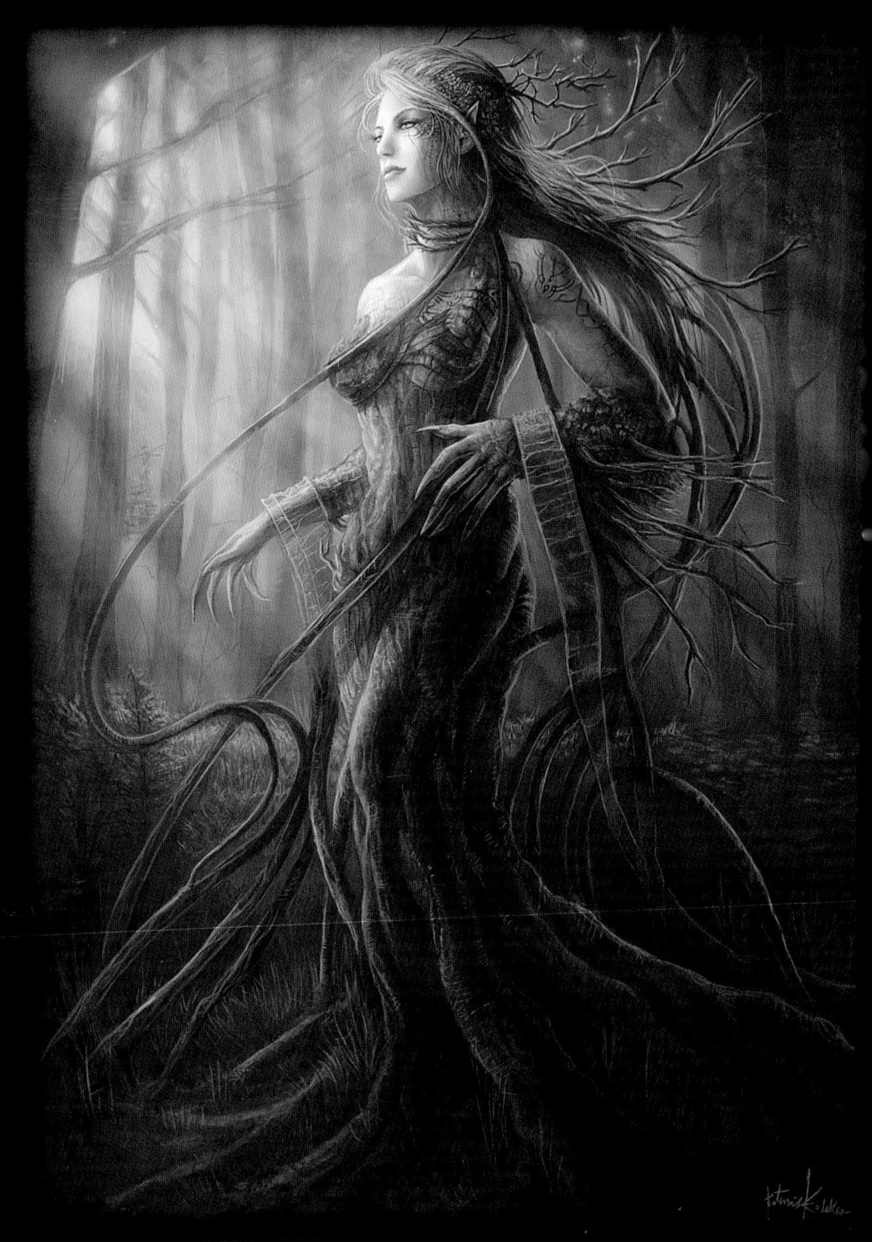

Dryad

TREE NYMPHS FROM ANCIENT GREEK MYTHOLOGY, DRYADS ARE BEAUTIFUL AND FROLICSOME FEMALE SPIRITS THAT WATCH OVER GROVES AND FORESTS. IF A CARELESS PERSON CAUSES ANY DAMAGE TO TREES THE DRYADS WILL PUNISH THEM. THESE EVER-YOUTHFUL SPIRITS LIVE EITHER ALONGSIDE OR ACTUALLY INSIDE TRESS, IN WHICH CASE THEY ARE CALLED HAMADRYADS. THEIR LIVES ARE SO CLOSELY CONNECTED TO THE TREES THEY INHABIT THAT IF THE TREE DIES, THE HAMADRYAD DIES WITH IT. IF THE TREE PERISHES AT THE HAND OF A HUMAN, THE GODS WILL TAKE VENGEANCE. DRYADS WERE OFTEN DEPICTED IN GREEK MYTH AND ART ACCOMPANIED, OR RATHER BEING PURSUED, BY THEIR MALE COUNTERPARTS, THE SATYRS.

Development

- To show their oneness with nature, depict a Dryad in mid-transformation between a faerie and a tree, rooted into the ground.
- Choose an appropriate lighting scheme for your image – here the light streaming in through the trees conjures a feeling of being deep in a wood.

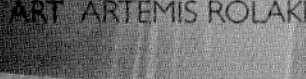
ART ARTEMIS ROLAKIS

Media and Execution

- Softimage XSI, Photoshop
- A 3D model was posed in XSI and then rendered.
- This was brought into Photoshop and edited to fix the proportions, then over-painted. The style of the trees in the background was changed to allow for a softer, more atmospheric lighting scheme.
- The final image was colour corrected and prepared for print in Photoshop.

FURTHER STUDY

Hamadryad, nymphs, Greek myths and legends, Daphne, CS Lewis (author) *The Chronicles of Narnia*, Terry Pratchett (author) *The Colour of Magic*.

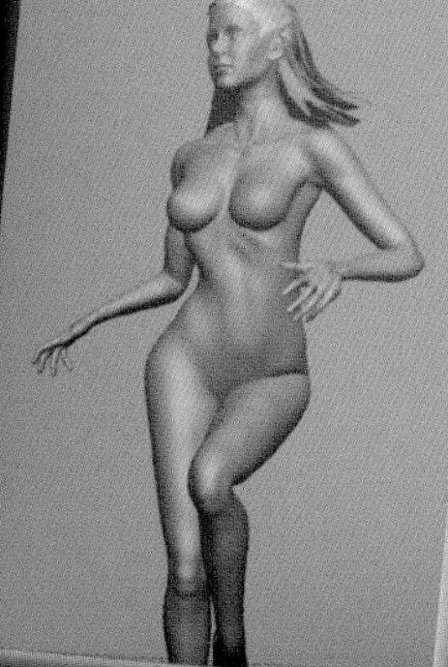

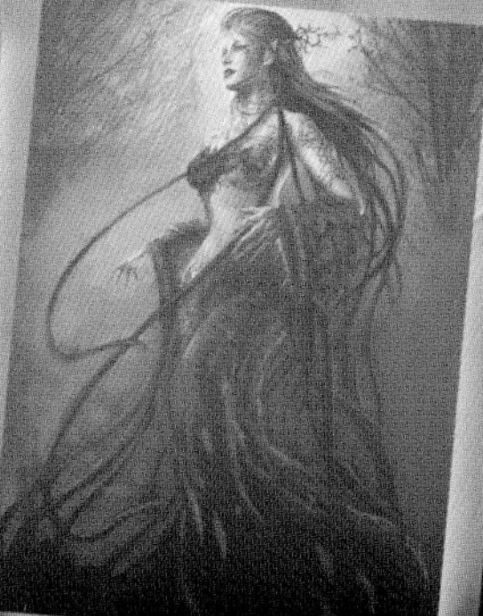

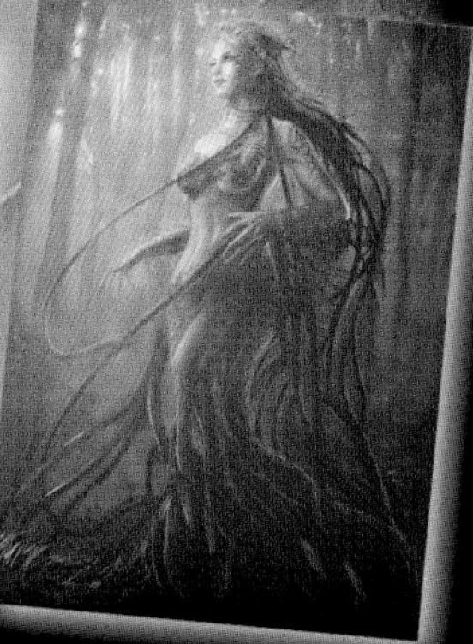

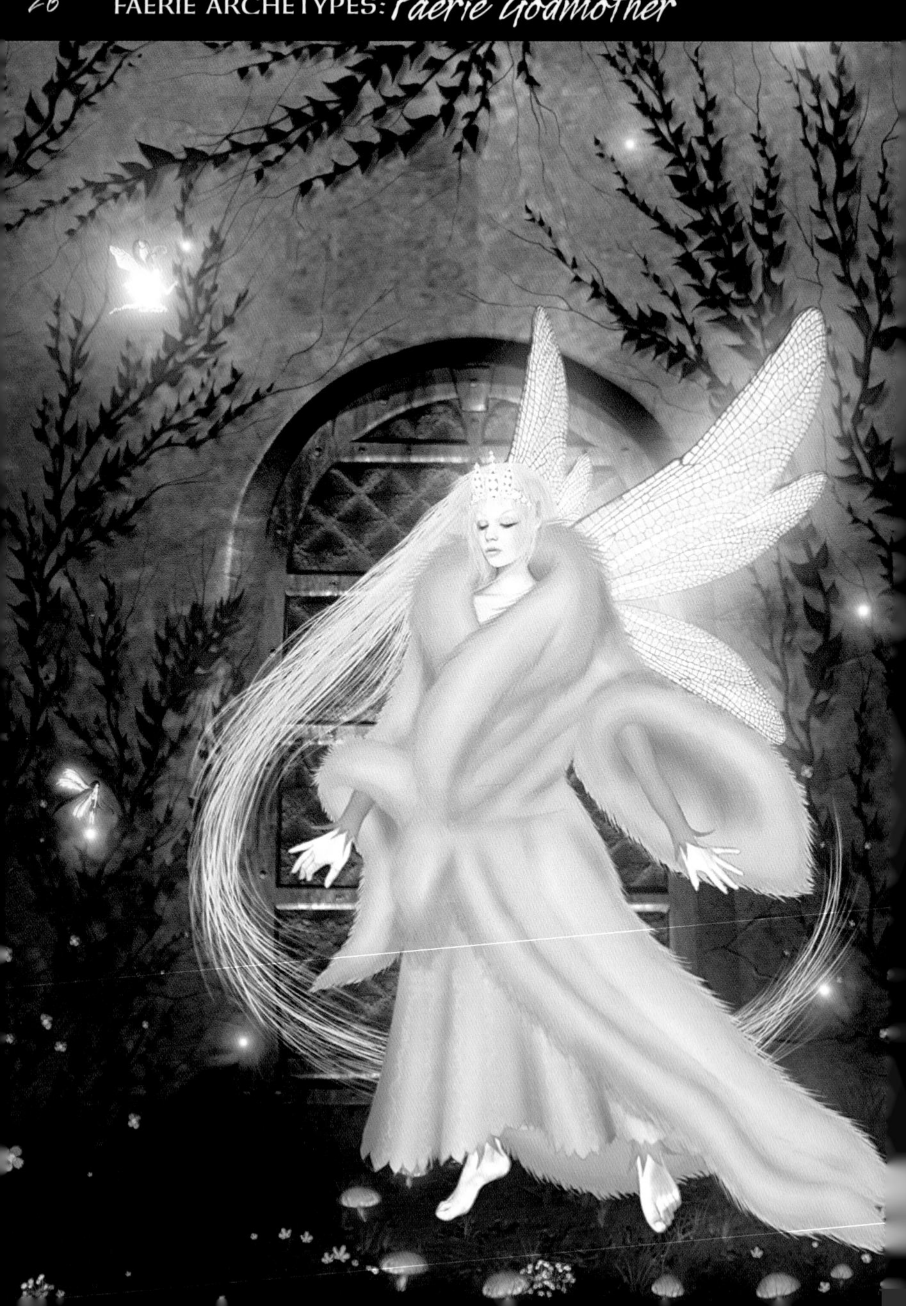

Faerie Godmother

A BEING WITH MAGICAL POWERS, A FAERIE GODMOTHER ACTS AS A MENTOR OR PATRON TO A FAERIE-TALE CHARACTER IN TIMES OF NEED. THE FAERIE GODMOTHER STEPS IN TO LEND HER ABILITIES, ADVICE AND WISDOM IN ENSURING THAT THE PROTAGONIST - USUALLY A YOUNG WOMAN - SUCCEEDS. IN MOST CASES THE HEROINE HAS BEEN ORPHANED AND IS LABOURING UNDER UNFAIR CIRCUMSTANCES, BUT AT OTHER TIMES, SHE IS THE VICTIM OF A CURSE, HOWEVER, A FAERIE GODMOTHER IS NOT ALWAYS ABSOLUTELY GOOD. IN FACT, IN MOST CASES SHE WILL PURSUE THE GOAL OF THE CENTRAL CHARACTER WITHOUT REGARD TO WHETHER THIS IS ACTUALLY RIGHT, AND OFTEN TRIES TO HELP HER PROTÉGÉS AT THE EXPENSE OF OTHERS.

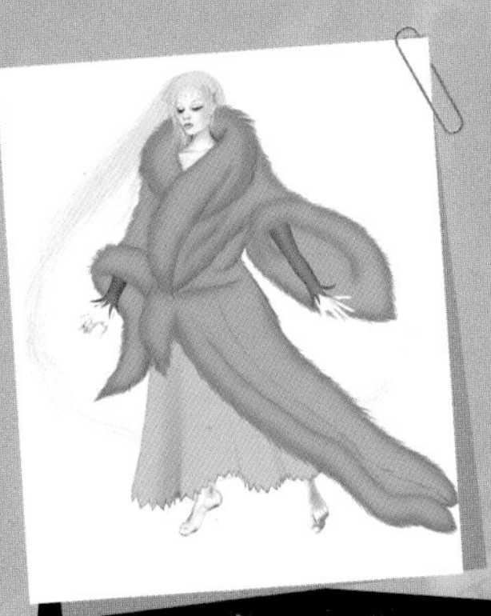

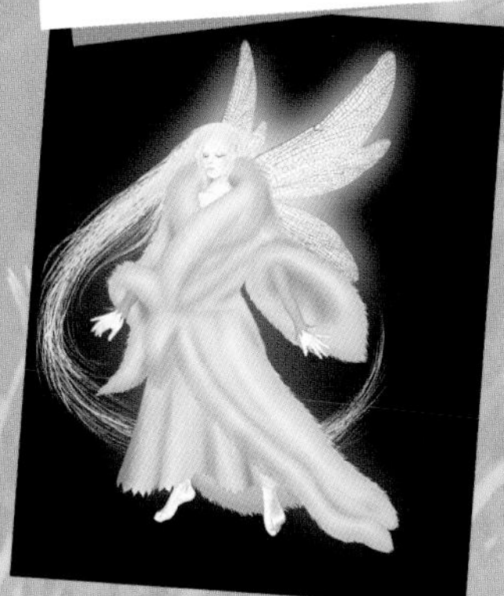

Development

- A Faerie Godmother should be beautiful and wise and wear white, which symbolizes her goodness.
- Tiny fairies and flowers can be used to give your main character scale and perspective and to further illuminate the scene.
- Use long hair to define of the direction of the composition.

ART ALAIN VIESCA

Media and Execution

- 3DS Max, Photoshop
- A simple 3D model was created in Max with custom textures and basic lighting, before being rendered and brought into Photoshop.
- The character was sketched out and then painted.
- The wings were painted on a separate layer so that their position, size and angle could be manipulated during the process.
- Finally, her outline was darkened and a few more shadows were added to her features.

FURTHER STUDY

The Brothers Grimm (authors) *Cinderella*, good witches, Weiss Frau.

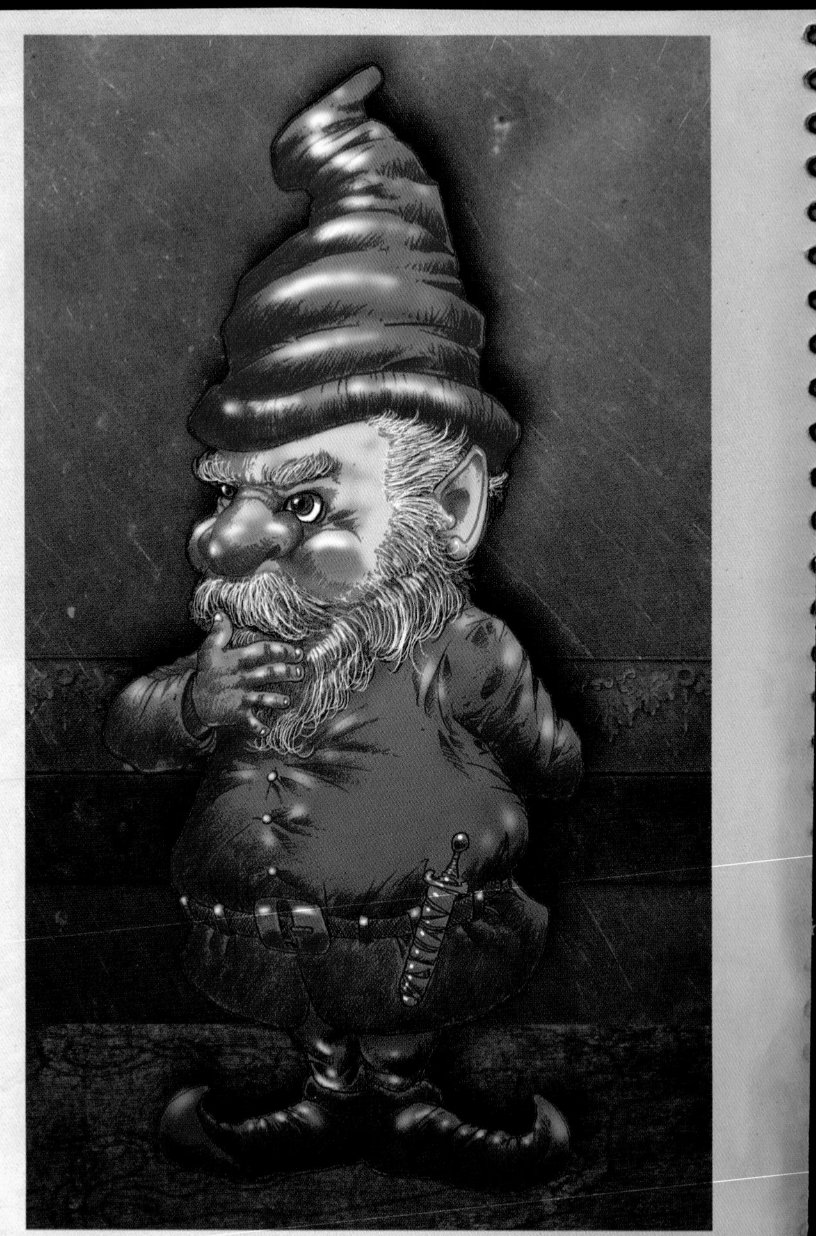

Gnome

THE WORD 'GNOME' IS DERIVED FROM THE GREEK *GENOMOS* MEANING 'EARTH-DWELLER'. GNOMES ARE CHARACTERIZED BY THEIR SMALL STATURE AND SUBTERRANEAN LIFESTYLE. THEY OFTEN APPEAR IN GERMANIC FAERIE TALES AS WELL AS THE FOLKLORE OF EASTERN, NORTHERN AND CENTRAL EUROPE. GNOMES ARE POPULAR CHARACTERS IN A LARGE NUMBER OF FANTASY STORIES, FILMS AND GAMES, AND ALSO APPEAR IN GARDENS AS LAWN DECORATIONS. GNOMES ARE USUALLY DEPICTED AS VERY SHORT, STOCKY OLD MEN WITH BEARDS AND RED HATS, SMOKING PIPES. THE FEMALES WEAR GRAY OR KHAKI CLOTHING, KNEE SOCKS AND GREEN HATS AND HAVE BRAIDED HAIR. GNOMES ARE SEVEN TIMES STRONGER THAN HUMANS, ARE QUICK RUNNERS AND HAVE EYESIGHT LIKE A HAWK.

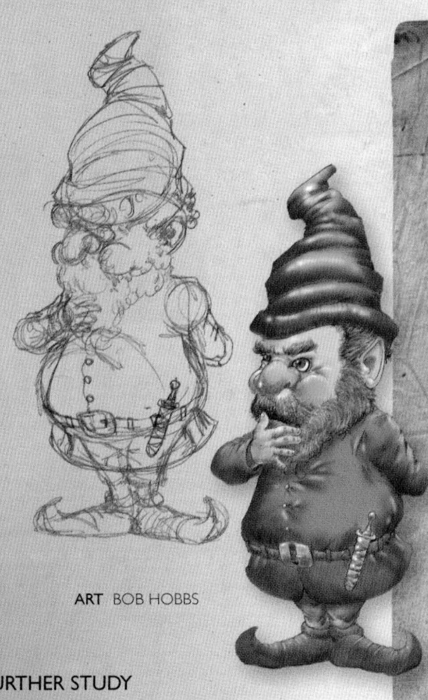

ART BOB HOBBS

Development

- Start with the archetype and then use your imagination to create your own take. The basic Gnome is short with a beard and red hat. From there, play with colours, clothing designs and facial features.
- Considering the old-world European origins of the Gnome, sticking to the staples of the folk tales of the Brothers Grimm and Hans Christian Anderson will ensure that you create a more believable Gnome when it comes to clothing designs, props and background settings.

Media and Execution

- Pencil, Photoshop
- The image was worked in a series of sketches, becoming more refined with each one.
- The final pencil image was scanned and opened in Photoshop.
- Various Photoshop tools and effects were then used to finalise the colourization.

FURTHER STUDY

The Brothers Grimm, Hans Christian Anderson, Germanic folklore, *Dungeons and Dragons*, JK Rowling (author) *Harry Potter*.

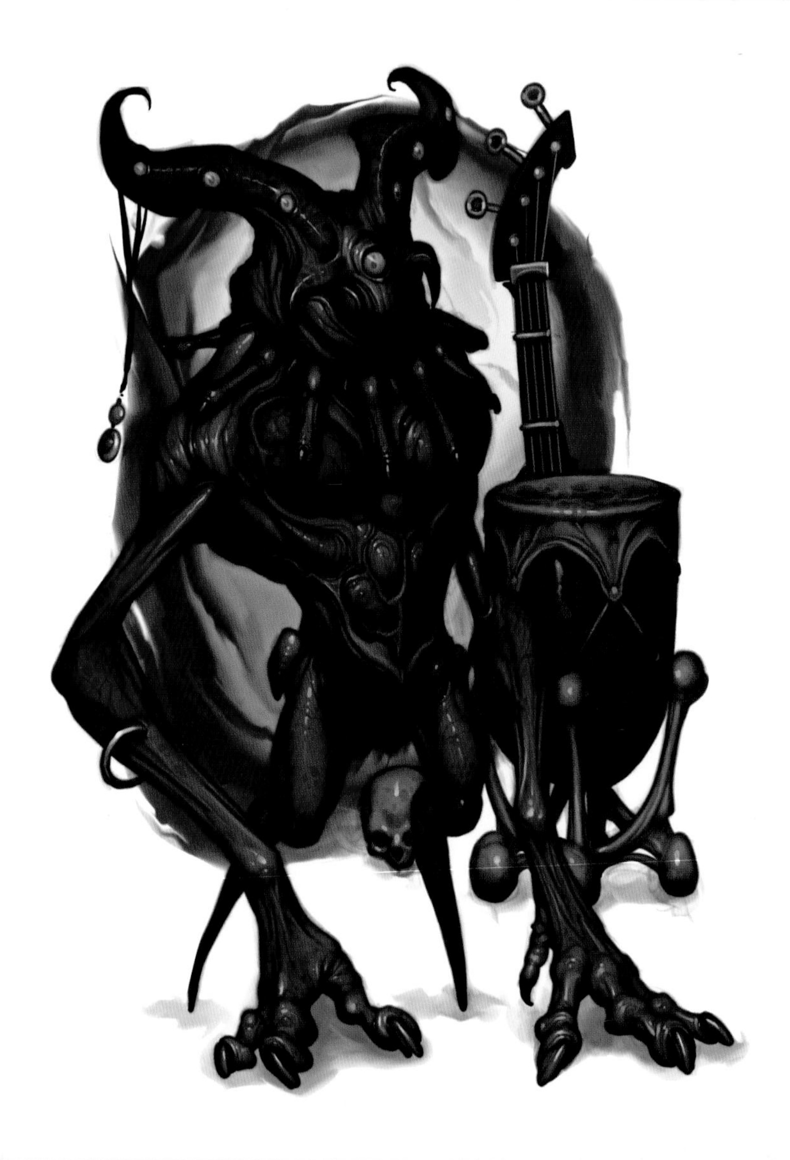

Imp

SMALL, LIVELY AND EXCEEDINGLY MISCHIEVOUS, IMPS ARE WINGLESS, GOBLIN-LIKE CREATURES FROM GERMANIC TRADITIONAL FOLKTALES. WHILE THEY HAVE ALWAYS BEEN SOMETHING OF A CROSS BETWEEN A FAERIE AND A DEMON, IN THE MIDDLE AGES, THEY BECAME ASSOCIATED WITH SATANISM, AND WERE DESCRIBED AS ATTENDANTS OF THE DEVIL. WITCHES WERE SAID TO HAVE IMPS AS THEIR FAMILIARS, SERVING THEIR EVIL WHIMS, BUT THEY ARE GENERALLY CONSIDERED TO BE MORE NAUGHTY THAN NASTY. IMPS CAN BE TAMED AND SEDUCED BY SWEET MUSIC, WHICH SEEMS TO CHARM THEM INTO DOING GOOD RATHER THAN DASTARDLY DEEDS. THEY ARE LONELY CREATURES AND WILL SOMETIMES GO OUT OF THEIR WAY TO BEFRIEND ANOTHER SOUL, BUT THEY WILL NEVER TOTALLY ABANDON THEIR IMPISH NATURE.

Development

- Use colour to play on the demonic aspect with different shades of red.
- Think about how your character will move – here the rear legs are not really functional except to support the weight of the body. Most of movement function is left to the forelegs.
- Including musical instruments in the image makes the imp less of a one-dimensional character by suggesting he has other interests aside from just being impish.

Media and Execution

- Pencil, Photoshop
- A mechanical pencil drawing was scanned and opened in Photoshop.
- The pencil was toned to a sepia hue and edited by erasing and smudging.
- The base tones were added on a Multiply layer, and the colours were pushed and pulled with the Smudge tool set to 70%.
- Once the basic hues were in place, a normal layer was placed on top and tones from a custom palette were painted in with brushes set at between 10 and 30%.

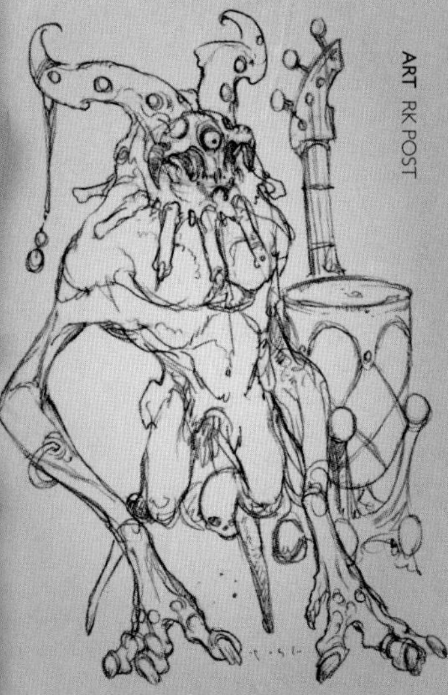

ART RK POST

FURTHER STUDY
Gremlin, demons, German folklore, witchcraft, devil worship.

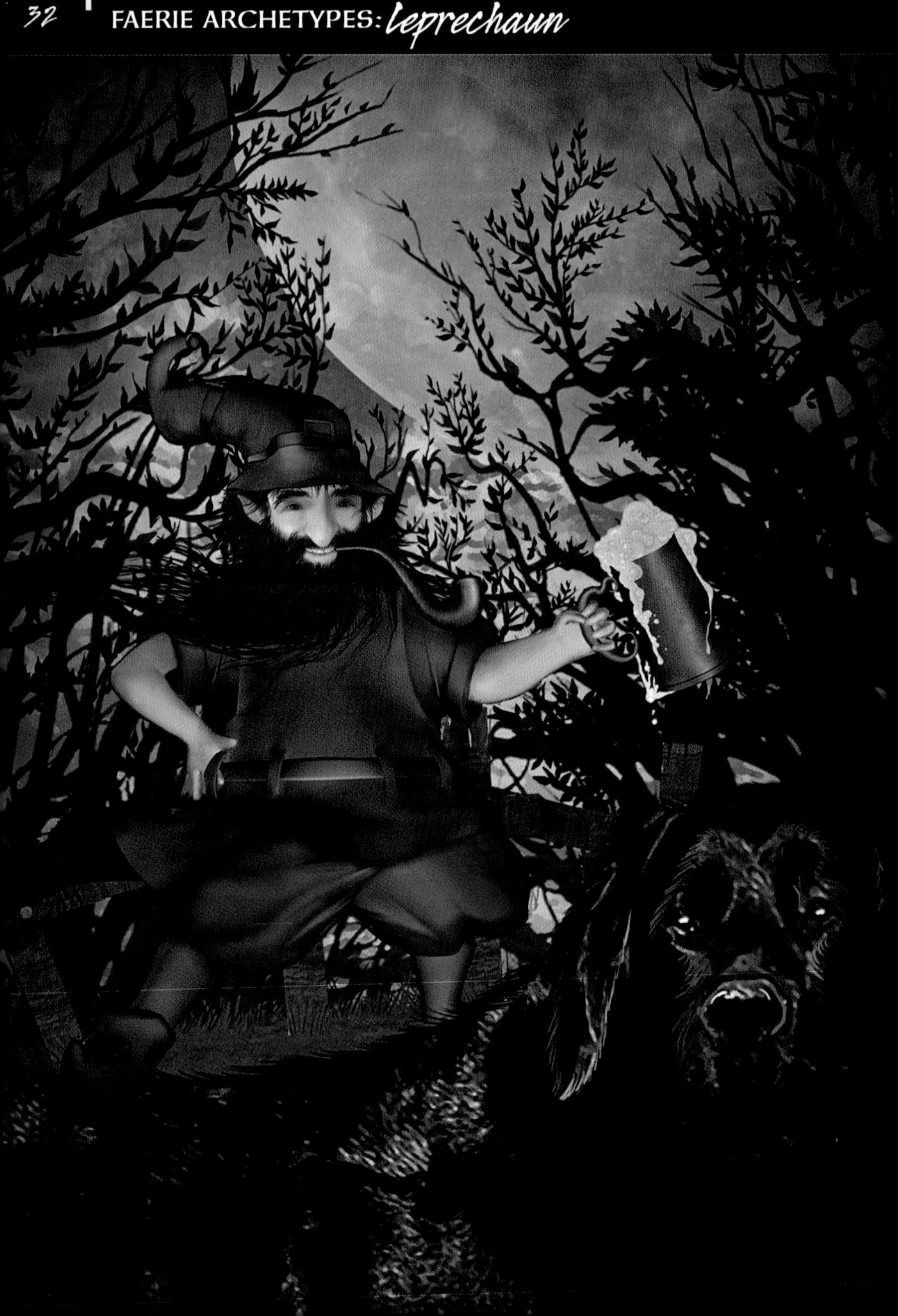

Leprechaun

MALE FAERIES FROM IRISH MYTHOLOGY, LEPRECHAUNS ARE HIGHLY MISCHIEVOUS BUT GENERALLY HARMLESS. THEY AVOID HUMAN CONTACT, AS THEY CONSIDER US TO BE GREEDY AND FOOLISH. IF YOU HAPPEN UPON A LEPRECHAUN, HE CANNOT ESCAPE WHILE YOUR EYE IS FIXED UPON HIM, BUT THE MOMENT YOUR GAZE WANDERS HE WILL DISAPPEAR. LEPRECHAUNS ARE TINY IN STATURE AND USUALLY HAVE BEARDS. THEY ARE FREQUENTLY FOUND IN AN INTOXICATED STATE, BUT ARE NONETHELESS VERY CLEVER AND CUNNING. THEY LIKE TO GATHER IN CIRCLES UNDER THE FULL MOON AND INDULGE IN WILD DRINKING, WHICH SOMETIMES LEADS TO THEM RIDING SHEEP DOGS AROUND ALL NIGHT, LEAVING THE DOGS EXHAUSTED. IT IS SAID THAT IF YOU FIND THE END OF A RAINBOW YOU WILL FIND A LEPRECHAUN AND HIS POT OF GOLD.

Development

- The concept of the Leprechaun is readily accepted but you may be surprised to find out that they are such drunkards and ride on dogs. Try to bring out the more unusual character traits in your image, rather than just portraying the stereotype with a pot of gold.
- Prior to the 20th century, it was generally agreed that Leprechauns wore red not green.

Media and Execution

- 3DS Max, Photoshop
- The background was created in Max, but kept fairly simple and then rendered and dropped into Photoshop.
- The Leprechaun was quickly sketched out then painted in on a new layer.
- The character, dog and background were all kept on separate layers so that they could all be manipulated without affecting the other layers.
- Finally, the outline was darkened, a few more strands were added to his hair and the textures of the dog were enhanced.

FURTHER STUDY
Irish folklore, Pixie, Portune, rainbow sprites.

ART ALAIN VIESCA

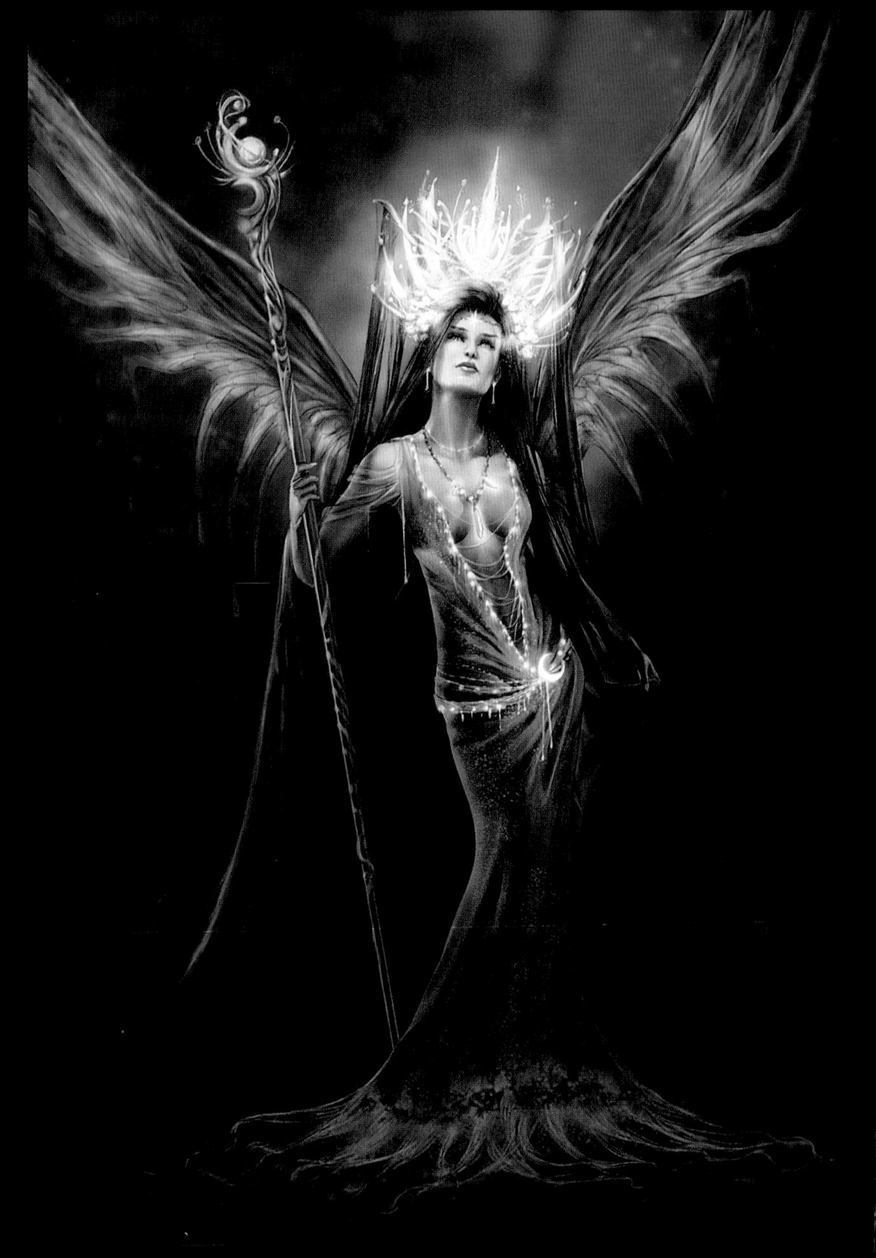

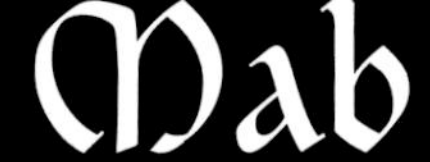

QUEEN OF THE FAERIES, MAB IS REFERENCED IN A COMEDIC SPEECH BY MERCUTIO IN WILLIAM SHAKESPEARE'S *ROMEO AND JULIET*. HERE SHE IS DESCRIBED AS A TINY CREATURE WHO DRIVES A CHARIOT MADE FROM A HAZELNUT SHELL ACROSS PEOPLE'S FACES AS THEY SLEEP, COMPELLING THEM TO DREAM ABOUT THEIR DEEPEST DESIRES. SHAKESPEARE MAY HAVE COINED THE NAME FROM THE CELTIC GODDESS MEDB OR HER WELSH COUNTERPART MABB. SHE WAS A MOTHER AND WAS SEEN AS A GODDESS OF FERTILITY, HEALING AND LOVE. SHE WAS ALSO A FIERCE WARRIOR WHEN IT CAME TO DEFENDING HER CHILDREN AND HER PEOPLE, AND SHE WAS KNOWN FOR HER WILLPOWER AND OVERWHELMING MAGICAL ATTRIBUTES.

Development

- Emphasize Mab's intense aura and portray her confidence of power over the creatures and spirits of the faerie world.
- Explore variations on crown designs and give the final crown a strong glow to ensure her head and face become the focal point of the image.

Media and Execution

- Softimage XSI, Zbrush, Photoshop
- The figure was modeled, posed and rendered in XSI.
- It was then brought into Zbrush for textures to be added.
- The image was then dropped into Photoshop where the colour and details were painted in and her staff was shortened to improve the composition.
- Finally the image was colour corrected and prepared for print in Photoshop.

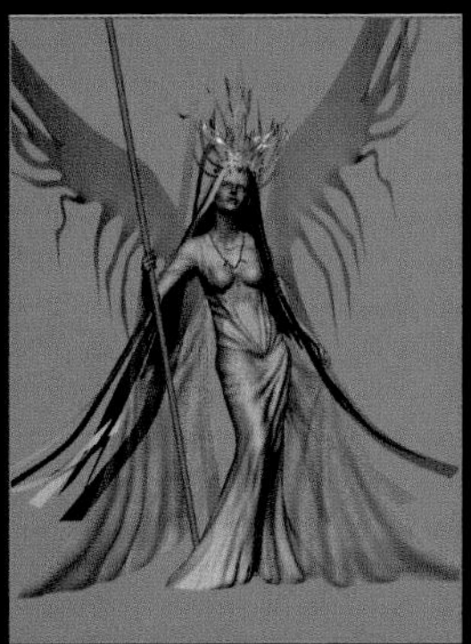

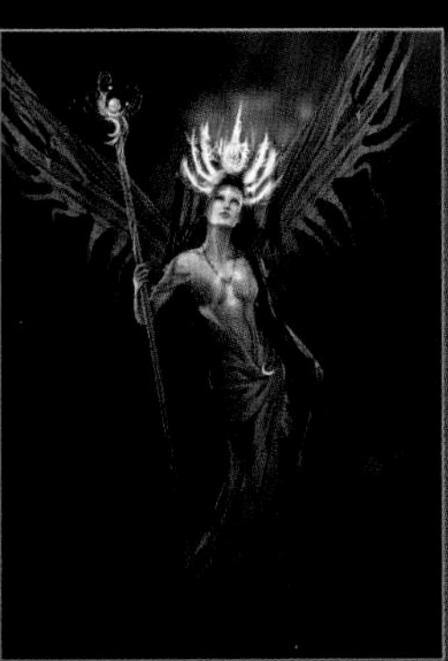

FURTHER STUDY
Queen Maeve, William Shakespeare (playwright) *Romeo and Juliet*, Shelley (poet) *Queen Mab: A Philosophical Poem*, Titania, Morrigan.

ART JULIANNA KOLAKIS

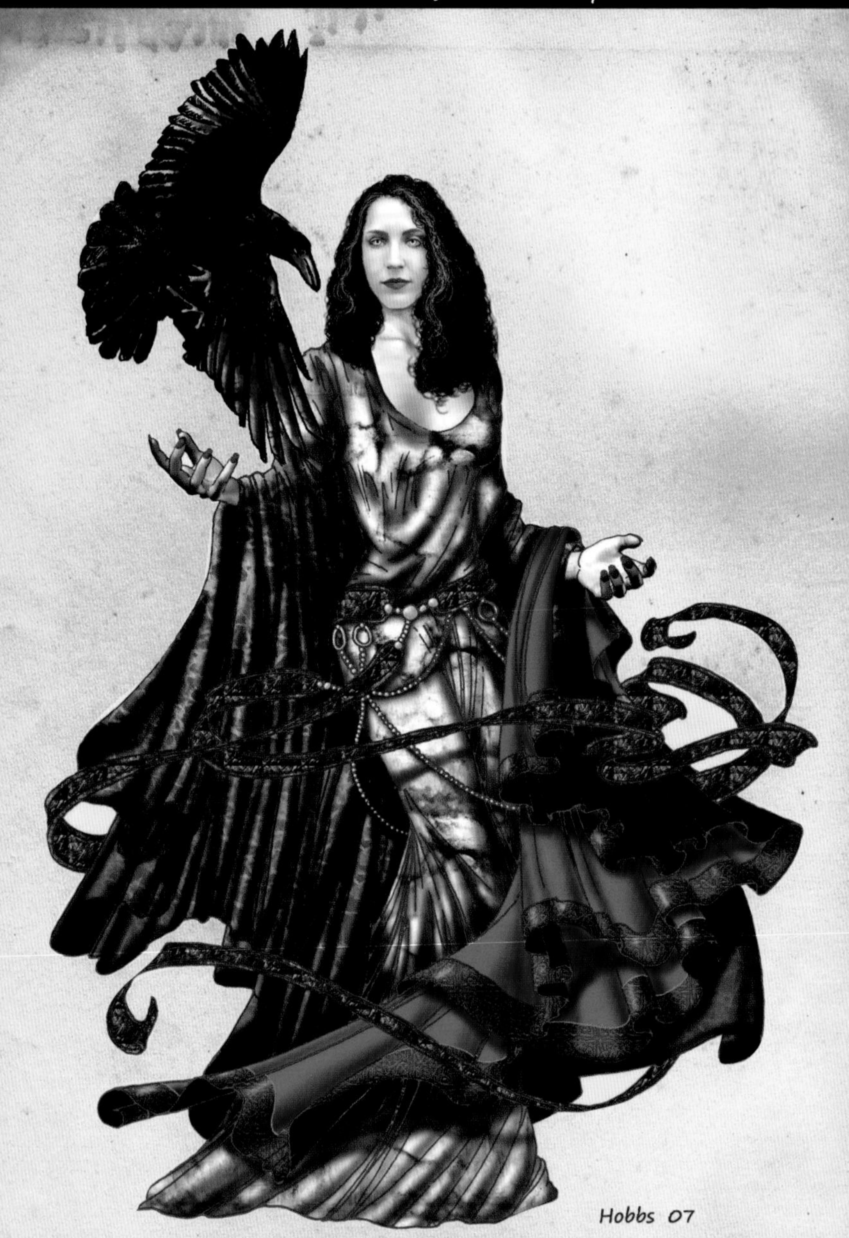
Hobbs 07

Morgan Le Fay

THE HALF-SISTER OF KING ARTHUR AND STUDENT OF MERLIN, MORGAN LE FAY WAS A FAERIE WHO LATER BECAME A WOMAN BUT RETAINED HER POWERS OF ENCHANTMENT. MORGAN WAS AN ENCHANTRESS, PRIESTESS, WITCH, SHAPE-SHIFTER, HEALER AND RULER OF AVALON. SHE ESCORTED ARTHUR TO AVALON AFTER HE FELL IN THE BATTLE OF CAMLANN. SHE HAS APPEARED IN STORIES AS EARLY AS THE *VITA MERLINI* BY GEOFFREY OF MONMOUTH IN 1150, AND AS RECENTLY AS THE TV SERIES *STARGATE SG-1*. HER ORIGINS CAN BE TRACED BACK TO THE FIGURE MODRON IN WELSH MYTHOLOGY. SHE CAN ALSO BE LINKED TO THE IRISH GODDESS MORRIGAN, WHICH MAY EXPLAIN THE IMPORTANCE OF THE RAVEN AS ONE OF HER FAMILIARS.

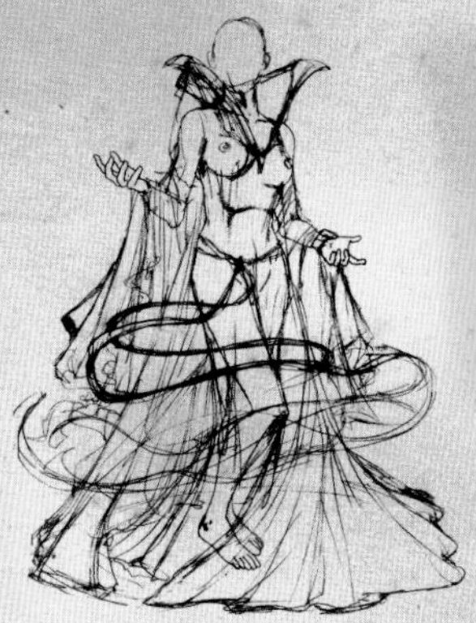

Development

- Be prepared to redraw elements several times to refine them. Here, the aim was to achieve a flowing motion to her robes – as if an unseen wind is blowing around her.
- Pay attention to how you pose the hands, as badly posed hands can ruin the piece. You can use your own or someone else's hands, or use Poser software.
- Experimentation is the key – it is up to you how you apply and manipulate the numerous digital tools available.

FURTHER STUDY

Arthurian Legends, Morrigan, *The Vulgate Cycle*, Merlin, Marion Zimmer Bradley (author) *The Mists of Avalon*, The Fay.

Media and Execution

- Pencil, pen and ink, Photoshop
- A face sketch was done in pencil based on a photo of the model. An otherworldly look was achieved using the Watercolour filter in Photoshop, with the pencil sketch then superimposed on top.
- The line art was scanned into Photoshop and basic colours were blocked in using Layers.
- Tones were then added using the Airbrush tool to create shadow and more definition to the flat colours.

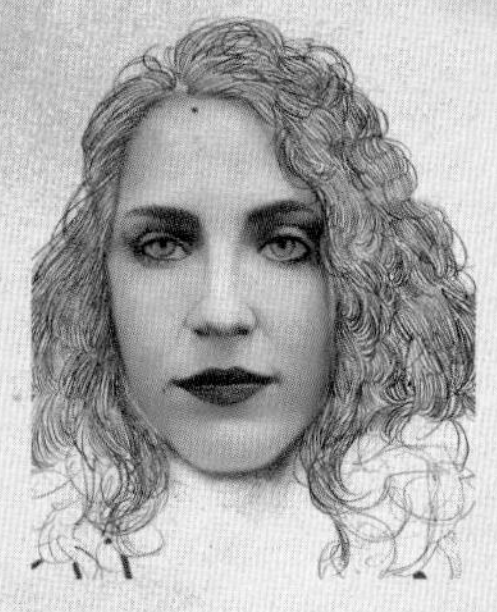

ART BOB HOBBS
MODEL JODI GOLDBERGER

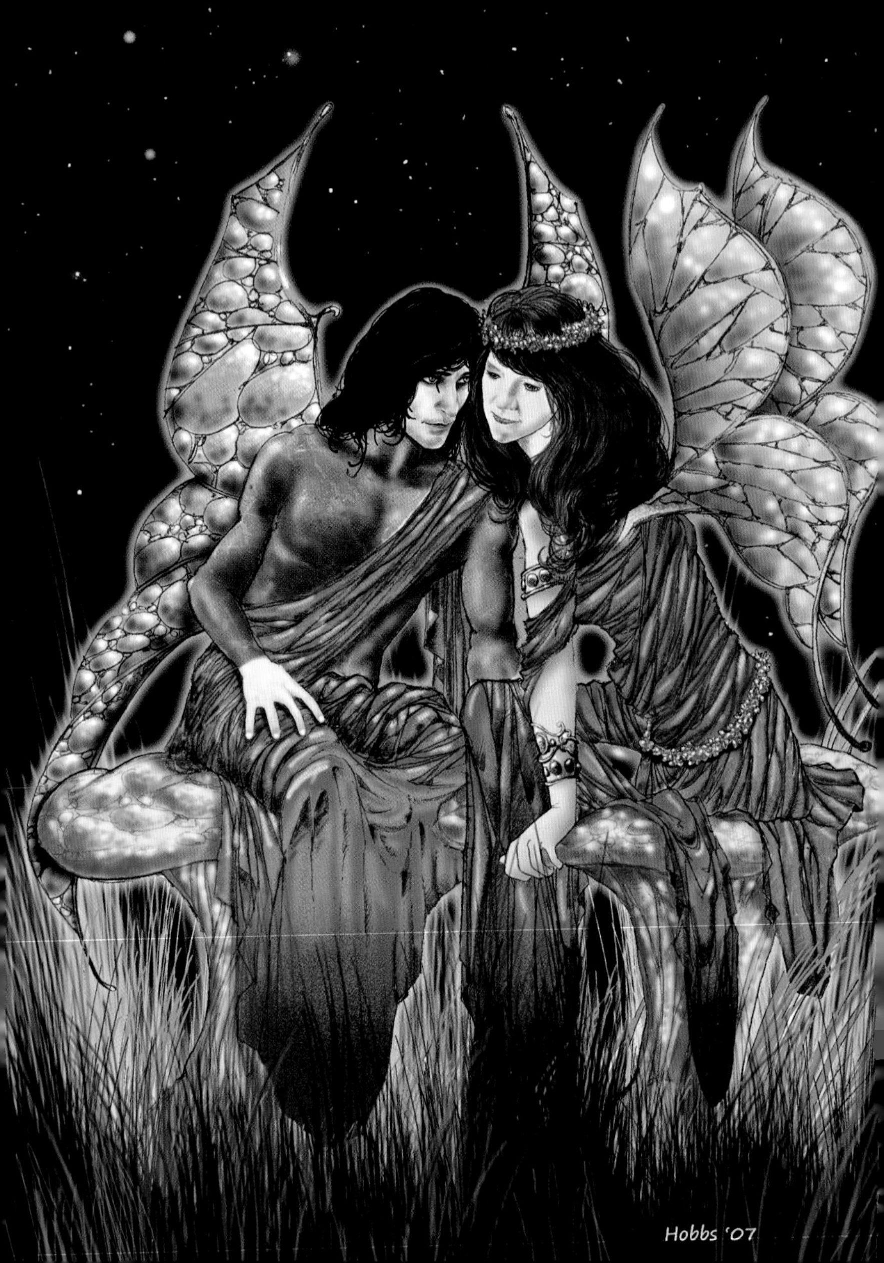
Hobbs '07

Oberon and Titania

THE KING AND QUEEN OF THE FAERIES FEATURE IN SHAKESPEARE'S *A MIDSUMMER NIGHT'S DREAM*. A QUARREL BETWEEN THEM OVER A LITTLE INDIAN BOY SETS NATURE OFF BALANCE. THE CONFLICT IS RESOLVED WHEN OBERON USES A MAGIC POTION TO FORCE TITANIA TO LOVE A CREATURE HALF-MAN, HALF-DONKEY. WHILE SHE IS UNDER THIS SPELL, OBERON ASKS HER TO GIVE HIM THE BOY, WHICH SHE DOES WITHOUT COMPLAINT. WHEN HE TAKES AWAY THE SPELL, TITANIA IS HAPPILY HIS AGAIN, DISGUSTED BY THE MONSTER SHE ONCE LOVED. IN THE 16TH CENTURY, FAERIES WERE CONSIDERED TO BE WINGLESS AND THE SAME SIZE AS HUMANS, BUT SHAKESPEARE PREFERRED TO MAKE THEM NATURE-LOVING, TINY CREATURES WITH WINGS, AND POPULAR MYTH WAS CHANGED FOREVER.

- Research archetypal faeries on the Internet as well as in books.
- The characters of *A Midsummer Night's Dream* were popular subjects for painters, so there is a wealth of visual reference material available. Since Shakespeare did not give full detailed physical descriptions of them, each artist has interpreted them differently. Here they are depicted as being tiny but very elegant with elaborate butterfly wings. They are posed upon toadstools under a star-lit sky sharing a moment of closeness, reunited at the end of the play.

Media and Execution

- Pencil, photograph, Photoshop
- Rough pencil sketches were used to work out the composition followed by detailed pencil renderings of the faces based on model photos.
- The pencil drawing was scanned and opened in Photoshop, and colours were built up in layers of varying Opacity.
- The hair and grass were enhanced with a fine Airbrush to build up volume.
- Finally, touches of highlights, blending and shading completed the image.

FURTHER STUDY
William Shakespeare (playwright) *A Midsummer Night's Dream*, Ovid (author) *Metamorphosis*, Elizabethan England, Puck/ Robin Goodfellow.

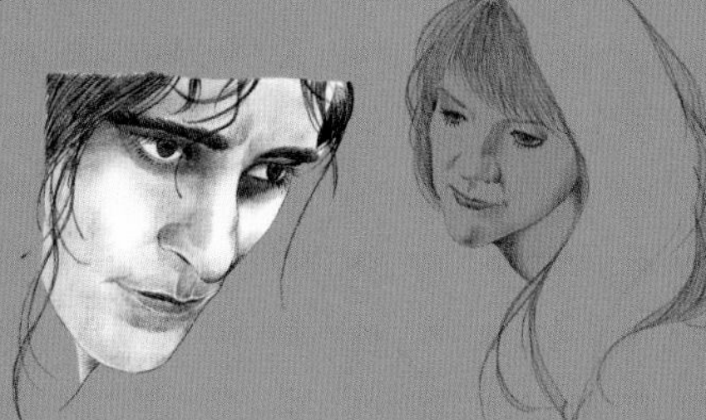

ART BOB HOBBS
MODEL LESLIE PARKER

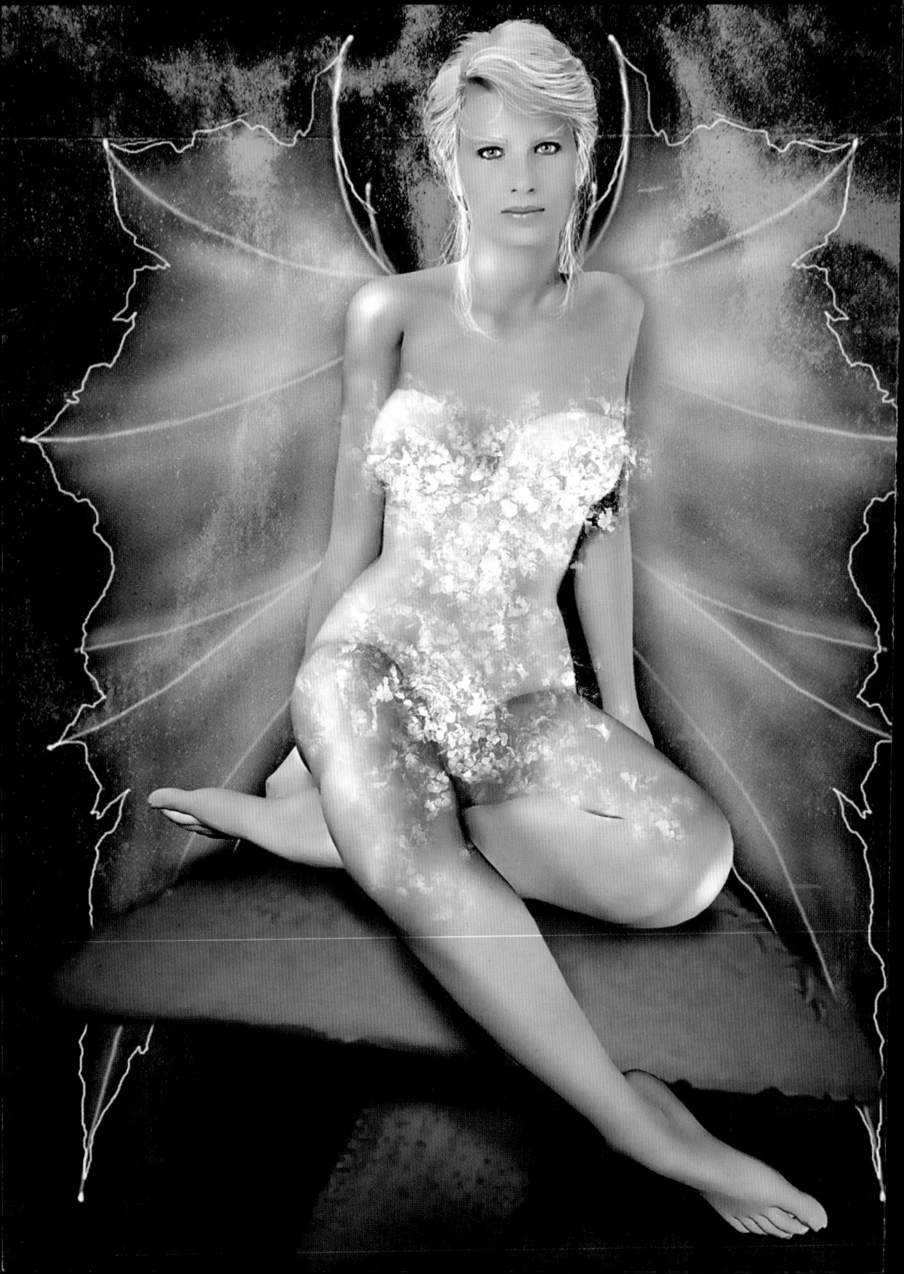

Pixie

ALSO CALLED PISKIES OR PIGSIES, PIXIES ARE WELL KNOWN IN DEVON AND CORNWALL IN SOUTHERN ENGLAND. IT IS SUGGESTED THAT THEY MAY BE OF CELTIC ORIGIN. SOME LEGENDS SAY THAT THE PIXIES WERE A RACE OF PEOPLE WHO WERE NOT GOOD ENOUGH FOR HEAVEN NOR BAD ENOUGH FOR HELL AND THUS REMAINED ON EARTH FOREVER, WHILE OTHER LEGENDS CLAIM THEY WERE DRUIDS WHO RESISTED THE COMING OF CHRISTIANITY AND WERE CURSED BY GOD TO SHRINK EVER SMALLER. OTHERS THEORIZE THAT THE ANCIENT PICTS OF SCOTLAND MAY BE THE SOURCE OF THE PIXIE LEGEND. PIXIES ENJOY PLAYING PRANKS ON PEOPLE BUT CAN BE REPELLED BY OBJECTS MADE OF SILVER TO WHICH THEY ARE ALLERGIC. THEY LIVE ON A DIET OF NECTAR AND POLLEN.

Development

- Many effects can be added in Photoshop via the Layer Styles dialog. The use of a drop shadow, as seen here, creates added depth, giving more of a three-dimensional feel.
- Photoshop Filters can be used to create a glowing effect, which is perfect to depict a Pixie's golden aura.
- Try creating a Custom Brush – here a leaf-shaped brush was used to paint her clothing.
- Reduce the Opacity of the layer with the wings on it for a more translucent look.

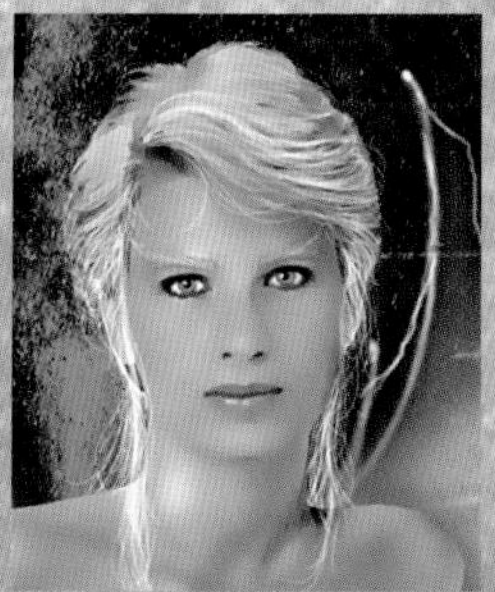

FURTHER STUDY
JK Rowling (author) *Harry Potter*, Korrigans, Heather Pixie, nature sprites, Cornish folklore.

Media and Execution

- Photograph, Poser, Photoshop
- The figure was created in Poser and rendered out to Photoshop.
- The model photo was scanned and opened in Photoshop, merged with the Poser body and airbrushed to match up the skin colours.
- All the other elements were painted in with the Pen, Brush and Airbrush tools.
- The background was imported from a collection of grunge textures with a filter lighting effect added.
- On a new layer, the hair was airbrushed in, followed by the wings and clothing. Finally a drop shadow was used for depth.

ART BOB HOBBS

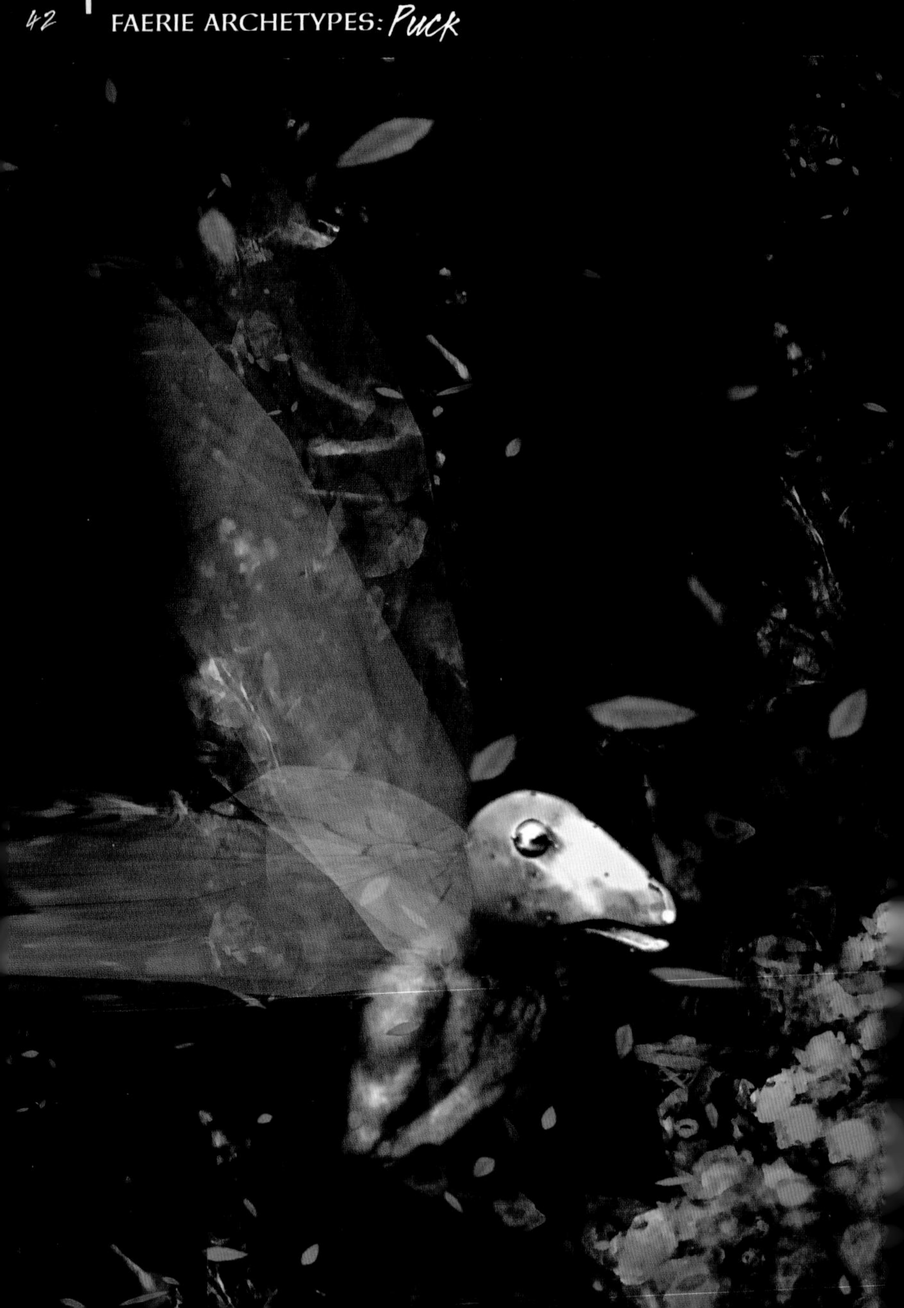

PUCK

THIS FUN-LOVING NATURE SPRITE IS A CONSUMMATE PRANKSTER AND LOVES MAKING MISCHIEF WHEREVER HE CAN. ALSO KNOWN AS ROBIN GOODFELLOW, PUCK WAS IMMORTALIZED BY HIS APPEARANCE IN SHAKESPEARE'S COMEDY *A MIDSUMMER NIGHT'S DREAM*, IN WHICH HE SERVES THE FAERIE KING OBERON, AND CAUSES THE MAYHEM OF THE PLOT WITH HIS MISTAKEN ACTIONS. BUT PUCK'S ORIGINS GO BACK MUCH FURTHER TO PRE-CHRISTIAN TIMES, WHERE HE WAS CONSIDERED AN UNPREDICTABLE WOODLAND SPIRIT WHO LIKED TO LEAD TRAVELLERS ASTRAY WITH LIGHTS AND ECHOES, MUCH LIKE PIXIES OR WILL 'O THE WISPS. SOME SAY HIS NAME COMES FROM THE OLD ENGLISH PUCA MEANING 'UNSETTLED'.

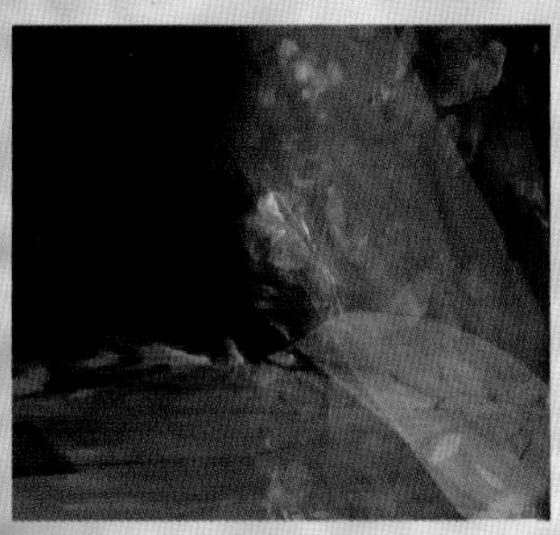

Development

- The use of a stylized ass's head serves as a reminder of Shakespeare's storyline – in the play it is the character Bottom who is transformed in this way by Puck.
- Suggest the transparent nature of faerie wings by keeping their Opacity level down, and lightening the background elements behind them.
- Woods are at their most beautiful and enchanting in the fall so setting woodland sprites amongst autumnal foliage makes for an evocative image.

Media and Execution

- Pencil, Photoshop
- A pencil sketch was scanned and opened in Photoshop.
- The sketch was over-painted on several layers.
- The wings were created on a new layer, with careful attention given to where they overlapped and the different levels of transparency between a single and double wing thickness.
- The flowers in the foreground were loosely worked to keep the main focus of attention on Puck.

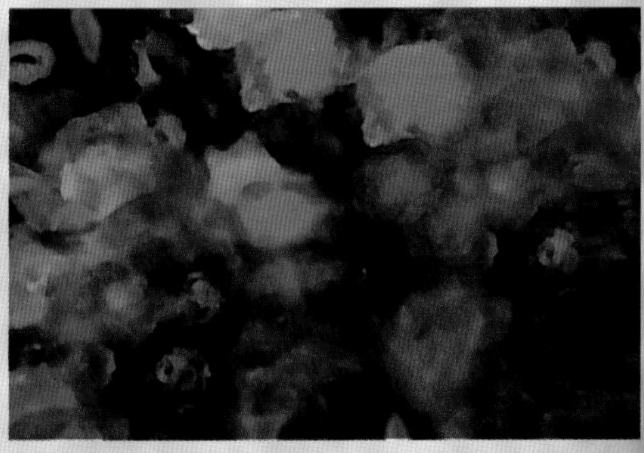

FURTHER STUDY

Pooka, Imp, William Shakespeare (playwright) *A Midsummer Night's Dream*, Rudyard Kipling (author) *Puck of Pook's Hill*, Bwca, Pixie.

ART CHRISTOPHER SHY

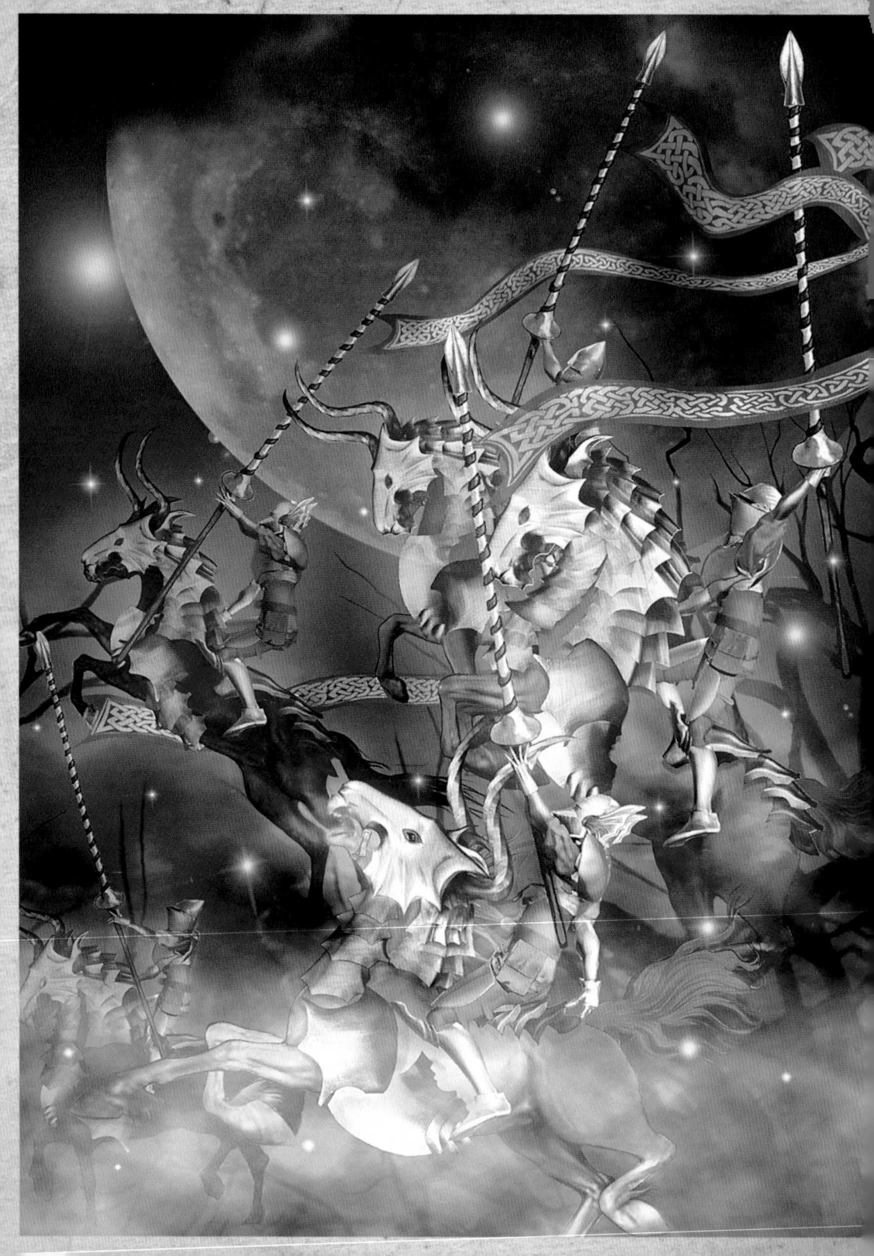

Seelie Court

MOST OF THE SEELIE FOLKLORE ORIGINATES FROM SCOTLAND, ALTHOUGH IT IS NOT LIMITED TO THESE SHORES. IN IRELAND THEY ARE THE DAOINE SÍDHE; IN FRANCE, THE PRÉCIEUSES; WELSH LEGEND CALLS THEM THE TYLWYTH TEG, AND THEY ARE ALSO KNOWN AS TROOPING FAIRIES AND THE BLESSED ONES. THE SEELIE COURT IS MADE UP OF THE MOST NOBLE, HEROIC AND BEAUTIFUL OF THE FAERIE WORLD. THESE BENEVOLENT SPIRITS ARE OFTEN DEPICTED AS A HOST OF LIGHT, TROOPING IN LONG PROCESSIONS. THE SEELIE HAVE A SENSE OF HUMOUR AND ARE PERPETUALLY SURROUNDED BY MUSIC. THEY INDULGE IN GAMES AND FEASTS AND PRANCE AROUND ON GREAT STEEDS. THE COUNTERPART TO THE SEELIE IS THE UNSEELIE COURT, WHICH CONSISTS OF SINISTER AND MALICIOUS FAERIES.

Media and Execution

• 3DS Max, Photoshop
• The background was composited in Photoshop using separate layers for the sky, clouds, moon and treetops.
• The knights, horses and armour were all rendered Max then composited in Photoshop.
• A new layer was created and the Cloud filter was applied, then much of the top and sides were erased to leave it heavier around the riders.
• The layers were merged and then the riders were worked over with a pale bluish/green brush to give more illumination.

Development

• Painting an entire court of faeries presents a real challenge, so pick a popular scene from folklore and let this guide you.
• Create all the different elements on separate layers to that each can be honed independently of the others, and only merge them when you are happy with everything.
• When painting horses use plenty of references for correct anatomy and musculature.

ART ALAIN VIESCA

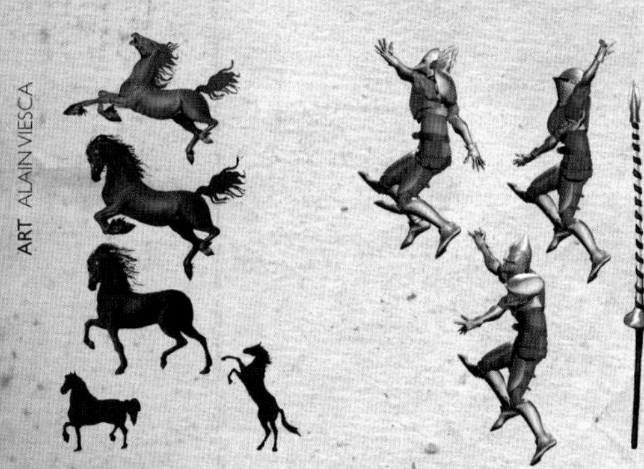

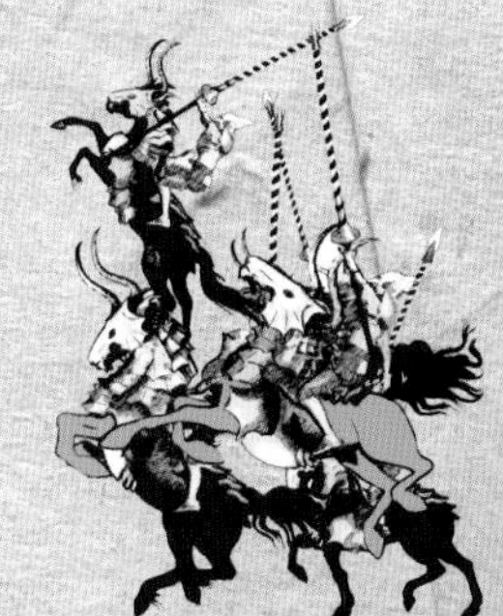

FURTHER STUDY

Daoine Sídhe, Précieuses, Tylwyth Teg, WB Yeats (poet), Trooping Fairies, Unseelie Court.

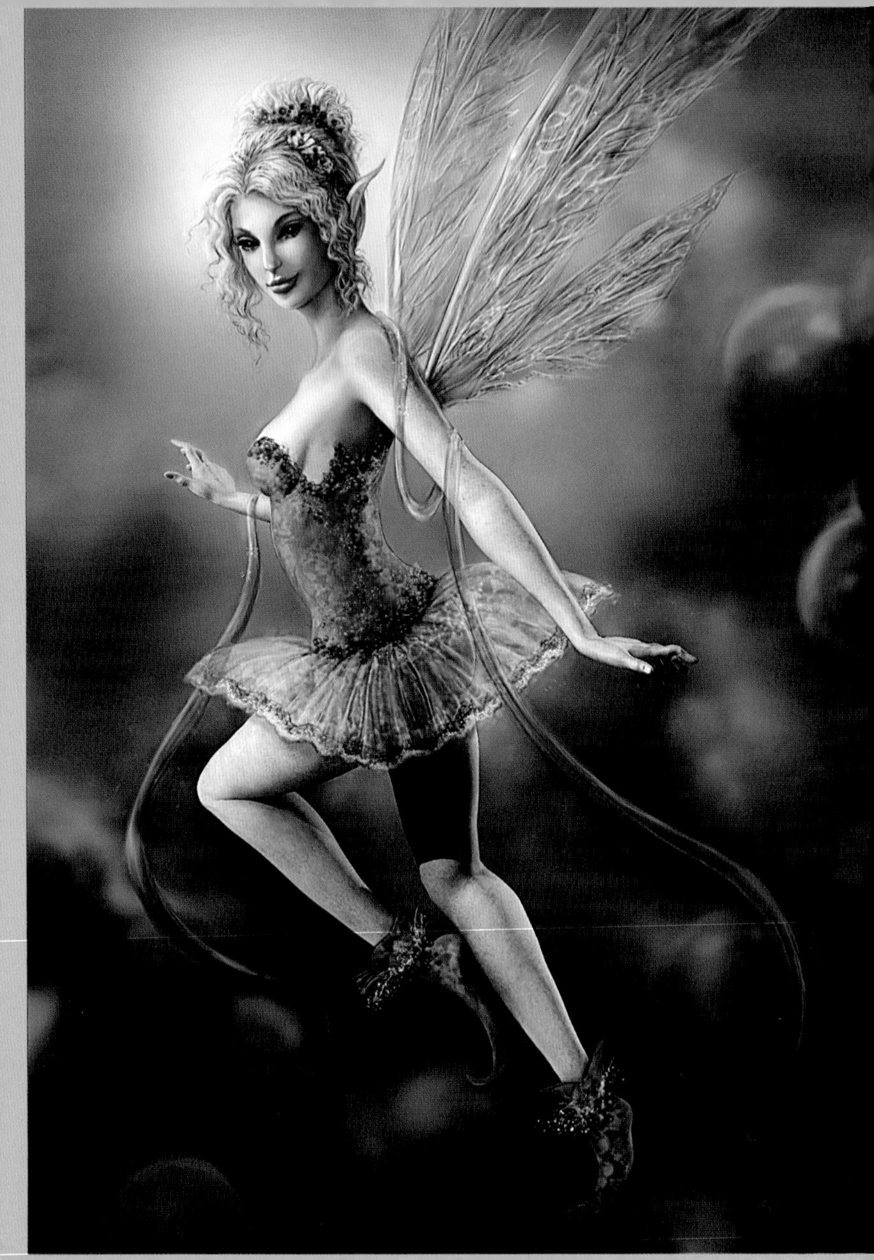

Sugar Plum Faerie

THESE RARE AND BEAUTIFUL FAERIES CAN OCCASIONALLY BE SEEN IN ORCHARDS AND PLUM GROVES AT DAWN, DANCING TO THE MORNING BIRDSONG. THEY LOVE SWEET RIPE FRUITS, BEES, BALLET AND CHRISTMAS. THEY ARE GRACEFUL DANCERS WITH A PLAYFUL ENTHUSIASM FOR ALL THINGS MUSICAL. THEY WERE THE INSPIRATION FOR TCHAIKOVSKY'S BALLET *THE NUTCRACKER SUITE* IN WHICH THE SUGAR PLUM FAERIE AND HER ATTENDANTS DANCE FOR CLARA AND THE PRINCE IN THE KINGDOM OF SWEETS. THEY DISLIKE MICE AND HATE MILDEW, WHICH SPOILS THEIR FAVOURITE FRUIT. THE BEST TIME OF YEAR TO SEE THEM IS LATE SUMMER, WHEN THE PLUMS ARE RIPE AND BEGINNING TO FALL FROM THE TREES.

Development

- Use a limited colour palette of pink and plum shades to ensure that the faerie blends in with its surroundings and appears harmonious.
- Choose a pose that captures the grace and poise of a ballet dancer.
- Showing plums in the image gives an impression of the faerie's tiny size.

Media and Execution

- Softimage XSI, Zbrush, Mudbox, Photoshop
- The female model was posed and rendered in XSI.
- It was then sculpted and textured in Zbrush and Mudbox before being taken into Photoshop.
- The Liquify filter was used to fix the proportions and it was then over-painted.
- The image was then colour corrected and prepared for print in Photoshop.

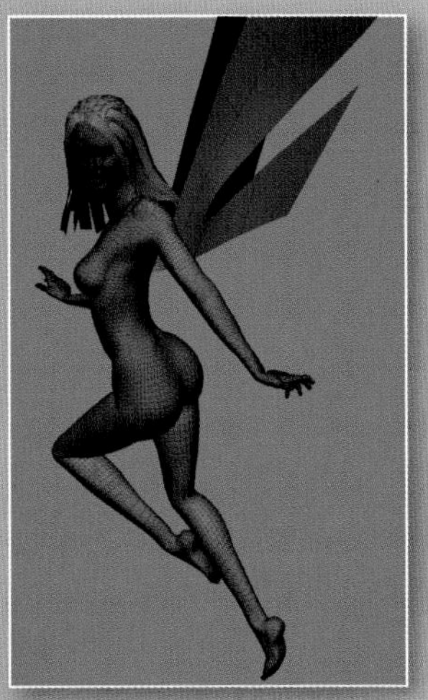

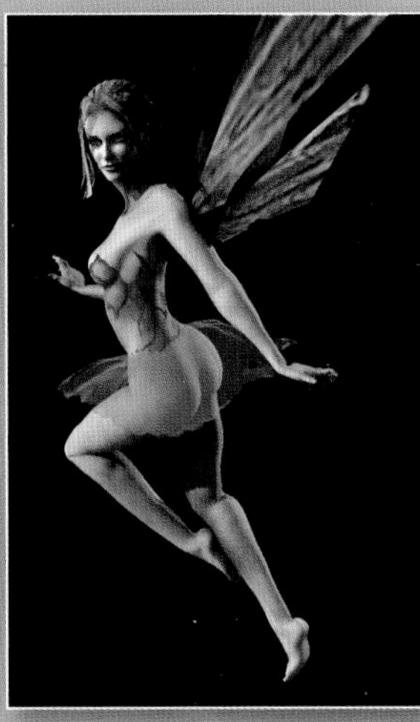

FURTHER STUDY
Pyotr Tchaikovsky (composer)
The Nutcracker Suite, Kingdom of Sweets, Mirabelle.

ART JULIANNA KOLAKIS

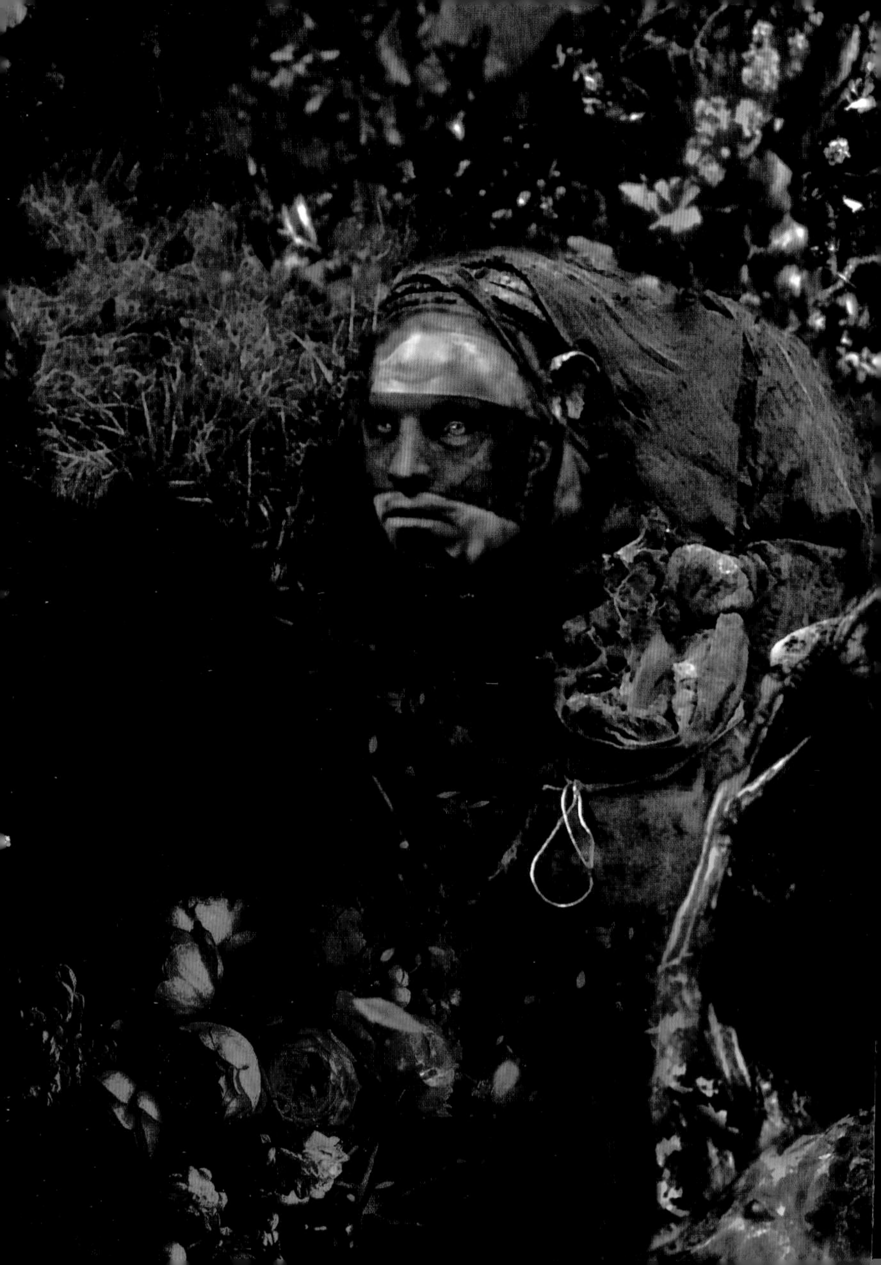

TROLL

A MYTHICAL RACE OF FEARSOME CREATURES FROM SCANDINAVIAN FOLKLORE, TROLLS RANGE IN SIZE FROM GIANTS TO VERY SMALL CREATURES. THEY LIVE IN COOL, DARK PLACES SUCH AS MOUNDS, CAVES, UNDER BRIDGES AND IN MOUNTAIN LAIRS. THEY ARE ONLY ACTIVE AT NIGHT AND MUST AVOID DAYLIGHT AT ALL COSTS, AS IF THE RAYS OF THE SUN CATCH THEM THEY WILL INSTANTLY TURN TO STONE. AFTER DARK, THESE MAGICAL AND SINISTER BEINGS TRAVEL AS SILENTLY AS THE WIND, AND SNEAK INTO VILLAGES TO KIDNAP PEOPLE TO BECOME THEIR SLAVES. THEY ARE ALSO KNOWN TO STEAL CHILDREN, SUBSTITUTING THEM WITH CHANGELINGS. TODAY TROLLS HAVE BECOME SOMEWHAT ROMANTICIZED AND TROLL DOLLS ARE A FAVOURITE WITH YOUNG CHILDREN, BUT THEIR DARKER SIDE SHOULD NEVER BE UNDERESTIMATED.

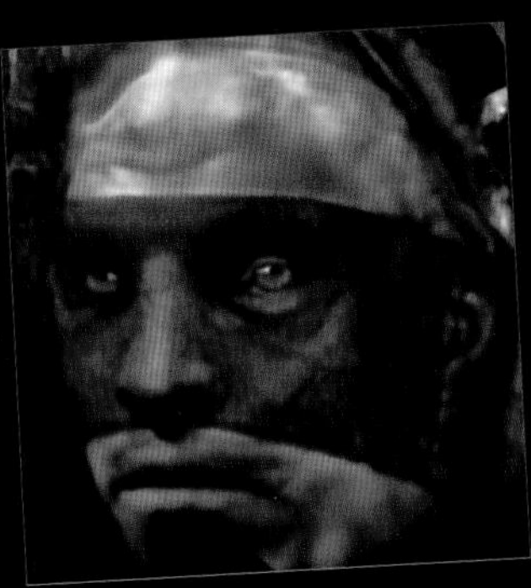

Development

• Trolls are staple characters in fantasy fiction, so there are many hundreds of descriptions of them for you to base an illustration on.
• Give yourself the freedom to explore ideas along the way and take chances. Here, the artist has brought out a demonic glow in the Troll's eyes, with a mask-like band across his face, which suggests he has something to hide.
• Try using a single-tone in your images, picking out details and textures with highlights and leaving what is in the shadows to the viewer's imagination.

Media and Execution

• Pencil, Photoshop
• The image began as a rough pencil sketch, which was scanned and opened in Photoshop.
• The sketch was heavily over-painted, with various shades of red smeared to leave some areas blurred and lower in detail than others.
• The Curves dialog was used to bring out the highlights and to strengthen the shadows.

FURTHER STUDY
Huldrafolk, *The Three Billy Goats Gruff*, changelings, John Bauer (artist).

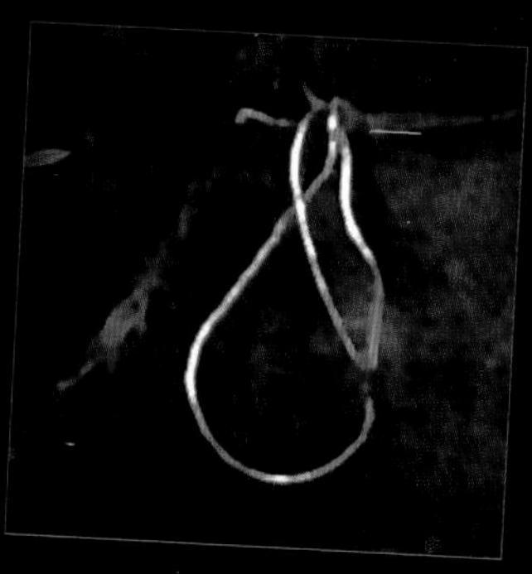

ART CHRISTOPHER SHY

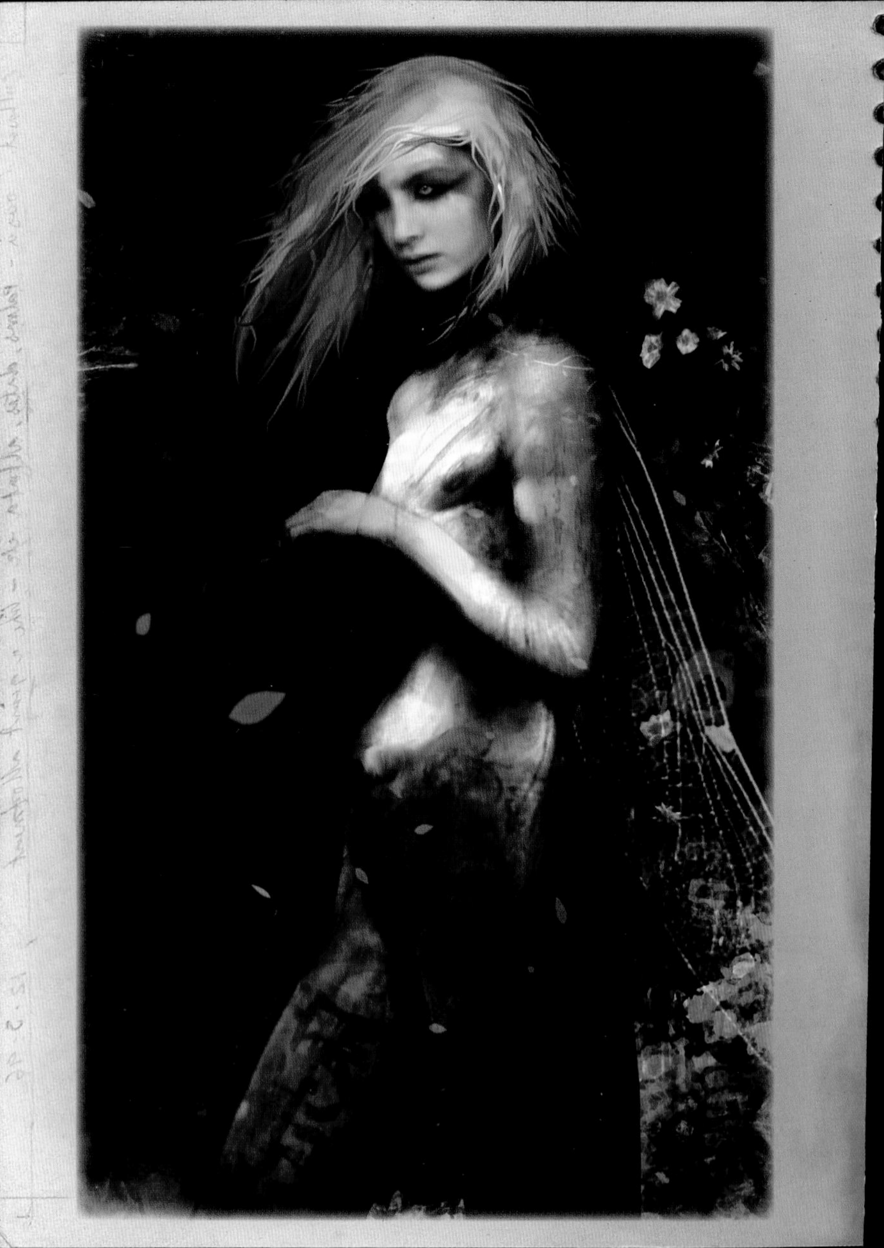

Tuatha De Danaan

ACCORDING TO THE *BOOK OF INVASIONS*, THE TUATHA DÉ DANAAN WERE THE FIFTH WAVE OF INHABITANTS TO SETTLE IN ANCIENT IRELAND. THEIR NAME MEANS 'TRIBE OR PEOPLE OF THE GODDESS DANU', AND THEY HAVE A DIVINE STATUS WITH MYSTERIOUS MAGICAL POWERS. THEY ARRIVED IN IRELAND ON THE DAY OF THE CELTIC FESTIVAL OF BELTANE, AND WENT ON TO FIGHT AND WIN MANY BATTLES, BUT THEY WERE EVENTUALLY DEFEATED AND FORCED TO RETREAT UNDERGROUND. OVER TIME THEY SHRUNK IN STATURE TO BECOME THE 'WEE FOLK' DWELLING IN MOUNDS THAT WE KNOW TODAY. THEY ARE THE KEEPERS OF FOUR MAGICAL TREASURES INCLUDING A MAGICAL CAULDRON AND A SWORD OF LIGHT.

Development

- Start with a basic humanoid figure and bring out different magical elements. Here, the distorted body shape and bright pink hair create a real sense of 'other'.
- Study ancient Celtic art and patterns and try to bring these into your picture.
- Give a certain glow to your faerie to suggest their divine power.

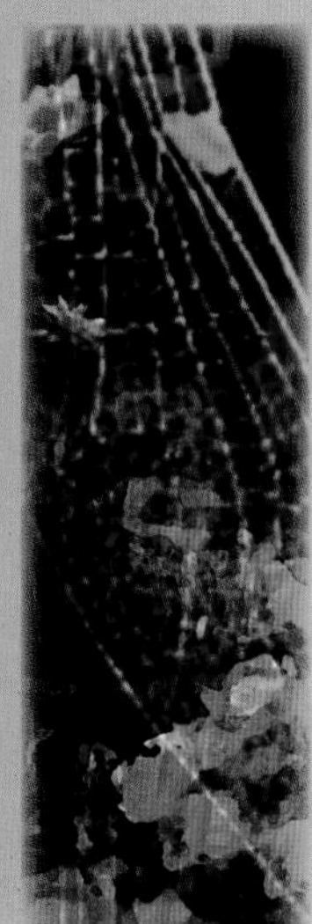

FURTHER STUDY
Irish mythology, Beltane, Danu, Morrigan, Nuada, High Kings.

ART CHRISTOPHER SHY

Media and Execution

- Photograph, Photoshop
- A model photograph was opened in Photoshop and heavily over-painted.
- The Liquify tool was used to push and pull the body into a more fantastical shape.
- Patterns and textures were overlaid on to the faerie and smeared and smudged.
- The wings were carefully drawn in on a new layer using a fine brush to create this mesh effect.
- The hair was created with a mixture of fine and soft brushes. It was then strongly toned pink to make it the focal point of the image.

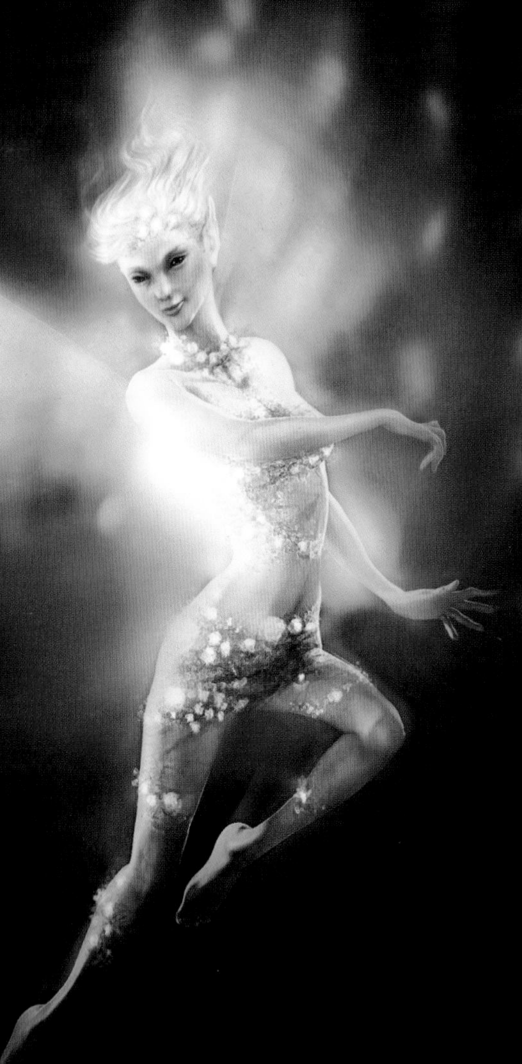

Will o' the Wisp

THE MYSTERIOUS LIGHTS THAT HANG OVER POOLS AND BOGS IN THE BRITISH ISLES HAVE LONG BEEN ATTRIBUTED TO FAERIE BEINGS, KNOWN AS WILL O' THE WISPS. THEIR FORM IS USUALLY HIDDEN BY THE GHOSTLY GREEN LIGHT THAT ENVELOPS THEM. LEGEND HAS IT THAT THEY ARE THE MISCHIEVOUS OR MALEVOLENT SPIRITS OF DEAD PEOPLE WHO CANNOT ENTER HEAVEN OR HELL, AND SO SPEND THEIR ETERNITY LURING TRAVELLERS AWAY FROM THE PATHS INTO TREACHEROUS MIRES AND MARSHES. HOWEVER, THERE ARE ALSO BELIEFS THAT WILL O' THE WISPS ARE THE GUARDIANS OF BURIED TREASURE AND WILL REWARD ANYONE WHO IS BRAVE ENOUGH TO FOLLOW THEM.

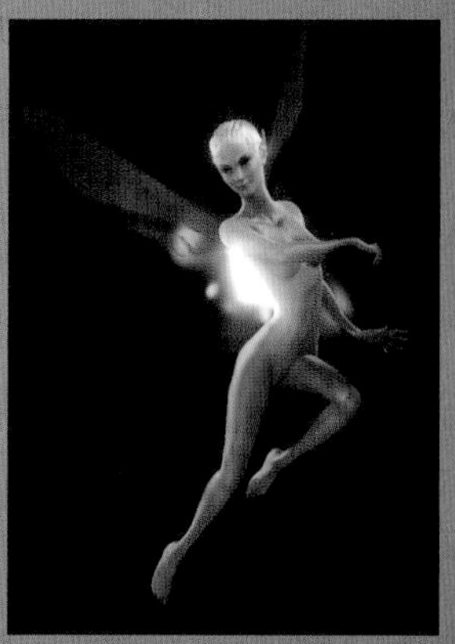

Development

- Study photographs of this natural phenomenon to inspire your faerie design – there are many examples on the Internet.
- Capturing this faerie's enigmatic nature is key to its portrayal; their eerie green glow should be the focus of your image.
- Facial expression is crucial for expressing a mischievous personality, particularly the eyes.

FURTHER STUDY

Ignis Fatuus, Jack o' Lantern, St Elmo's Fire, Feux Follets, Samuel Taylor Coleridge (poet) *The Rime of the Ancient Mariner.*

ART JULIANNA KOLAKIS

Media and Execution

- Softimage XSI, Mudbox, Zbrush, Photoshop
- The figure was modelled, and posed in XSI.
- It was then brought into Mudbox to be sculpted, and texture was added in Zbrush.
- It was taken back into XSI to be rendered, then dropped into Photoshop.
- The proportions were fixed with the Liquify filter, and details were painted in.
- Finally the highlights were strengthened and the image was colour corrected.

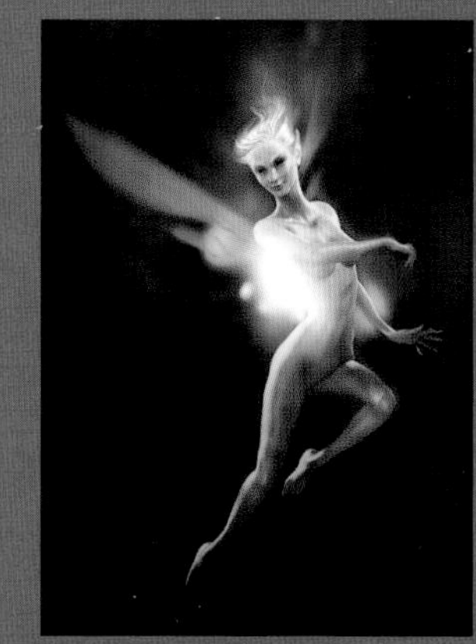

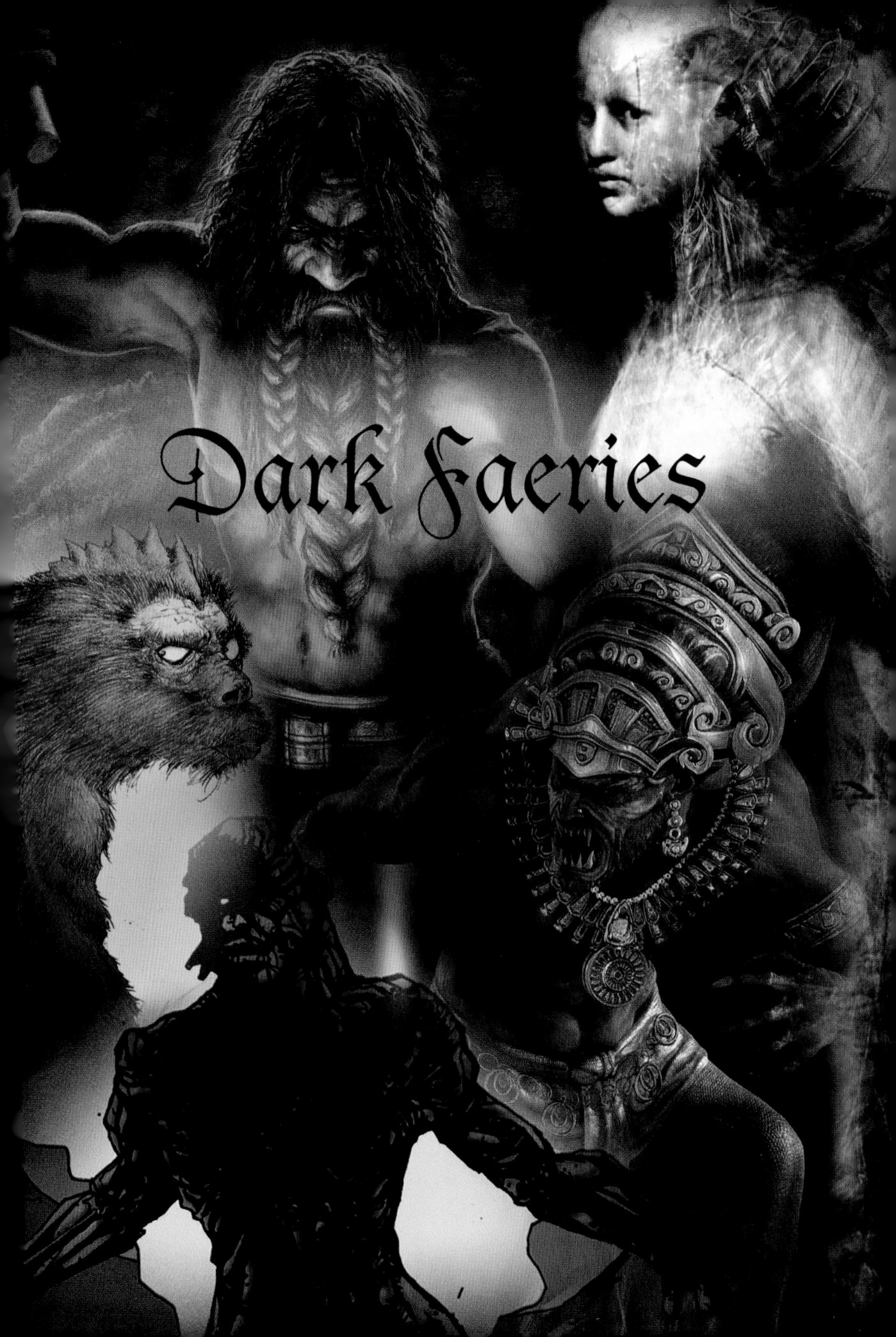
Dark Faeries

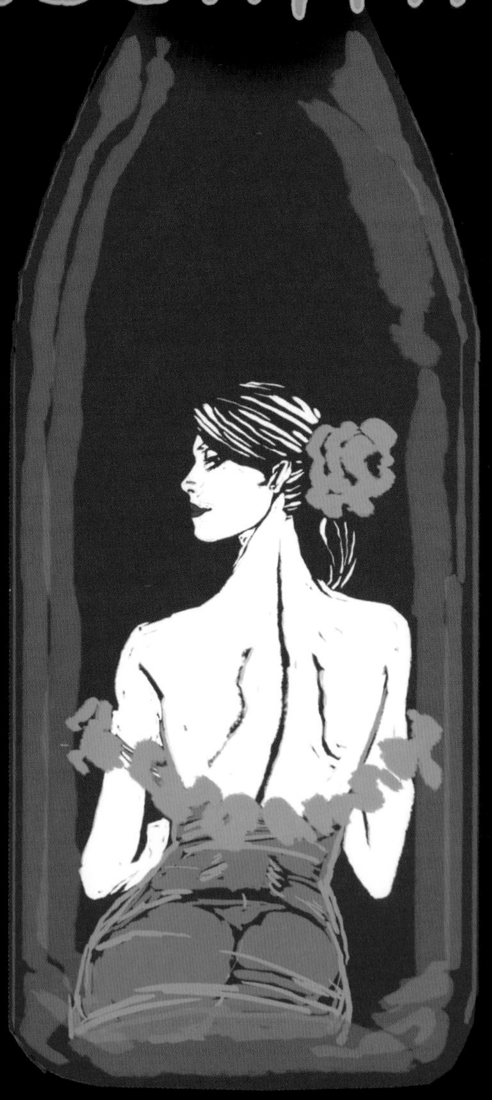
ABSINTHE

Absinthe Faerie

A POTENT ALCOHOLIC DRINK THAT BECAME MOST POPULAR DURING THE 19TH CENTURY, ABSINTHE WAS SAID TO CAUSE POWERFUL HALLUCINATIONS, MOSTLY ON ACCOUNT OF ITS ACTIVE INGREDIENT: WORMWOOD. IT BECAME A TERRIBLE SCOURGE AND CLAIMED THOUSANDS OF VICTIMS UNTIL IT WAS EVENTUALLY MADE ILLEGAL. THE NIGHTMARES THAT IT INDUCED LED TO THE MYTH OF THE ABSINTHE FAERIE OR GREEN FAERIE WHO WAS SAID TO LURE DRINKERS FURTHER INTO ADDICTION AND MADNESS. NOTABLE ABSINTHE DRINKERS WERE VAN GOGH, GAUGUIN, MANET, RIMBAUD, PICASSO, OSCAR WILDE AND TOULOUSE LAUTREC, MANY OF WHOM PRODUCED WORK INSPIRED BY THIS FAERIE.

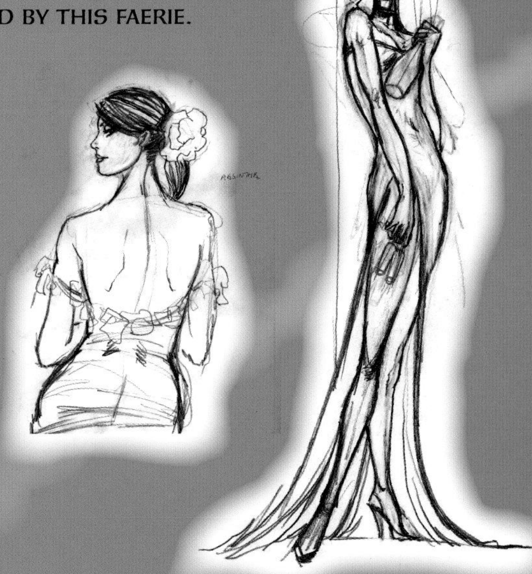

Development

- As the faerie originates from the 19th century, use the contemporary imagery of French poster design for the style of your illustration.
- Use terms such as 'devil in a bottle' to inspire you. Here, the Absinthe Faerie lurks in a bottle and looks seductively over her shoulder in an alluring manner, tempting you to try the deadly liquid.
- Early drawings featured the figure carrying the bottle and striking an elegant pose but these were discarded in favour of the final composition, which is more graphic and has a stronger message.

FURTHER STUDY

Toulouse Lautrec, Guy de Maupassant, Arthur Rimbaud, Paul Verlaine, Belle Epoche, Henri-Louis Pernod, *Moulin Rouge*.

ART FINLAY COWAN

Media and Execution

- Pencil, Photoshop
- The original line drawing was scanned in and then filled with white on a layer in Photoshop.
- The pencil line layer was then switched off leaving just the white paint layer.
- The rest of the colour layers were done in the same way, before merging the layers to finish.

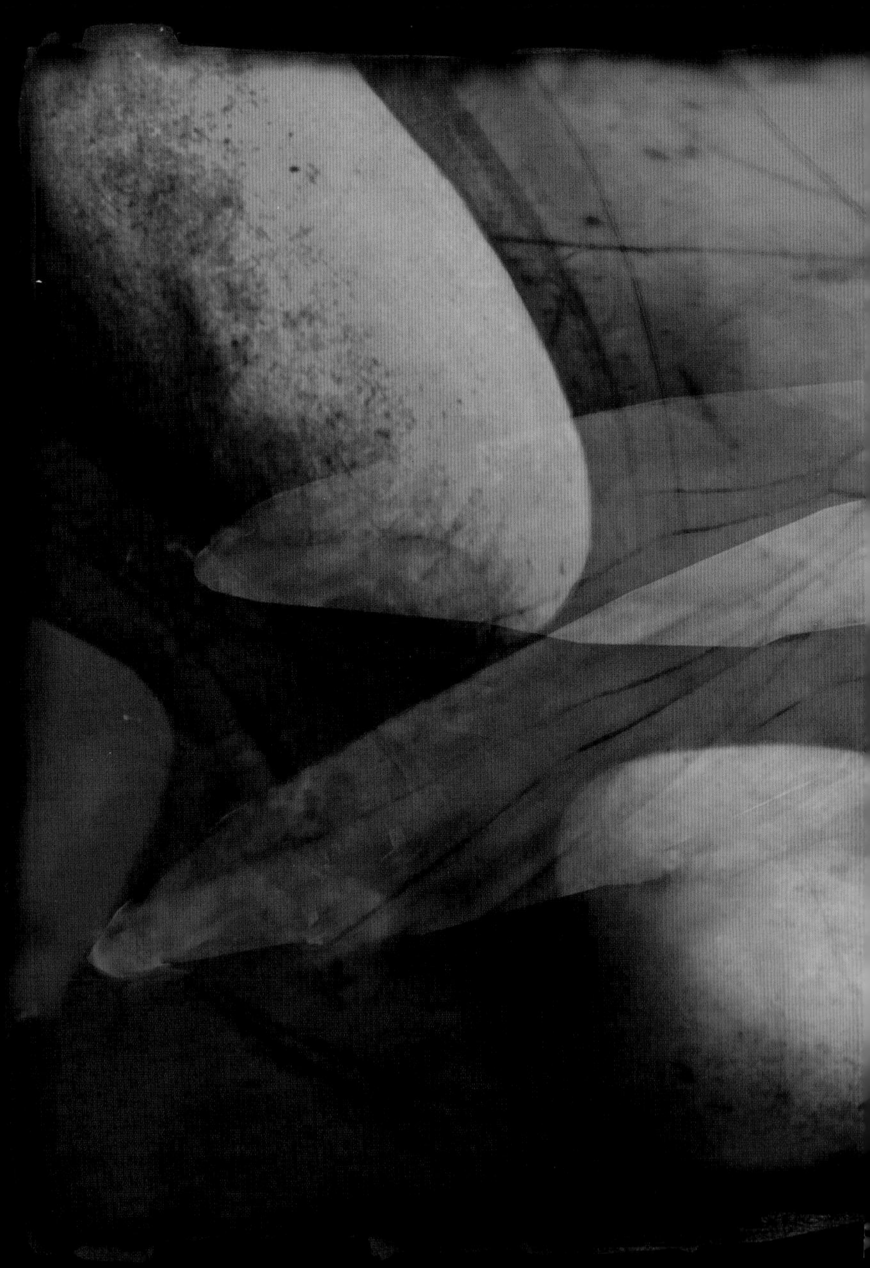

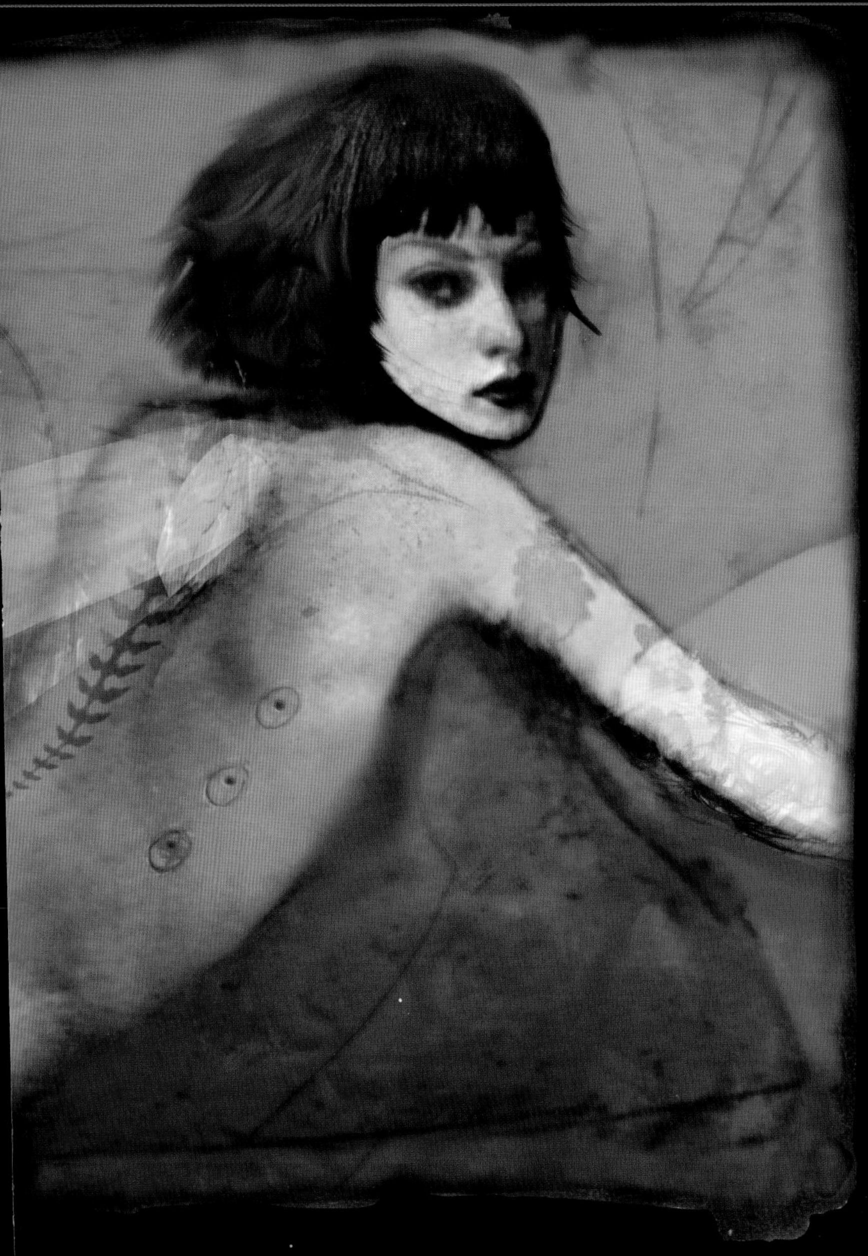

GLAISTIG

A SOLITARY, SHAPE-SHIFTING SPIRIT OF SCOTTISH ORIGIN, A GLAISTIG HAS THE UPPER BODY OF A WOMAN WITH THE LOWER HALF OF A GOAT, BUT CAN TRANSFORM HERSELF INTO EITHER HUMAN OR ANIMAL. WHEN SHE APPEARS IN HER HUMAN FORM, SHE IS THE MOST BEAUTIFUL WOMAN IMAGINABLE, CAPABLE OF ENCHANTING ALL MEN. SHE LURES UNSUSPECTING MALE VICTIMS INTO HIGHLAND CAVES WITH BEAUTIFUL SONGS AND SUGGESTIVE DANCING, AND THEN DISPATCHES THEM QUICKLY BY DRAINING THEIR BLOOD IN THE MANNER OF A VAMPIRE. SOME ACCOUNTS SUGGEST SHE CAN BE BOTH MALEVOLENT AND BENEVOLENT THOUGH, AND SAY THAT SHE SHOWS KINDNESS TO THE ELDERLY AND CHILDREN, BUT HER DARKER, BLOOD-THIRTY NATURE IS WHAT EARNS HER A FORMIDABLE REPUTATION.

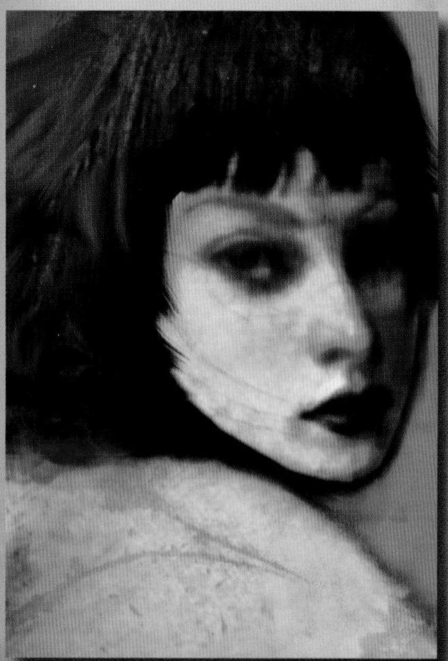

Development

• When depicting shape-shifting faeries you have the freedom and choice to show them in whatever form you like. Here, the artist was drawn to the description of a beautiful vampire-like spirit and has chosen to paint this aspect.
• Use a strong red colour to suggest blood and the interior of a cave, adding to the narrative of the image.
• Use the Quick Mask mode in Photoshop to create a border effect such as this, roughly masking out areas with a large brush to leave a loose 'painted' border.

ART CHRISTOPHER SHY

Media and Execution

- Photograph, Photoshop
- A model photograph was taken for the pose, opened in Photoshop and then over-painted.
- The face and hair were painted in from imagination to create a very strong and sinister look, but still very alluring.
- The image was printed out and the paper was folded roughly to create creases, then it was scanned back in. The creases were cloned out in other parts leaving them just visible in the background.
- The Quick Mask mode was used to create the 'painted' border to the image.

FURTHER STUDY
Scottish folklore, vampires, sirens.

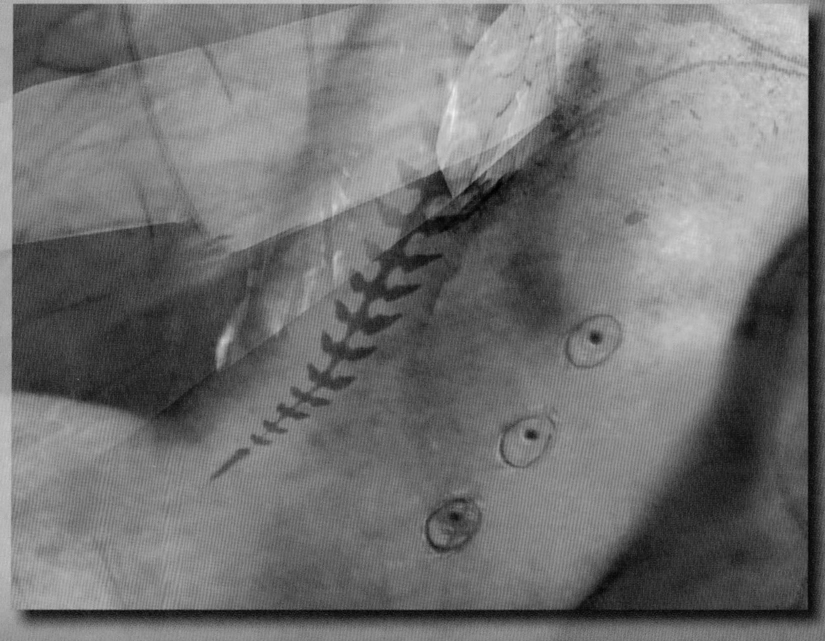

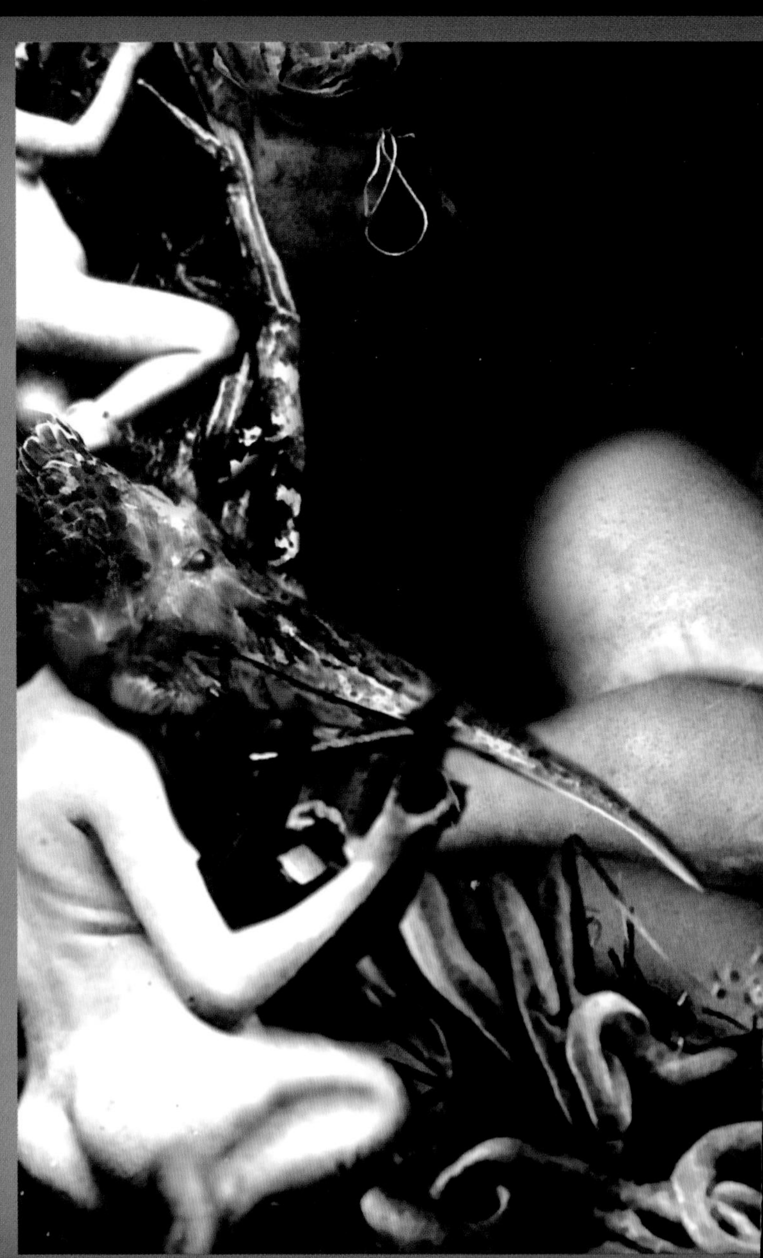

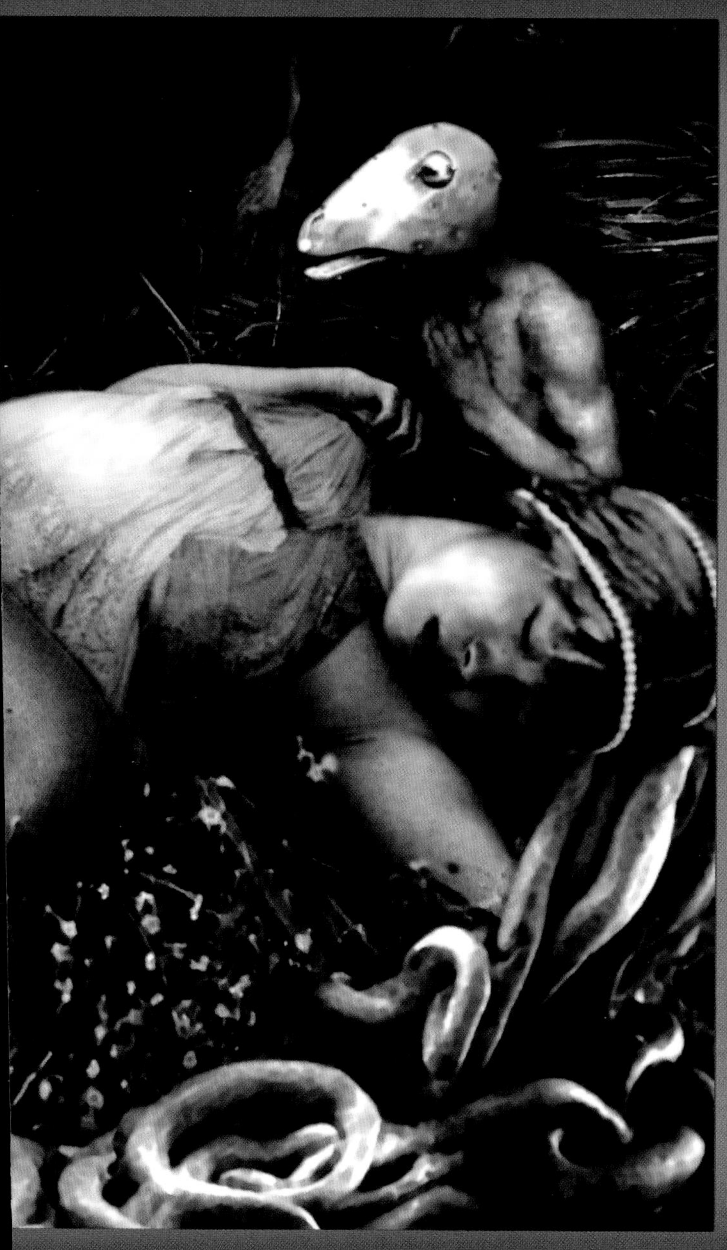

Goblins

APPEARING IN A WIDE VARIETY OF FORMS, GOBLINS ARE GENERALLY CONSIDERED TO BE NASTY-NATURED, BAD-TEMPERED SPIRITS WHO CAUSE MINOR CHAOS AND HARM WHEREVER THEY GO. THEY GRAVITATE TOWARDS HUMANS AND LIKE TO TAKE UP RESIDENCE IN HOUSES, WHERE THEY WAIT FOR THE INHABITANTS TO FALL ASLEEP AND THEN CREATE MISCHIEF BY MESSING UP ROOMS AND PINCHING OR MOLESTING THEIR HOSTS. DESCRIPTIONS OF THEIR PHYSICAL CHARACTERISTICS VARY FROM LEGEND TO LEGEND, BUT THEY ARE USUALLY PORTRAYED AS GROTESQUE OR DISFIGURED IN SOME WAY, AND AS BEING SMALL IN STATURE. IT IS SAID THAT A SMILE FROM A GOBLIN CAN CURDLE THE BLOOD, AND A LAUGH CAN TURN MILK SOUR.

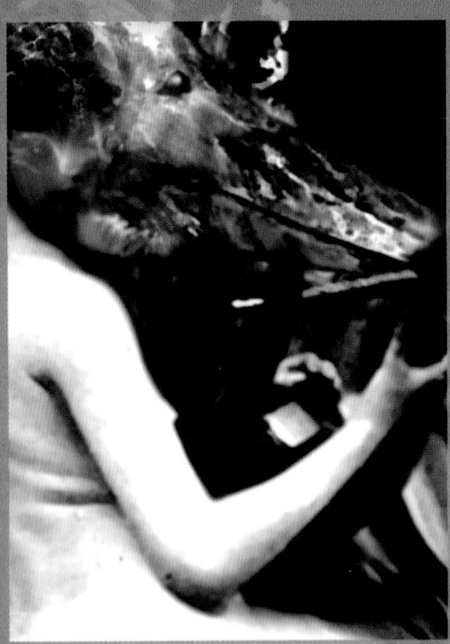

FURTHER STUDY
Hobgoblin, Boggart, Imp, Gremlin, demons.

Development

- Set your goblins in context and give a clear indication of their scale by including a human in the illustration.
- An absence of colour and a realistic depiction of the human figure makes it seem as though the scene was caught on black-and-white film, rather than being a purely imaginary event.
- Experiment with different head shapes, taking inspiration from nature and applying your own spin.
- If you make a mistake, don't bin it, use it – try to keep things fluid and let the image go where it wants to go.

Media and Execution

- Photographs, Photoshop
- Various model photographs were used and layered together in Photoshop to create the composition.
- The heads of the goblins were over-painted to create grotesques, using photographic references then distorted to make them more fantastical.
- The image was desaturated then toned with a cool sepia hue to create a sense of realism.

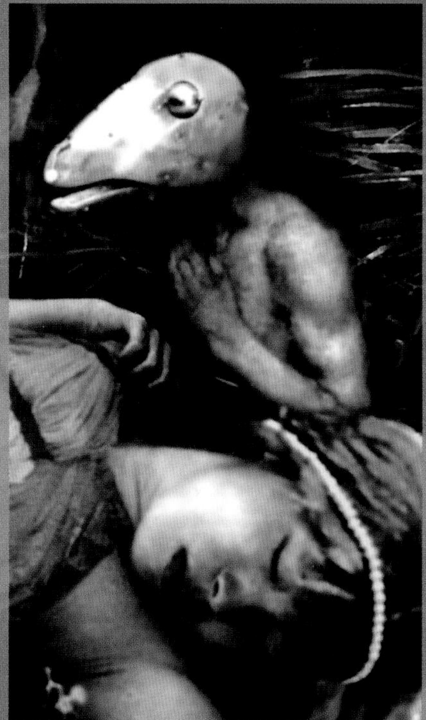

ART CHRISTOPHER SHY

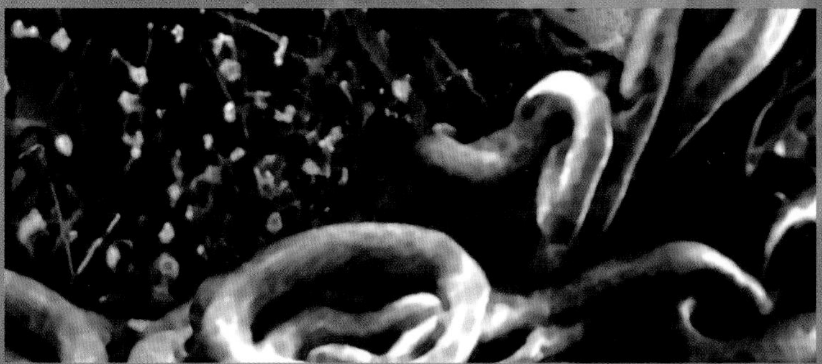

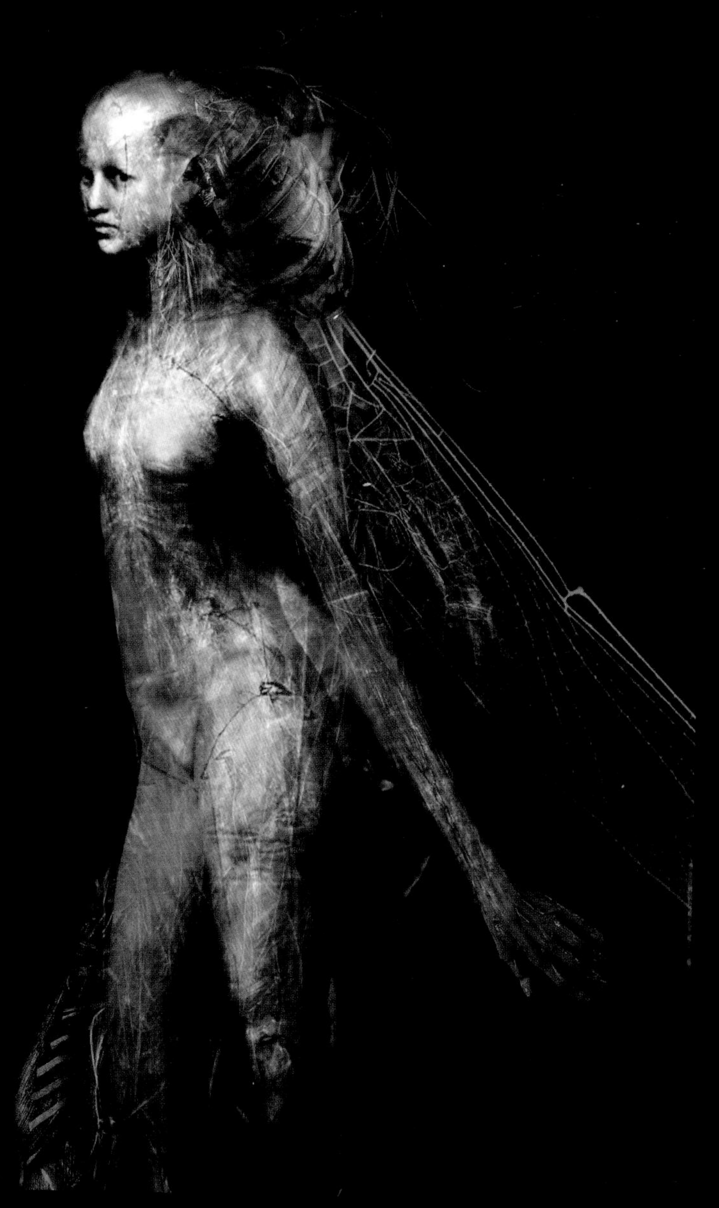

IELE

THESE CRUEL AND DANGEROUS SPIRITS HAIL FROM ROMANIAN FOLKLORE AND ARE SAID TO HUNT HUMANS RELENTLESSLY. LIKE VAMPIRES, THEY DRAIN THE BLOOD OF THEIR UNFORTUNATE VICTIMS, FOR WHICH THEY HAVE AN INTENSE AND INSATIABLE THIRST. THEY STALK REMOTE ROADS AT NIGHT AND USE STEALTH AND SPEED TO BRING DOWN PREY MUCH LARGER THAN THEY ARE. DISMEMBERED, SHRIVELLED-UP BODY PARTS ARE OFTEN THE ONLY EVIDENCE TO BE FOUND OF THE PRESENCE OF AN IELE. IF YOU FIND YOURSELF ON A LONELY ROAD IN EASTERN EUROPE AND THINK THERE MAY BE AN IELE ABOUT, HEAD FOR THE NEAREST CROSSROADS AND STAY IN THE CENTRE OF IT WHERE YOU WILL BE SAFE. SOME ACCOUNTS DESCRIBE THEIR CAT-LIKE CHARACTERISTICS, AND SAY THAT NO MATTER HOW MANY PEOPLE THEY KILL AND CONSUME THEY REMAIN EXTREMELY THIN.

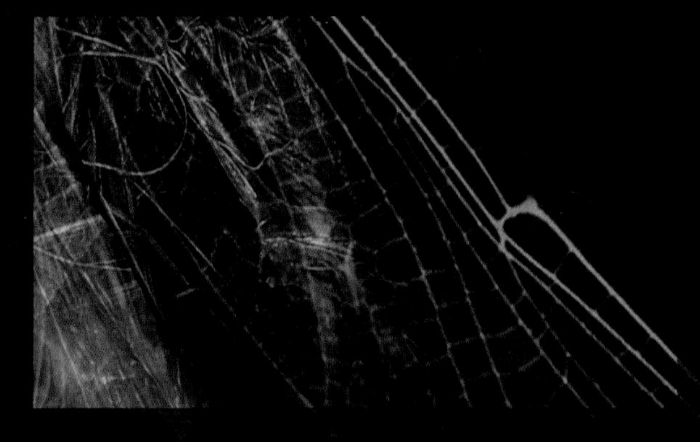

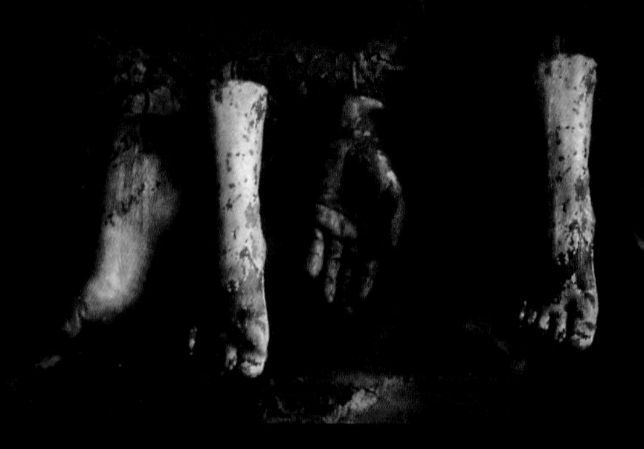

FURTHER STUDY
Eastern European folklore, vampires, cat-spirits.

ART CHRISTOPHER SHY

Development

- Although the description of the lele is very gory, don't assume you have to use red in your illustration. The green hue used here gives a far more sinister and unsettling feel to the image.
- Use photographic references when rendering hands and feet, as they are difficult to get right – even if they are dismembered!
- Try overlaying different textures on top of your characters to enhance their otherworldly feel.
- For a disturbing effect, keep the face of your character very human and close to the original model photo, then distort the body as much as you want, playing with the viewer's expectations.

Media and Execution

- Photographs, Photoshop
- Photographs were used for the faerie's face and the hands and feet hanging on the wall. These were over-painted fairly subtly to keep them instantly recognizable to the viewer. The body of the faerie was also taken from the model photograph, but was manipulated heavily to lengthen and slim the neck, arms and hands.
- Texture from another image was overlaid on to the faerie and then blended, smeared and smudged to create this effect.

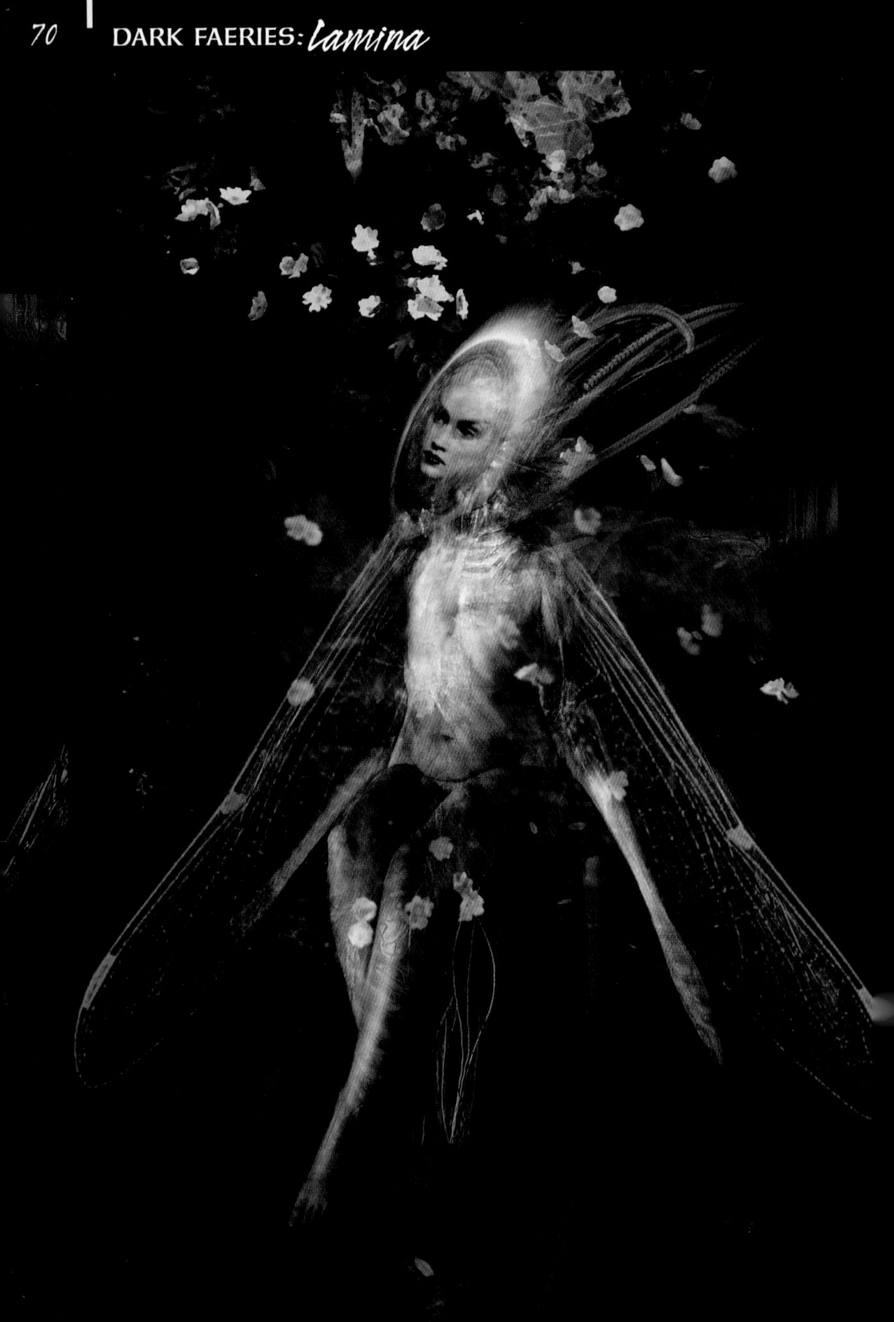

Lamina

HAILING FROM THE MYTHOLOGY OF THE BASQUE COUNTRY, LAMINAS ARE EVIL FAERIES THAT LIVE IN THE WOODS AND ON RIVERBANKS. THEY APPEAR IN THE FORM OF A BEAUTIFUL WOMAN, ALTHOUGH THEY OFTEN EXHIBIT STRANGE DISTORTIONS IN THEIR LIMBS. THEY ARE SAID TO SPEND THEIR TIME COMBING THEIR HAIR WITH GOLDEN COMBS AND OFTEN FALL IN LOVE WITH MORTAL MEN, BUT ARE UNABLE TO GET MARRIED AS THEIR WICKED NATURE MEANS THAT THEY CANNOT SET FOOT INSIDE A CHURCH. TO STEAL THE COMB OF A LAMINA WILL RESULT IN INCURRING THEIR FURIOUS WRATH, ALTHOUGH THEY HAVE AT TIMES BEEN KNOWN TO BE HELPFUL TO HUMANS, HELPING THEM BUILD BRIDGES ACROSS RIVERS.

Development

- Use colour to bring out the evil nature of your faerie – black, red and purple can all have this effect when used correctly.
- A harsh, no-nonsense facial expression helps to underpin the severe character of the Lamina.
- Fire is a motif that can be used to suggest intense anger. Here, fire can be seen above the faerie's head and is also used to add texture and colour to her torso.

Media and Execution

- Pencil, Photoshop
- A quick pencil sketch was scanned and opened in Photoshop.
- Colours were overlaid on top of the sketch, and smeared and smudged around.
- The Liquify tool was used to elongate the arms and a fine brush was used to create the hair and mesh-like wings.
- The contrast was carefully controlled using the Curves dialog.

FURTHER STUDY

Basque folklore, Lamin, sirens.

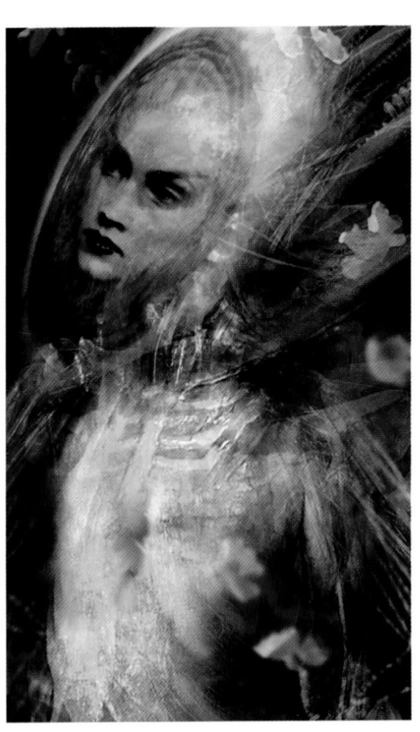

ART CHRISTOPHER SHY

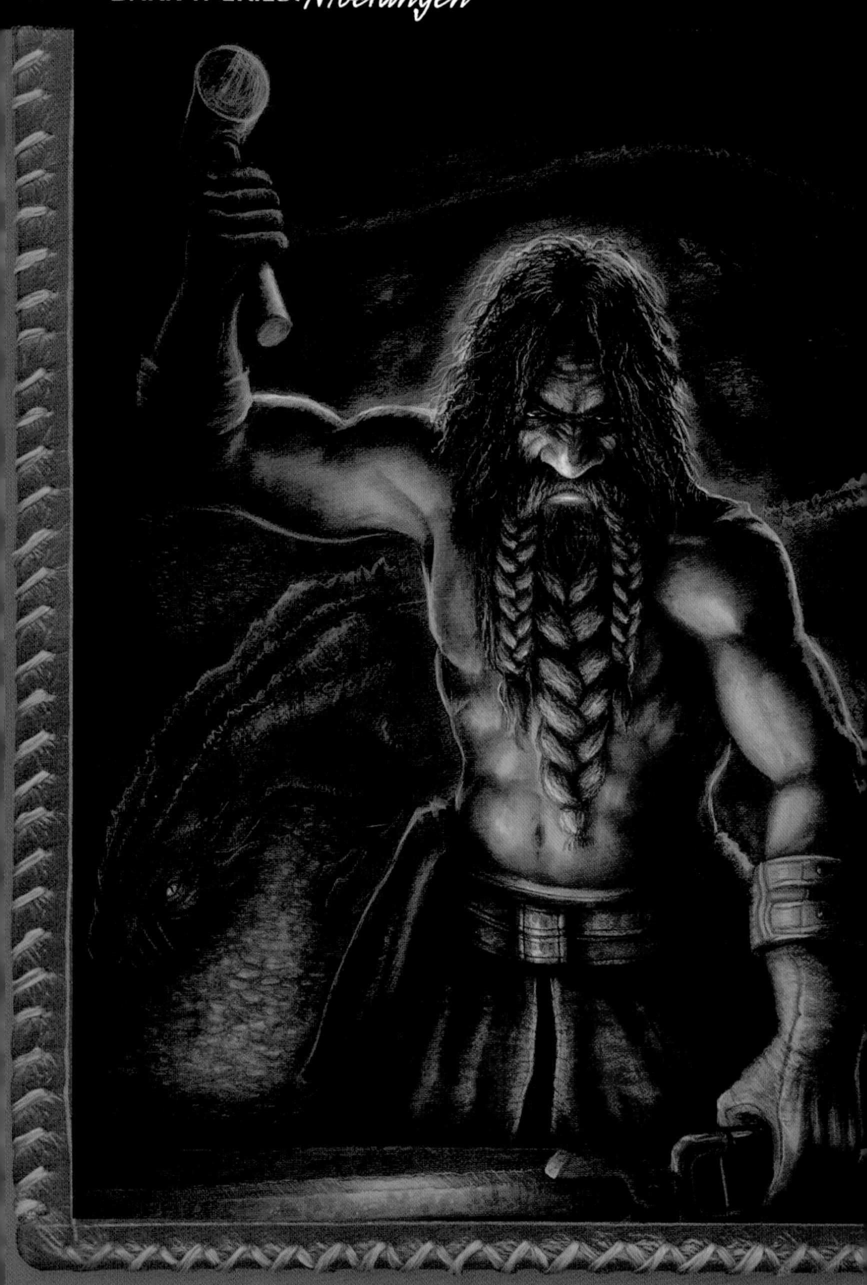

NIBELUNGEN

THE LEGEND OF A RACE OF DWARVES WHO FORGED A RING FROM STOLEN GOLD THAT GIVES MASTERY OVER ALL THE WORLD GOES BACK TO TEUTONIC FOLKLORE AND FURTHER TO NORSE MYTHOLOGY IN THE FORM OF NIBELUNGEN. THE HOARD OF GOLD THEY GUARD IN THEIR SUBTERRANEAN PALACES DOES NOT BRING HAPPINESS, BUT WILL RUIN ANYONE WHO DESIRES IT, AND THE RING IN PARTICULAR IS A HIGHLY DESTRUCTIVE FORCE FOR EVIL. ALSO KNOWN AS CHILDREN OF THE MIST, THESE EXCESSIVELY HAIRY CREATURES ARE SKILLED GOLDSMITHS, AND ALSO SHOW GREAT SKILL AT MINING AND METALLURGY. THEY HAVE STRONG ASSOCIATIONS WITH GREED, DARK DESIRES AND DEATH.

Development

- Try to capture their greedy passion through a fixed, concentrated expression.
- Use physique to reveal something about the character's lifestyle – this Nibelungen clearly works hard to have such a finely toned body.

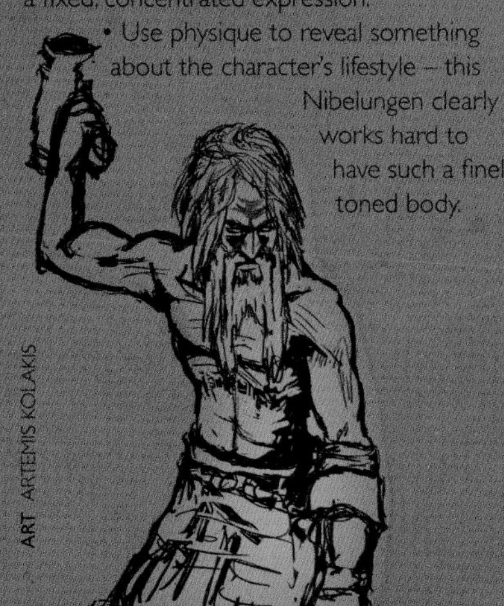

ART ARTEMIS KOLAKIS

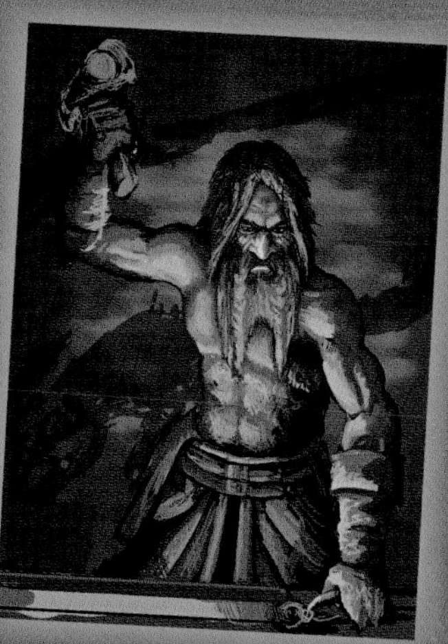

Media and Execution

- Photoshop
- The composition was sketched out digitally in Photoshop.
- Proportions were corrected with the Lasso tool and Liquify filter.
- The image was then colour corrected and prepared for print in Photoshop.

FURTHER STUDY

Dwarf, Richard Wagner (composer) *Der Ring des Nibelungen*, Alberich, Kobold, JRR Tolkien (author) *The Lord of the Rings*.

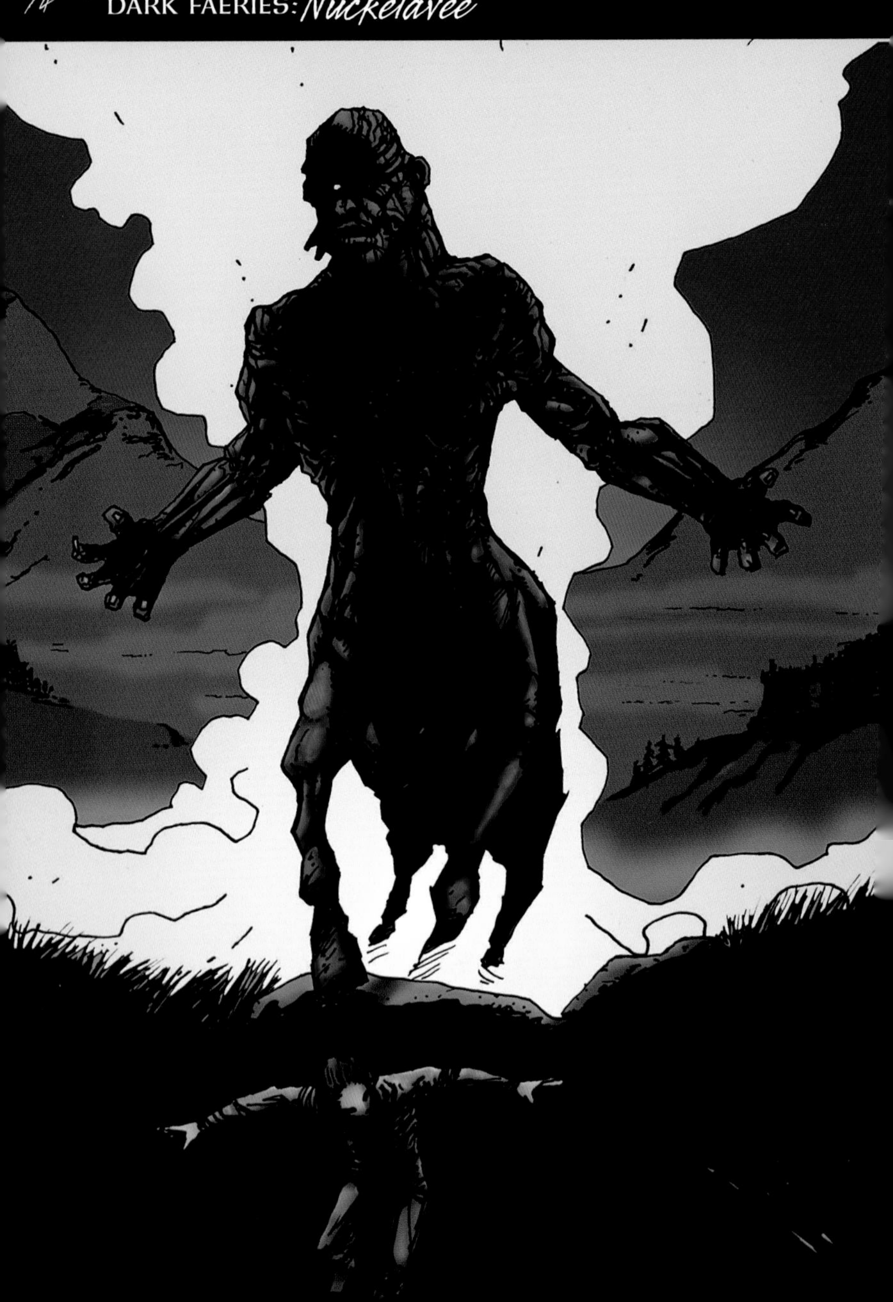

Nuckelavee

THE MOST HORRIBLE AND FEARED OF ALL THE CREATURES IN SCOTTISH FOLKLORE, THE NUCKELAVEE IS A LOATHSOME MONSTER. IT WAS SAID TO BE HAIRLESS AND APPEARED TO BE A MASS OF RAW, WRITHING FLESH WITH YELLOW BLOOD PULSING THROUGH THE VEINS THAT CRISSCROSSED THE SURFACE OF ITS SKIN. IT HAD LONG ARMS AND A HUGE HEAD IN WHICH PULSED A GLOWING RED EYE. THE CREATURE WAS RESPONSIBLE FOR THE DEATHS OF LONE TRAVELLERS AND WAS ALSO BLAMED FOR THE FAILURE OF CROPS AND ANY PESTILENCE THAT AFFECTED LIVESTOCK. THE NUCKELAVEE HAD ONLY ONE WEAKNESS: A FEAR OF WATER, AND ANYBODY UNLUCKY ENOUGH TO BE PURSUED BY THE BEAST COULD ONLY ESCAPE IT BY LEAPING OVER A STREAM.

Development

- Try using technical ink pens to achieve a graphic novel look.
- The use of a low vanishing point and perspective lines will help to emphasize the creature's size by creating a view from a low angle.

Media and Execution

- Pencil, pen and ink, Photoshop
- Pencil sketches were used to work out the shadows and get all the compositional elements right.
- Each element was then inked separately on a light box.
- All the different elements were then brought into Photoshop on separate layers – this made it quicker to select and colour each object in the final picture.
- Although the colours are quite flat, there are subtle variations in light and darkness achieved using the Burn tool.

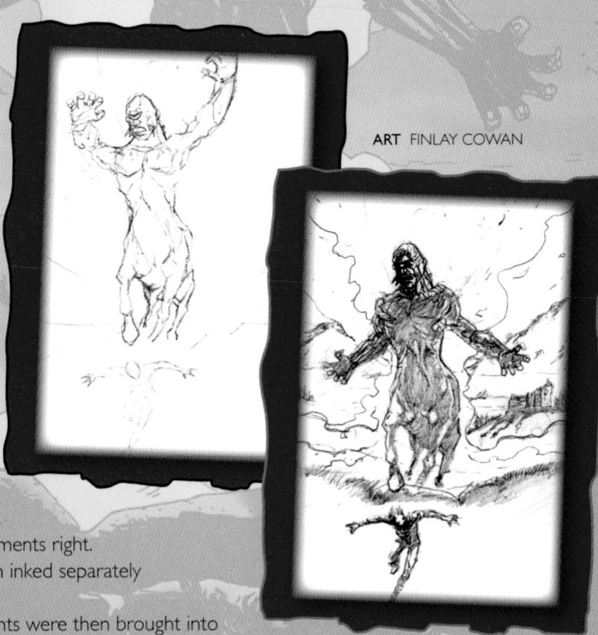

ART FINLAY COWAN

FURTHER STUDY
Scottish folklore, Kelpie, Backahasten, Sloagh, Red Cap, Awd Goggie.

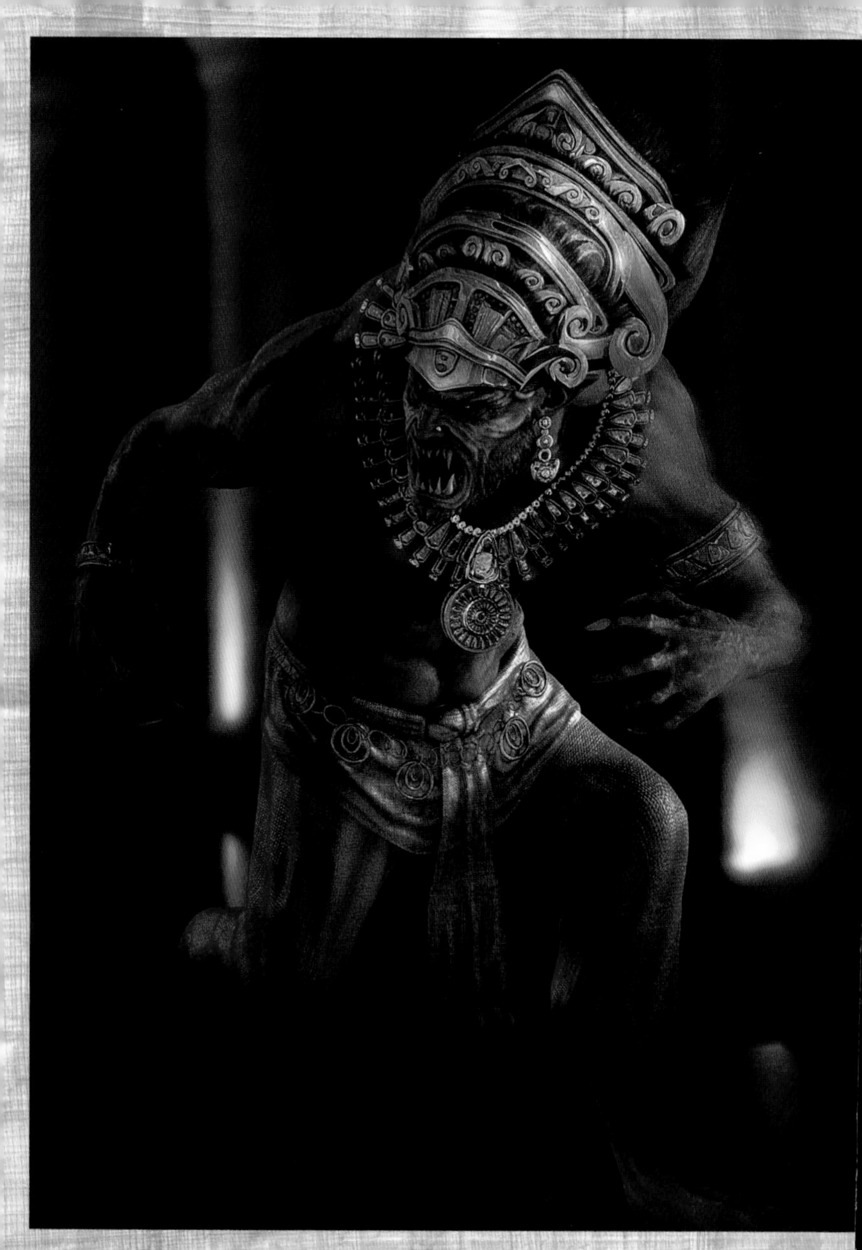

Raksha

MALICIOUS, DIM-WITTED DEMONS THAT SERVE THEIR TEN-HEADED, TWENTY-ARMED KING RAVANA, RAKSHA HAIL FROM INDIAN FOLKLORE. THEY ARE BELIEVED BE THE REINCARNATIONS OF WICKED HUMANS AND ARE ETERNAL ENEMIES OF VISHNU. THEY DISTURB SACRIFICES, HARASS PRIESTS, POSSESS HUMAN SOULS AND DESECRATE GRAVES. THEY HAVE THE ABILITY TO CHANGE THEIR SHAPE AND FORM AT WILL AND CAN CONJURE POWERFUL ILLUSIONS. THEY HAVE VENOMOUS FINGERNAILS AND FEED ON HUMAN FLESH, FREQUENTLY MATERIALIZING ON BATTLEFIELDS AND FEASTING ON THE SLAUGHTERED. RAKSHA MASKS ARE USED IN PROCESSIONS AND FESTIVALS IN INDIA AND SRI LANKA.

Development

- Give your demonic figures a foul and savage sense of disfigurement – this Raksha has similar qualities to a vampire, as he is known to be a voracious man-eater.
- Obtain as much visual reference material as possible to help in rendering Indian-style costume and jewellery.

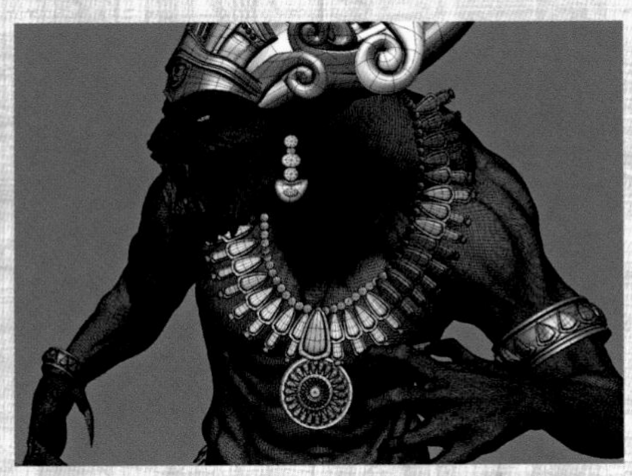

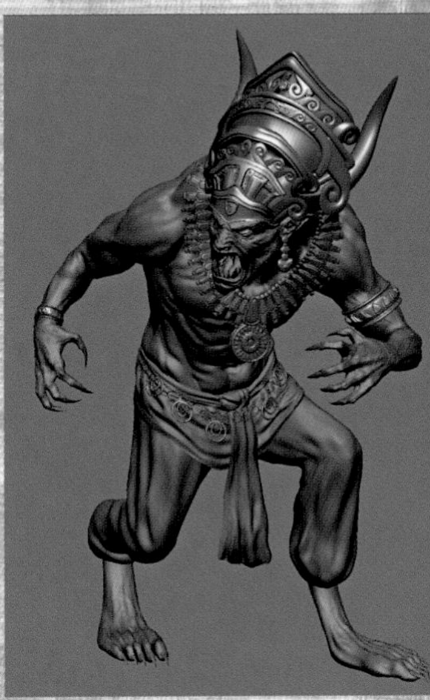

ART JULIANNA KOLAKIS

Media and Execution

- Softimage XSI, Zbrush, Photoshop
- The figure was modelled and posed in XSI.
- He was brought into Zbrush to be sculpted, and then taken back into XSI for rendering.
- Finally he was dropped into Photoshop for detailing, motion blurring and colour correction.

FURTHER STUDY

Hindu mythology, Rakshasa, Ramayana, Ravana, *The Mahabharata*.

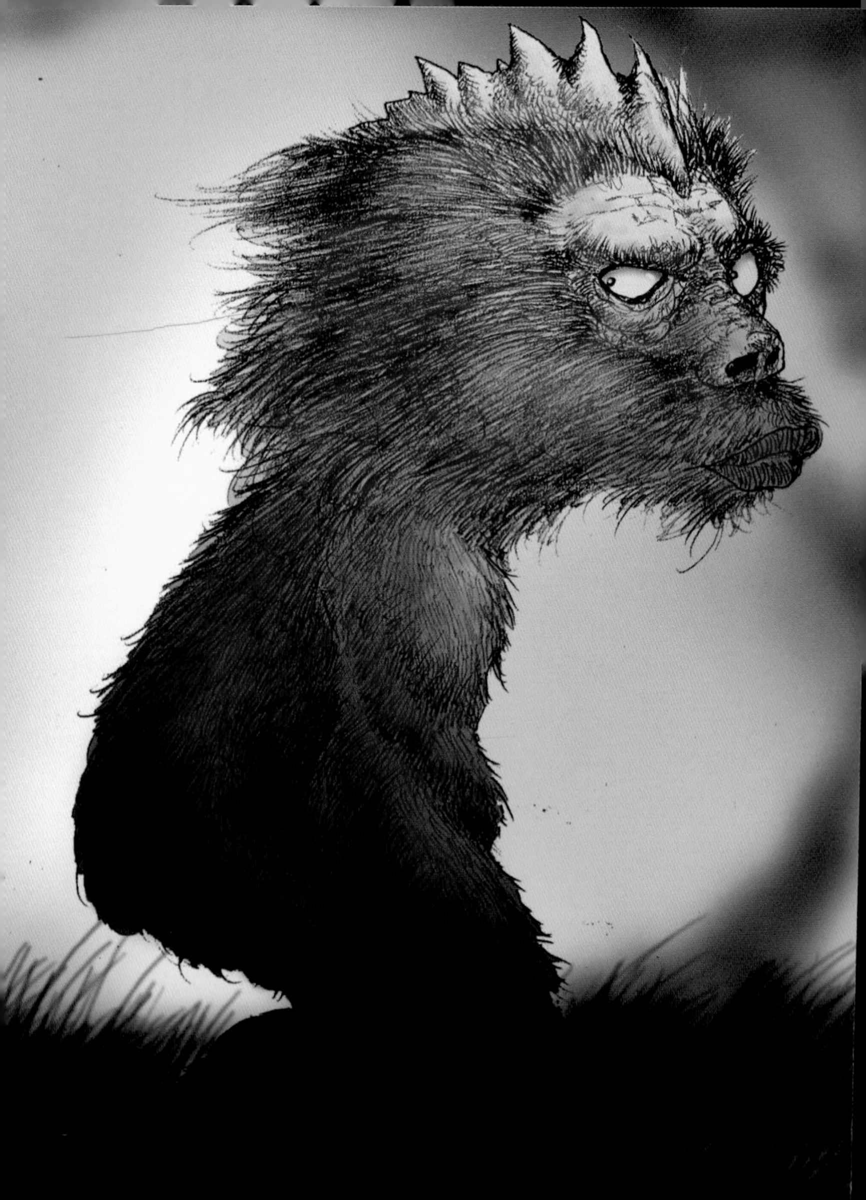

Hobbs '07

Tikoloshe

BELONGING TO THE MYTHOLOGY OF THE AFRICAN ZULU, A TIKOLOSHE, ALSO KNOWN AS TOKOLOSHE OR HILI, IS A DWARF-LIKE WATER SPRITE. IT IS SAID TO HAVE ONLY ONE ARM AND ONE LEG, AND IS FOND OF WOMEN AND MILK. A MISCHIEVOUS AND OFTEN EVIL SPIRIT, HE CAN BECOME INVISIBLE BY SWALLOWING A PEBBLE. THE TIKOLOSHE IS A BEAR-LIKE HUMANOID WITH A THICK BONY RIDGE ON TOP OF ITS HEAD WITH SHAGGY HAIR ALL OVER, RATHER LIKE THE BIGFOOT OF AMERICAN LEGEND. IN SOME AFRICAN FOLKLORE THE TIKOLOSHE IS A MIXTURE OF ZOMBIE, POLTERGEIST AND GREMLIN AND IS OFTEN IN THE SERVICE OF A WITCH DOCTOR OR WIZARD.

Development

- Develop your characters through a series of sketches, refining with each one.
- Use references found on the Internet of apes and bears. Exaggerate the features, particularly the hands, feet and face to create a more otherworldly look.
- Use facial expressions to convey your character's attitude. Here the character has been given not so much an evil look but certainly an unfriendly one – he is not to be messed with.

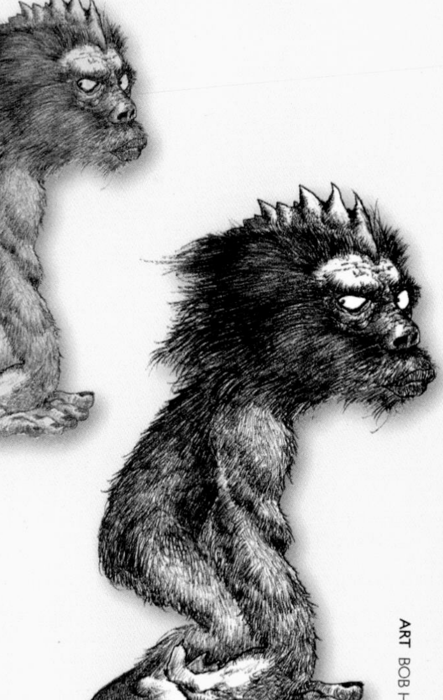

Media and Execution

- Pencil, Photoshop
- Preliminary sketches were made and the final pencil drawing was scanned and opened in Photoshop.
- The white background was deleted and the pencil lines were enhanced using the Levels dialog, contrast and sharpness.
- The image was coloured using the various Paint tools, and a background was created and blurred so that the figure stood out more.
- The image was finished off by applying a lighting effect that highlighted the upper torso and face.

ART BOB HOBBS

FURTHER STUDY

Zulu mythology, Credo Mutwa, Bigfoot, witch doctor, zombies.

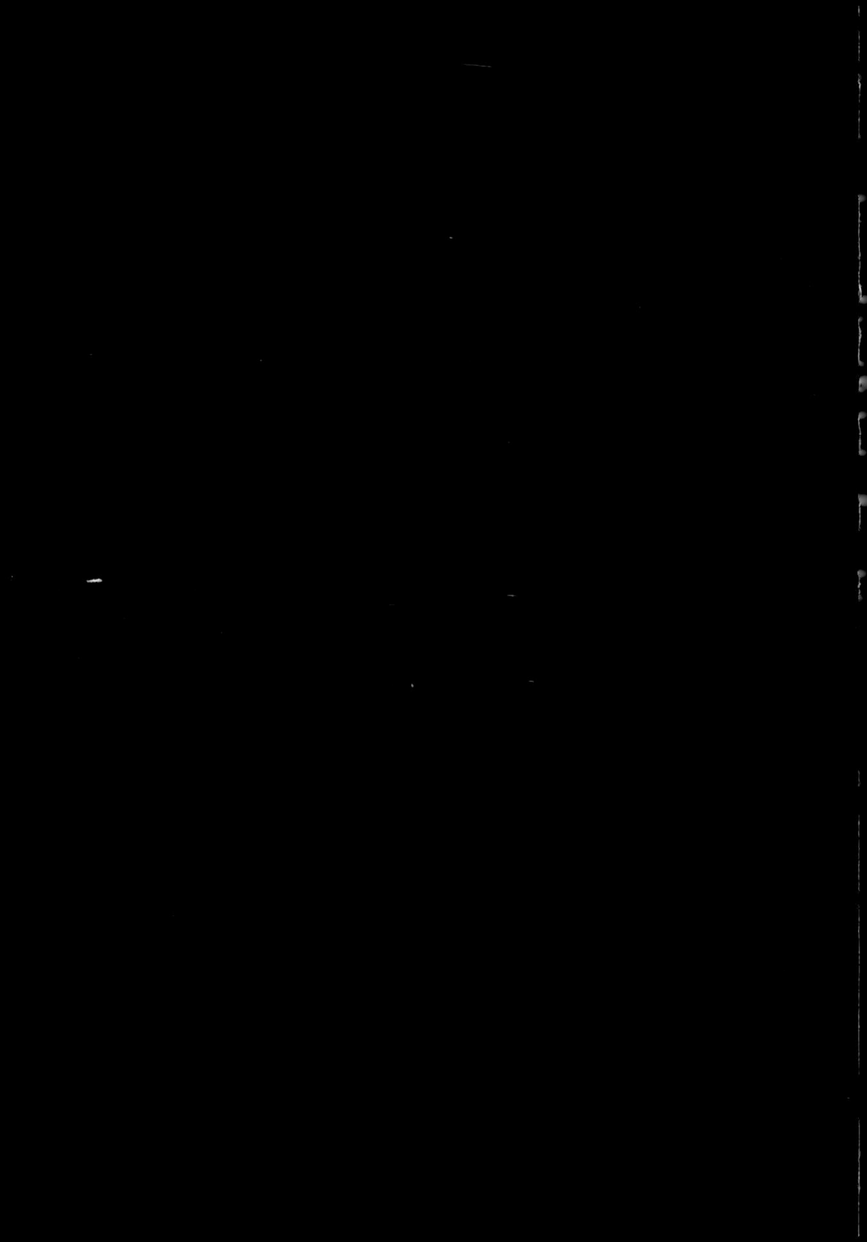

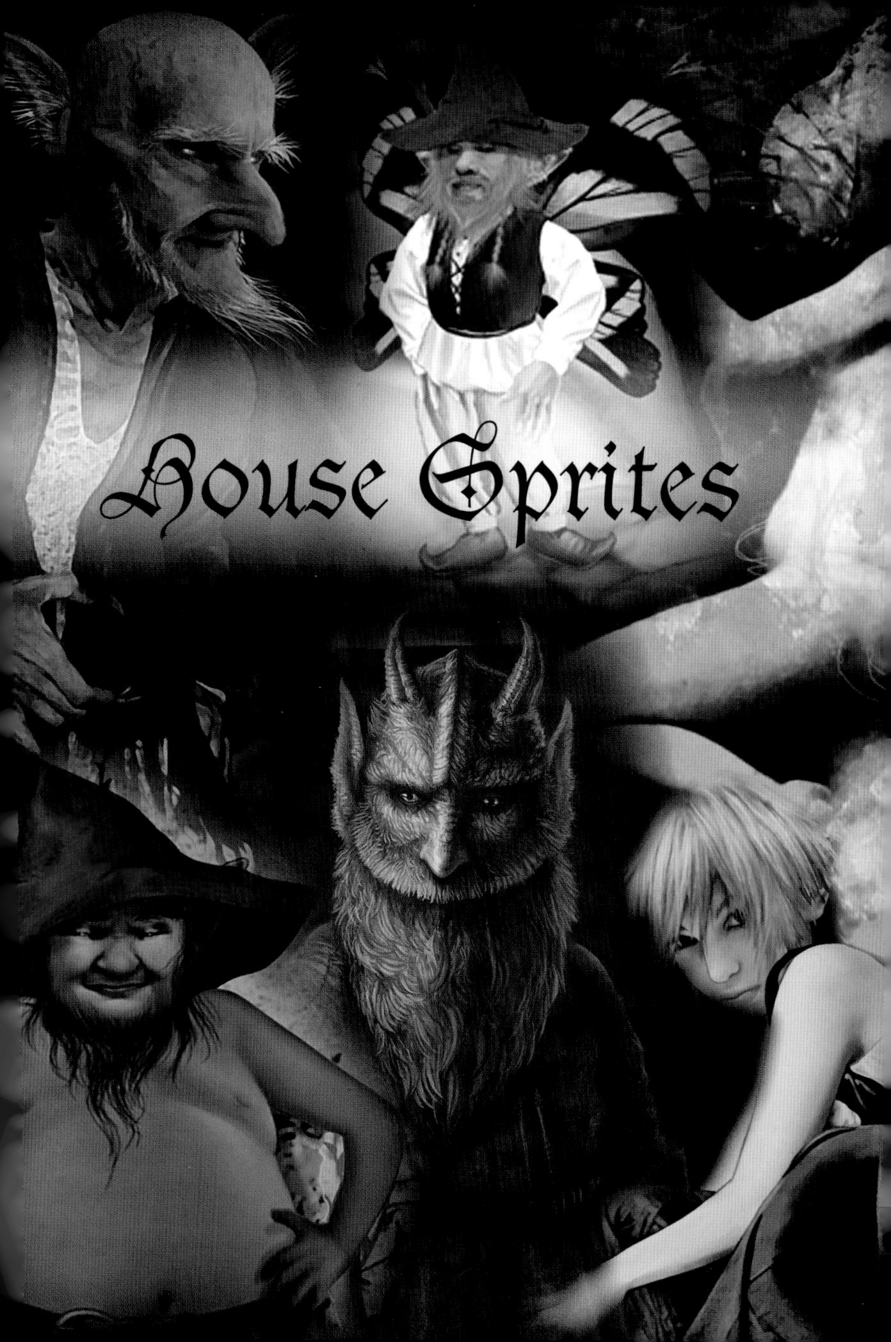
House Sprites

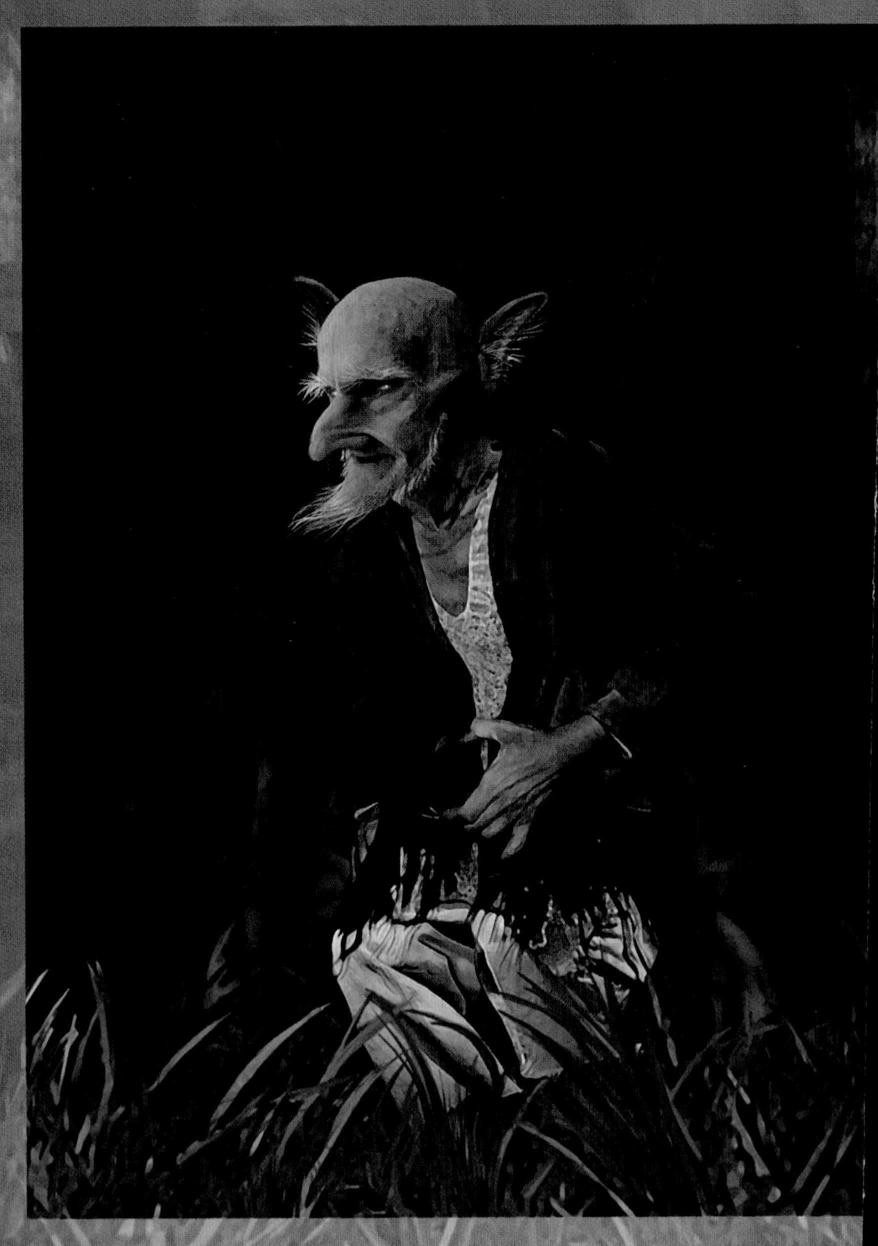

Boggart

MALEVOLENT, CLUMSY HOUSEHOLD SPIRITS, BOGGARTS CAUSE MILK TO TURN SOUR, THINGS TO DISAPPEAR AND DOGS TO GO LAME. THEY ARE SAID TO CRAWL INTO PEOPLE'S BEDS AND PLACE THEIR CLAMMY HANDS ON THEIR FACES, PULL ON THEIR EARS AND STRIP THE BED SHEETS OFF THEM. THERE IS NO WAY TO APPEASE A BOGGART; IT WILL ATTACH ITSELF TO A FAMILY AND FOLLOW THEM EVEN IF THEY TRY TO FLEE. BOGGARTS ARE DARK AND HAIRY AND DRESS IN RAGS AND TATTERED CLOTHES. WHEN NOT OCCUPYING HOUSES, THEY LIVE UNDER BRIDGES AND ON DANGEROUS SHARP BENDS ON ROADS. HANGING A HORSESHOE ON THE DOOR OF YOUR HOUSE IS SAID TO KEEP A BOGGART AWAY.

Development

- Read up on your character and its basic folklore, finding any interesting stories to fire your imagination.
- If your character is a nocturnal creature, a dark and gloomy atmosphere should prevail. Creepy-looking trees help to convey menace.
- Choosing an outdoor setting adds to the narrative, as if the Boggart is searching for a new home and a new family to bother.

Media and Execution

- Pencil, Photoshop
- A rough sketch was scanned and opened in Photoshop, and the outlines were redrawn.
- The tree, fence and grass were painted in on several layers so that the character could be placed in between. Once combined, the Liquify filter and the Clone tool were used to smooth and blend the layers.
- Colour was added then the light, shadows and textures were enhanced.
- Finally, the layers were merged and drop shadows and other shading effects were applied.

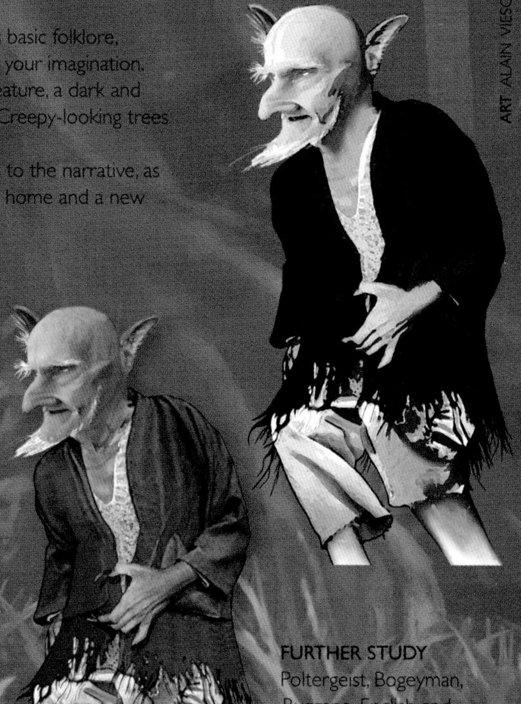

ART ALAIN VIESCA

FURTHER STUDY
Poltergeist, Bogeyman, Buggane, English and Manx folklore.

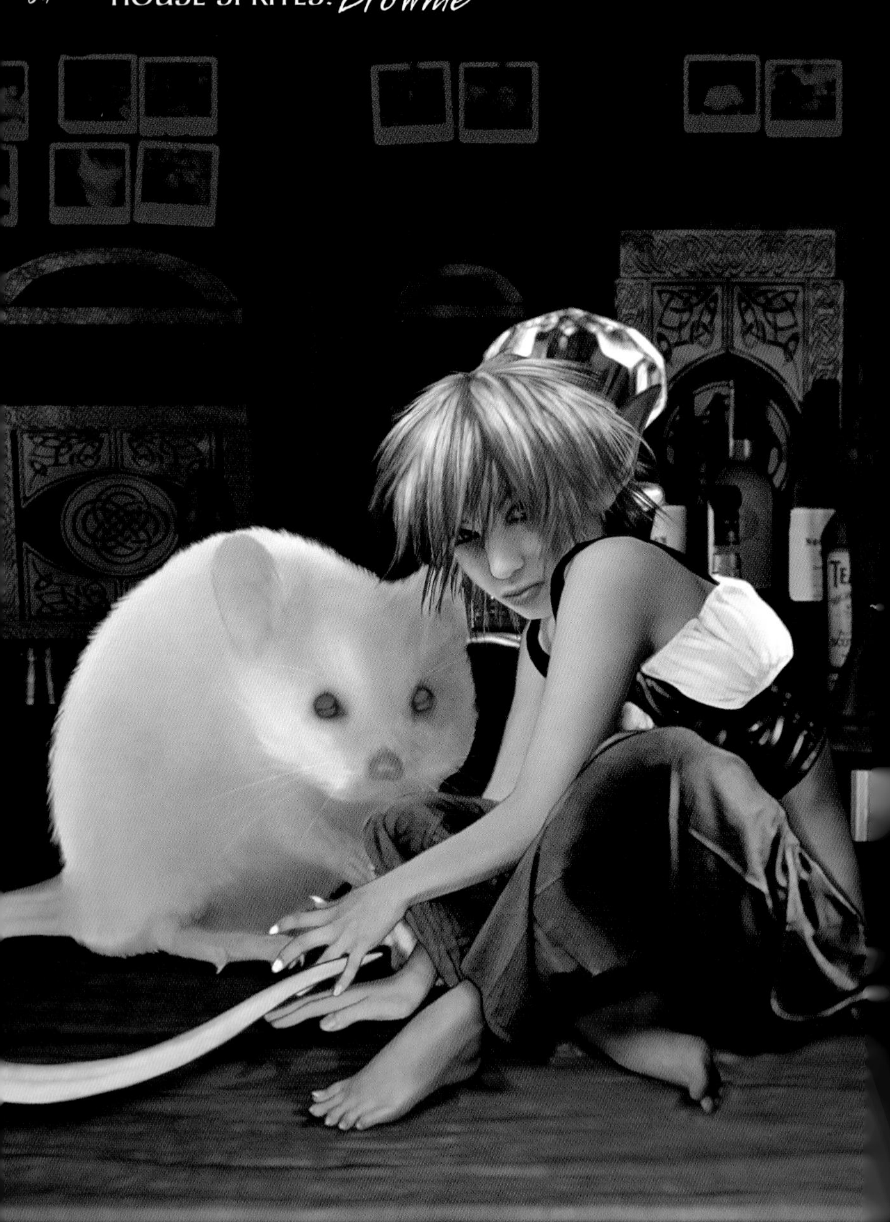

Brownie

GOOD-NATURED SPIRITS THAT AID IN TASKS AROUND THE HOUSE, BROWNIES ARE VERY SHY, DO NOT LIKE TO BE SEEN AND ONLY WORK AT NIGHT WHEN THE RESIDENTS ARE ASLEEP. THEY PERFORM THEIR CHORES IN EXCHANGE FOR GIFTS AND FOOD. THEY WILL ABANDON A HOUSE IF THEY ARE SPIED UPON, SPOKEN OF, OR IF THE GIFTS ARE CALLED PAYMENTS. IF TREATED CRUELLY THEY WILL TURN INTO BOGGARTS. BROWNIES ARE SMALL WITH CURLY HAIR AND WEAR EARTH-COLOURED CLOTHES. WHEN THERE IS NO HOUSE TO CALL HOME THEY MAKE THEIR RESIDENCE IN HOLLOW TREES AND RUINED CASTLES. BROWNIES ATTACH THEMSELVES TO FAMILIES AND CAN RESIDE IN THE SAME HOME FOR MANY GENERATIONS.

Development

- Do some background research on your character and its folklore then use your imagination to create your own variation. In most stories Brownies are male, but a cute female version was created here instead.
- Refer back to old sketchbooks to see if you have any suitable material that can be reused in your new work.
- Use props and other creatures to help describe the scale of tiny characters.

Media and Execution

- 3DS Max, pencil, Photoshop
- This piece began with a 3D modelled background.
- A pencil sketch of the Brownie was scanned in and the outline was redrawn in Photoshop with tints and shades added on a new layer.
- The Liquify filter and Clone tool were used to smooth and blend the layers; then the highlights on the skin, hair and mouse's fur were enhanced to bring out more of a glow.
- The layers were merged and the entire image was outlined to achieve the illustrative look.

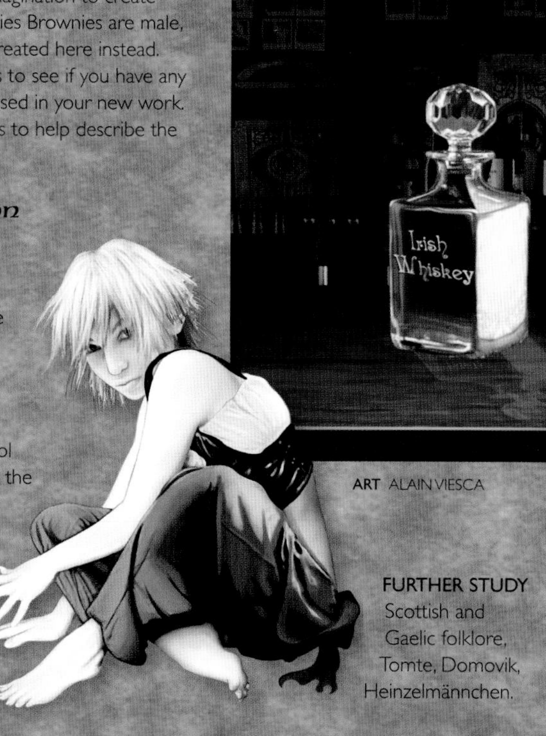

ART ALAIN VIESCA

FURTHER STUDY
Scottish and Gaelic folklore, Tomte, Domovik, Heinzelmännchen.

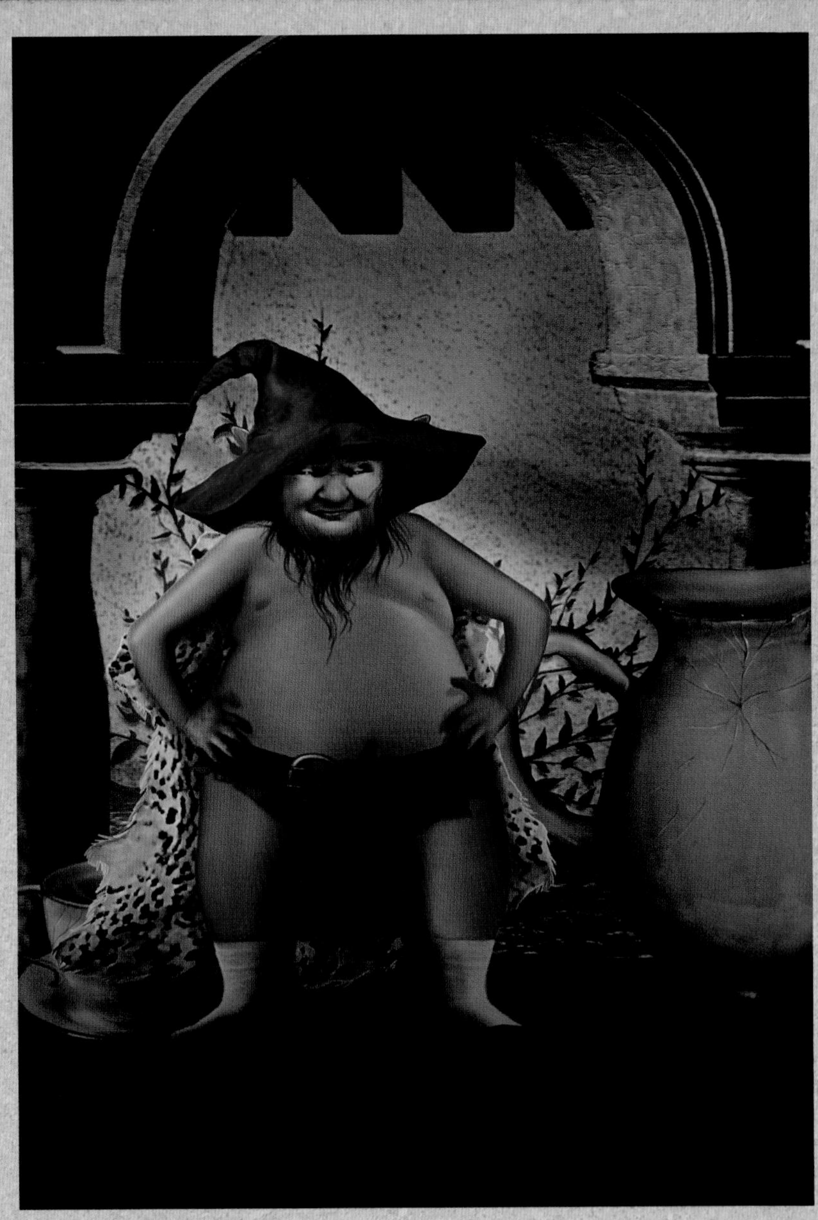

BWBACH

THESE SOLITARY HOUSE FAIRIES ARE SMALL, ROUND AND WEAR LARGE HATS AND ANIMAL FUR CLOAKS. NOT AS HELPFUL AS BROWNIES, THEY ARE MISCHIEVOUS, SOMEWHAT UNTRUSTWORTHY AND VERY TERRITORIAL, THOUGH THEY DO NOT WISH TO HARM THEIR HOST FAMILIES. BWBACHS ARE PROTECTIVE TOWARDS THE HOME AND WILL CHASE AWAY INTRUDERS. THEY ARE PRANKSTERS BUT CAN BE PACIFIED WITH REGULAR FEEDING. IT IS SAID THAT A BWBACH CAN TRANSPORT A HUMAN THROUGH THE AIR, BUT CAUTION IS NEEDED: FIRST HE WILL GIVE YOU A CHOICE ON THE MANNER OF TRAVEL – ALWAYS CHOOSE 'MID-WIND' TO AVOID BEING DRAGGED THROUGH BRIAR OR THROWN INTO CLOUDS. THEY HATE NOSEY PEOPLE AND HAVE A VIOLENT DISLIKE OF MEDDLESOME FOLK.

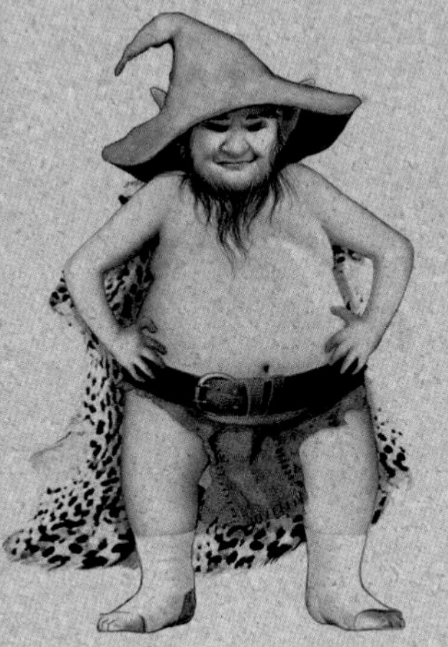

Development

- If a faerie is mischievous and territorial, give them a darker nature.
- Many faeries have become overlapped in different folk tales, so it can be difficult to find specific information about more obscure faeries. Just go with whatever basic descriptions you can find and use your own imagination to take it further.
- Try out the Liquify filter in Photoshop to distort your characters into fantastical shapes.

FURTHER STUDY
Welsh folklore,
Brownie,
Boggart,
Domovik.

Media and Execution

- 3DS Max, Photoshop
- This piece began as separate 3D background and foreground images, which were then rendered and composited in Photoshop.
- The character was roughed out in Photoshop and the Liquify filter was used to exaggerate the body shape.
- Colours were added on a new layer. The character was dropped on to the background and the lighting and shadows were matched up.
- A dark red was used to deepen and texture the shadows, and a glow was added to make the character stand out.

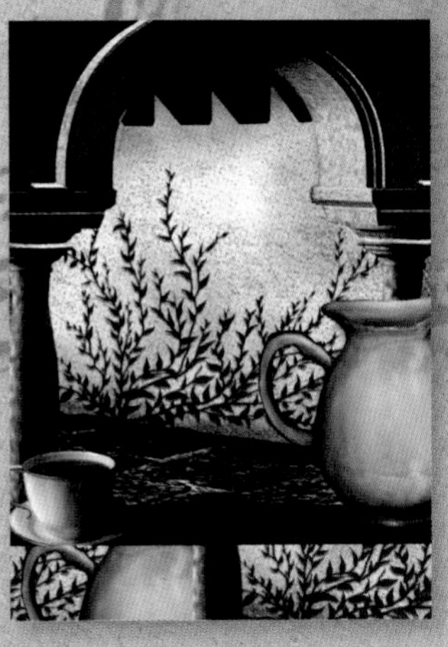

ART ALAIN VIESCA

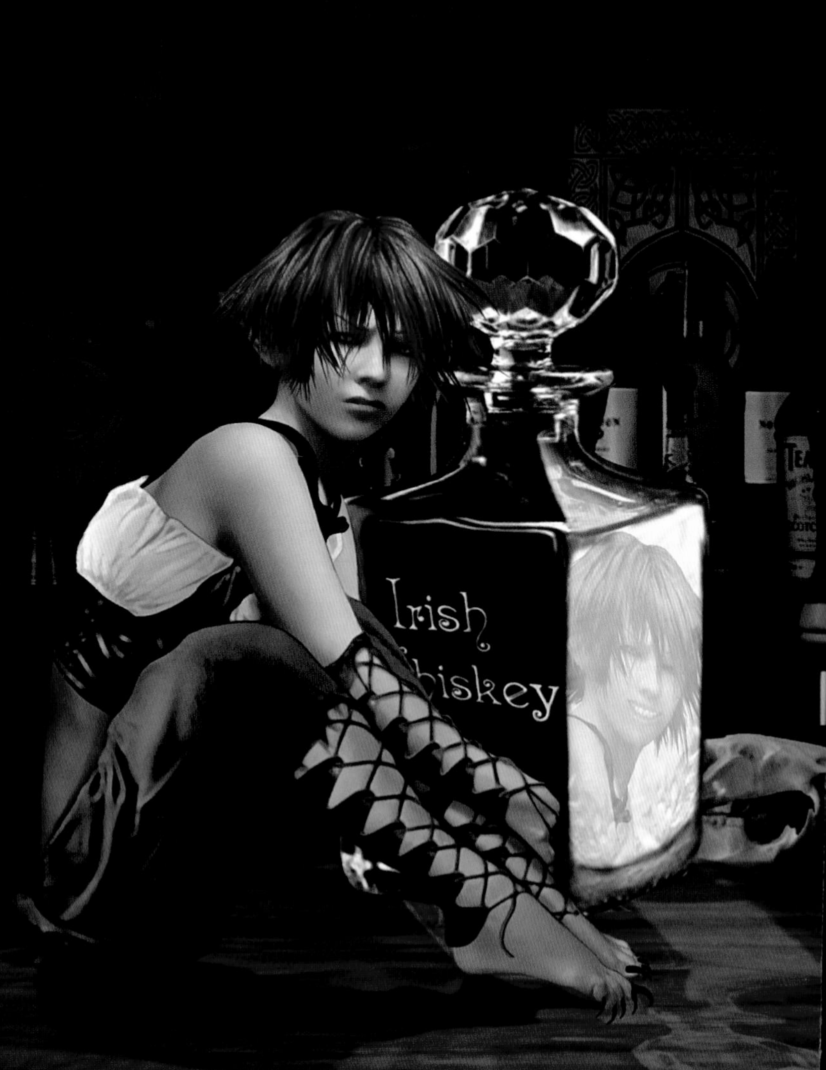
Irish
hiskey

BWCA

POSSESSING MANY OF THE SAME CHARACTERISTICS AS BROWNIES (SEE PAGE 84), BWCAS ARE WELSH FAERIES WITH A MUCH DARKER AND FIERIER TEMPERAMENT THAN THEIR ENGLISH COUSINS. LIKE BROWNIES, THEY ASSIST WITH HOUSEHOLD CHORES IN EXCHANGE FOR A BOWL OF CREAM BUT IF THEIR WORK IS CRITICIZED THEY ARE PRONE TO THROWING TANTRUMS BY POUNDING WALLS, DESTROYING CLOTHES, THROWING OBJECTS AND PINCHING PEOPLE WHILE THEY SLEEP. THE DOMESTIC DUTY THEY EXCEL AT IS CHURNING BUTTER. THEY DESPISE 'TATTLETALES' AND PEOPLE WITH LONG NOSES, DESPITE THE FACT THAT THEY ARE NOT VERY GOOD AT KEEPING SECRETS THEMSELVES. BWCAS CAN BECOME INVISIBLE AND UNLIKE BROWNIES ARE NOT TIED TO ONE PARTICULAR FAMILY.

Development

- As the Bwca is similar in appearance to the Brownie, a mirror image of that faerie was created, but with a more menacing look.
- Change the pose to give your faerie a stance akin to that of a wary animal.
- Instead of the friendly mouse that features in the Brownie painting, a half-hidden rat skull creates a more morbid air here.
- Using more robust fabrics such as leather also adds to the darker nature.

Media and Execution

- Pencil, 3DS Max, Photoshop
- An initial pencil sketch was worked over to create a greyscale version then colour was added on a new layer.
- The faerie was dropped on to the previously finished background and the lighting, shadows and colours were matched up.
- The layers were then combined and the Clone tool was used to smooth and blend the layers together.
- The Brush tool set to Colour Burn was used to deepen and texture the shadows. Colour Dodge with a light purple shade was used to bring out a slight metallic highlight to her hair and eyes.

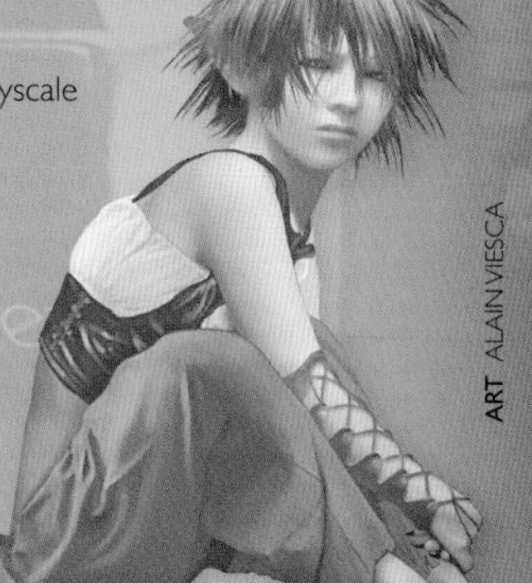

ART ALAIN VIESCA

FURTHER STUDY

Welsh folklore, Brownie, Boggart, Domovik.

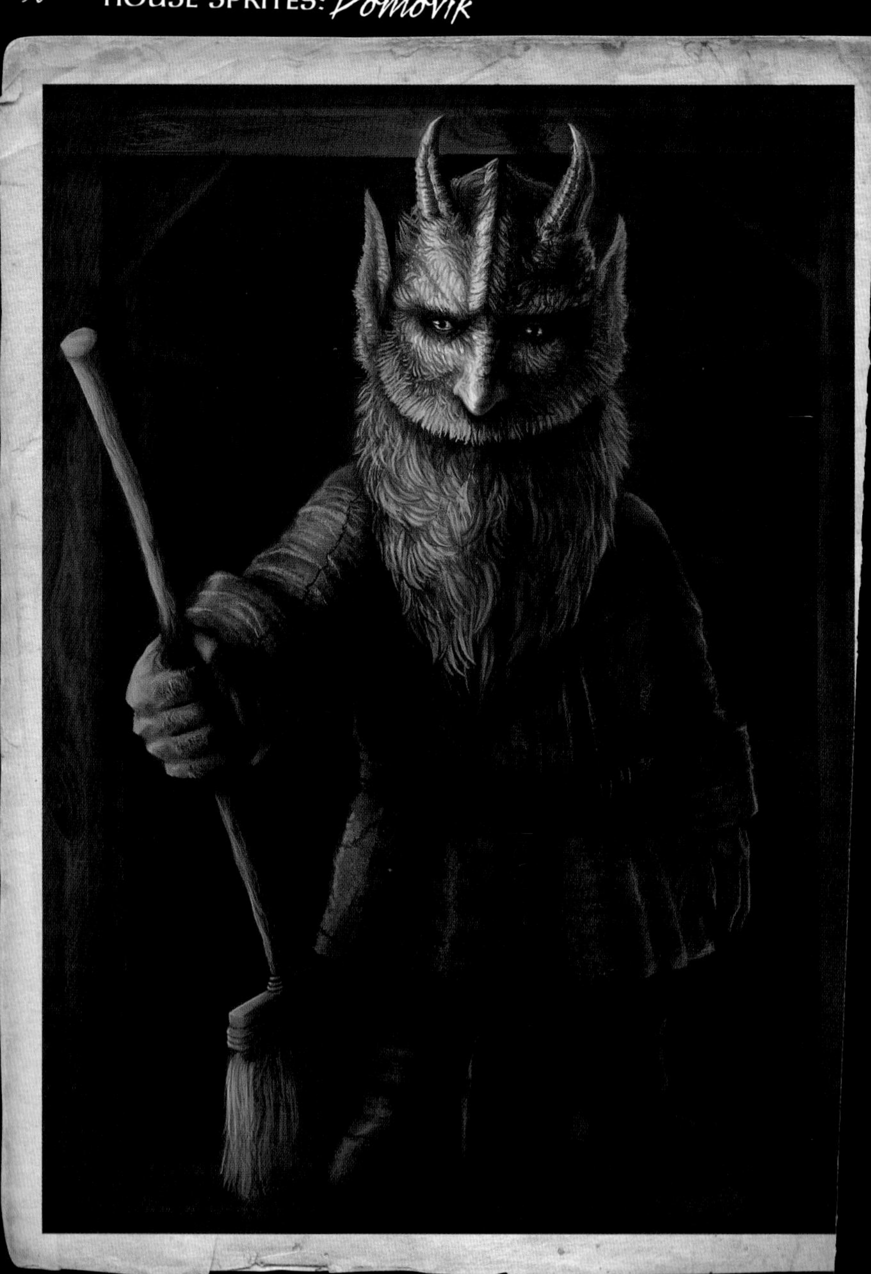

Domovik

DOMESTIC SPIRITS FROM SLAVIC AND BALTIC FOLKLORE, DOMOVIKS ARE SMALL MALE FAERIES THAT CLEAN AND LOOK AFTER HOUSES AND THEIR OCCUPANTS. THEY LIVE UNDERNEATH DOORSTEPS OR BEHIND OVENS AND ACT AS WATCHMEN. A DOMOVIK WILL REMAIN IN RESIDENCE AS LONG AS THE HOUSE IS RESPECTED BY ITS OWNERS, BUT IF IT FEELS THE HOME IS BECOMING NEGLECTED IT WILL BE BEGIN TO PLAY TRICKS, SUCH AS HIDING THINGS OR MOVING THEM AROUND. IF HE GETS REALLY ANGERED HE MIGHT EVEN BURN THE HOUSE DOWN. THEY ARE SAID TO BE VERY HAIRY CREATURES THAT SOMETIMES HAVE HORNS OR A TAIL.

Development

- Try to create a design that reflects its friendliness, but could easily transform to become threatening when angry.
- Use props to suggest a character's preoccupations – here a brush tells us he likes things clean and tidy.

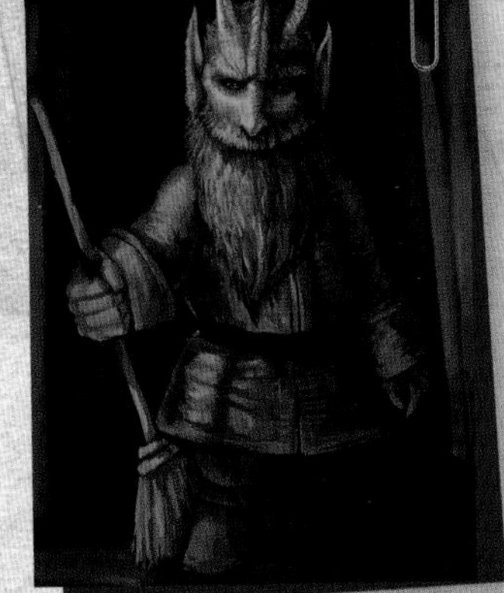

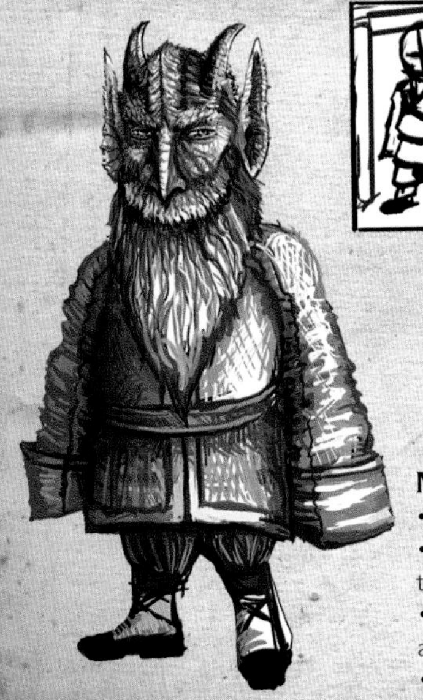

FURTHER STUDY

Kikimora, Domovoi, household deity, Brownie, Boggart.

Media and Execution

- Painter, Photoshop
- The faerie was sketched digitally in Painter and then colours were applied.
- Photoshop was used to correct the proportions and to add a definitive lighting scheme.
- Colour correction was also carried out in Photoshop, and finally filters were used to perfect the textures.

ART ARTEMIS KOLAKIS

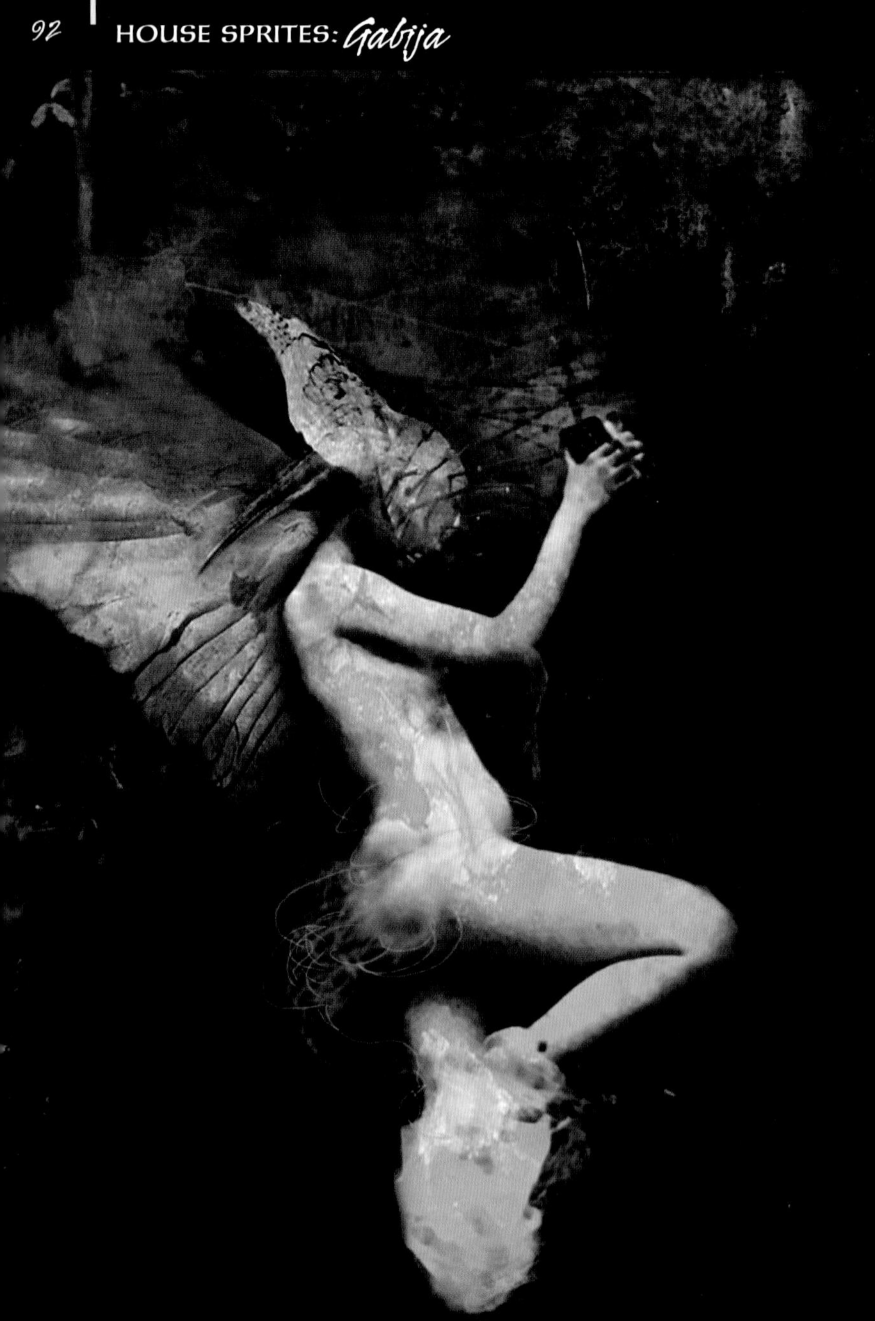

Gabija

STEMMING FROM LITHUANIAN TRADITION, THE GABIJA IS THE GODDESS OF FIRE AND THE HEARTH. SHE IS TO BE BOTH RESPECTED AND FEARED, PRAYED TO AND OFFERED LIBATIONS. SHE CAN TAKE THE FORM OF A CAT OR A BIRD AND LIKES TO BATHE HER FACE, SO A CUP OF WATER SHOULD ALWAYS BE LEFT OUT FOR HER. IF BOTH SHE AND THE HEARTH ARE KEPT CLEAN, THE FIRE WILL PROVIDE PROTECTION FROM THIEVES AND OTHER SINFUL FOLK. IF THE FIRE SHOULD BE NEGLECTED HER WRATH WILL BE SEVERE. SHE IS ALSO KNOWN AS GABIETA OR GABETA, AND IS NOW IDENTIFIED WITH ST AGATHA IN CHRISTIAN BELIEF.

Development

- Create a sense of a pious spirit with a devout pose. Here, the faerie clasps what could be a Bible, with a shadowy cross protruding from it.
- Study vintage photographic toning and colouring techniques and try to bring a sense of this into your digital work to bring out an aged effect.
- Explore different ways of revealing the zoomorphic forms of your faeries. A bird's head is used here, but rotated to face in the opposite direction and transformed into a less defined shape.

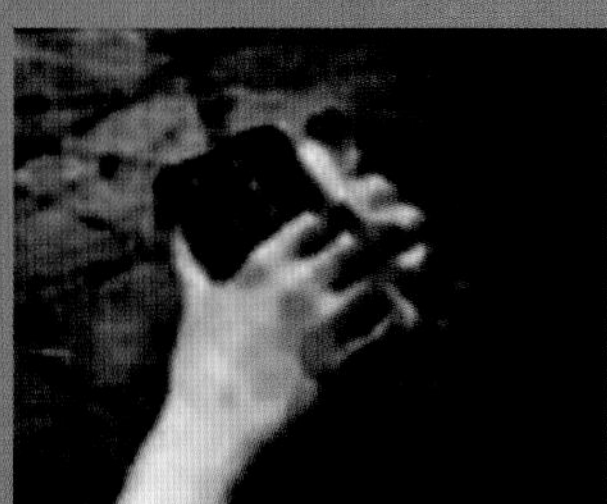

FURTHER STUDY
Domovik, household deity, Eastern European folklore.

Media and Execution

- Photograph, Photoshop
- A model photograph was used for the pose, and over-painted to create the bird-like headgear and wings.
- The fire was painted in at her feet and then parts of it overlaid on to her body, to create further highlights and textures.
- The image was desaturated and then toned with a warm sepia hue to create an old-fashioned look.

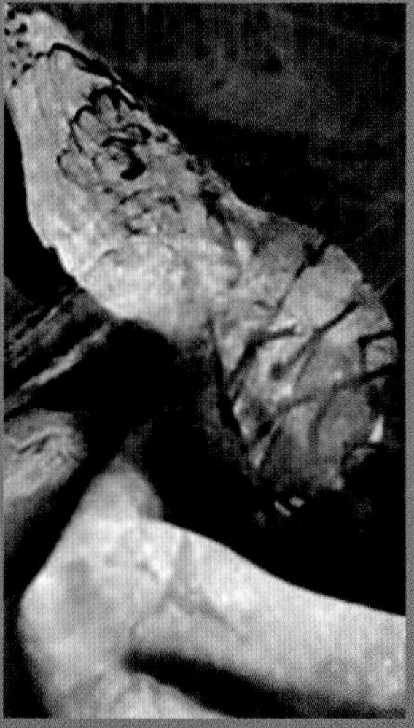

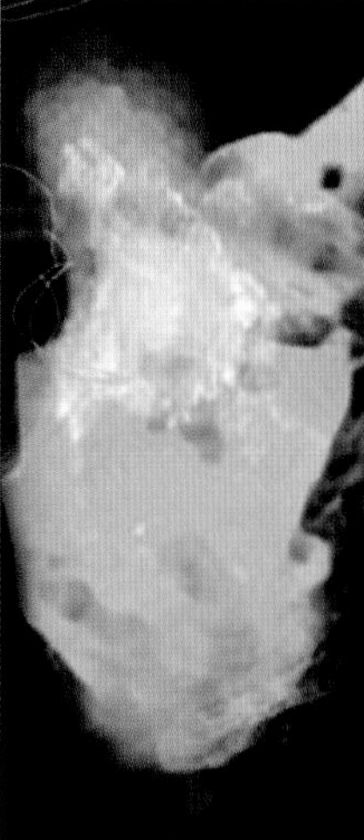

ART CHRISTOPHER SHY

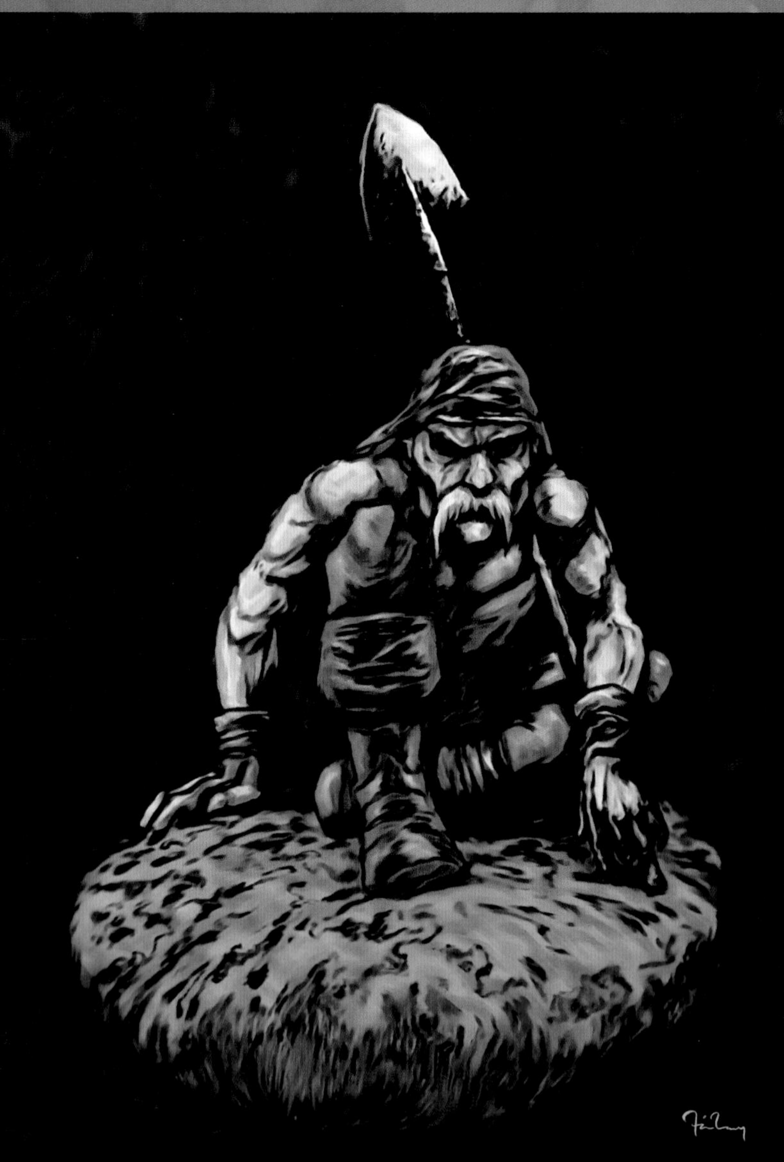

Kobold

A KOBOLD IS A TYPE OF HOBGOBLIN FROM GERMAN FOLKLORE, WHOSE NAME DERIVES FROM *KOBE* MEANING HOUSE OR HUT, AND *HOLD* MEANING GOOD. THERE ARE MANY SUBCATEGORIES OF KOBOLD, MOST OF WHICH ARE BENEVOLENT HOUSEHOLD SPRITES, SUCH AS THE HEINZELMANNCHEN, THAT PERFORM DOMESTIC CHORES BUT CAN TURN MALICIOUS IF MALTREATED. HOWEVER, ONE TYPE OF KOBOLD IS MORE SIMILAR TO A GNOME, AND IS SAID TO INHABIT MINES, STEALING THE TOOLS OF WORKERS AND CAUSING OTHER MISHAPS. THE ELEMENT COBALT TAKES ITS NAME FROM THE KOBOLD, AFTER THE POISONOUS NATURE OF THE METAL, WHICH ALSO POLLUTED OTHER ELEMENTS IN MINES.

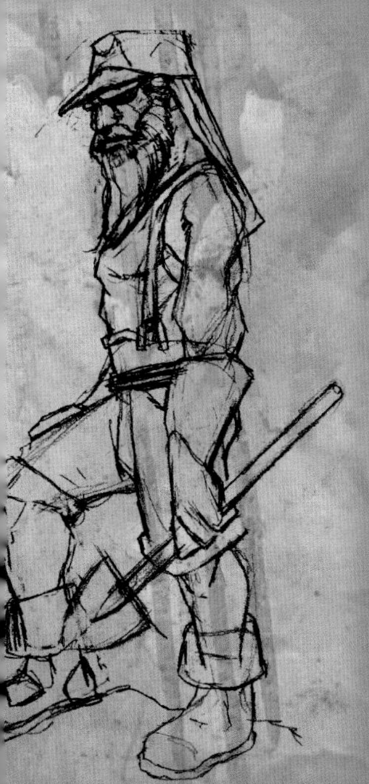

Development

- Always consider how a character's working environment will affect their appearance – in this case a miner would be stocky with powerful musculature and strong features.
- In order to make the character more sprite than human, over-exaggerate the features.
- The striking blue of Cobalt provided the inspiration for the colour palette of the character.

Media and Execution

- Pencil, Photoshop
- A series of rough sketches determined the composition, then the final version was drawn in pencil with a heavy black background on rough cartridge paper to ensure extra texture.
- The image was scanned and opened in Photoshop, where the background shadow was darkened using the Curves dialog then cloned to give it extra depth.

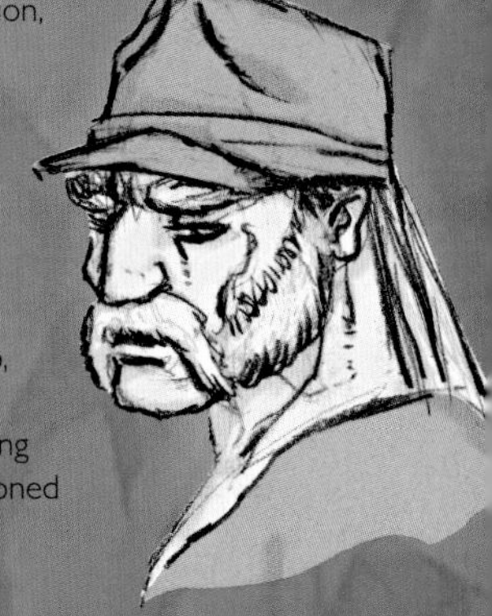

FURTHER STUDY
Biersal, Heinzelmannchen, Brownie, Gnome.

ART FINLAY COWAN

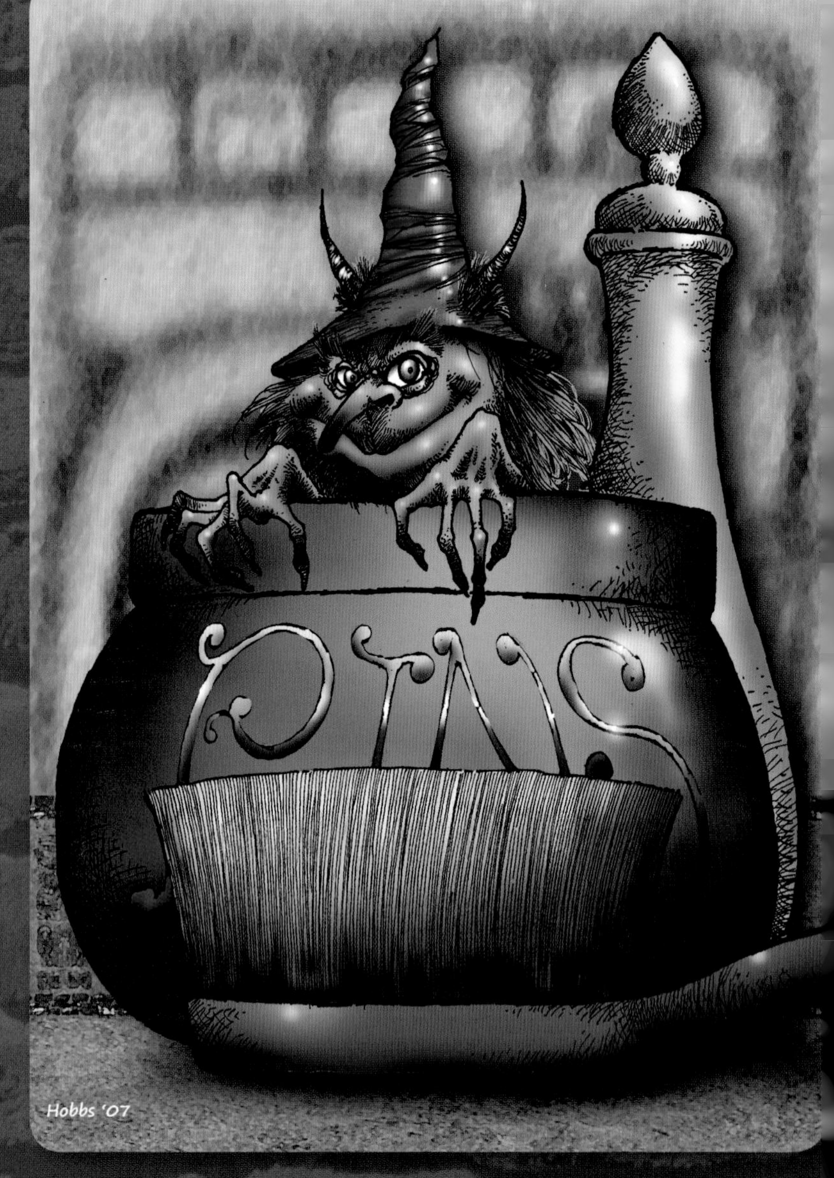
Hobbs '07

Mamur

A TYPE OF SPANISH IMP OR SMALL DWARF, MAMURS HAVE DIFFERENT NAMES IN DIFFERENT REGIONS OF SPAIN. THEY ARE CALLED DIABLILLO IN GALICIA, PAUTO IN ASTURIAS, MENGUE IN CANTABRIA AND CARMENO IN ANDALUSIA. MAMURS ARE SO SMALL THAT THEY CAN FIT INSIDE A PIN BOX. THEY ARE HELPFUL AROUND THE HOUSE AND WORK HARD. THEY ARE CHILDLIKE AND MISCHIEVOUS BUT NEVER MALICIOUS. THEY HAVE HORNS AND WEAR RED POINTED HATS. TO CATCH ONE, PUT A PIN BOX OVER A BRAMBLE, LOOK INSIDE IT AT MIDNIGHT AND THERE YOU'LL FIND A MAMUR; HE NOW BELONGS TO YOU.

Development

- To create a sense of scale, include recognizable objects, such as the brush in the foreground. Props such as this can either be scanned in from photo references or you can be sketched from life using everyday items around your house.
- Creating a mischievous but non-malicious facial expression requires careful balance.

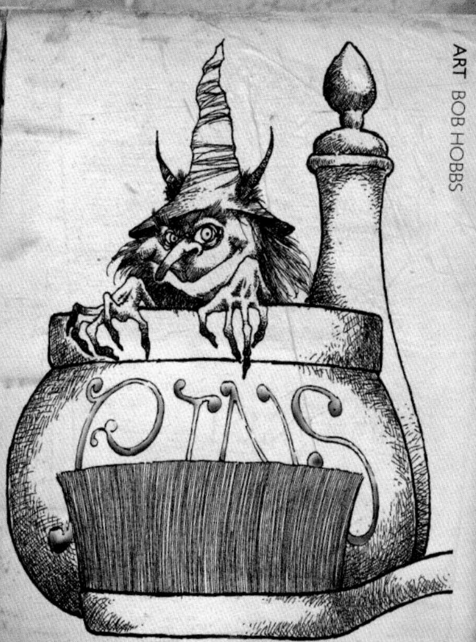

ART BOB HOBBS

Media and Execution

- Pencil, pen and ink, Photoshop
- Preliminary sketches were made with the final sketch rendered in pen and ink.
- The ink drawing was scanned into Photoshop, the edges were cleaned up, the white background was deleted and the black lines were enhanced with the Levels dialog.
- The image was coloured using the various Paint tools, keeping the ink layer semi-transparent on top.

FURTHER STUDY
Diablillo, Spanish folklore, Pauto.

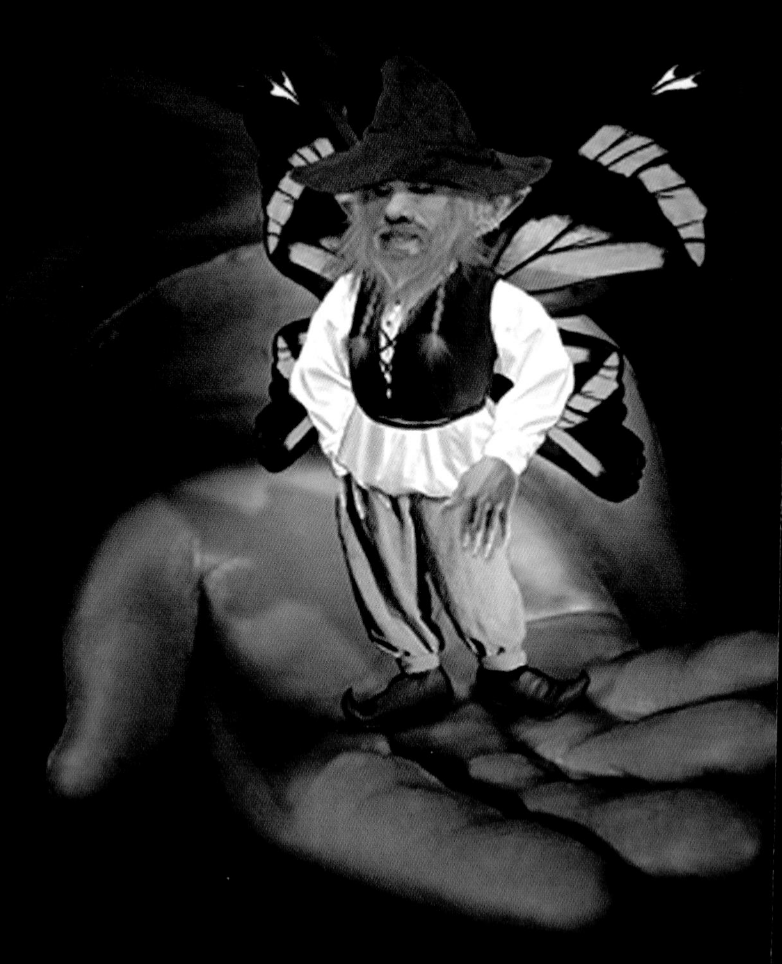

Portune

THESE TINY MEDIEVAL FAERIES ARE NOTORIOUS PRANKSTERS AND TRICKSTERS. THEY APPEAR AS OLD MEN, AND DURING THE DAY CAN BE VERY HELPFUL AS THEY CAN BE PERSUADED TO ASSIST WITH CHORES AROUND THE FARMSTEAD. IT'S AT NIGHT WHEN THEY CANNOT RESIST PLAYING THEIR ANNOYING AND OFTEN HUMILIATING PRANKS. PORTUNES ARE CAPABLE OF GRANTING WISHES IF CAPTURED OR OUTWITTED. THEY ARE SOMETIMES BELIEVED TO GUARD TREASURE. THEY LOVE MISCHIEF ABOVE ALL ELSE, AND ONE PARTICULARLY BOTHERSOME PRANK IS THEIR PENCHANT FOR DRIVING HORSES AND RIDERS INTO PONDS AND LAKES. WHEN NOT OCCUPYING A FARM THEY CAN BE FOUND IN BURGHS AND WOODLANDS.

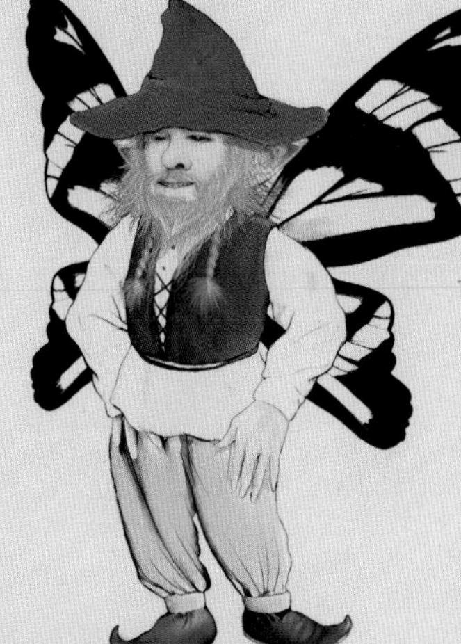

Development

- Portunes are sometimes described as English Leprechauns. They share many features, but Portunes have wings.
- Using a human hand in the piece creates a powerful scale reference.

Media and Execution

- Pencil, 3DS Max, Photoshop
- The faerie began as a sketch that was scanned and opened in Photoshop and then worked over several times.
- A second layer was used for the tints and colours and then a third layer for the shadows.
- The glow and drop shadows were made on yet another layer.
- After merging the layers, tints were added to balance the faerie with the background and the Clone tool was used with a low Opacity setting to blend them together.

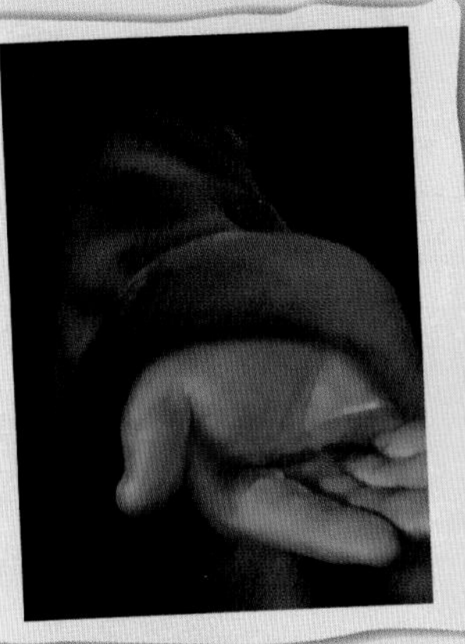

ART ALAIN VIESCA

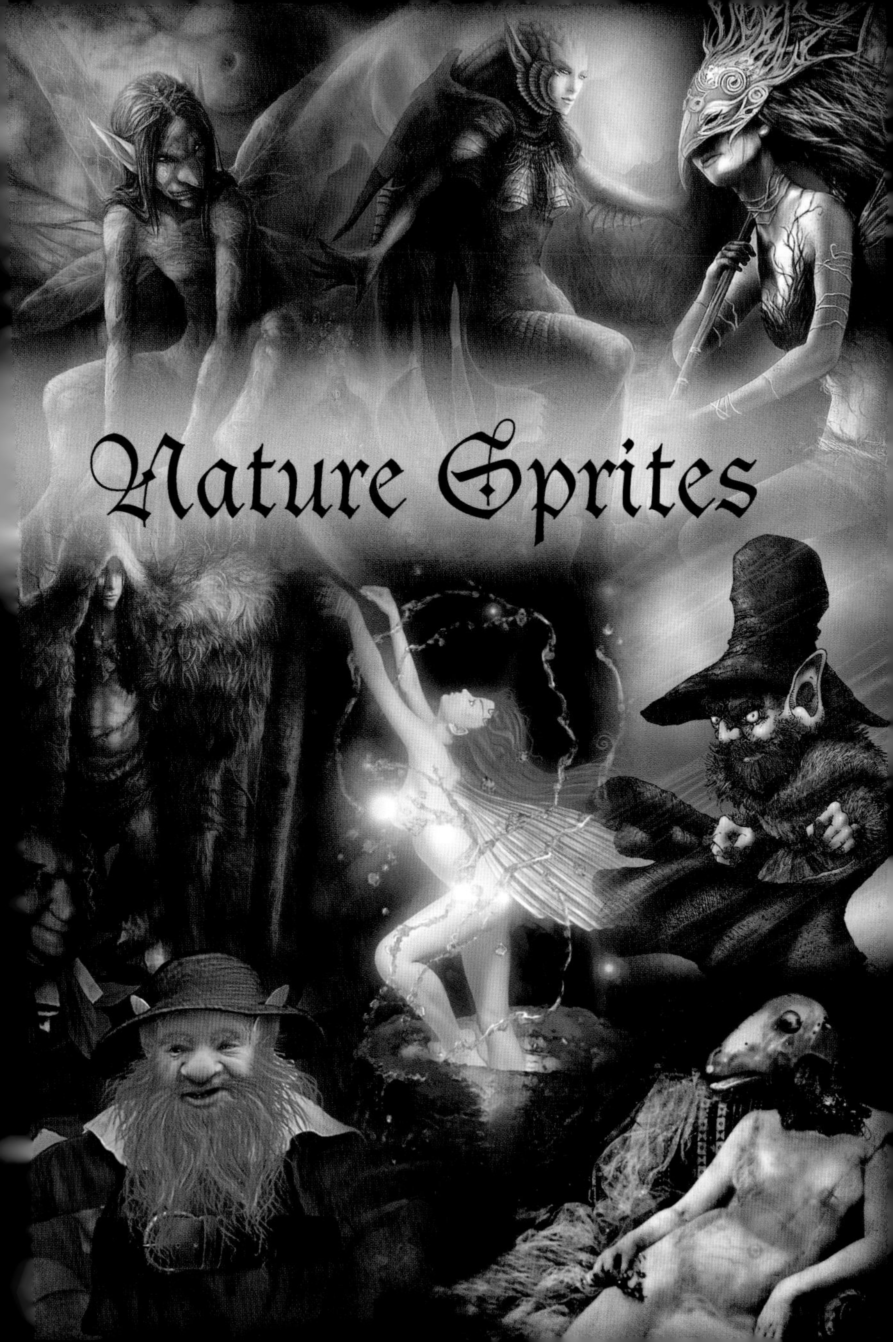
Nature Sprites

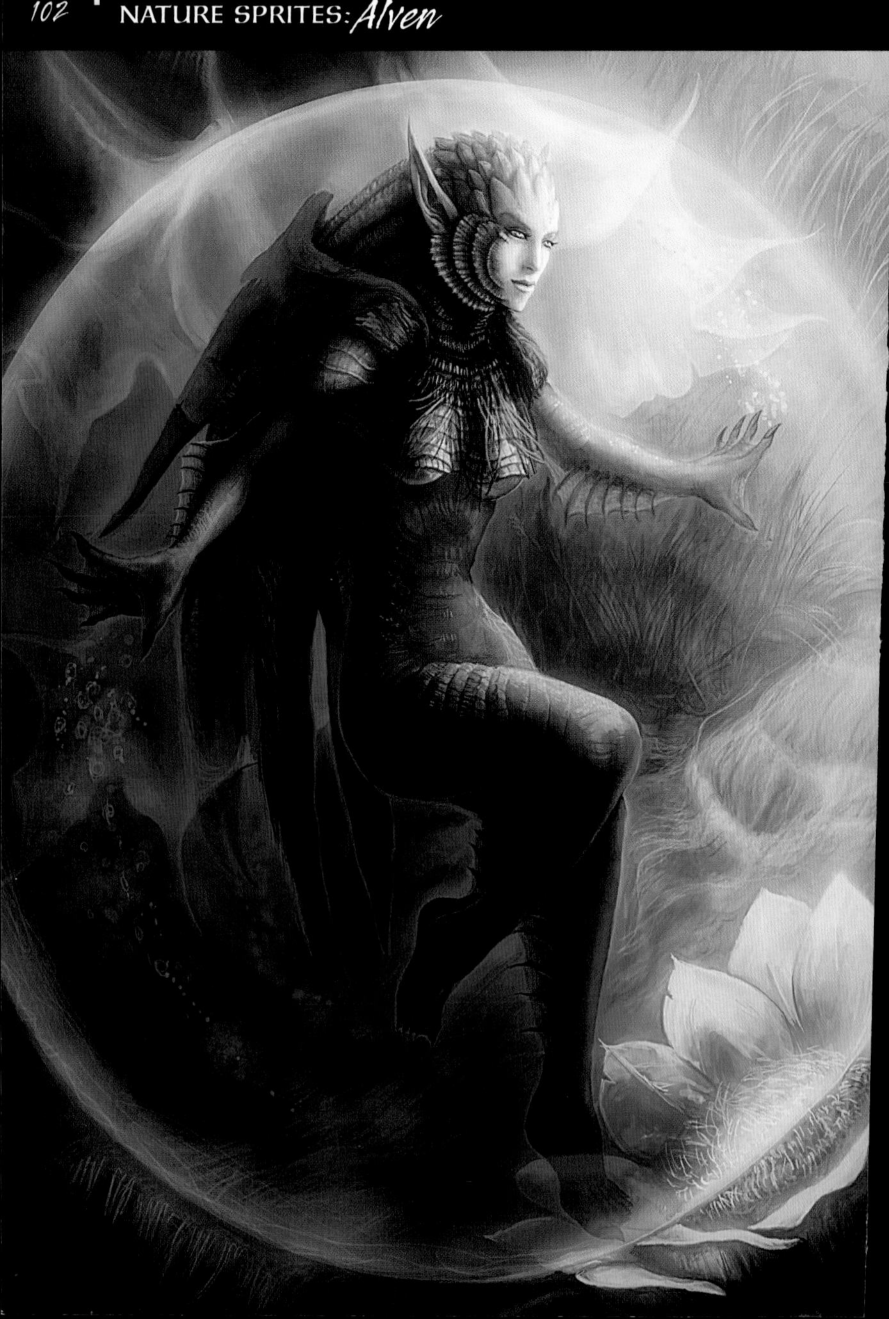

Alven

SO LIGHT THAT YOU CAN HARDLY SEE THEM, ALVEN ARE SHY WATER SPIRITS FROM DUTCH FOLKLORE THAT LIVE IN PONDS, RIVERS AND LAKES AND ENJOY DANCING UNDER MOONLIGHT. THEY CHERISH NIGHT-BLOOMING FLOWERS AND SHOW MALICE TO THOSE THAT PICK THEM. DURING THE SPRING AND SUMMER THEY SUBSIST ON A DIET OF NECTAR AND DEW, WHILE IN WINTER THEY EAT FROST. THEIR ONLY REAL ENEMIES ARE THE FISH THAT TRY TO EAT THEM, AND SO THEY DO THEIR UTMOST TO AVOID THEM. AS ALVEN DO NOT HAVE FUNCTIONING WINGS, THEY TRAVEL FROM POND TO POND ENCASED IN A SHIMMERING BUBBLE.

Development

- Try to incorporate an amphibious nature into your water spirit designs through skin textures and features such as webbed fingers and toes, gills and fish-like fins.
- Experiment with filter effects in Photoshop to achieve an ethereal quality.

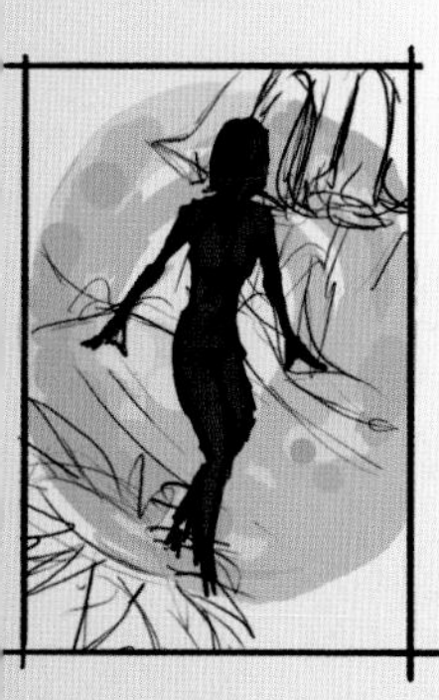

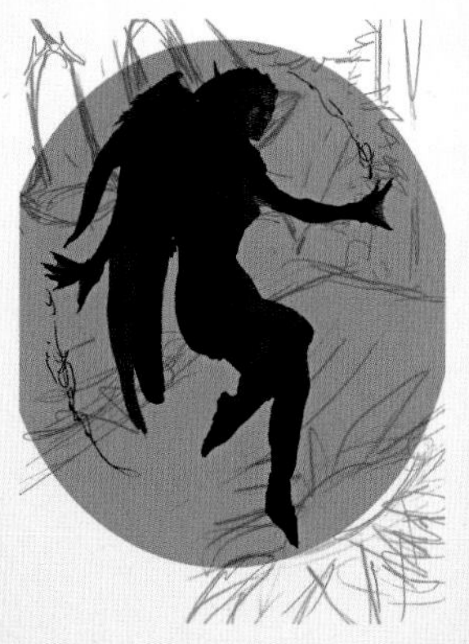

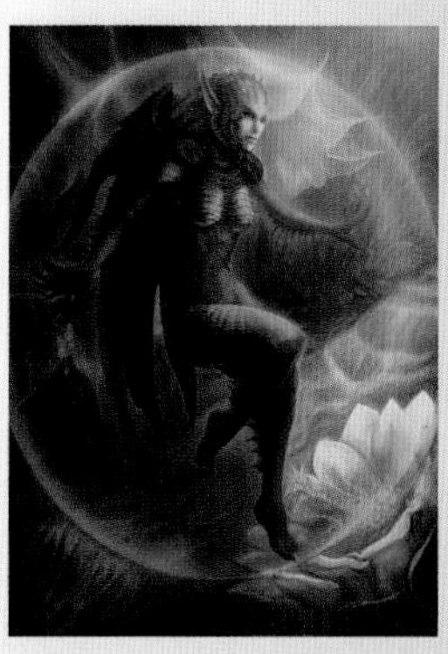

Media and Execution

- Photoshop
- The initial faerie and composition were digitally sketched out in Photoshop.
- Proportions were corrected and then Brush tools were used to colour the image.
- The final image was colour corrected and then filters were used to create her beautiful glow.

FURTHER STUDY

Otteermaaner, Dutch folklore, water sprites.

ART ARTEMIS KOLAKIS

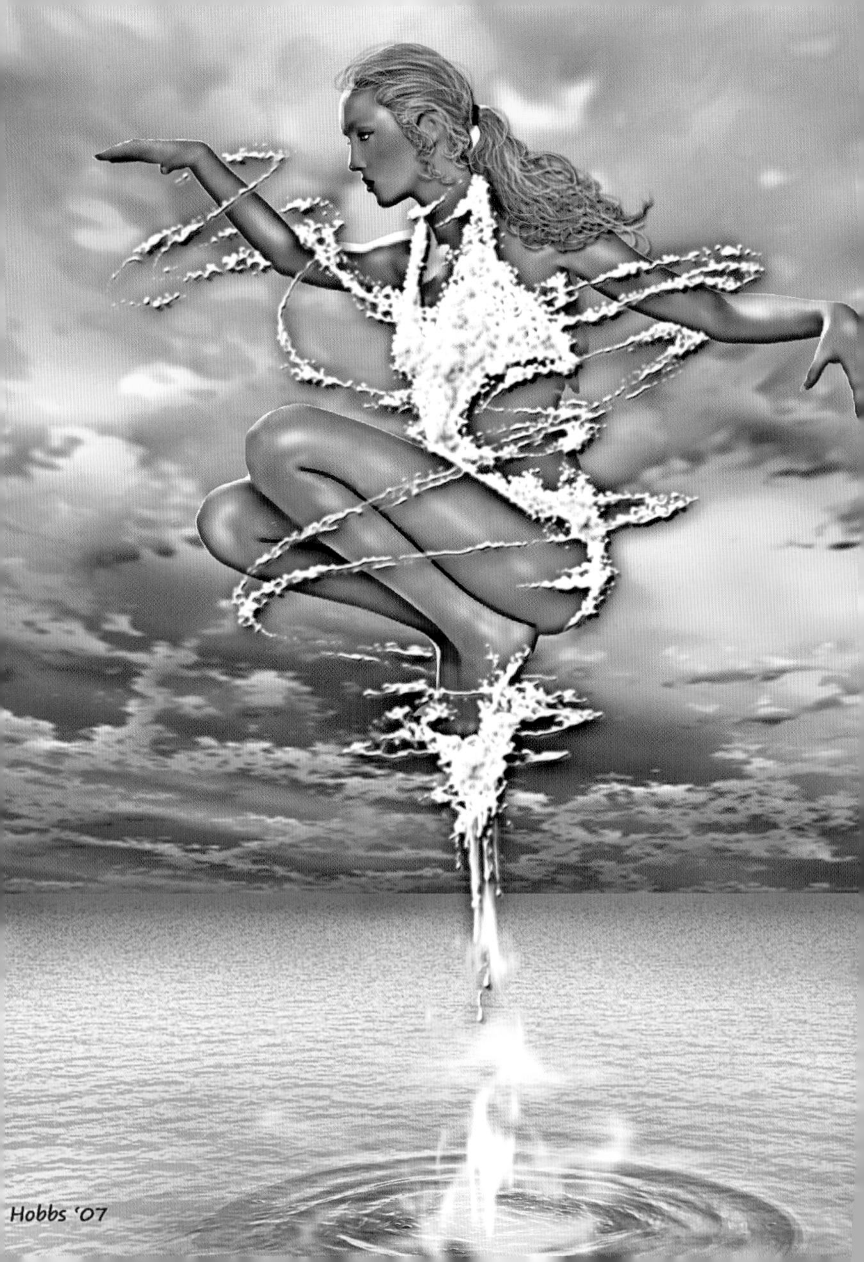
Hobbs '07

Asrai

SMALL, DELICATE WATER FAERIES FROM ENGLAND AND SCOTLAND, ASRAI ARE EXCEPTIONALLY BEAUTIFUL AND GENTLE CREATURES THAT MELT AS THE SUN COMES UP, BUT COME OUT AGAIN AT THE FULL MOON. TOTALLY NOCTURNAL, EACH ASRAI CAN RISE FROM THE DEPTHS OF THE SEA ONLY ONCE A CENTURY. ALWAYS DEPICTED AS FEMALE (ALTHOUGH THERE ARE MALES), ASRAI HAVE LONG GREEN HAIR, TRANSLUCENT SKIN AND WEBBED FEET. ONE LEGENDARY TALE IS ABOUT A FISHERMAN WHO CAPTURED AN ASRAI IN HIS NETS. IGNORING ITS CRIES, HE WAS DETERMINED TO BRING IT BACK TO SHORE, BUT IT HAD MELTED AWAY INTO A PUDDLE BY THE TIME HE REACHED LAND. ALL THAT REMAINED WAS A BLISTER ON HIS HAND WHERE HE HAD TOUCHED HER.

Media and Execution

- Photograph, Vue d'Esprit, Photoshop
- The photograph was cropped to leave only the figure.
- The background was created in Vue d'Esprit then imported into Photoshop, where whites and various shades of blue were used to create swirls of water, mist, bubbles and foam.

ART BOB HOBBS
MODEL KRISTEN PEOTTER

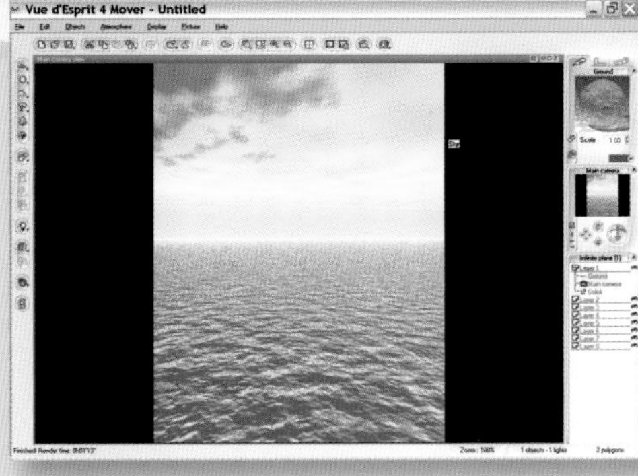

Development

- Working from a photo is always a time-saver, sometimes even meaning that no preliminary sketches are needed.
- Digital backgrounds can be created using 3D software Vue d'Esprit, which features highly realistic landscape-creation capabilities.
- Using an orange sky adds an element of warmth to what is otherwise a very cool-toned image.

FURTHER STUDY
English folklore, water faeries, Scottish folklore, sea ghosts.

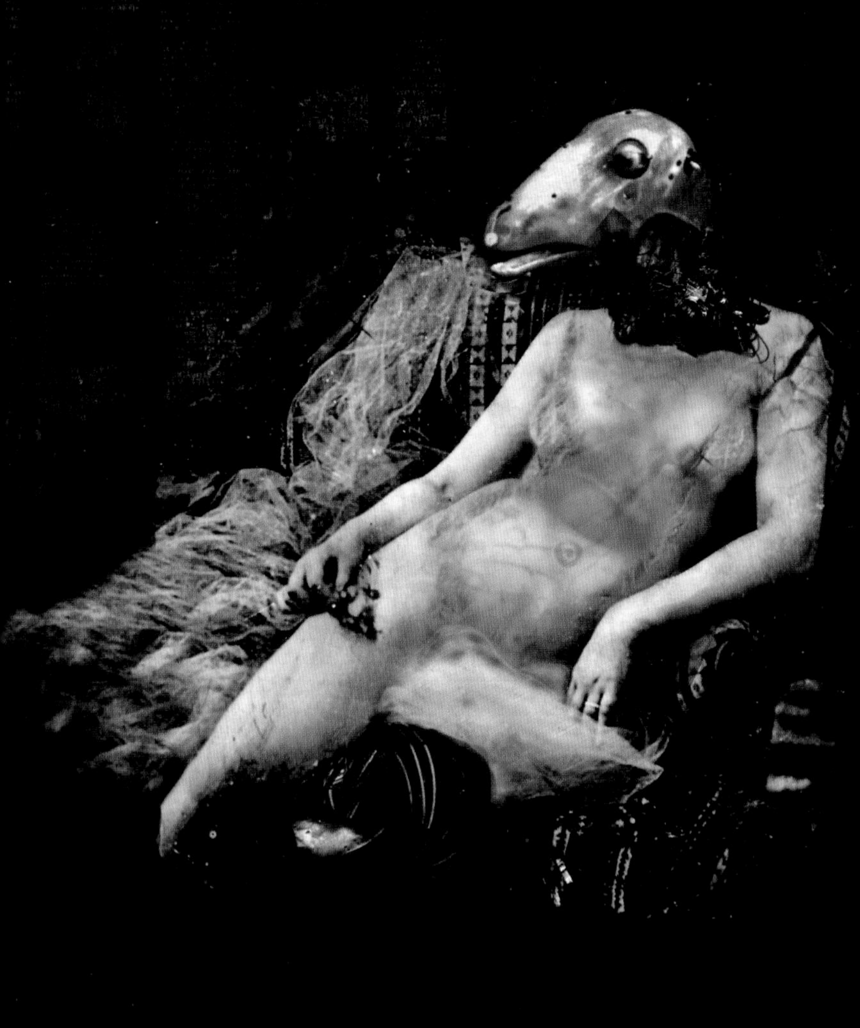

Bucca

CAPABLE OF TRANSFORMING INTO AN AMAZING VARIETY OF FORMS, A BUCCA IS TO BE BOTH RESPECTED AND FEARED. ORIGINATING IN WELSH FOLKLORE, BUCCAS ARE SAID TO BE ABLE TO ASSUME THE SHAPE OF A HUMAN, A DOG, A HORSE, A RABBIT AND A GOAT, AND ARE SOMETIMES SEEN WITH DIFFERENT COMBINATIONS OF THESE PARTS. THEY ARE CLOSELY ASSOCIATED WITH SAMHAIN, THE PAGAN HARVEST FESTIVAL AND ARE CONSIDERED TO BE BENEVOLENT ALTHOUGH THEY ARE HIGHLY MISCHIEVOUS. THEY HAVE THE ABILITY TO SPEAK TO HUMANS AND WILL OFTEN TRY TO LURE YOU ON TO THEIR BACKS WHERE THEY WILL GIVE YOU A WILD RIDE, BUT THEIR POWERS OF SPEECH CAN ALSO HELP TO GUIDE YOU AWAY FROM DANGER.

Development

- Learn about vintage hand-colouring techniques and try out different ways of replicating them digitally, overlaying colour on top of a mono-chrome image.
- The use of a straw-like texture alludes to hay-bales and the harvest, which is so important in the portrayal of a Bucca.
- Study old paintings of nudes for ideas on posing and then try to simulate these with a live model.

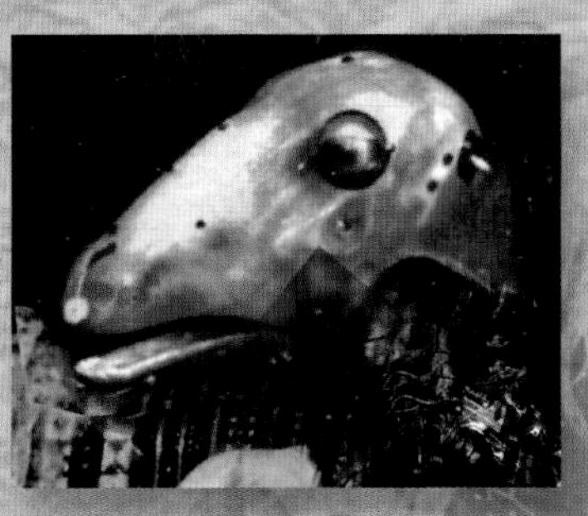

Media and Execution

- Photograph, Photoshop
- A model photograph was used for the pose then heavily over-painted in Photoshop.
- The paint was smeared and smudged to create an impressionistic feel.
- The image was desaturated and then shaded and toned to resemble an old-fashioned hand-tinted image.
- A vignette effect was created by darkening the edges of the frame.

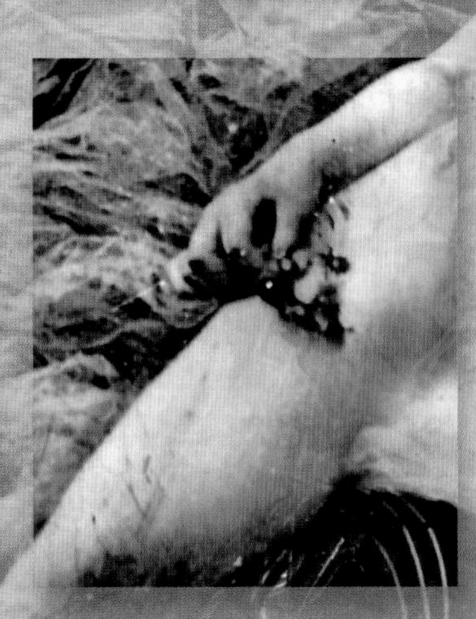

FURTHER STUDY

Puck, Pwca, Phooka, Welsh folklore, Samhain festival.

ART CHRISTOPHER SHY

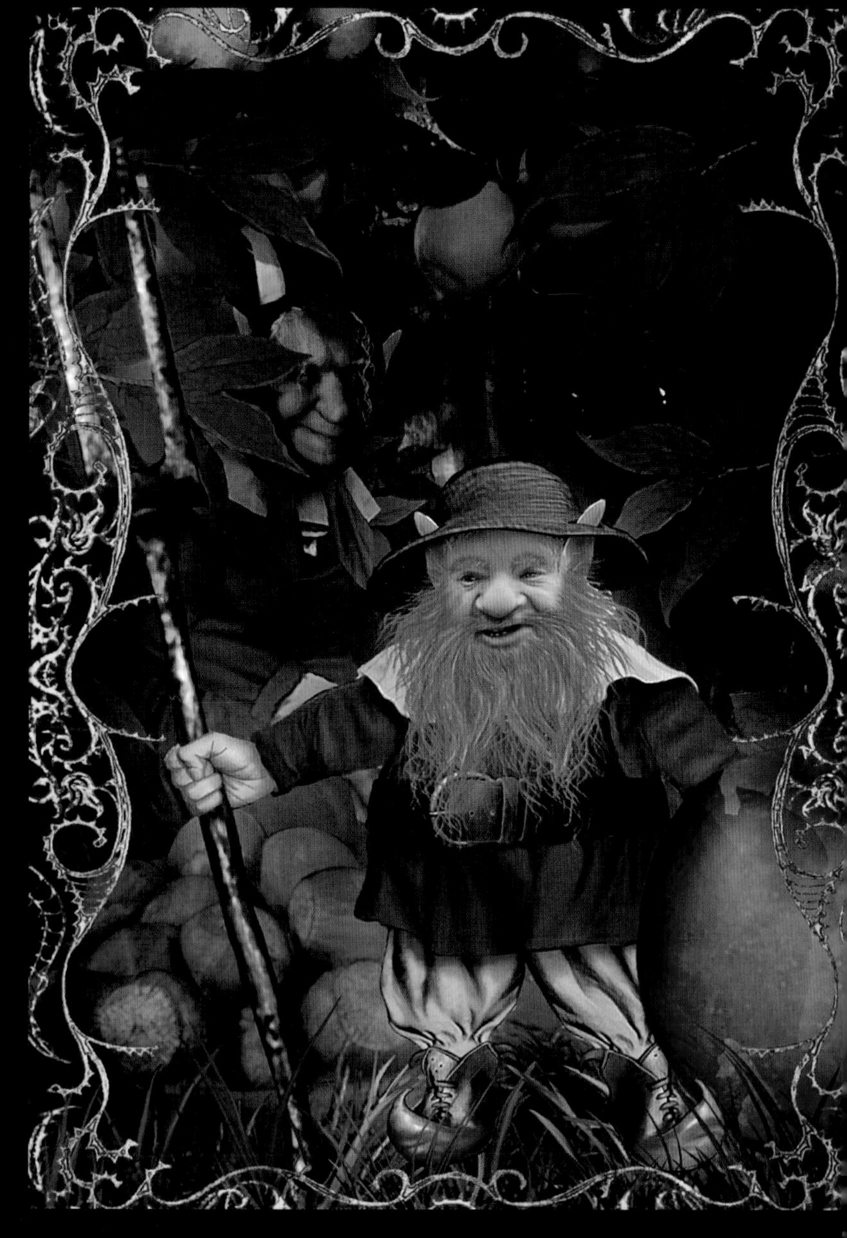

Churn Milk Peg & Melch Dick

THESE ENGLISH DWARF FAERIES ARE CAPRICIOUS, LAZY AND SPITEFUL, BUT THEY LOATHE THESE QUALITIES IN HUMANS AND PLAY CRUEL PRANKS ON THE SLOTHFUL BY INFLICTING FLATULENCE, BLOATING AND CRAMPS. MOSTLY ACTIVE FROM SPRING TO AUTUMN, BOTH PEG AND DICK AND ARE CLOSELY TIED TO THE EARTH, AS GUARDIANS OF FRESH MILK, ORCHARDS AND NUTS, AND THUS PEG IS ALSO KNOWN AS THE ACORN LADY. THEY ARE NOMADIC, MOVING FROM TREE TO TREE WATCHING FOR THIEVES, AND WEAR 15TH-CENTURY PEASANT CLOTHING. IT IS BELIEVED THAT THEY ORIGINATE FROM FERTILITY SPIRITS ASSOCIATED WITH THE ANCIENT CELTIC BELTANE FESTIVAL.

Development

- Begin by researching characters and folklore, and then draw inspiration from other sources such as Grimms' Faerie Tales and Gothic fantasy.
- Colour is important to lead the viewer's eye through the image. Here, the eye lingers on the bright tempting apples and nuts; then the viewer gauges Dick and finally sees Peg in the shadows.
- To develop the characters further, try bringing them into a more contemporary setting.

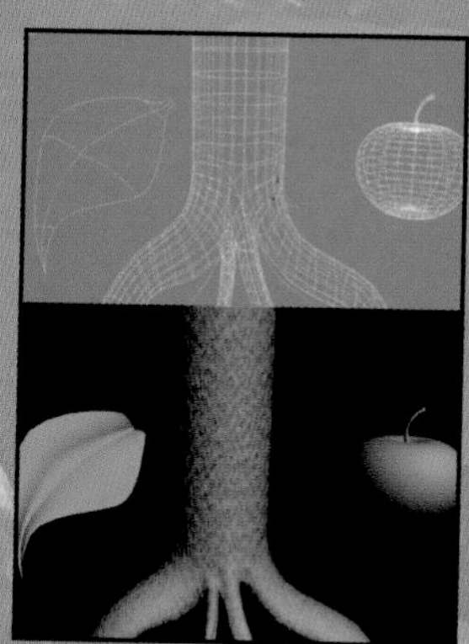

FURTHER STUDY
Beltane (Celtic festival), Acorn Lady, 15th century costume.

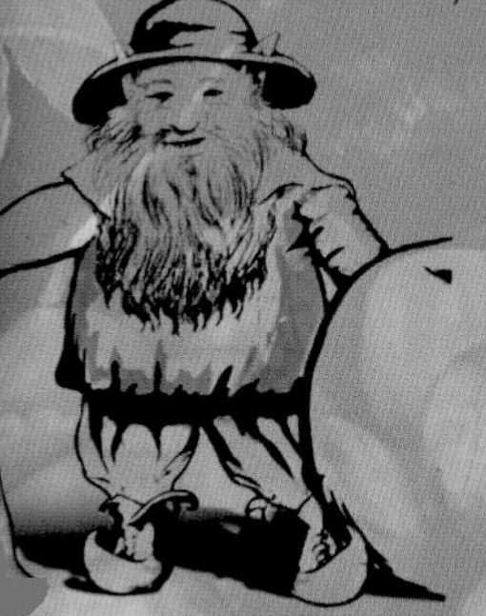

Media and Execution

- 3DS Max, Photoshop
- The tree, apple and leaf were quickly modelled in Max, without worrying about textures or advanced lighting.
- In Photoshop the Liquify and Clone tools were used to introduce changes.
- Colour was then added and enhancements made to the light and shadows, and the textures for the background and characters.
- As a final touch, a spiky golden frame was placed around the entire piece.

ART ALAIN VIESCA

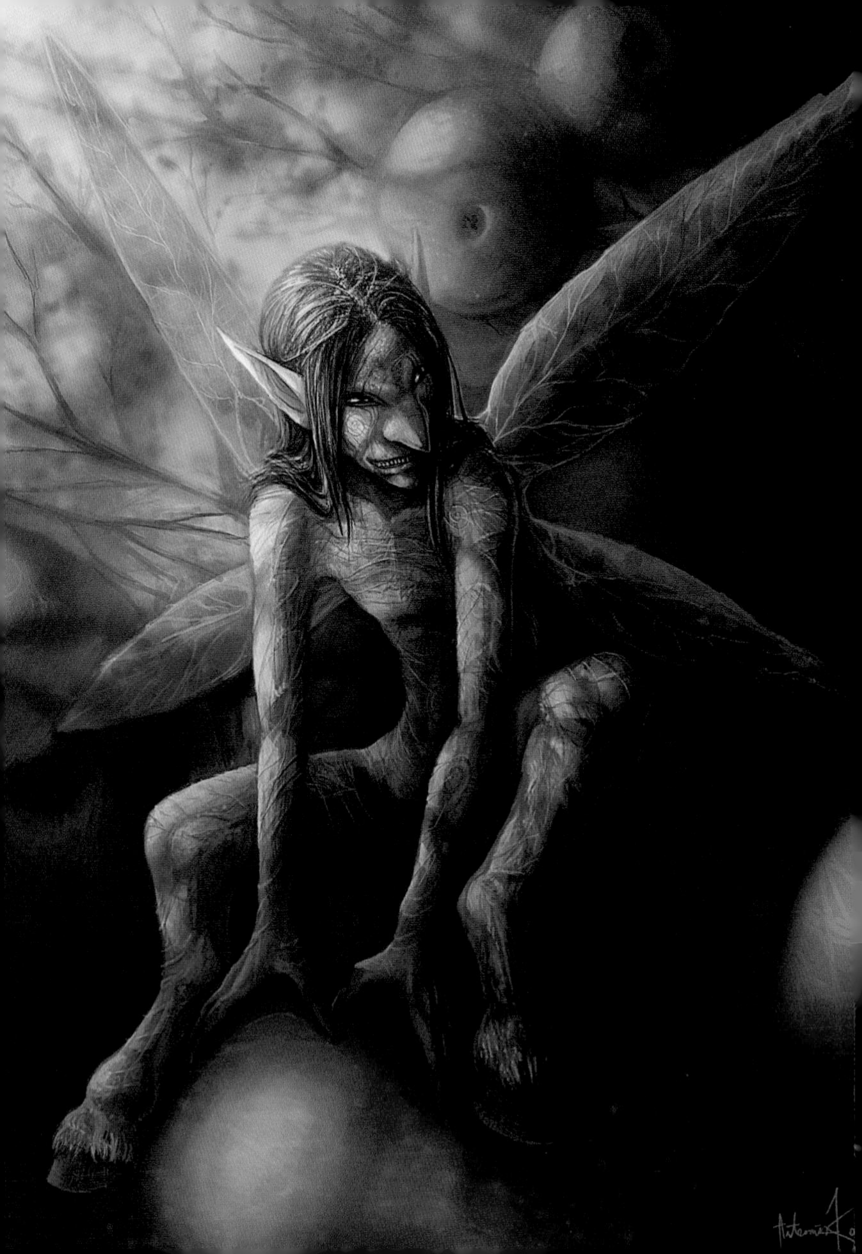

Colt Pixie

LIKE ALL VARIETIES OF PIXIE, COLT PIXIES ARE MISCHIEVOUS AND PLAYFUL SPRITES. THEIR PASTIMES ARE ANNOYING TO HUMANS, ALTHOUGH THEY ARE NOT INTENDED TO CAUSE HARM. THE MOST COMMON OF THEIR GAMES IS TO CONFUSE TRAVELLERS WITH ELABORATE ILLUSIONS, HENCE THE TERM TO BE 'PIXIE-LED'. IT IS SAID THAT WEARING YOUR COAT INSIDE OUT WILL CONFUSE A PIXIE AND STOP IT FROM MISGUIDING YOU. COLT PIXIES IN PARTICULAR ARE CONSUMMATE SHAPE-SHIFTERS WHOSE FAVOURITE PRANK IS TO TAKE ON THE FORM OF HORSES AND NEIGH TO THROW CARRIAGE HORSES OFF COURSE. THEY LIVE IN ORCHARDS AND WILL ATTACK ANYONE WHO TRIES TO STEAL THEIR APPLES.

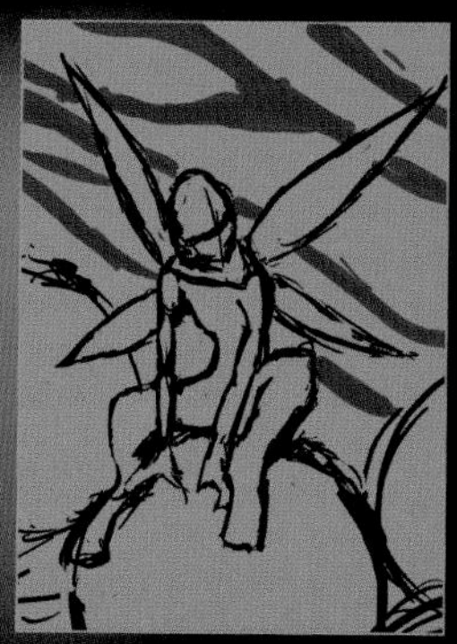

Media and Execution

- Painter, Photoshop
- The initial sketch was made in Painter software and then brought into Photoshop to fix the proportion issues.
- Once amended, the image was taken back into Painter for colouring and detailing.
- It was then brought back into Photoshop to be colour corrected and prepared for print.

FURTHER STUDY
Cornish folklore, Pixie, Heather Pixie, Puck.

Development

- The key aspect in depicting Pixies is incorporating a sense of mischief into their pose and facial structure.
- Always try to use the character's natural environment as a backdrop to your image.
- Use whatever software packages you feel most at home in for different aspects of your image, even if it means swapping between programs at several stages.

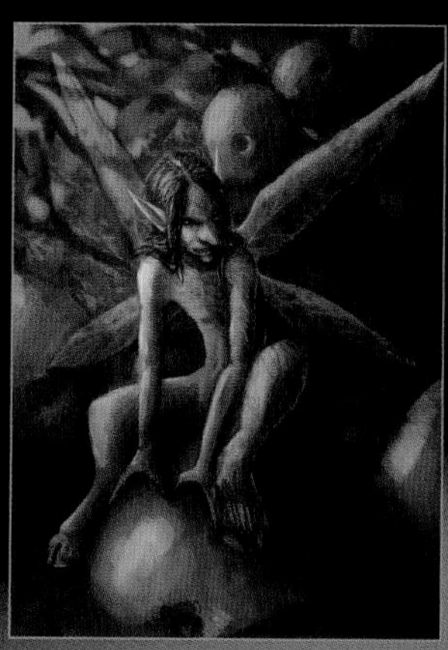

ART ARTEMIS KOLAKIS

DEVA

FROM THE SANSKRIT WORD MEANING 'A BEING OF BRILLIANT LIGHT', DEVA IS USED TO INDICATE A VARIETY OF NON-PHYSICAL BEINGS IN BOTH BUDDHIST AND HINDU MYTHOLOGY. HAILING FROM AN ASTRAL REALM, THEY HAVE NO TRUE FORM AND ARE INVISIBLE TO HUMANS. THEY HAVE BEEN DESCRIBED AS OPEN VORTEXES OF COSMIC CONSCIOUSNESS. SOME DEVAS REPRESENT THE FORCES OF NATURE, AND ARE RESPONSIBLE FOR FIRE, AIR, RAIN AND TREES, WHILE OTHERS EMBODY MORAL VALUES. THEY ARE CAPABLE OF MOVING GREAT DISTANCES AT SPEED AND OF FLYING. HUMANS ARE SAID TO HAVE ORIGINALLY HAD MANY OF THE DEVAS' POWERS: NOT NEEDING FOOD, THE ABILITY TO FLY, AND SHINING BY OUR OWN LIGHT. HOWEVER, OVER TIME AS WE BEGAN TO EAT FOOD, OUR BODIES BECAME CRUDER AND OUR POWERS VANISHED.

Development

- Depicting an invisible formless being is impossible, so instead focus on the organic aspect of these spirits and portray their oneness with nature.
- Show the glow these spirits have by contrasting them against a dark background.

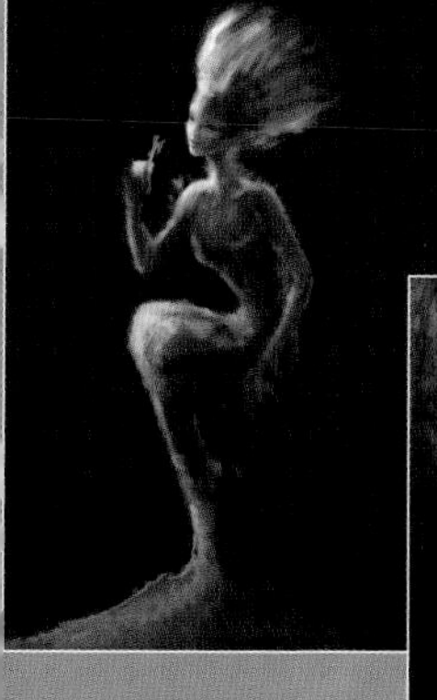

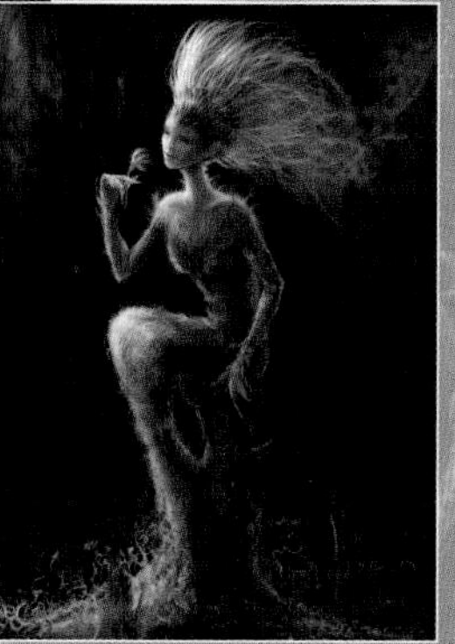

ART JULIANNA KOLAKIS

Media and Execution

- Photoshop
- The general shape and initial colours were blocked out digitally in Photoshop.
- Details and highlights were then painted in using the Brush tool.
- The details were refined through many hours of work, and then the Liquify filter was used to mesh things together.
- Finally the image was darkened to increase the atmosphere and focus the attention on the glowing being.

FURTHER STUDY
Hindu mythology, Buddhist mythology, Geoffrey Hodson (mystic).

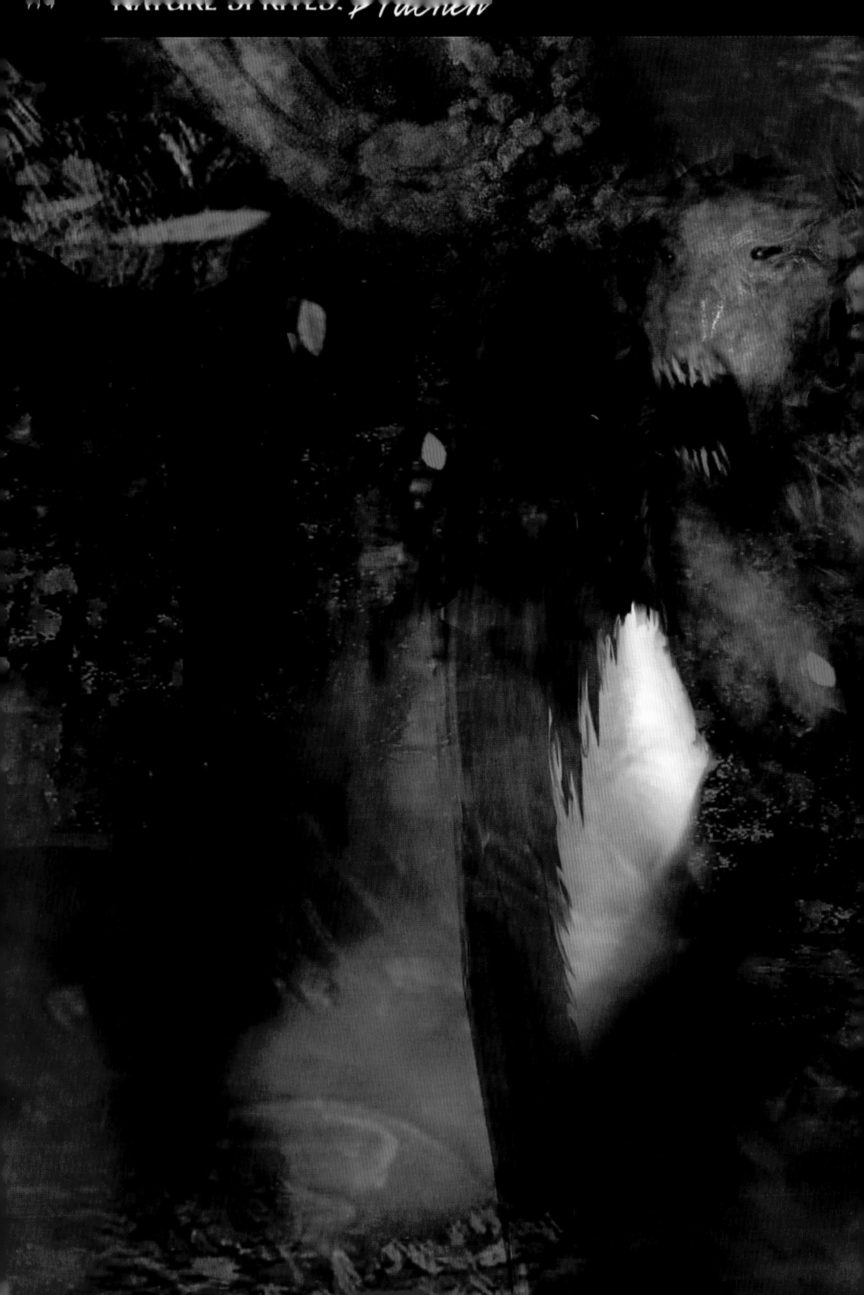

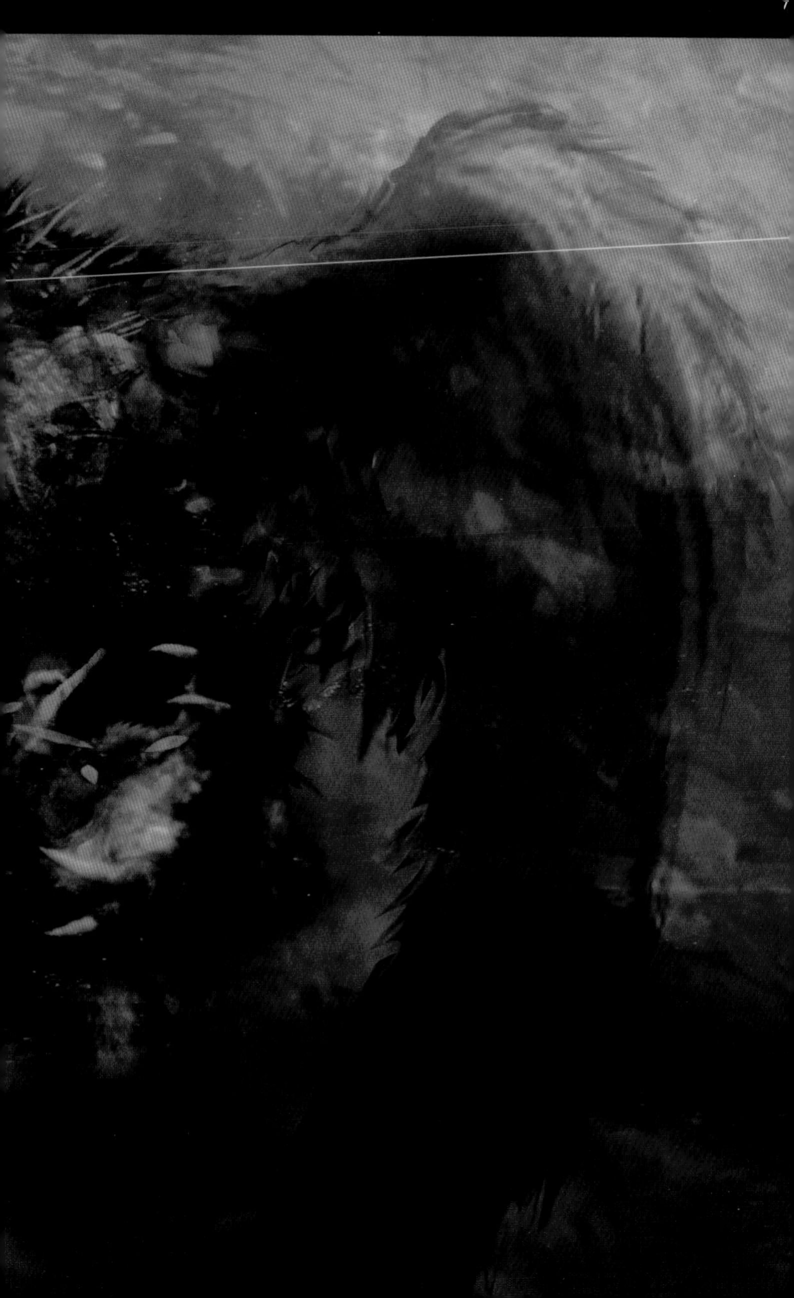

DRACHEN

FOUND ACROSS THE BRITISH ISLES AND NORTHERN EUROPE, DRACHENS OR DRAKES ARE FIRE SPIRITS THAT RESEMBLE BALLS OF FIRE STREAKING THROUGH THE NIGHT SKY. A RANCID SMELL OF SULPHUR, SIMILAR TO THE STENCH OF ROTTEN EGGS, TRAILS THEIR EVERY MOVE AND GIVES AWAY THEIR PRESENCE TO ANYONE WITHIN A FIVE-MILE RADIUS. SOME ACCOUNTS SUGGEST THEY ARE DRAGONS, AND THE NAME IS CERTAINLY CLOSE ENOUGH TO MAKE THIS LINK. THEY ALSO DISPLAY DRAGON-LIKE CHARACTERISTICS, WITH SHARP CLAWS, THE ABILITY TO BREATHE FIRE AND A HOSTILE TEMPERAMENT. FIGHTS BETWEEN MALE DRACHENS OVER FOOD, TERRITORY AND FEMALES ARE COMMON, BUT THEY WILL JOIN FORCES WHEN NECESSARY TO FIGHT OFF OUTSIDE THREATS.

Development

- When working up fire spirits, remember to use plenty of smoke. Here, the choking fumes fill the image and obscure many of the finer details, making the shape of the creature somewhat enigmatic.
- Use a restricted colour palette of red and black to emphasize the blistering heat surrounding a Drachen and to give the image an aggressive edge.
- Think about where to place the light sources – both primary and secondary – for maximum impact in your image.

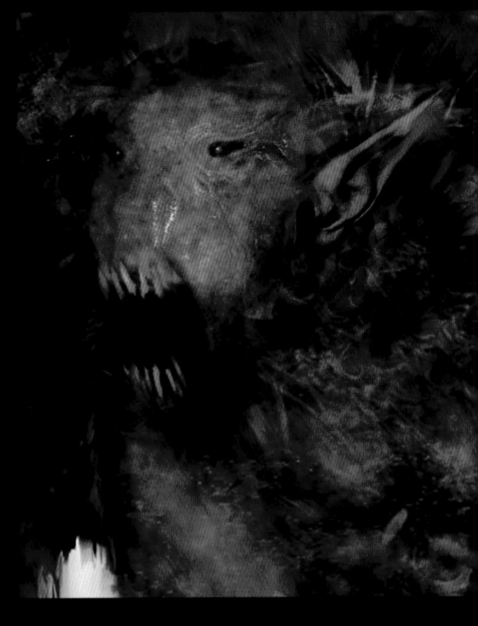

Media and Execution

• Photoshop
• The creature was created entirely in Photoshop with no sketches or photographs.
• Paint was built up in stages and smeared using the Smudge tool.
• The smoke was airbrushed in and developed with filter effects.
• A degree of Gaussian Blur was applied to the whole image to make it less sharp and to further enhance the ambiguity of the Drachen's shape.

FURTHER STUDY
Fire spirits, dragons, drakes.

ART CHRISTOPHER SHY

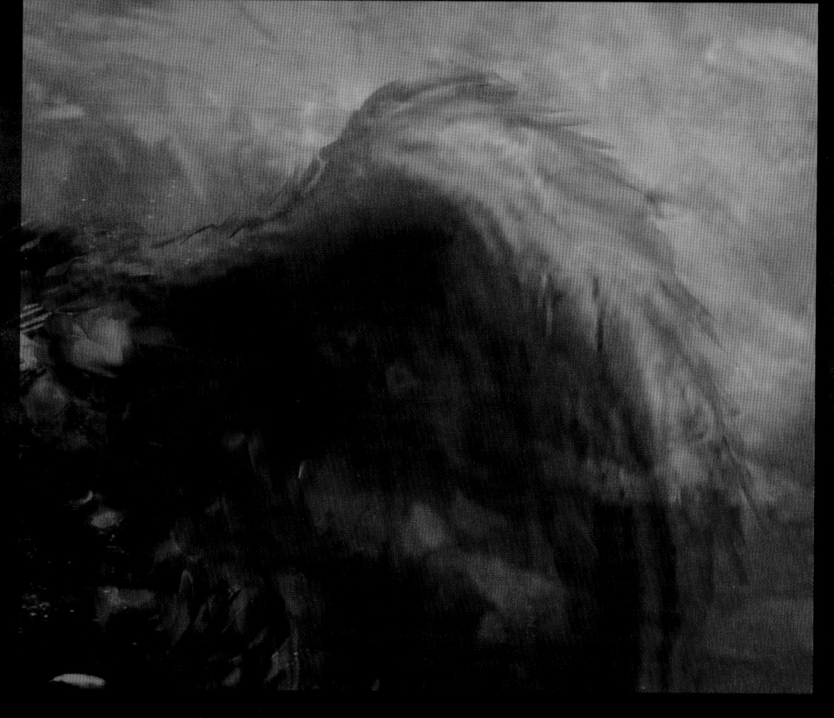

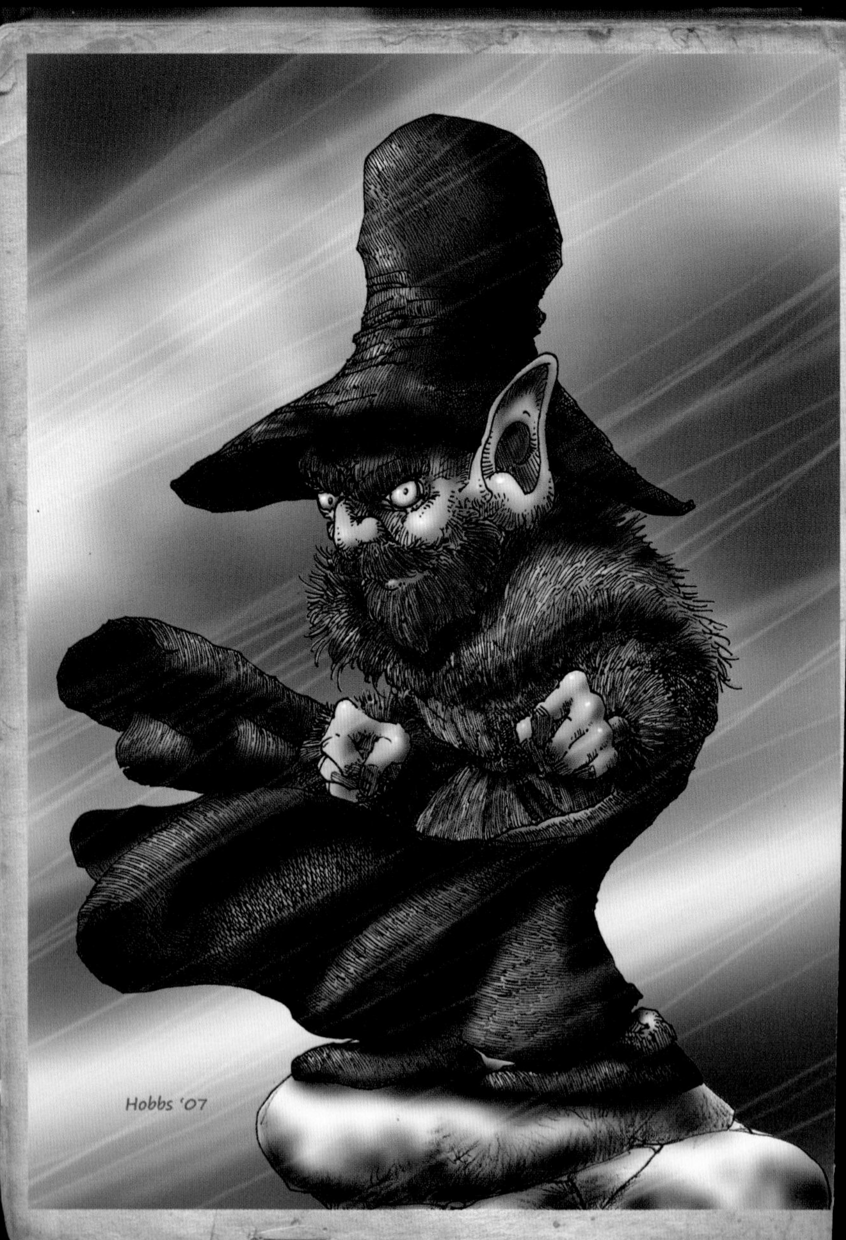
Hobbs '07

El Nuberu

ORIGINATING IN SPAIN, PARTICULARLY IN ASTURIAS, EL NUBERU IS CALLED 'THE LORD OF THE TEMPEST', AND IS CONSIDERED A WIND SPIRIT. HE APPEARS AS A DARK-SKINNED OLD MAN SPORTING BIG EARS, A THICK BEARD, GOAT LEATHERS, A FUR CLOAK AND A LARGE HAT, AND HE CAN EITHER BE SMALL OR GIANT. HIS BEHAVIOUR DEPENDS ON HOW HE IS TREATED BY OTHERS. FARMERS TAKE GREAT PAINS TO BE GOOD TO HIM SO THAT HE WILL BRING RAIN TO NOURISH THE CROPS. TO ANGER HIM WILL BRING DESTRUCTIVE STORMS OF WIND, RAIN, ICE OR EVEN FROGS.

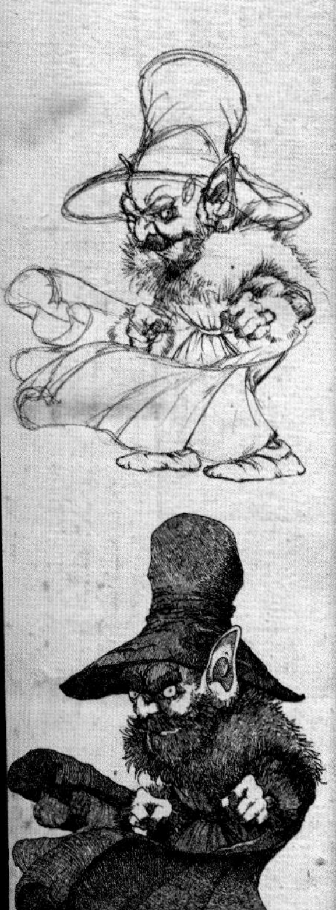

Development

- Use pencil sketches to work out the composition and details, then finalize your composition with a full rendering in pen and ink.
- For the appearance of a cranky little old man, the character has been drawn tensed up and glaring at the viewer, obviously angry.
- His cloak billowing about him in the raging wind adds movement and narrative to the image.
- Try adding a textured background, a blurred image background or simply a solid colour.

Media and Execution

- Pencil, pen and ink, Photoshop
- Preliminary sketches were made, with the final sketch rendered in pen and ink.
- The ink drawing was scanned into Photoshop, where the edges were cleaned up, the white background was deleted and the black lines were enhanced with the Levels dialog.
- The image was coloured using the various Paint tools, keeping the ink layer semi-transparent on top.

FURTHER STUDY

Asturian folklore, John Goat, Reñubreiru, Taranis, wind spirits.

ART BOB HOBBS

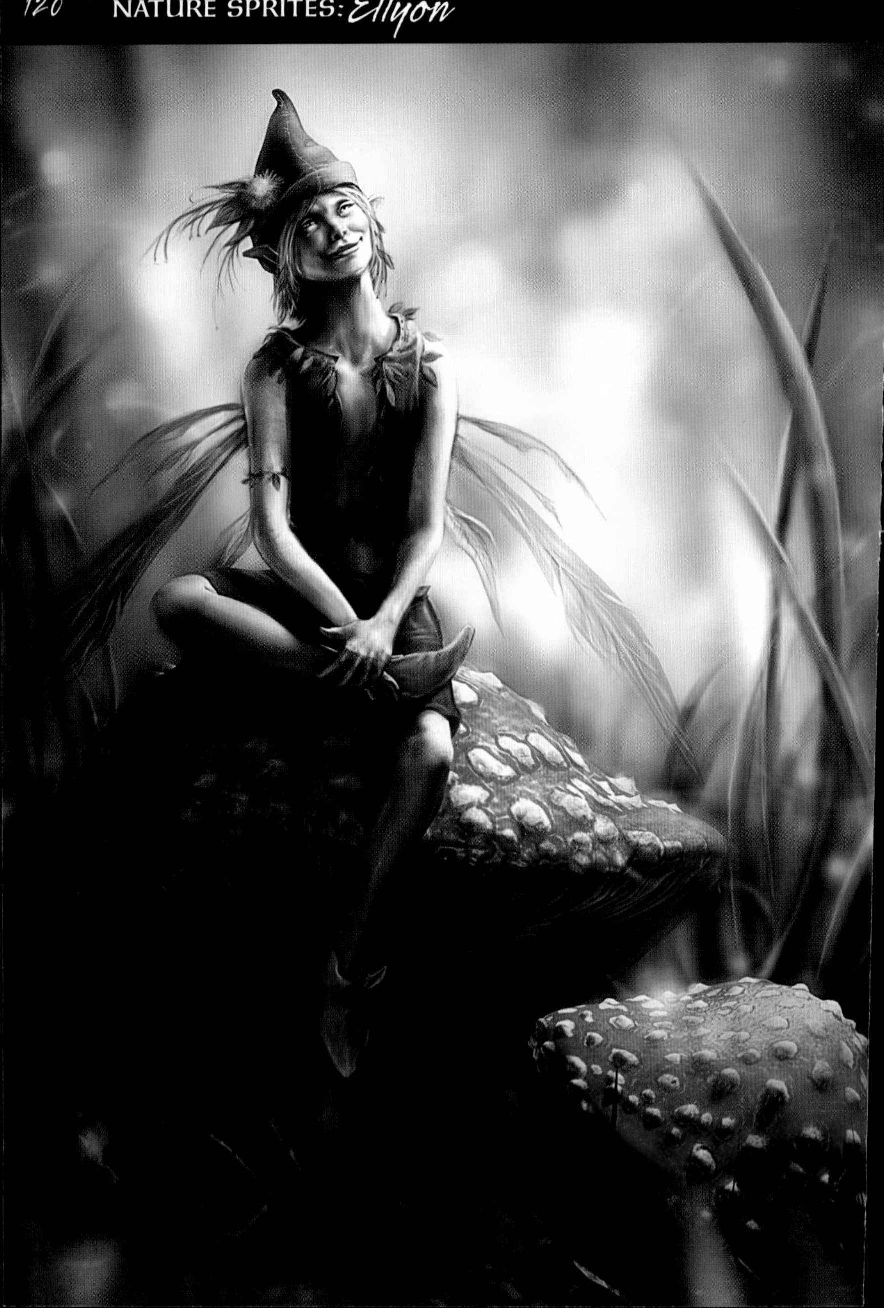

Ellyon

THESE DIMINUTIVE FAERIES APPEAR IN WELSH FOLKLORE. THEY FORM PART OF THE TYLWYTH TEG AND ARE FAITHFUL SERVANTS TO THEIR QUEEN, MAB (SEE PAGE 35). THEY SUBSIST ON A DIET OF TOADSTOOLS AND FAERIE BUTTER – A YELLOW TREE-FUNGUS – AND ARE ALWAYS CHEERFUL AND FRIENDLY. ELLYONS THRIVE ON HELPING OTHERS, AND LOOK AFTER OTHER LESS FORTUNATE FAERIES IN TIMES OF NEED. THEY WEAR SIMPLE OUTFITS DECORATED WITH LEAVES AND FLOWERS FROM THE FOREST. THEY HELP MAINTAIN A PEACEFUL ENVIRONMENT, AND MAKE GREAT TEACHERS ON ACCOUNT OF THEIR ENTHUSIASM AND PATIENCE.

Development

• Play on the classic toadstool theme by sitting the faerie on top of one. Use photographic references to ensure you make the fungus look believable.

• Use Photoshop Blur filters around the edges of the frame to create a soft, dream-like image. Make sure you keep your character in focus though.

Media and Execution

• Softimage XSI, Mudbox, Zbrush, Photoshop

• The figure was modelled and posed in XSI, and then sculpted further in Mudbox.

• Texture was added in Zbrush and then taken back into XSI to be rendered.

• The image was then brought into Photoshop, where it was painted over, liquified, blurred and colour corrected.

FURTHER STUDY

Tylwyth Teg, Mab, Seelie Court, Bendith Y Mamau.

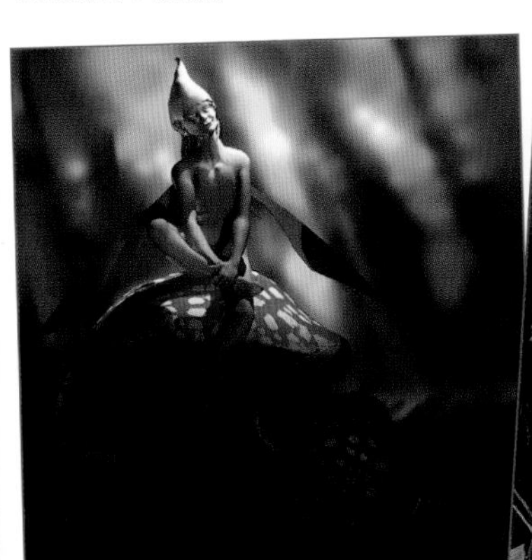

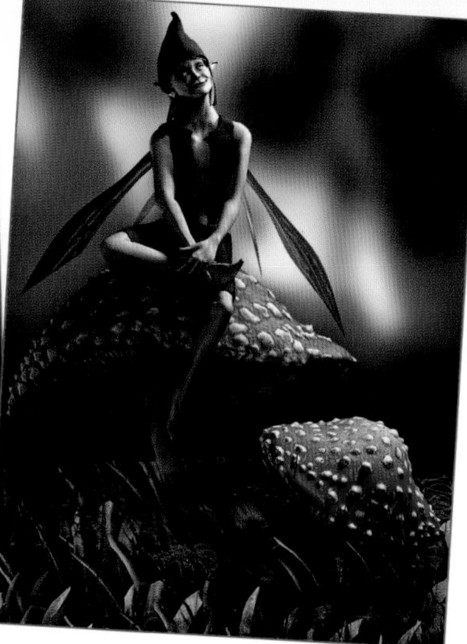

ART JULIANNA KOLAKIS

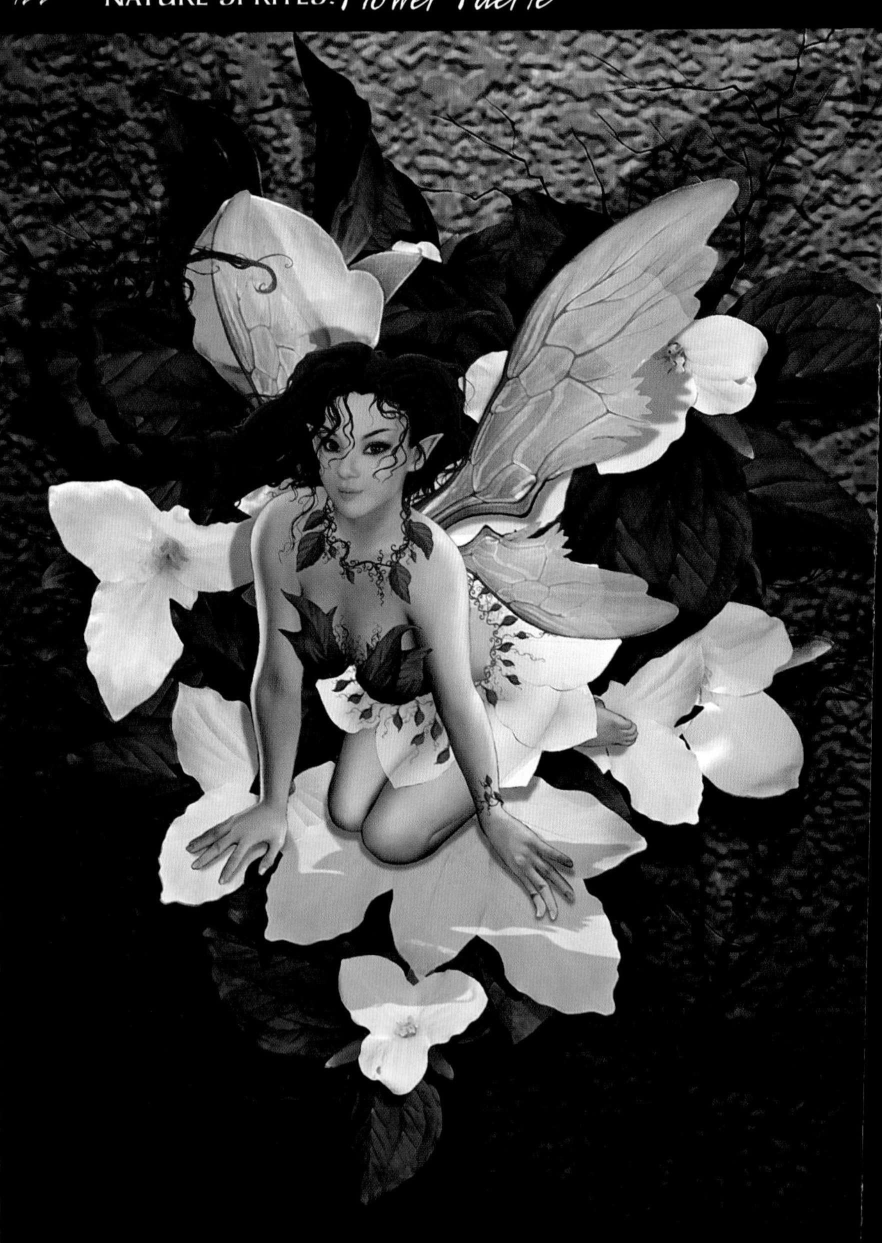

Flower Faerie

THESE TINY SPIRITS CARE FOR GARDENS, PARKS, MEADOWS AND FIELDS. THEY LIVE AND SLEEP AMONG THE FLOWERS OR PLANTS THEY GROW. EACH AND EVERY FLOWER FAERIE IS RESPONSIBLE FOR LOOKING AFTER ITS CHARGES AND KEEPING THEM STRONG AND HEALTHY WITH PLENTY OF SUN, WATER AND GOOD SOIL. THEY MUST ALSO SWEEP AWAY LITTER AND DEAD LEAVES, AND EVEN POLISH FLOWER STEMS AND LEAVES. FLOWER FAERIES ARE VERY SHY AND WARY OF HUMANS AND ANIMALS. THEY WEAR CLOTHING MADE FROM LEAVES AND FLOWERS AND THEY ARE VERY ADEPT AT HIDING. THEY ARE MOST ACTIVE JUST BEFORE DAWN AND DUSK, BUT CAN OCCASIONALLY BE SEEN AT MIDDAY.

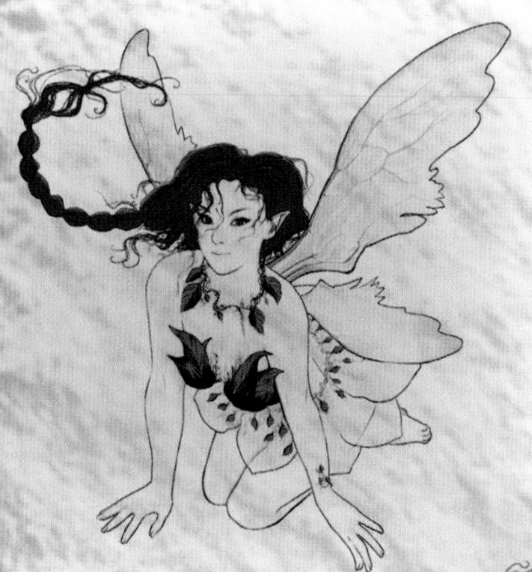

Media and Execution

- Pencil, 3DS Max, Photoshop
- A 3D plane was used to render the background texture, which was then brought into Photoshop to incorporate the shadows, plants and cracks.
- A pencil sketch of the faerie was scanned and cleaned up in Photoshop.
- Colours and tints were applied to the character on a new layer.
- At the final stage the layers were merged and some touch up work was done on the outline and facial features.

Development

- Use other characters in myth or folklore that have a resemblance to what you're working on when you can't find enough background information.
- If history or folklore is scarce, keep your characters generic and straightforward – this will give you more freedom to design and render your piece.

FURTHER STUDY
Dryad, tree spirits.
Heather Pixie.

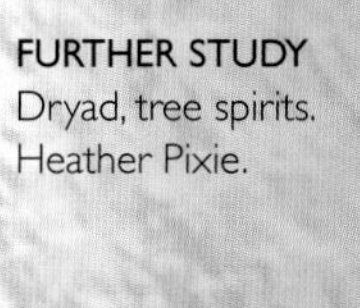

ART ALAIN VIESCA

Forest Faerie

ENCHANTED WOODLANDS ARE A COMMON FEATURE IN BOTH TRADITIONAL FAERIE TALES AND CONTEMPORARY FANTASY FICTION. THE DARK AND MYSTERIOUS NATURE OF FORESTS GIVES RISE TO MANY MYTHS AND LEGENDS, OF WHICH THE PRESENCE OF FOREST FAERIES IS A CORNERSTONE. THE FOREST FAERIE IS A GENERIC WOODLAND SPRITE WHO DANCES IN RINGS OF TOADSTOOLS KNOWN AS FAERIE RINGS, AND CAUSES PEOPLE TO LOSE THEIR BEARINGS IN THE FOREST. THEY HAVE A HUMAN APPEARANCE, BUT ARE TINY AND HAVE DELICATE WINGS. THEY CAN CAST MANY SPELLS, INCLUDING LOVE SPELLS, AND CAN FORESEE AND INFLUENCE THE FUTURE. GENERALLY BENIGN BUT FREQUENTLY MISCHIEVOUS, THEY ARE MOSTLY SEEN AT DUSK AND DAWN.

Development

- Don't always show your faeries in an active state; a sleeping faerie curled up on the forest floor is an equally enchanting sight.
- Use the colours found in nature for inspiration in your colour palette, particularly when representing nature sprites.
- Try to create an organic frame to your composition using the flowers and foliage of the background. The effect here is of a leafy bower where the faerie can doze undisturbed, but it also helps to focus the viewer's attention on her.

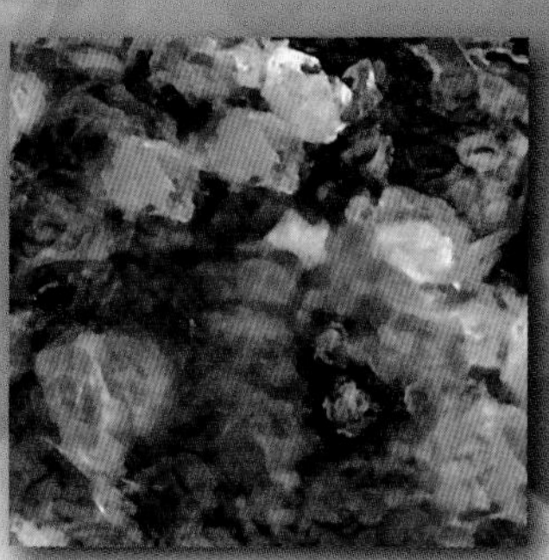

ART CHRISTOPHER SHY

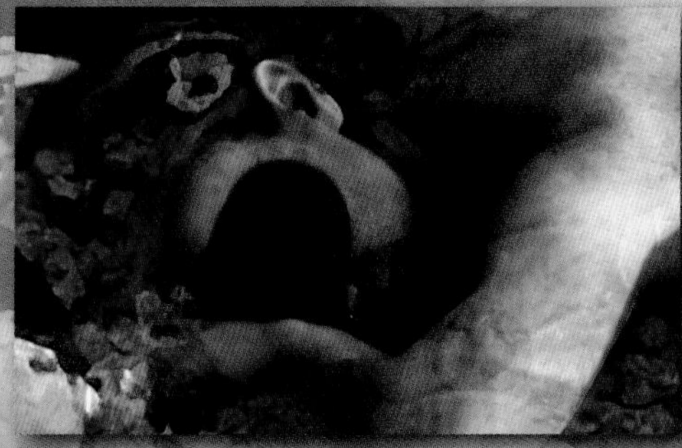

FURTHER STUDY

Puck, Bucca, Pixie, Titania, Dryad, nymphs, woodland spirits.

Media and Execution

- Photograph, Photoshop
- The background was painted in Photoshop, with the Burn tool used to darken the centre of the image to make a natural frame.
- The faerie began as a model photograph, which was over-painted to suggest the dappled light from between the branches falling on her body.
- The wings were created on a separate layer with the Brush tool set to a very low Opacity.

Ghillie Dhu

SHY CREATURES FROM SCOTTISH FOLKLORE, GHILLIE DHU WERE FORCED INTO ISOLATION AND ARE NOW BELIEVED TO BE EXTINCT. IN THE PAST, THEY JEALOUSLY GUARDED BIRCH TREES FROM HUMANS, WHO THEY DISLIKED INTENSELY. ANYONE TRAVELLING THROUGH THE WOODS AT NIGHT, WHEN THE GHILLIE DHU WERE MOST ACTIVE, NEEDED TO TAKE CARE NOT TO APPROACH THESE FAERIES, OR THEY WOULD BE FOREVER ENSLAVED BY THEM. THEY WORE CLOTHES WOVEN FROM MOSS, LEAVES, BRANCHES AND GRASSES AND HAD LONG BLACK HAIR AND LIGHT GREENISH COLOURED SKIN. THEIR ARMS AND FINGERS EXTENDED MUCH FURTHER THAN THOSE OF A HUMAN, MAKING IT EXTREMELY DIFFICULT TO GET OUT OF THEIR CLUTCHES ONCE CAUGHT.

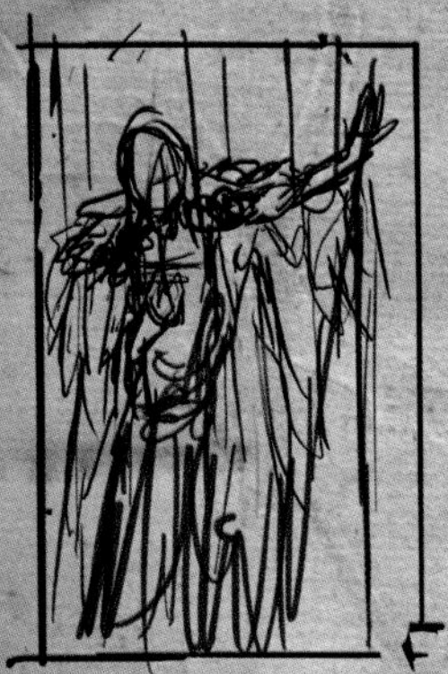

Development

- Create a feeling of night by keeping your background fairly monochromatic, picking out highlights in white as if caught in the moonlight.
- Test your composition by flipping the image during the design process – this is a simple way to check that the overall balance is working.
- Create a sense of perspective using converging verticals – the trees here bend outwards towards the edges of the frame, suggesting an upward view.

ART ARTEMIS KOLAKIS

Media and Execution

- Photoshop
- The composition was digitally sketched using the Brush tool in Photoshop.
- The original sketch was refined and then flipped to test the composition.
- Colour was added and the Liquify and Warp filters used to adjust the character's proportions.
- The image was then colour corrected and prepared for print.

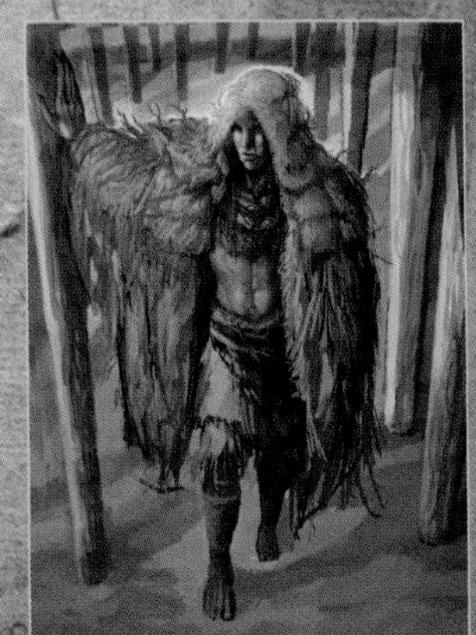

FURTHER STUDY

Scottish folklore, Ghillie Dubh, Loch Druing.

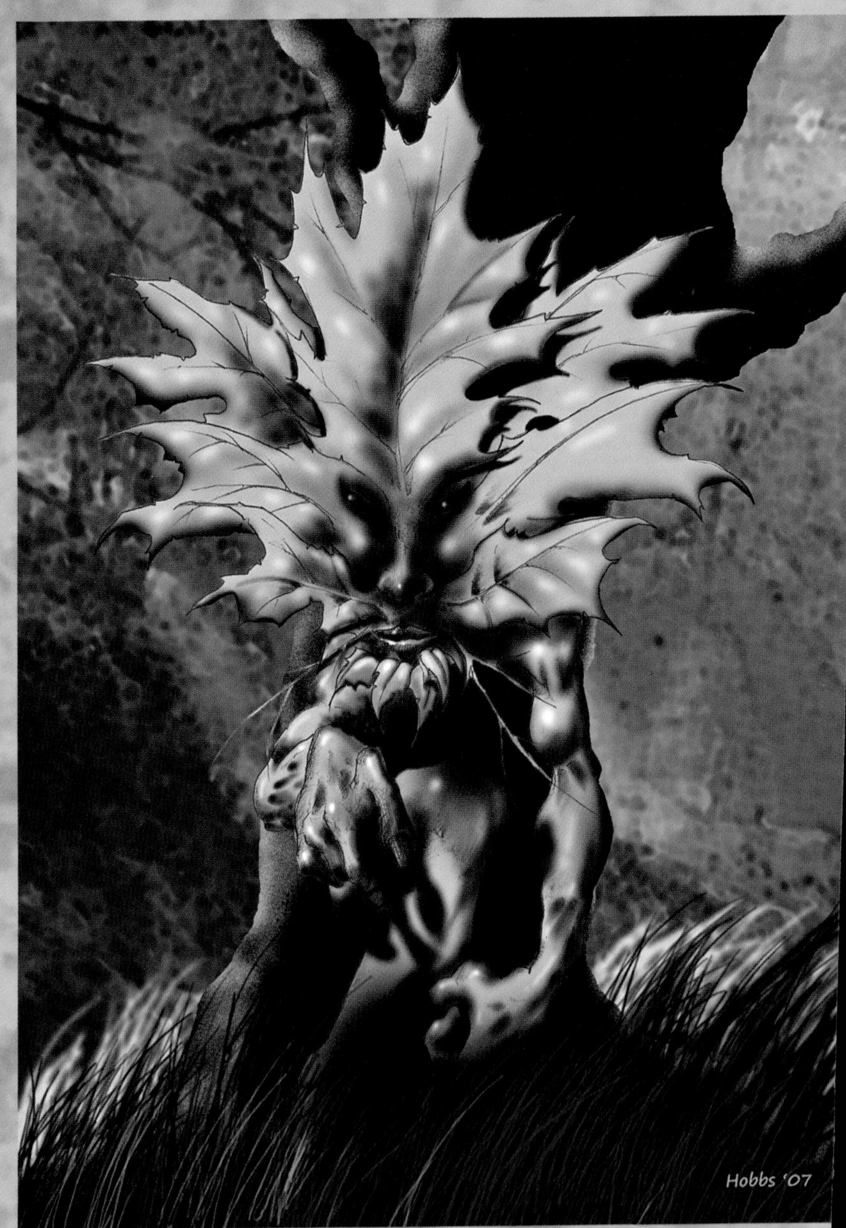
Hobbs '07

Green Man

A WELL-KNOWN PAGAN DEITY, THE GREEN MAN CAN BE FOUND IN THE WOODLANDS OF THE BRITISH ISLES AND EUROPE. HE IS NORMALLY DEPICTED AS A HORNED BEING WITH A MASK OF OAK FOLIAGE. HE IS ALSO KNOWN AS GREEN JACK, JACK-IN-THE-GREEN AND GREEN GEORGE. ALTHOUGH HE IS A PAGAN SPIRIT, HIS IMAGE IS OFTEN SEEN IN CHURCH DECORATIONS. AN IMPORTANT FIGURE IN PAGAN CEREMONIES, PEOPLE FREQUENTLY DRESS UP AS HIM FOR RITES AND FESTIVALS. THE GREEN MAN IS A PROTECTOR OF THE FOREST AND THE TREES AND ANIMALS THAT LIVE THERE. IN THE MODERN RELIGION OF WICCA, THE GREEN MAN REPRESENTS THE HORNED GOD, A MIXTURE OF THE CELTIC CERNUNNOS AND THE GREEK PAN.

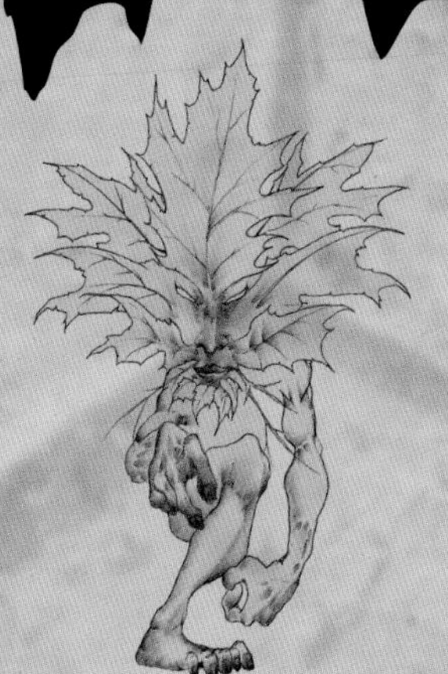

Media and Execution

- Pencil, photograph, Photoshop
- Preliminary sketches were made and the final pencil line drawing was scanned and opened in Photoshop.
- Using the Brush tool, grass was drawn in the foreground and the silhouette of a large oak tree was added behind the figure for contrast.
- A photo of a forest was placed in the background, blurred and then treated with a Watercolour filter.
- Finally touches of shading and highlights were added.

Development

- The Green Man is normally depicted as just a face, but you can choose to render him with a body, as here. He would naturally be naked or covered in leaves much like the Swamp Thing character in comic books.
- Finding a good reference for oak trees is vital unless you've got one growing nearby that you can photograph yourself.
- Be as detailed with foliage as you like, or keep it simple.

FURTHER STUDY
Wicca, Paganism, Romanesque architecture, Green Knight, English folklore, Cernunnos, Pan.

ART BOB HOBBS

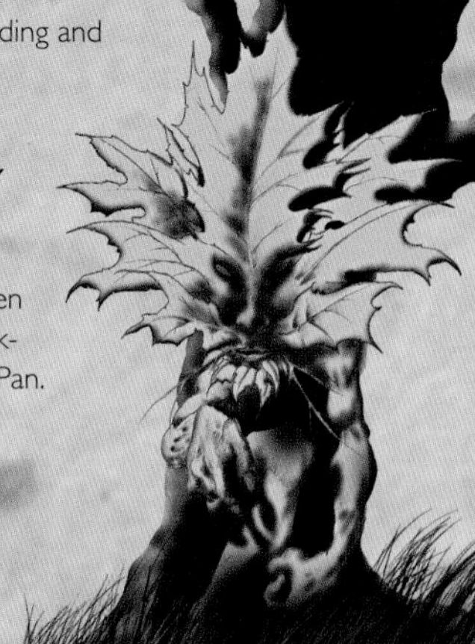

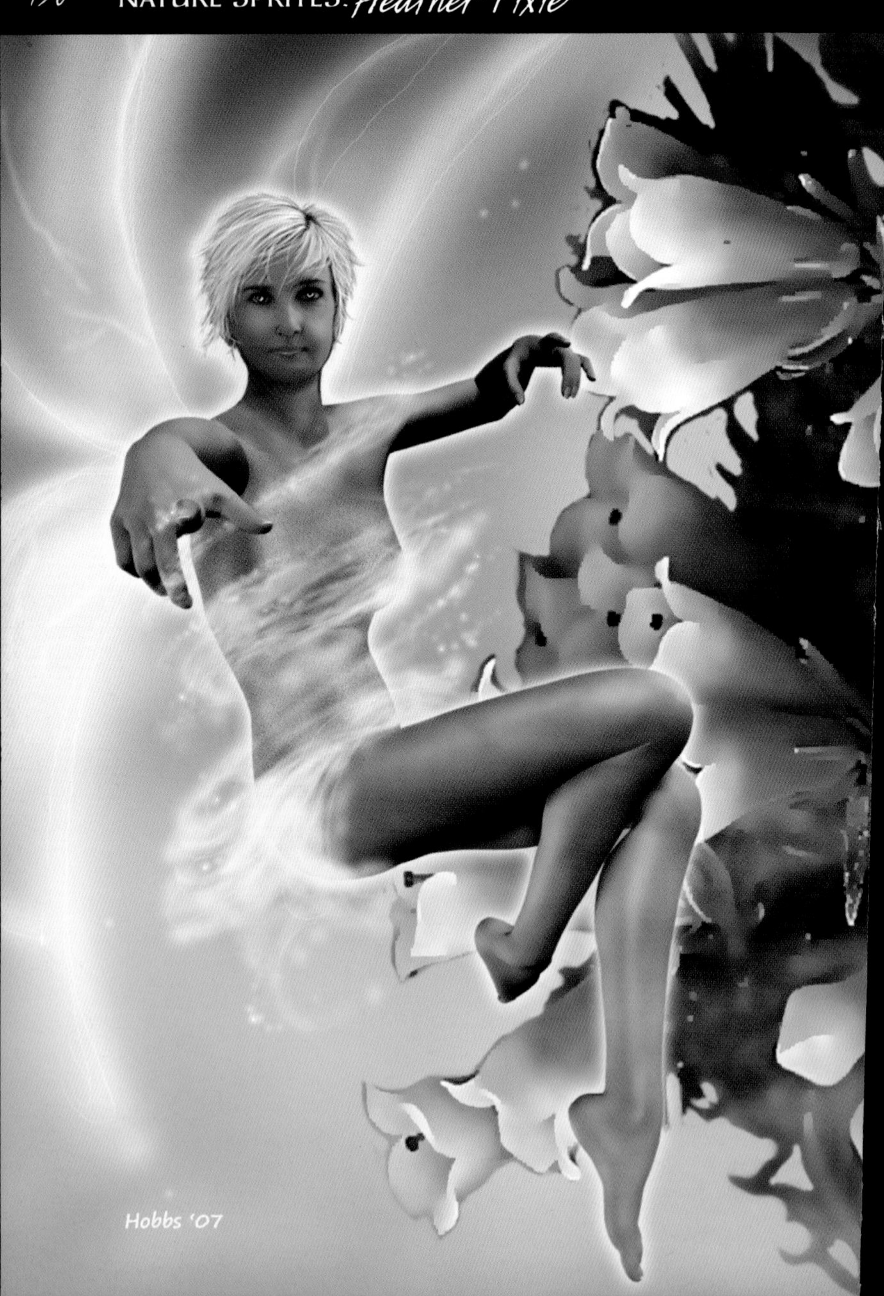
Hobbs '07

Heather Pixie

THESE EARTHY SPIRITS ORIGINATED IN SCOTLAND WHERE, IN THE LOWLANDS, HEATHER GROWS PLENTIFULLY. THEY ARE STRONGLY RELATED TO THE REGULAR PIXIES OF NORTHERN ENGLAND AND SCOTLAND, BUT DEPEND ON THE HEATHER FOR THEIR SURVIVAL. LIKE OTHER PIXIES, THEY HAVE CLEAR OR GOLDEN AURAS AND DELICATE, TRANSLUCENT WINGS. THEY ARE SAID TO ENJOY SPINNING FLAX AND ARE USUALLY FOUND ON HEATHER-COVERED MOORS, WHICH GIVES THEM THEIR OTHER NAME – MOOR SPRITES. THEY ARE NOT ADVERSE TO HUMANS, BUT ARE SOMEWHAT SHY AND DO NOT SEEK MEN OUT. WHEN THEY DO COME IN CONTACT WITH HUMANS, THEY ARE CONSUMMATE PRANKSTERS, SO A CAREFUL APPROACH IS REQUIRED.

Development

- Find a model with a Pixie-like face and hairstyle to photograph and create the body in Poser software. Then merge the two elements together in Photoshop.
- Use photographic references for greater accuracy and believability when depicting plants and flowers.
- Airbrushing in Photoshop can be used create shimmering, vaporous clothing.

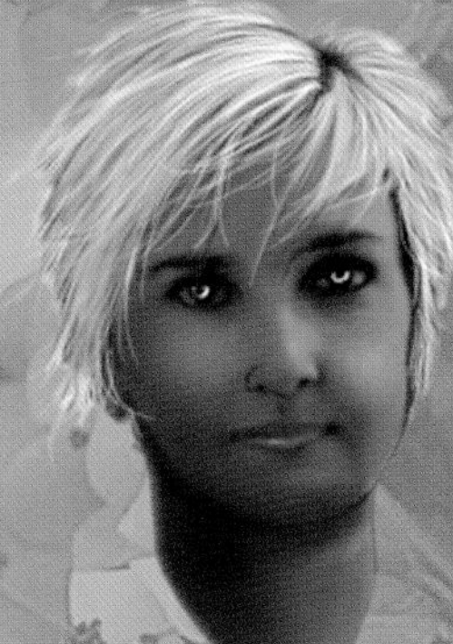

FURTHER STUDY
Moor Sprites, Yorkshire folklore, Scottish folklore.

ART BOB HOBBS
MODEL AMY GUINN

Media and Execution

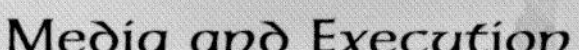

- Photograph, Poser, Photoshop
- The figure was created in Poser and rendered out to Photoshop.
- The model photo was scanned and opened in Photoshop, merged with the Poser body and airbrushed to match up the skin colours.
- The hair, wings, clothing and background were painted in with the Pen, Brush and Airbrush tools.
- Based on a photo, the heather flowers are added then a Smart Blur filter was used several times to smooth them out.

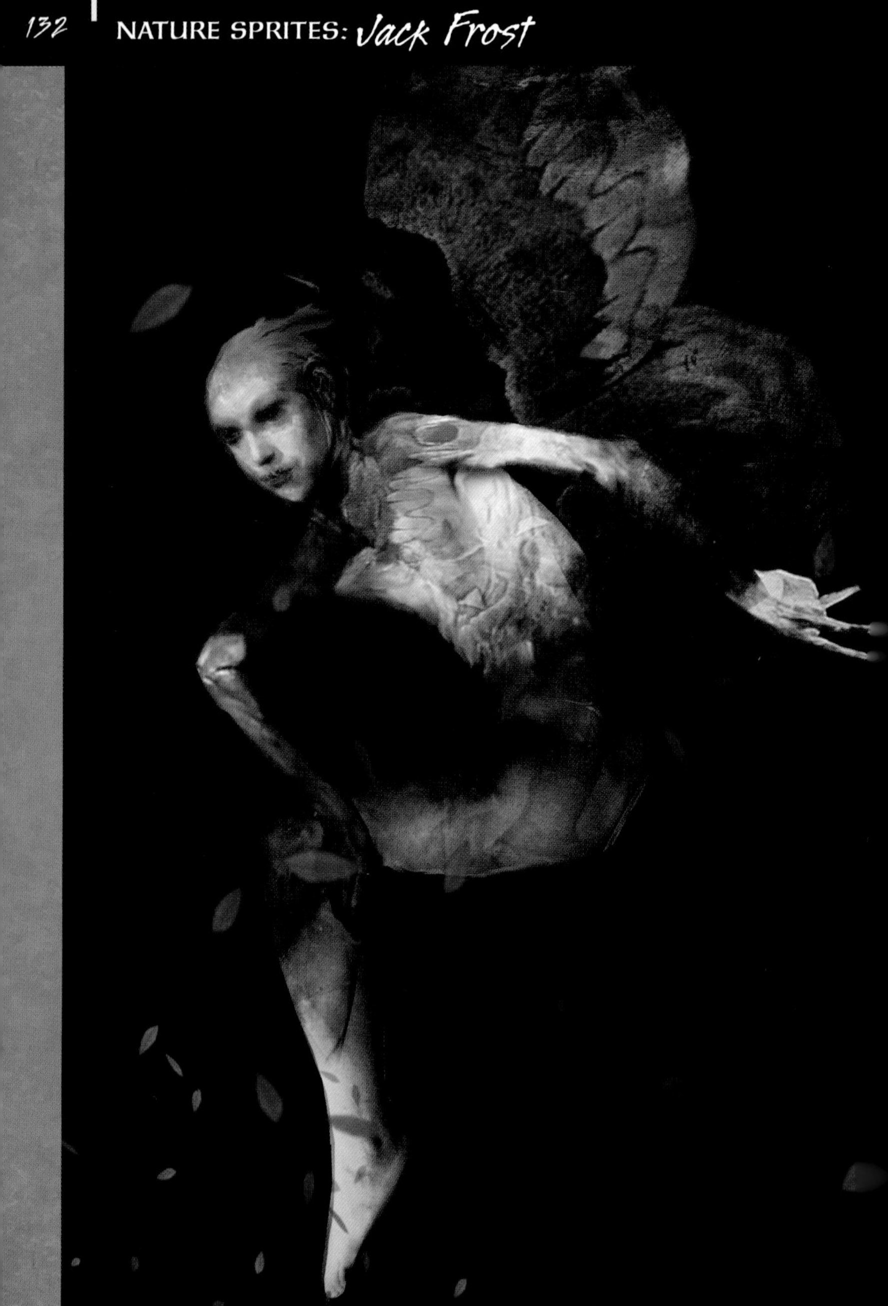

Jack Frost

'LOOK OUT, LOOK OUT! JACK FROST IS ABOUT, HE'S AFTER YOUR FINGERS AND TOES,' GOES THE FIRST LINE OF A CHILDREN'S NURSERY RHYME. AN ELF-LIKE BEING ASSOCIATED WITH COLD WINTER WEATHER, JACK FROST HAS ORIGINS IN VIKING, RUSSIAN AND ENGLISH FOLKLORE. IT IS HE WHO IS RESPONSIBLE FOR THE PATTERNS OF ICE-CRYSTALS THAT APPEAR ON WINDOWPANES ON FROSTY MORNINGS. ALTHOUGH HIS ORIGINS ARE ANCIENT, JACK FROST CONTINUES TO APPEAR IN MODERN FICTION AND POPULAR CULTURE, AND THE NAME WAS EVEN USED A PSEUDONYM BY BOB DYLAN. JACK IS OFTEN ACCOMPANIED BY HIS FEMALE COUNTERPART, JILL FROST, AND TOGETHER THEY ARE ALSO KNOWN AS FATHER AND MOTHER WINTER, OR OLD MAN AND OLD WOMAN WINTER.

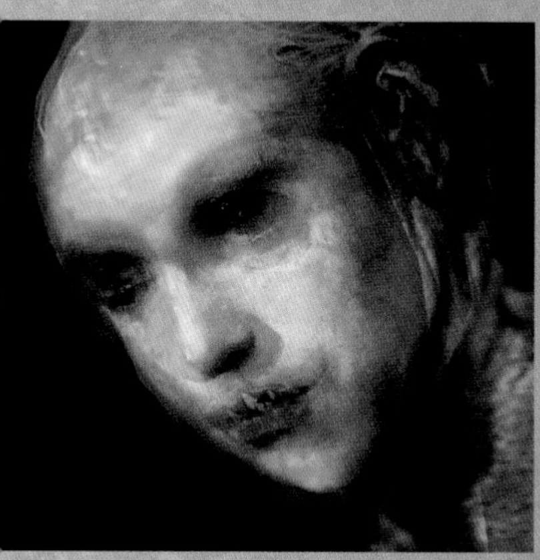

Development

- Skinny arms, long fingers and spiky hair are all elements that encapsulate Jack Frost, so try as many different variations on these as you wish.
- Lighting is crucial in faerie art – try to think about lighting your characters as though they are actors on a stage.
- Always carry a camera and keep your eyes open for interesting textures or details that can be used in your paintings.

FURTHER STUDY

Snow sprites, sky people, Old Man Winter.

Media and Execution

- Photographs, Photoshop
- A model photograph was used for the basic pose, but was heavily manipulated in Photoshop, particularly around the arms, hands and torso.
- The photograph was over-painted, smearing and smudging the colours to create interesting surface textures.
- The wings were taken from a photographic reference of moth wings, which was transformed and over-painted to work with the shades and tones of the character.

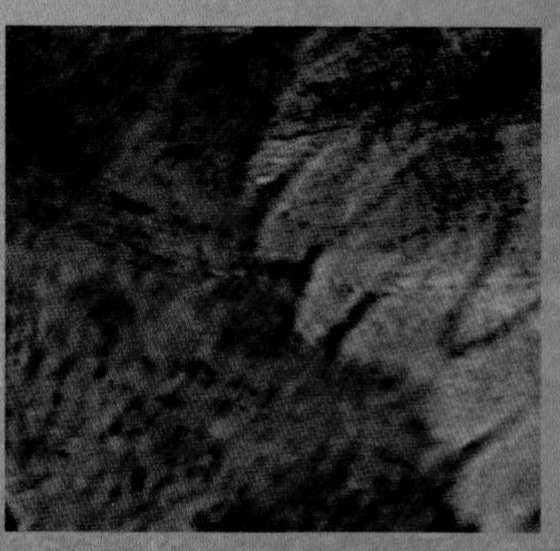

ART CHRISTOPHER SHY

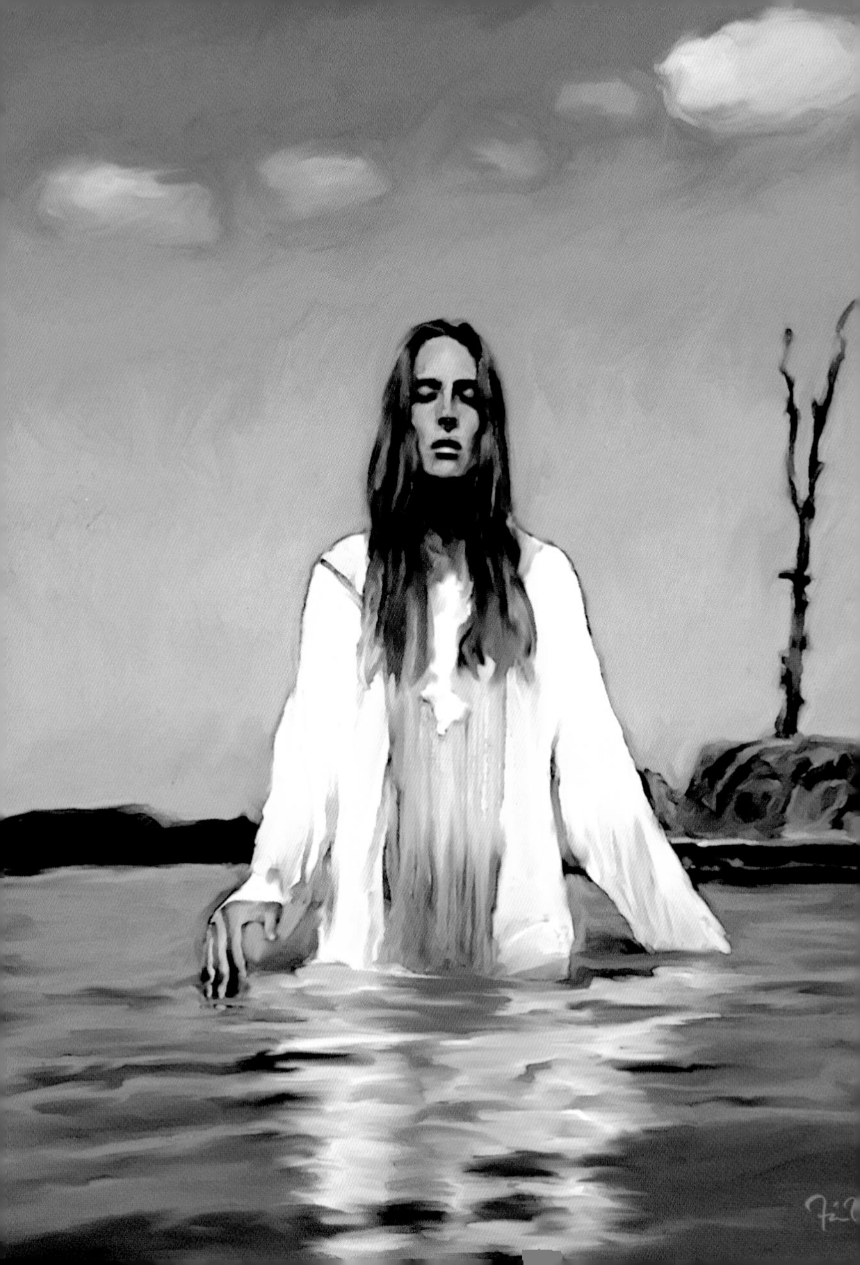

Kallraden

THESE SWEDISH WATER SPIRITS HAVE VERY LITTLE RECORDED GENEALOGY. SOME ACCOUNTS SUGGEST THEY ARE BEAUTIFUL, WHILE OTHERS IMPLY THEY ARE HIDEOUS. SWEDEN IS A COUNTRY OF MANY LAKES, SO THE LARGE NUMBER OF FAERIES ASSOCIATED WITH WATER IS NOT SURPRISING. KALLRADENS' BEHAVIOUR IS TYPICAL OF MANY WATER SPRITES - LONELY HUNTERS OR WOODSMEN FALL IN LOVE WITH THESE BEGUILING CREATURES ON SIGHT AND ARE LURED TO THEIR DEATHS IN THE ICY WATERS. WHEN TREATED WITH RESPECT THOUGH, THEY WILL HELP LOST TRAVELLERS FIND THEIR WAY AND RETURN THEM SAFELY HOME. KALLRADENS ARE THE EMBODIMENT OF BOTH THE MYSTERIOUS BEAUTY AND THE LURKING DANGER OF THE VAST SWEDISH HINTERLAND, AN ALLURING METAPHOR FOR THE POETRY AND POWER OF NATURE ITSELF.

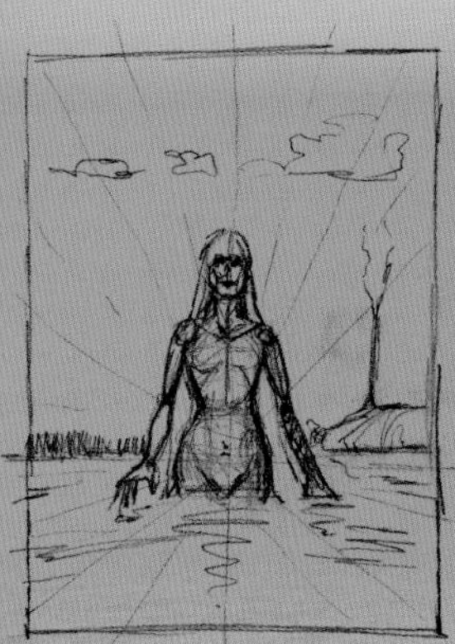

Development

- Producing numerous sketches will help you 'find' your character. Quick studies may bear little resemblance to the final image but help you immerse yourself in the personality of the sprite.
- Facial features will vary from drawing to drawing until certain features will start to 'settle', such as the shape of the mouth or the type of eyes.
- Exercises like this help you get into the flow of your creativity, allowing you to let your pencil wander, to stop thinking and just see what emerges.

FURTHER STUDY

Rusalka, Vodyanoy's Daughters, Nix, Morgens.

Media and Execution

- Photograph, pencil, Photoshop
- The image was based on a model photograph, which was then sketched out in pencil.
- After laying basic colours over the pencil drawing the whole image was passed through a Watercolour filter in Photoshop before being manually painted with the Smudge tool. The effect of the filter created a painterly look that was too obvious and so then had to be replicated by hand to make the final image look convincing.

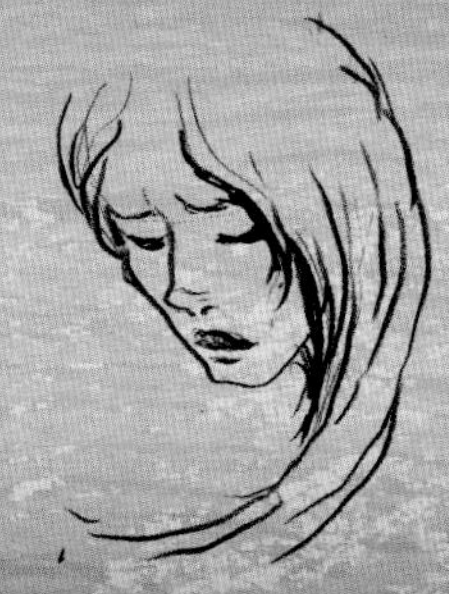

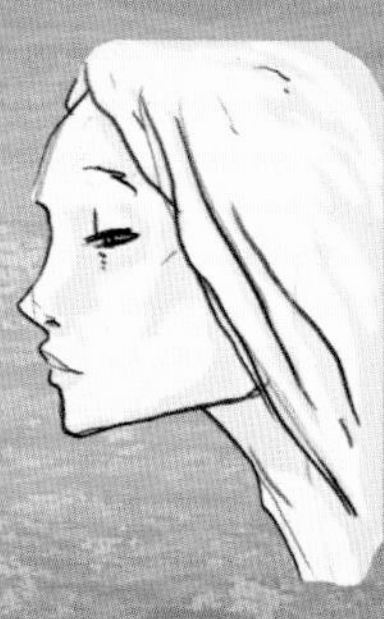

ART FINLAY COWAN **MODEL** IDA OLSEN

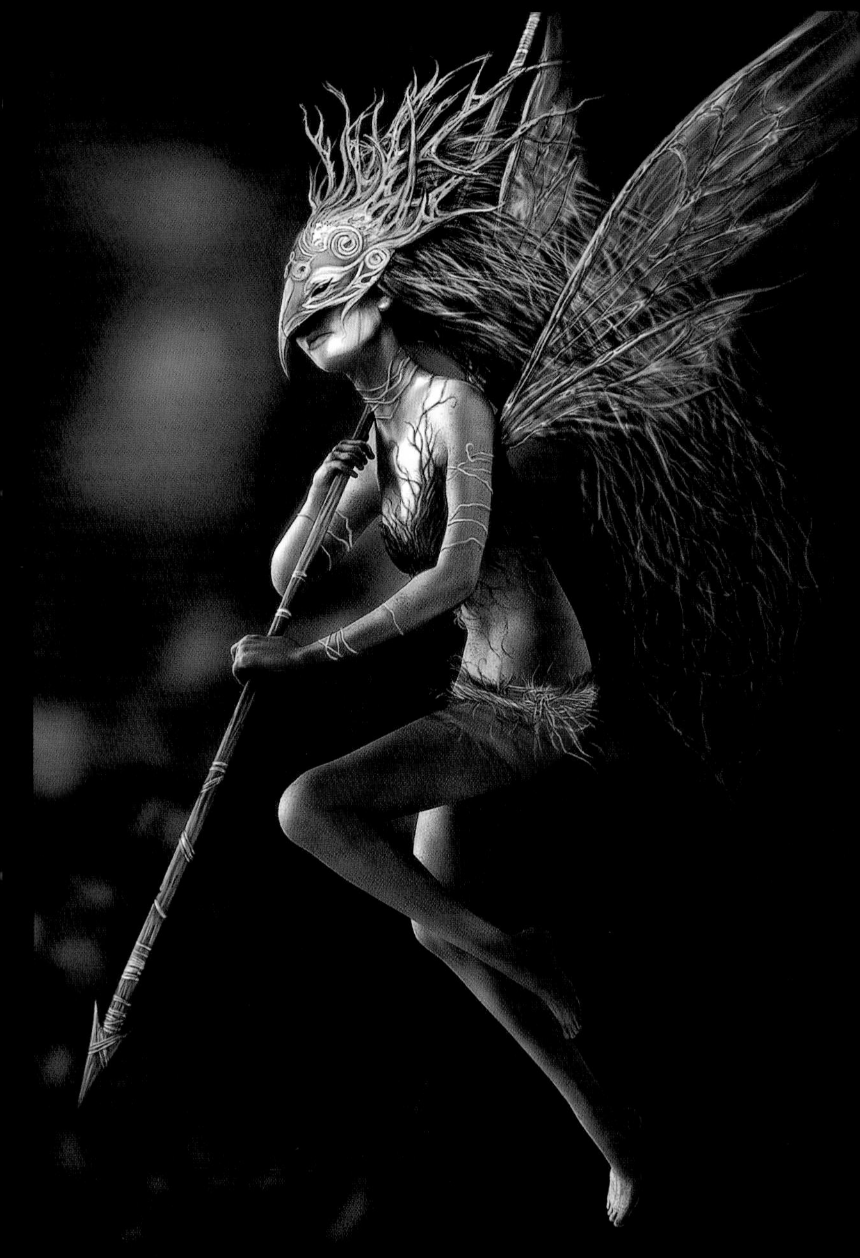

Lunantishee

THIS TRIBE OF FAERIES FROM THE FOLKLORE OF IRELAND ARE STALWART GUARDIANS OF BLACKTHORN BUSHES FROM WHICH *SHILLELAGHS*, TRADITIONAL IRISH WALKING STICKS, ARE MADE. THEIR NAME DERIVES FROM *LUNA*, THE LATIN WORD FOR MOON, AND *SIDHE*, MEANING FAERIE IN GAELIC. THEY HATE HUMANS WITH A PASSION FOR ENCROACHING ON THEIR BELOVED BLACKTHORN, AND WILL NOT ALLOW IT TO BE CUT ON 11 MAY, WHICH WAS MAY DAY IN EARLIER TIMES, OR 11 NOVEMBER, ORIGINALLY ALL HALLOWS EVE. IF YOU DO CUT THE BLACKTHORN ON THOSE DAYS, TERRIBLE MISFORTUNE WILL BEFALL YOU. LUNANTISHEE USUALLY SEEM NON-THREATENING, BUT THEIR TRUE NATURE IS REVEALED WHEN THEY FEEL THE URGENCY TO PROTECT AGAINST A POTENTIAL DANGER, SO CONTACT IS NOT ADVISED.

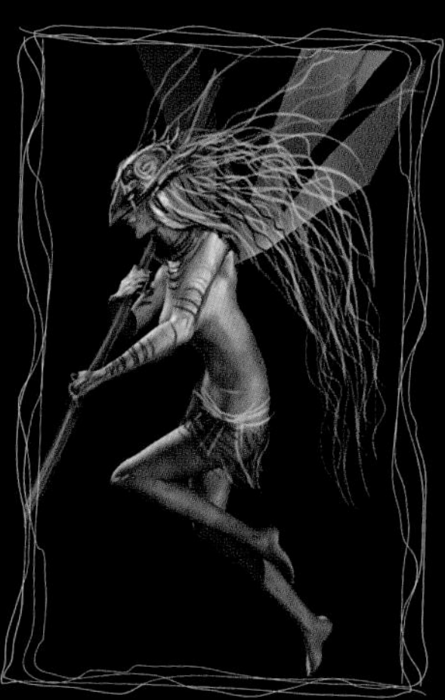

Media and Execution

- Softimage XSI, Zbrush, Photoshop
- The figure was modelled, posed and rendered in XSI.
- It was brought into Zbrush to be textured, then dropped into Photoshop, where the Liquify filter was used to edit its proportions.
- The figure was then painted over using the Brush tool.
- The highlights were added and the details were refined before the whole image was colour corrected.

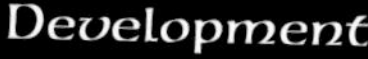

FURTHER STUDY
Lunantisidhe, Irish folklore, blackthorn faeries, moon goddess.

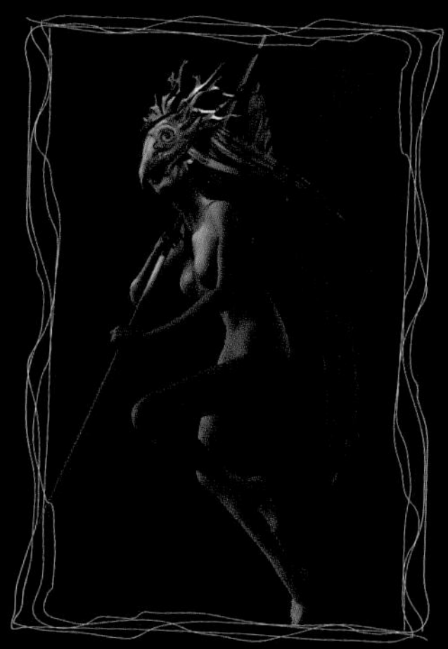

Development

- Show the Lunantishee's fierce defense of the blackthorn, by depicting them as faerie warriors, with weapons and armour.
- Create a sense of photorealism by using a blurred background, which alludes to the photographic technique of using a wide aperture for shallow depth of field.

ART JULIANNA KOLAKIS

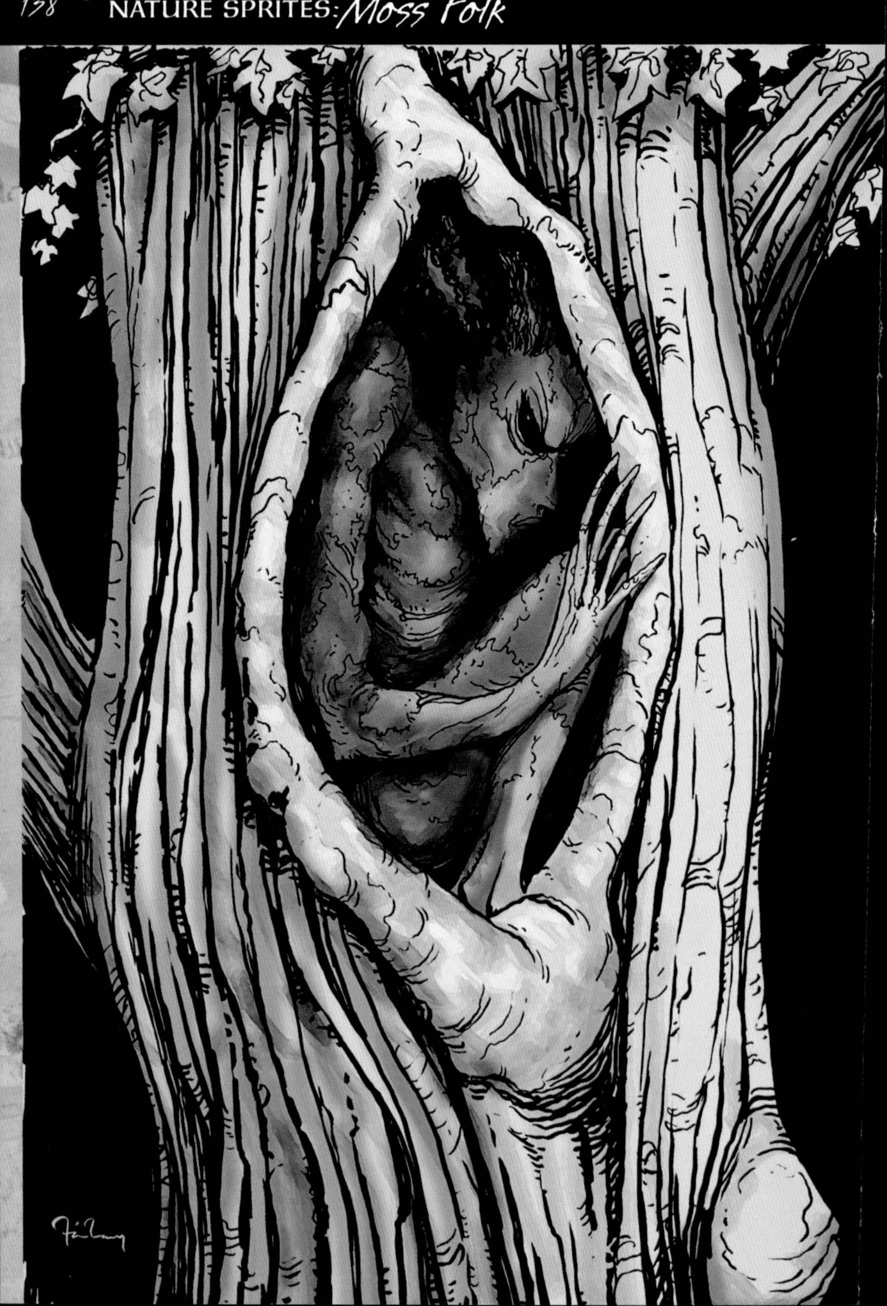

Moss Folk

APPEARING IN SCANDINAVIAN FOLKLORE, MOSS FOLK ARE FOREST-DWELLING FAERIES THAT BORROW ITEMS FROM HUMANS BUT ALWAYS REPAY THE FAVOUR. IN SOME STORIES THEY WOULD ASK HUMANS FOR MILK TO FEED THEIR YOUNG. IN SOUTHERN GERMANY THEY ARE A TYPE OF TREE SPIRIT, ALSO KNOWN AS WOOD PEOPLE AND MOSS MAIDENS. THEY ARE SOMETIMES DESCRIBED AS BEING SMALL AND BEAUTIFUL WITH FAERIE WINGS BUT ARE ALSO DEPICTED AS BEING OLD AND HAIRY AND COVERED IN MOSS. THEY AVOID HUNTERS BY HIDING IN TREES THAT WOODSMEN HAVE MARKED WITH A CROSS, DESIGNATING THAT THE TREE WILL BE CHOPPED DOWN. THEIR LIVES ARE LINKED TO SPECIFIC TREES AND IT IS SAID THAT IF THE TREE DIES THEN SO WILL THE FAERIE.

Development

- Keep the tonal range to one colour with highlights and shadows so that the faerie appears to blend in with its environment.
- Always begin by tackling the part of the drawing you are least confident about getting right – for most artists it's usually the face, but in this case it was the bark of the tree that required bold brush strokes.
- Moss Folk are often described as being beautiful, so try variations that depict more delicate nature spirits.

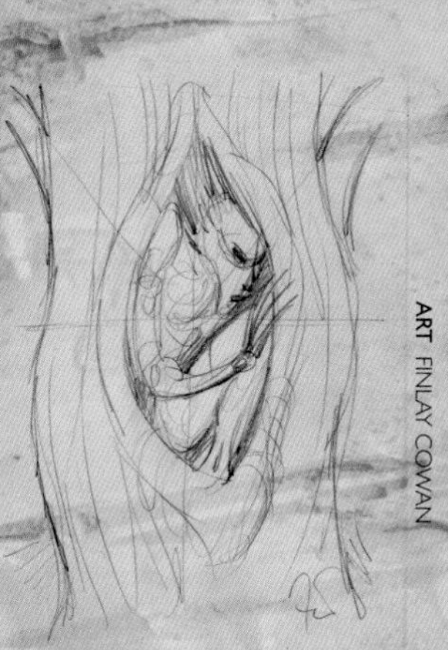

ART FINLAY COWAN

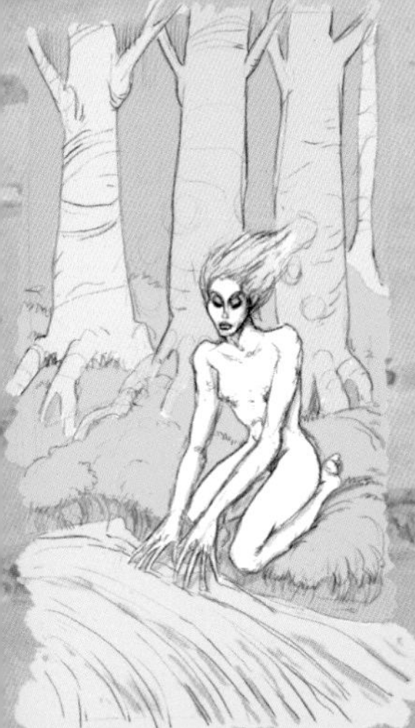

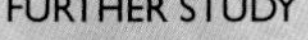

FURTHER STUDY

Hamadryad, Dryad, Askefreur, Huldrafolk, Skogsfru, *Legend of the Wooden Shoes.*

Media and Execution

- Pencil, brush pens, watercolours, Photoshop
- The drawing was executed with brush pens using bold fluid strokes to begin with before adding finer details.
- A rough watercolour wash was scanned into Photoshop then cloned to match the shape of the tree and figure.
- The Dodge and Burn tools were used at low Exposure to add shadow in the colour layer.

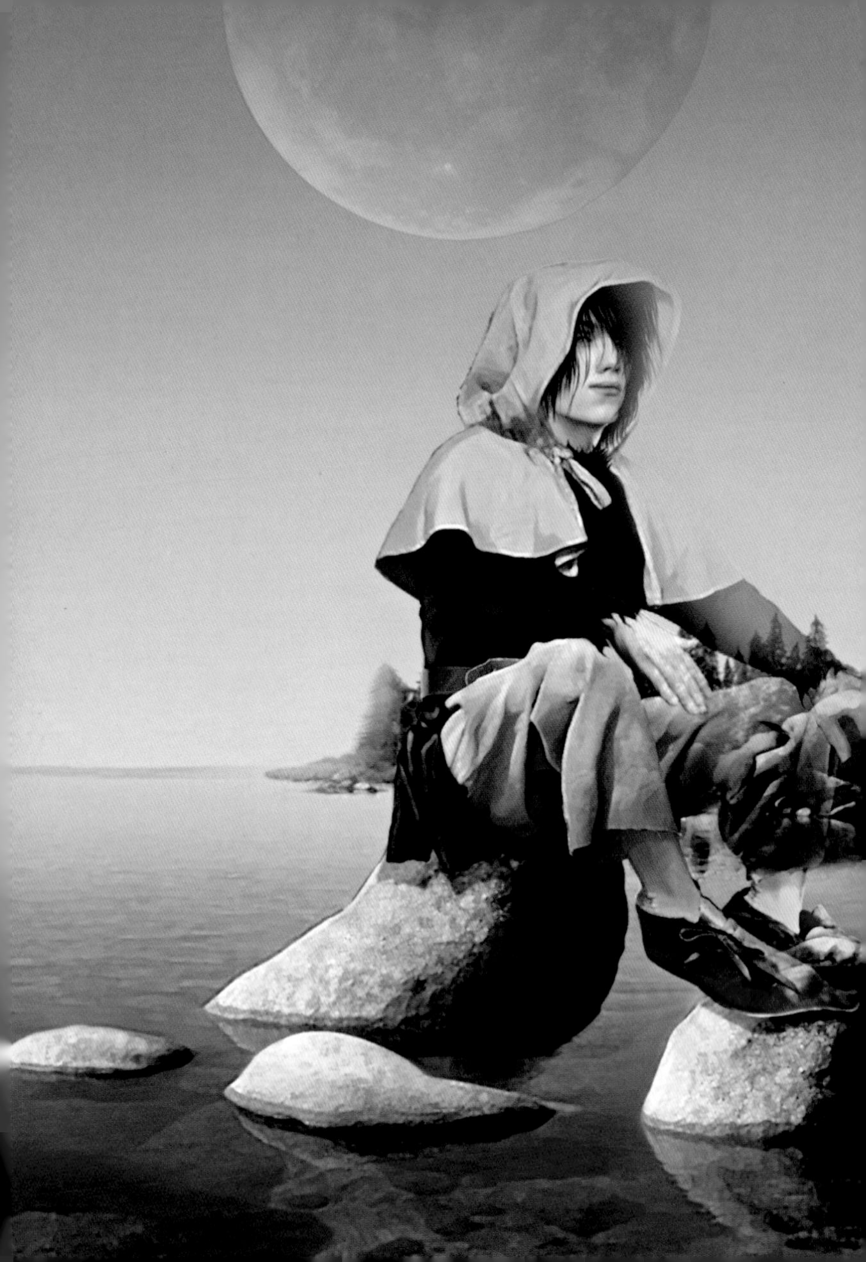

Plant Rhys Dwfen

THIS TRIBE OF FAERIES INHABITS AN ISLAND THAT IS INVISIBLE DUE TO A SPECIAL HERB THAT GROWS THERE. PLANT RHYS DWFEN, MEANS 'CHILDREN OF THE DEEP RHYS' IN WELSH. THEY OFTEN FREQUENT THE MAINLAND, WHERE THEY APPEAR IN HUMAN FORM BUT OF LESS THAN AVERAGE HEIGHT AND VERY HANDSOME. WHEN ON THE MAINLAND THEY VISIT MARKETS AND AUCTIONS, WHERE THEY DRIVE THE PRICES OF GOODS UP SO HIGH THAT NO ONE CAN COMPETE WITH THEM. UNLIKE MANY FAERIE CREATURES, SPIRITS OF THIS TRIBE ARE FAITHFUL, GENEROUS, HONEST AND COURTEOUS. PEOPLE WHO ARE KIND TO THEM WILL BE REWARDED WITH A VISIT TO THEIR MAGICAL ISLAND, WHERE TREASURES FROM ALL OVER THE WORLD CAN BE FOUND.

Development

- Depicting a character that takes a human form makes the task a little easier.
- Use a photo reference of a lake for inspiration, and choose a good palette of water-like colours.
- In the folktales it is the island that's invisible but try making the character fade away around the edges as the tale-tell attribute of his home.

Media and Execution

- 3DS Max, Photoshop
- The background was the starting point, consisting of a gradient from light to dark blue, with a number of boulders at the water's edge.
- The Liquify filter was used to re-shape the boulders in the foreground.
- The character was sketched out and then coloured on a new layer.
- Another layer was created for the shadows, with some Gaussian Blur to soften them. The final touches were to bring out the details of his face.

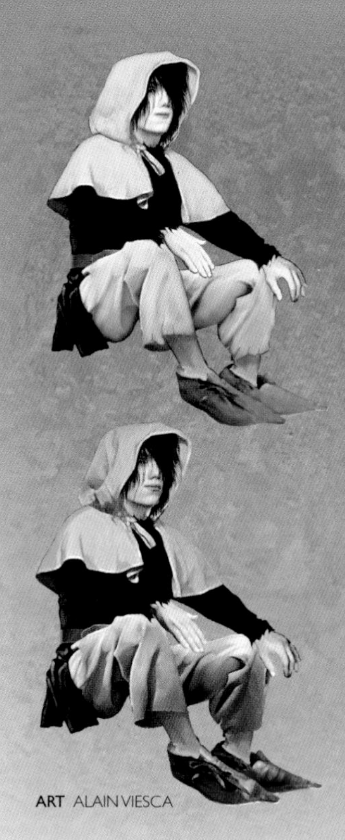

ART ALAIN VIESCA

FURTHER STUDY
Celtic mythology, Welsh folklore, herb of invisibility.

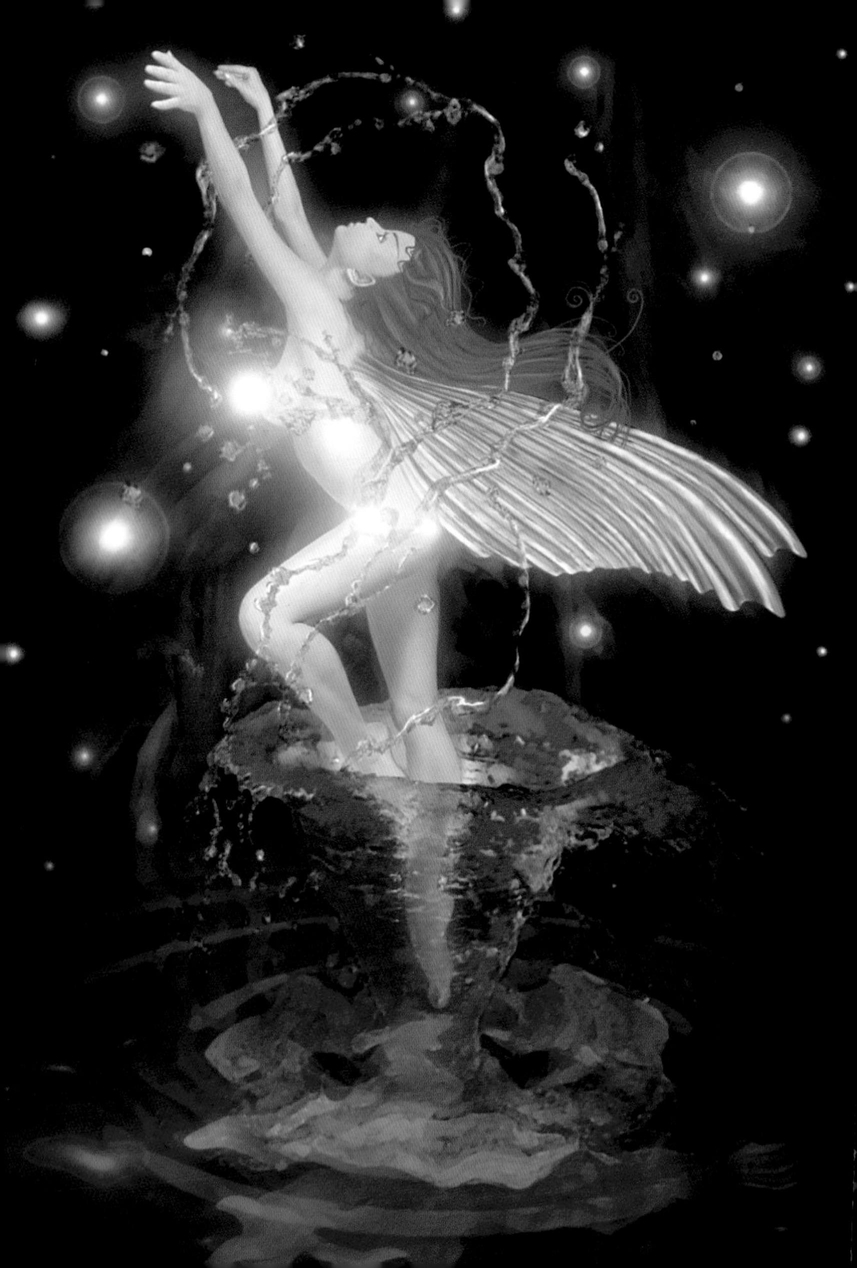

RIPPLE FAERIE

THIS WATER SPIRIT LEAVES UNEXPLAINED RIPPLES IN THE WATER AND A SUDDEN CHILL, OFTEN THE ONLY MARK OF ITS PRESENCE. IN ANCIENT TIMES, SPRINGS AND WELLS WERE GREATLY VALUED, AND IN SOME CASES THEY WERE EVEN WORSHIPED. IT WAS SAID THAT NYMPHS AND NAIDS LINGERED BY SUCH WATER SOURCES. AT ESPECIALLY DEEP POOLS DEMONS WERE BELIEVED TO RESIDE, AND SO ANXIOUS PARENTS WOULD WARN THEIR CHILDREN AGAINST PLAYING TOO CLOSE OR BATHING, IN CASE A MYSTERIOUS BEING DRAGGED THEM INTO THE WATER. SPRINGS AND WELLS REPLENISH THEMSELVES ALMOST MAGICALLY, AND HAVE OFFERED REFRESHMENT TO MAN THROUGHOUT THE AGES. THEY BECAME THE CENTRES AROUND WHICH VILLAGES GREW, A PLACE TO PASS GOSSIP AND STORIES, AND THEREFORE OFTEN FEATURE IN LOCAL LEGENDS.

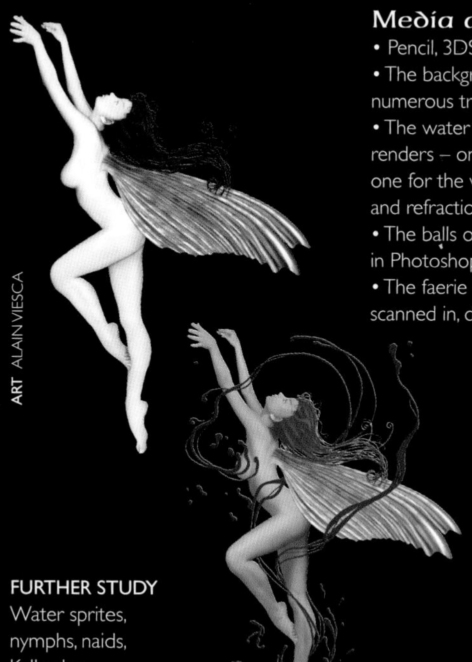

ART ALAIN VIESCA

Media and Execution

- Pencil, 3DS Max, Photoshop
- The background is a Photoshop painting of numerous tree roots dropping into the water.
- The water was created in Max in three different renders – one plane for the water with the ripple, one for the water splash and one for the reflection and refraction.
- The balls of light were created on a black layer in Photoshop using the Lens Flare filter.
- The faerie began as a sketch, which was then scanned in, detailed and softened up in Photoshop.

Development

- A straightforward anatomy study with simple composition provides a generic water sprite that will be enjoyable to work on.
- Restrict the colour palette to greys, blues and greens to achieve a suitably watery look.

FURTHER STUDY
Water sprites, nymphs, naids, Kallraden.

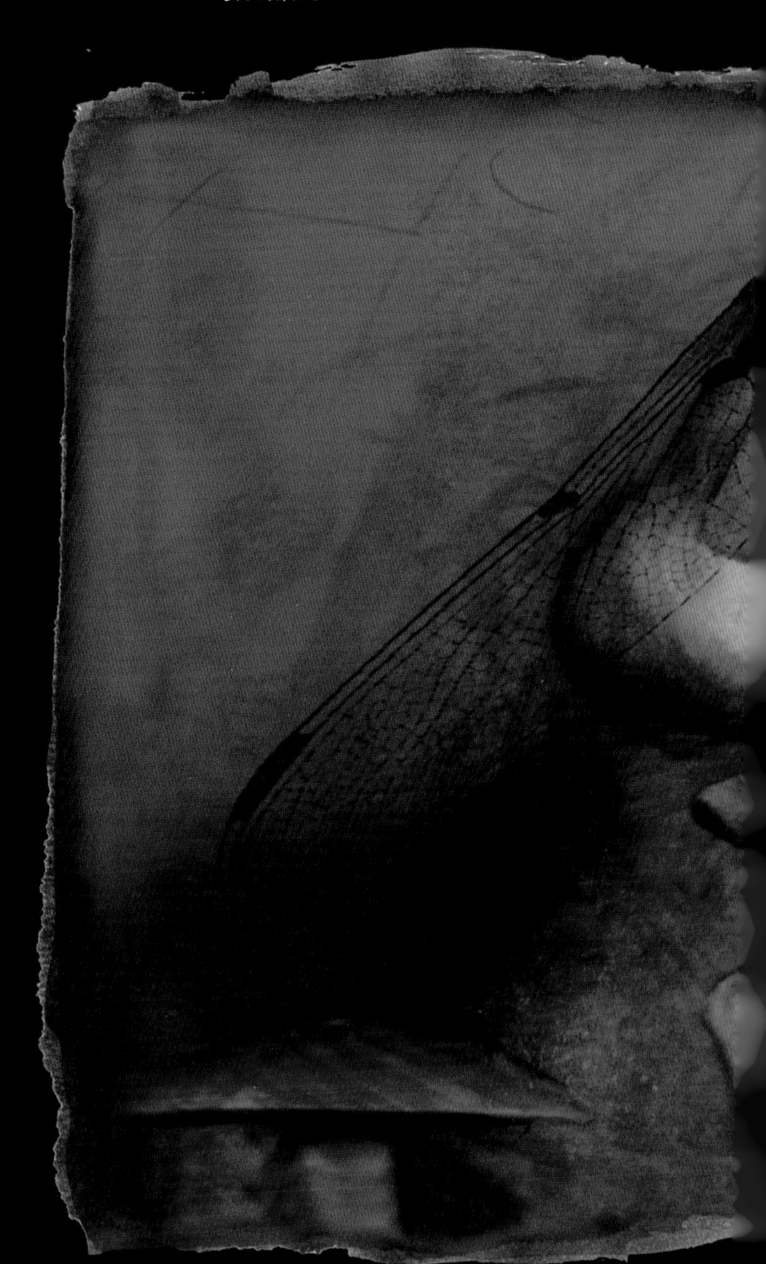

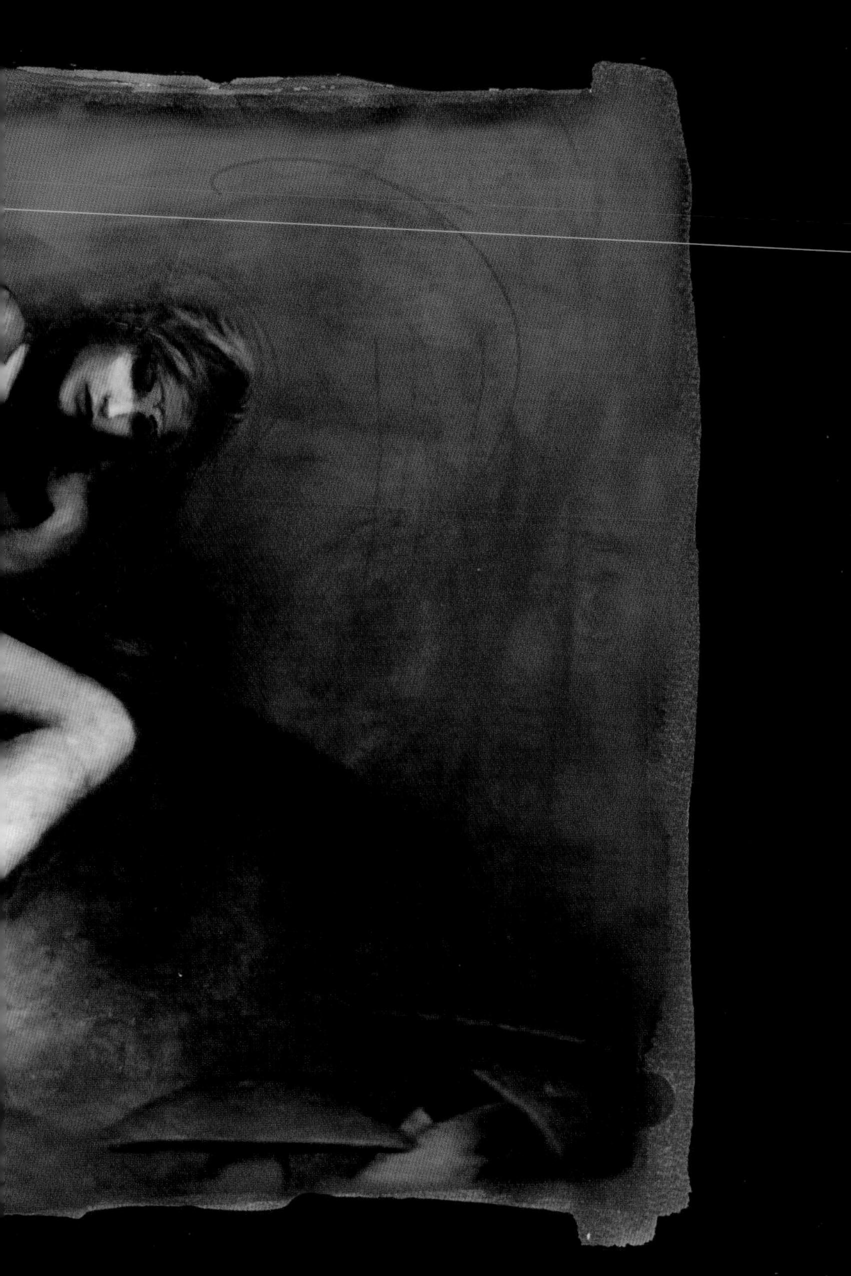

UNDINE

EXQUISITE YET WRETCHED, UNDINES OR ONDINES ARE WATER SPIRITS THAT CAN BE FOUND IN FOREST POOLS AND WATERFALLS IN WESTERN EUROPE. THEY HAVE ACHINGLY BEAUTIFUL SINGING VOICES AND ARE IMMORTAL, BUT TRAGICALLY THEY HAVE NO SOULS. IN ORDER TO OBTAIN A SOUL THEY MUST MARRY A HUMAN AND HAVE HIS CHILD, BUT FROM THAT MOMENT THEY LOSE THEIR GIFT OF ETERNAL LIFE AND AGE AS ANY NORMAL WOMAN DOES. AS THE UNDINE'S GOOD LOOKS FADE, IF HER HUSBAND IS EVER UNFAITHFUL TO HER SHE WILL CURSE HIM, MAKING IT IMPOSSIBLE FOR HIM TO EVER SLEEP AGAIN – IF HE FALLS ASLEEP HE WILL NOT BE ABLE TO BREATHE AND WILL DIE OF SUFFOCATION.

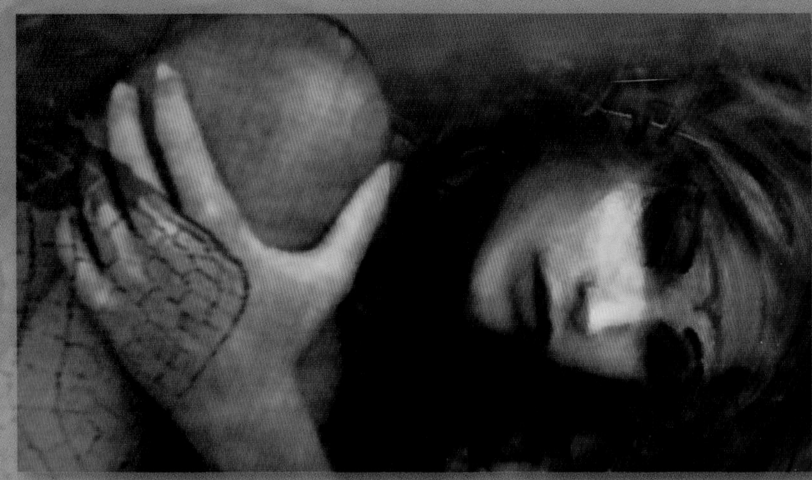

Development

- Use posture to convey a suitably tragic air – here the faerie adopts an almost foetal position, which suggests her vulnerability and desire for a soul.
- For figure studies such as this, a model photograph is essential to obtain a realistic and natural result.
- Study the way core shadows work with the lighter areas to define body shapes, such as the faerie's thigh.
- Try using a rough painted frame to add a further sense of intrigue to your illustration.

Media and Execution

- Photograph, Photoshop
- A model photograph was opened in Photoshop and heavily over-painted.
- A natural palette of reds, browns and flesh tones was chosen to create a warm, intoxicating image.
- Fine lines were drawn on to the wings using a very fine brush to give them a delicate mesh-like structure.
- Detail was kept down in other parts, such as the hair, to focus the attention on the powerful message contained in the pose.

FURTHER STUDY
Sirens, nymphs, Ondine, John William Waterhouse (artist).

ART CHRISTOPHER SHY

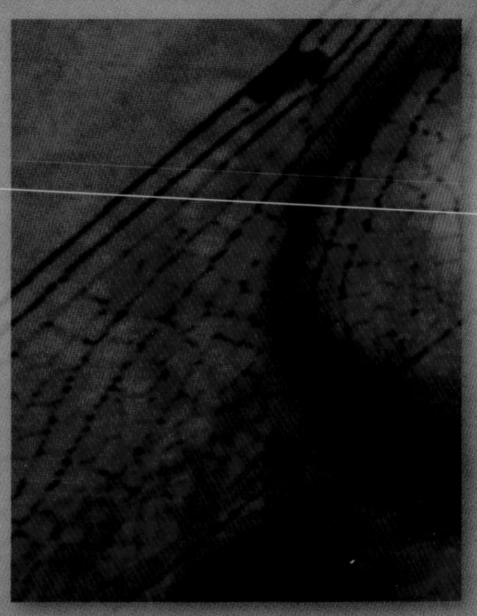

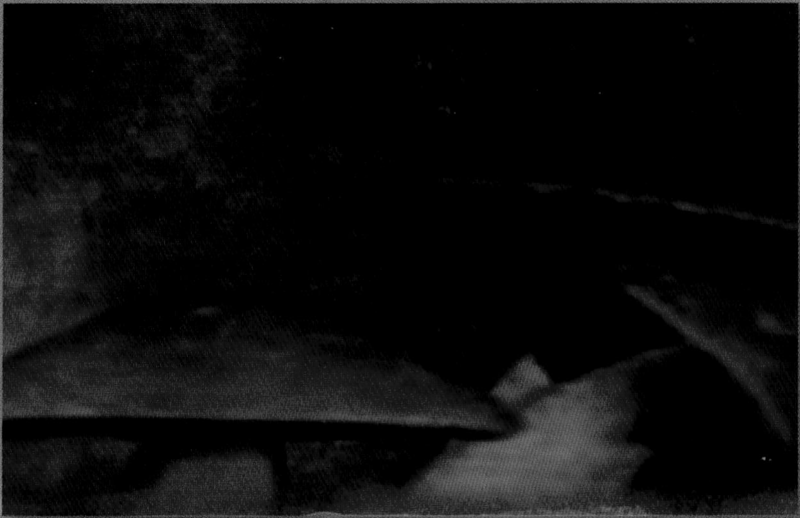

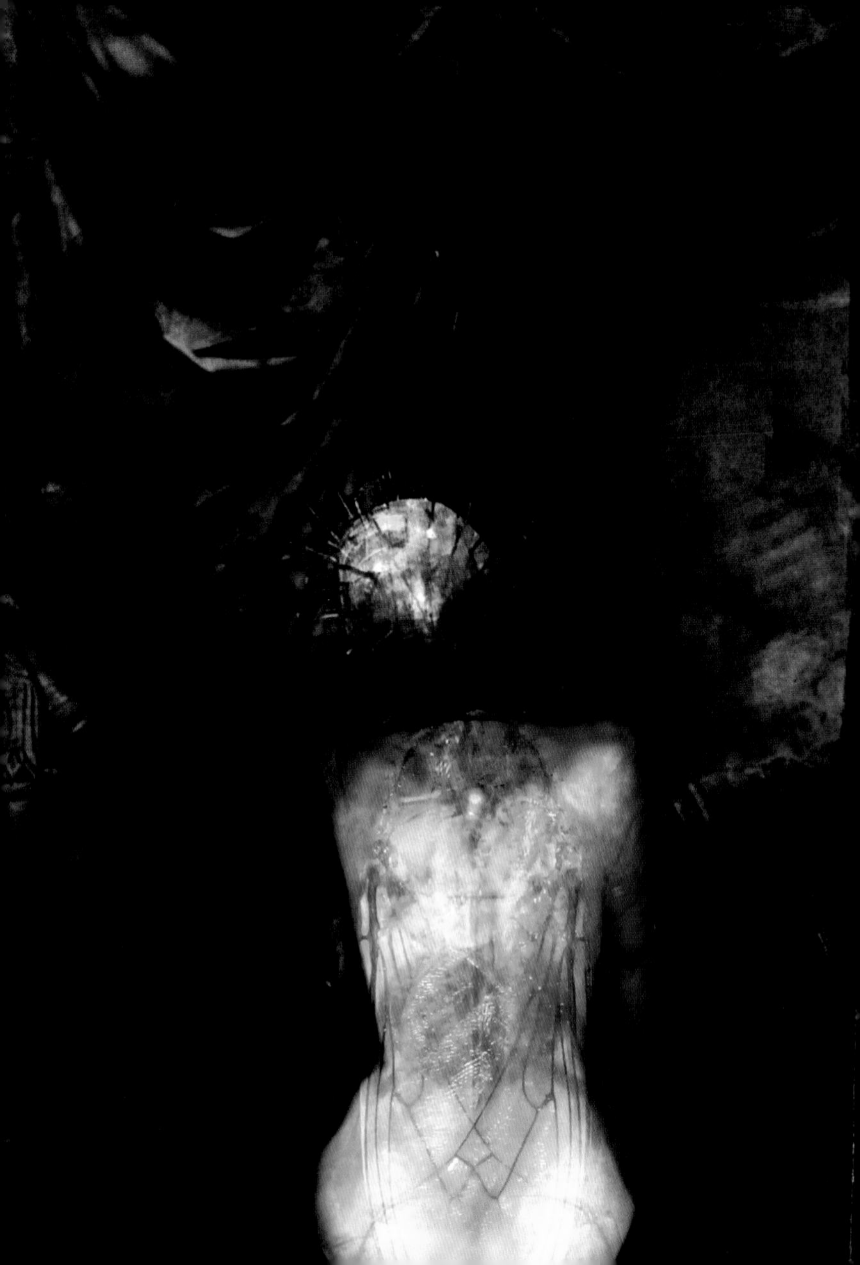

URISK

FOUND IN ISOLATED WOODLANDS AND NEAR REMOTE POOLS IN THE HIGHLANDS OF SCOTLAND, URISKS ARE THOUGHT TO BE SO HIDEOUS THAT THEY CAN KILL A PERSON WITH FEAR BY THEIR APPEARANCE ALONE. BECAUSE OF THIS, THEY ARE TRAGIC AND LONELY SOULS WHO CRAVE COMPANIONSHIP BUT RARELY GET IT. INSTEAD THEY ARE AT BEST FLED FROM AND AT WORST VICIOUSLY ATTACKED WHENEVER THEY MAKE CONTACT WITH HUMAN BEINGS. THEY ARE EXTREMELY INTELLIGENT AND ARE THOUGHT TO HAVE INTENSE PSYCHIC POWERS. SOME ACCOUNTS SUCH THEY ARE VERY HAIRY, WHILE OTHERS TALK OF THEIR DEEPLY WRINKLED SKIN.

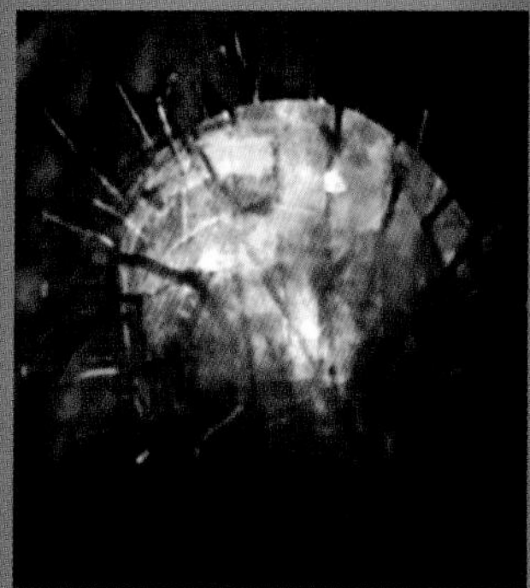

Development

- Showing the creature turned away from the viewer as if to hide its ugliness creates a strong sense of story to the image.
- The head position suggests a tormented soul, and the spikes reinforce this idea and play on our sense of revulsion.
- A strong downlight is used to spotlight the character and to create a disturbing feeling of isolation.

ART CHRISTOPHER SHY

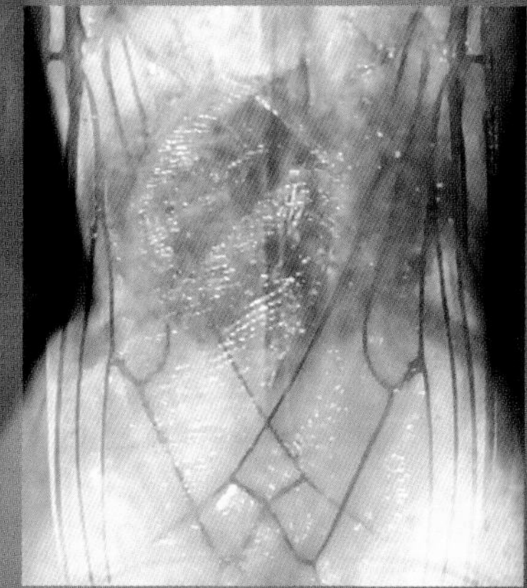

Media and Execution

- Pencil, Photoshop
- A pencil sketch was scanned and opened in Photoshop.
- The lighting was the primary consideration, creating areas of highlight and deep shadow to draw you into the image.
- Colour was used sparingly to pick out elements of the wings and to create nasty boil-like lesions on the scalp.

FURTHER STUDY

Scottish folklore, satyr, solitary faeries.

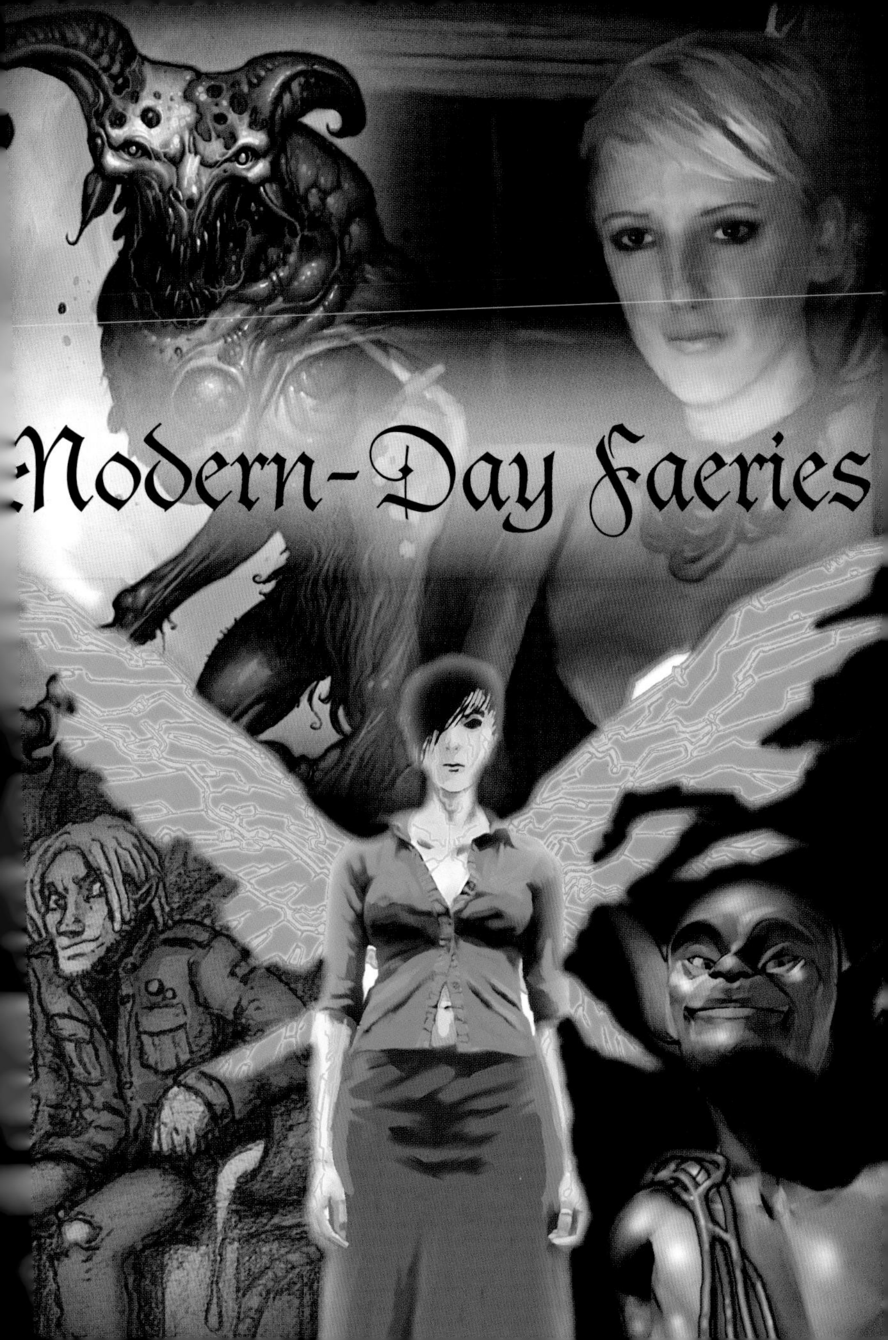
Modern-Day Faeries

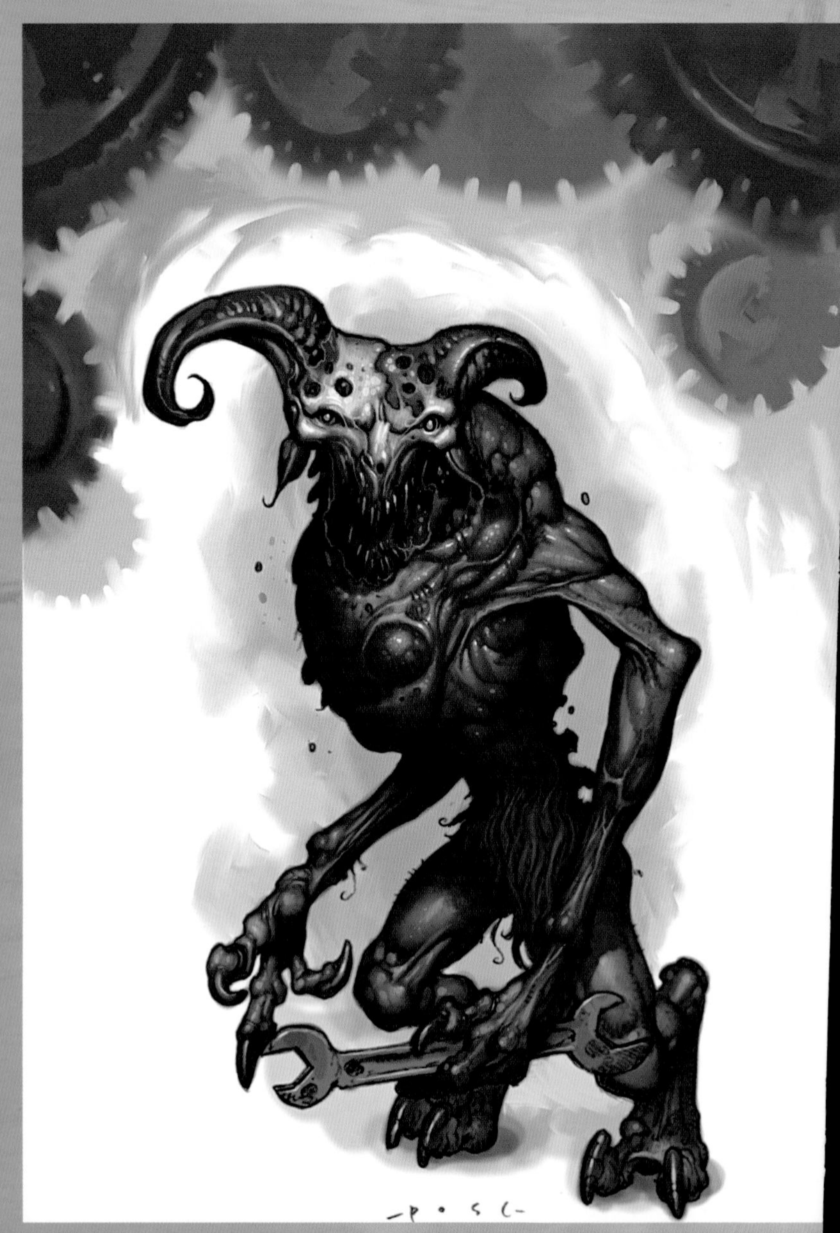

GREMLIN

MISCHIEVOUS, MECHANICALLY ADEPT AND IMPISH CREATURES, GREMLINS ARE USUALLY ASSOCIATED WITH SABOTAGE, SPECIFICALLY ON AIRCRAFT. THESE HAVOC-WREAKING CRITTERS ORIGINATED DURING WORLD WAR II AND WERE A COMMON COMPLAINT AMONGST THE RAF, BUT THEY DID NOT TAKE SIDES IN THE CONFLICT AND WERE EQUALLY DESTRUCTIVE TO THE LUFTWAFFE. THE TALE WAS SPREAD BY EX-RAF PILOT AND AUTHOR ROALD DAHL IN THE CHILDREN'S BOOK, *THE GREMLINS*, PUBLISHED IN 1943. GREMLINS ARE SMALL IN STATURE ALLOWING THEM ACCESS INSIDE MACHINERY. THEY HIDE IN THE SHADOWS AND TAKE ON A DEMONIC APPEARANCE. THEIR MOTIVATION IS TO MAKE LIFE HARD FOR MAN AND HIS MACHINES, LEAVING THE DOOR OPEN TO MANY SUBCATEGORIES OF GREMLINS.

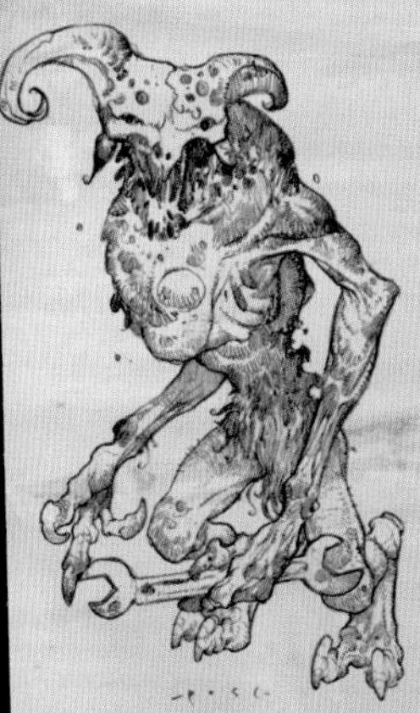

Development

- Start with a rough notion of the general attitude and approach of the character, and try a rough blocky drawing.
- List all the characteristics you want to portray – in this case a demonic skull-like head, humped back, arms with shoulders pinned back almost to the spine, long spindly arms, a wrench in hand, smallish squat legs with simple clasping toes, a greenish cast to the flesh and nasty needle-like teeth.
- Purposely bathing the character in shadow helps to leave something to the viewer's imagination.

FURTHER STUDY

RAF, Roald Dahl (author)
The Gremlins, widgets, fifinellas.

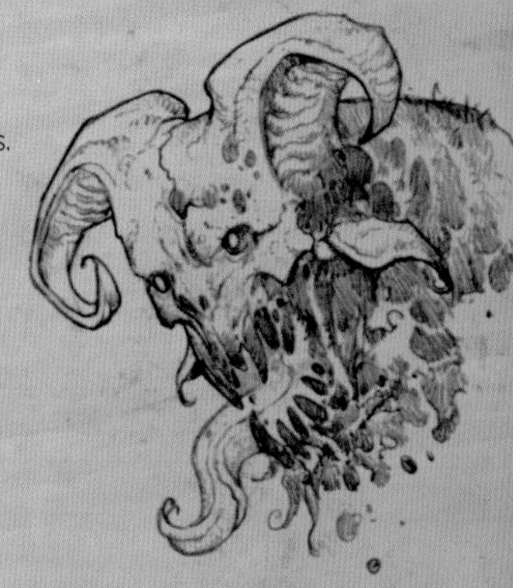

Media and Execution

- Pencil, Photoshop
- A mechanical pencil drawing was scanned in then toned to a reddish sepia hue and edited by erasing and smudging.
- A Multiply layer was created above that to add the base tones and push and pull the colour with the Smudge tool set at 70% Opacity.
- Once the basic hues were in place, a normal layer was placed on top and tones painted in from a custom palette with brushes set at a lower percentage Opacity.

ART RK POST

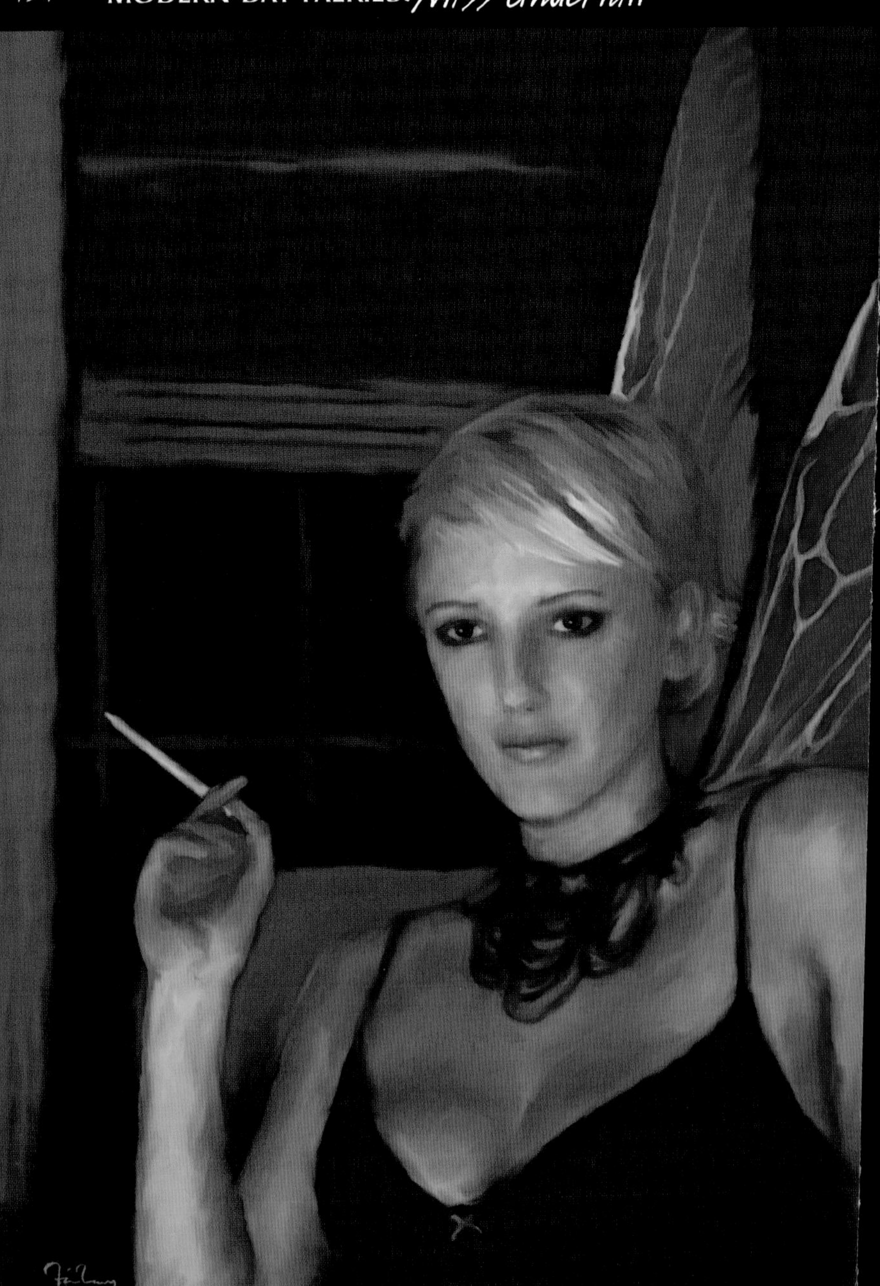

Miss Underhill

A FAERIE MUCH BELOVED OF GRAPHIC DESIGNERS AND ARTISTS, MISS UNDERHILL IS THE LATE NIGHT VISITOR WHO SNEAKS INTO THE STUDIO WHEN DEADLINES ARE APPROACHING AND SAVES THE DAY. SHE IS PARTICULARLY ADEPT AT LAYING OUT VAST NUMBERS OF PAGES IN A VERY SHORT SPACE OF TIME AND IS ALSO KNOWN AS THE ART DIRECTOR FAERIE, DUE TO HER CONSIDERABLE TALENT. SHE IS A TRUE CRAFTSMAN, PATIENT AND DEDICATED, AND CAN BE KEPT HAPPY WITH COMPLIMENTS AND A GENUINE APPRECIATION OF THE WORK SHE DOES. LIKE MANY DESIGNERS, MISS UNDERHILL IS AN INSOMNIAC AND THRIVES ON COFFEE AND NICOTINE, WHICH SHE BORROWS FROM THE DESIGNERS SHE VISITS, A LOGICAL EXPLANATION FOR THE REGULARITY WITH WHICH ARTISTS FIND THEIR STORES DEPLETED.

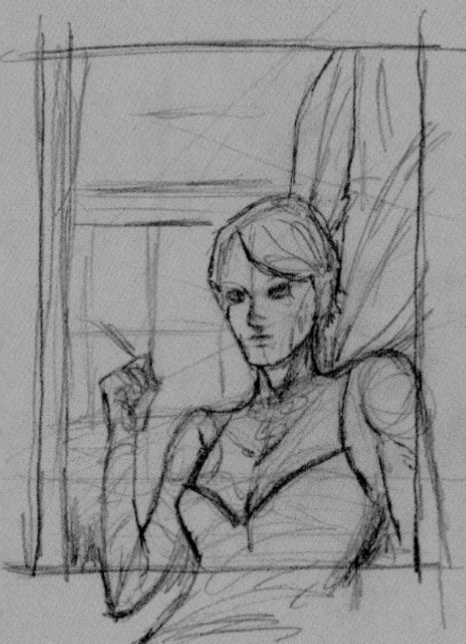

Development

- Use costume and props to clearly convey the occupation of the faerie. Here Miss Underhill is an elegant and stylish designer, who holds a stylus for digital drawing, an essential tool for all modern artists.
- Early studies for the character attempted to show a figure that was clearly nocturnal, almost vampiric with dark eyes and pale skin.
- When using photos it is important to be daring with the computer work in order to get as far away from the original source material as possible.

ART FINLAY COWAN
MODEL NICOLA GROVES

Media and Execution

- Photograph, Photoshop
- The painting was all done manually on a single layer in Photoshop.
- The brush widths and strokes were executed so as to be visible – if the strokes were too fine the image would have appeared too photographic.

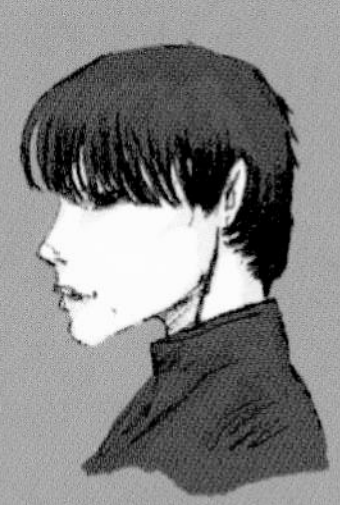

FURTHER STUDY

The nine poetic muses, Menmosyne, The White Goddess.

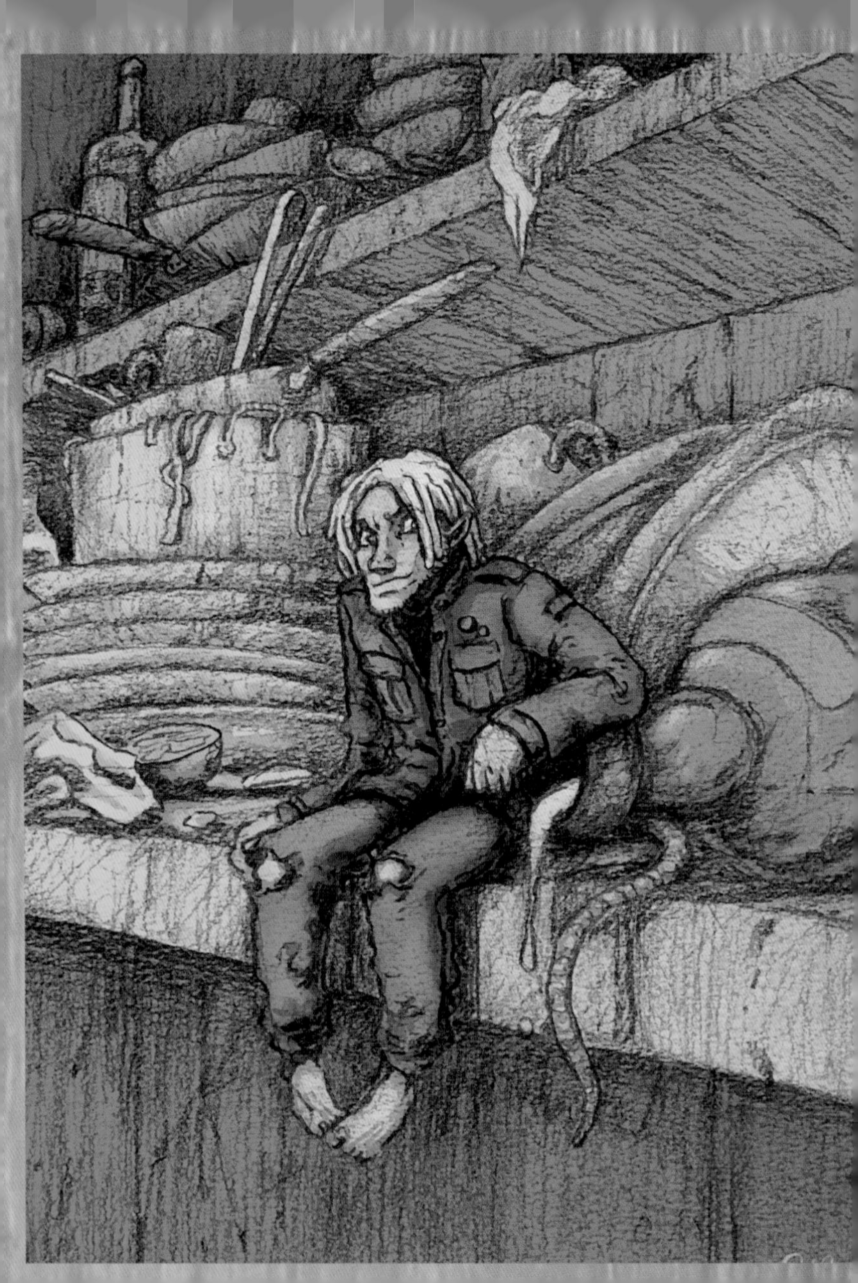

SKANK

THIS SOLITARY FAERIE INHABITS TOWER BLOCKS AND LARGE HOUSING ESTATES IN URBAN INNER CITY AREAS. THERE ARE MANY STORIES OF FAERIES THAT APPEAR AT NIGHT AND CLEAN THE HOUSE, BUT A SKANK IS THE TOTAL OPPOSITE. HE LEAVES THE SINK FULL OF DIRTY DISHES AND STREWS BOTTLES, CANS AND ASHTRAYS ALL OVER THE FLOOR. A SKANK IS NOT MALEVOLENT BUT HE JUST LOVES MESS. HE CAN BE KEPT HAPPY BY LEAVING OFFERINGS OF CDS AS HE IS VERY FOND OF MUSIC; BUT BE CAREFUL, HE IS VERY PARTICULAR AND EASILY OFFENDED – HE WILL ONLY ACCEPT HARDCORE, INDUSTRIAL, REGGAE AND OTHER FORMS OF UNDERGROUND MUSIC. ANYTHING HE CONSIDERS COMMERCIAL OR CORPORATE WILL ENRAGE HIM.

Development

- The image of the character is based on the 'crusty' movement of the 1980s, which grew out of a crossover between hippies and punks and eschewed materialism in favour of an anarchic form of environmentalism and extreme left-wing politics. It seemed appropriate that a Skank would have similar values.
- Use cartridge paper with a rough surface and a soft pencil to get the maximum amount of shadow and tone.

Media and Execution

- Pencil, Photoshop
- The pencil drawing was scanned and opened in Photoshop. The original layer was duplicated and the new layer made translucent.
- The new layer was put through the Watercolour filter at a very low setting then the two layers were blended so the integrity of the original pencil drawing was retained.
- Colour was added on a single layer then areas were selected with the Lasso tool and the colour was varied using the Hue/Saturation dialog.
- Shadows were added with the Brush tool on a separate layer and kept very light.

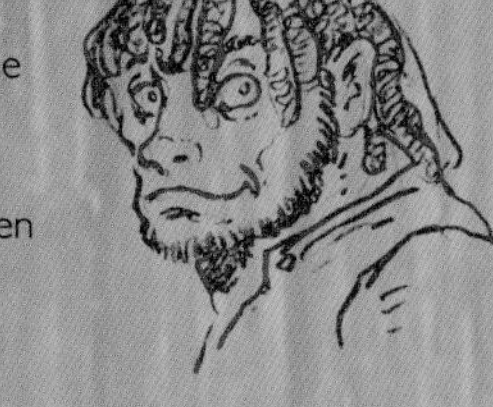

FURTHER STUDY
Crusties, Crass commune, Anarcho punk.

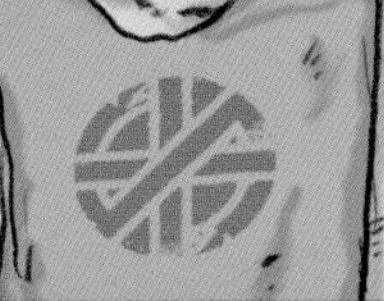

ART FINLAY COWAN

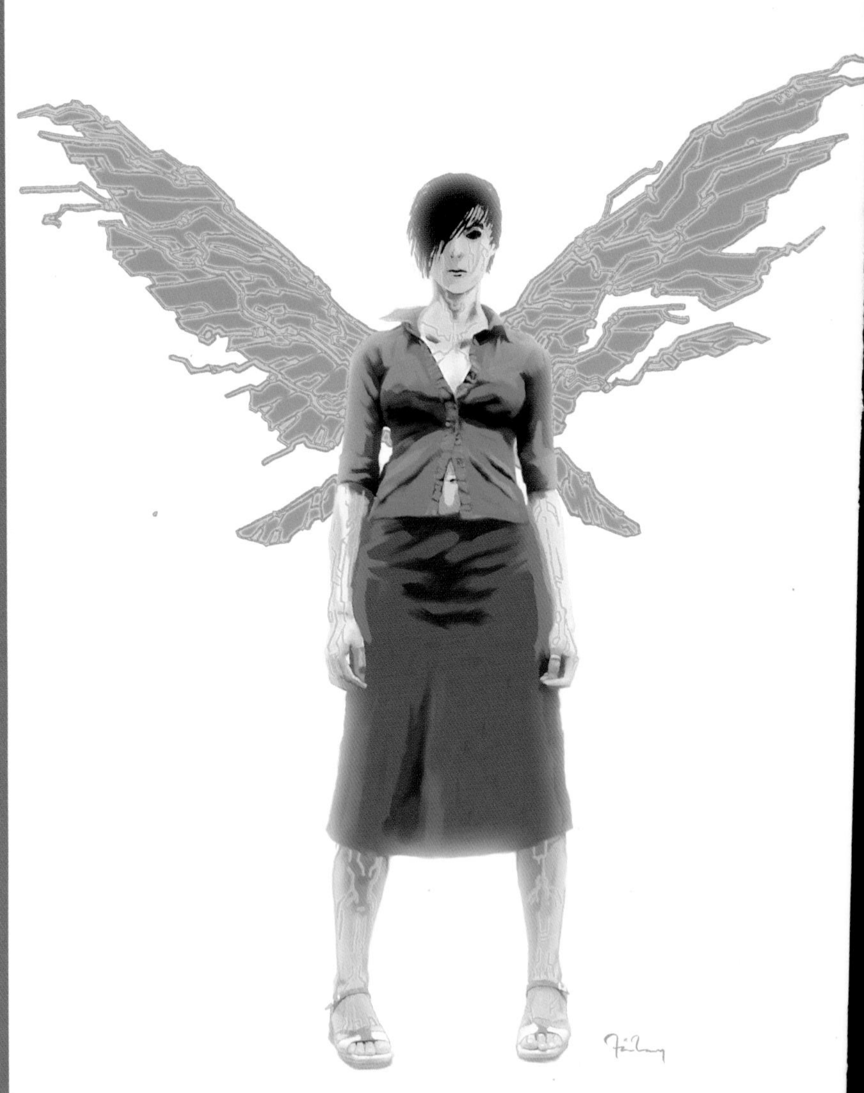

Syba

THE BELIEF IN FAERIES THAT INHABIT COMPUTERS HAS BEEN AROUND AS LONG AS MODERN TECHNOLOGY ITSELF. IN THE SILICON AGE IT HAS BECOME COMMON TO SPEAK OF THE SPIRITS THAT CAUSE INEXPLICABLE EVENTS IN OUR PCS. SYBA IS VERY SIMILAR TO THE TRADITIONAL GENIE IN THAT SHE IS ALMOST A CAPTIVE IN YOUR COMPUTER. IF SHE IS KEPT HAPPY WITH OFFERINGS OF SOFTWARE AND REGULAR SYSTEM OVERHAULS SHE IS GENERALLY BENIGN. HOWEVER, SHE WILL BECOME ANNOYED IF YOU OVERLOAD OR OVERWORK HER OR ADD APPLICATIONS THAT SHE DOES NOT APPROVE OF. SHE CAN BE DIFFICULT TO PLEASE AS SHE CHANGES HER MIND AS REGULARLY AS THE COMPUTER CORPORATIONS, WHO CONTINUOUSLY FRUSTRATE HER WITH THEIR INCESSANT UPGRADES AND INCOMPATIBLE PERIPHERALS.

Development

- This rough shows an early design for Syba, which was produced as an idea for an album sleeve for the rock group Jane's Addiction. She was intended to look 'alternative' and slightly disturbing.
- The concept of Deus Ex Machina – the god in the machine – dates back to antiquity. This conceptual sketch (far right) shows a more god-like figure.
- A basic pencil drawing can be quickly adjusted using filters and layer effects. Here, Syba's wings were enhanced with a mixture of simple glow effects.

Media and Execution

- Photograph, pencil, Photoshop
- A model photograph was painted over using the Brush tool in Photoshop.
- The numerous layers were flattened and the colours were adjusted before a variety of filters were used.
- This version was printed out so the wings and electronic patterns could be drawn on a separate sheet of paper using a light box.
- These were then scanned, added to the original and the colours were manipulated before layer effects were added.

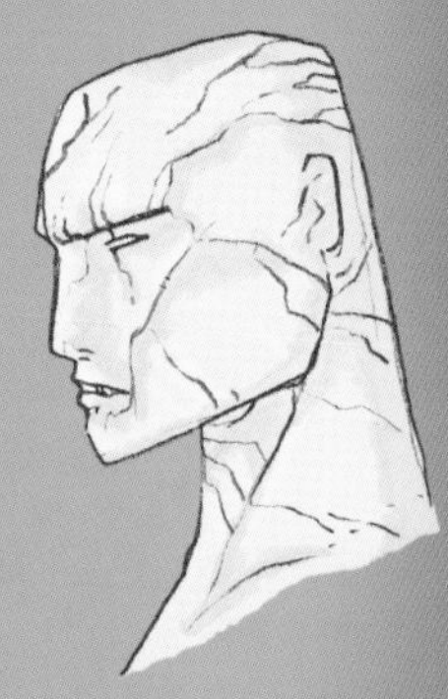

FURTHER STUDY
Deus Ex Machina, Tron, William Gibson (author) *Neuromancer, The Matrix.*

ART FINLAY COWAN
MODEL CHIARA GIULIANINI

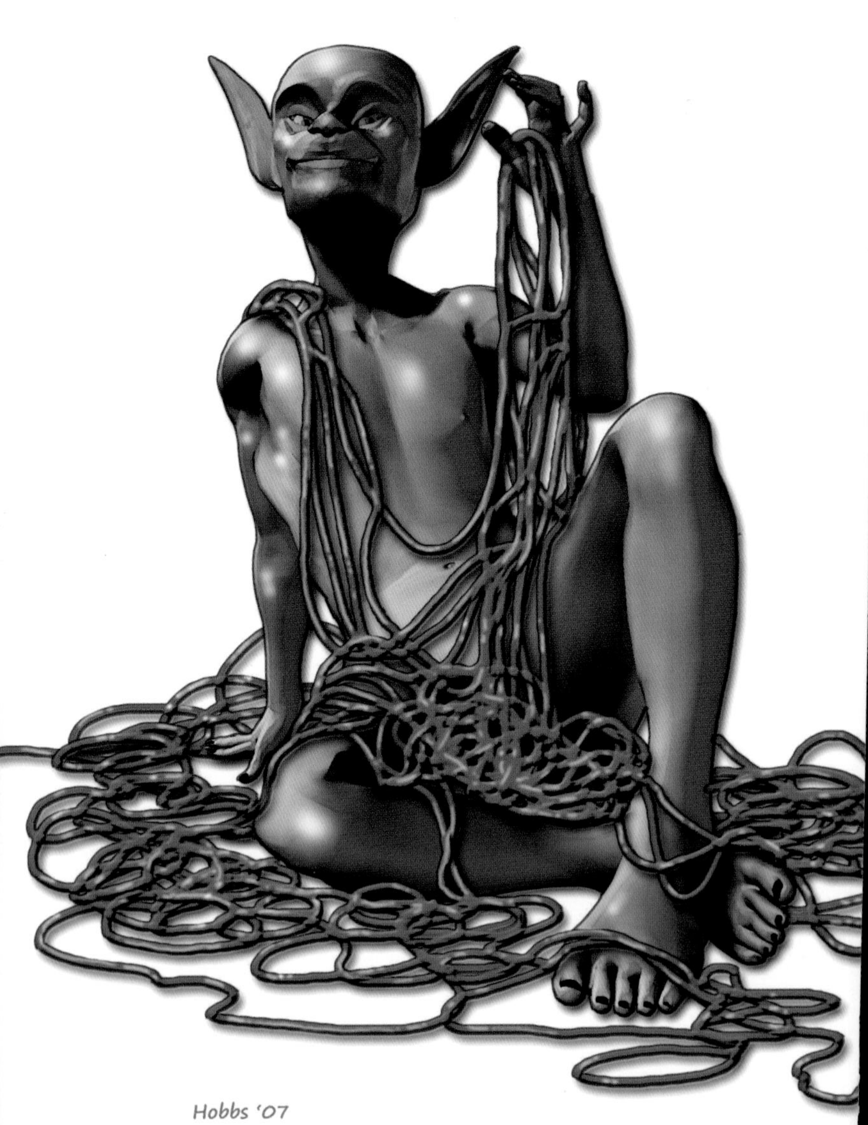
Hobbs '07

Tangle Sprite

ALTHOUGH HE'S CONSIDERED A PRESENT-DAY FAERIE BORN OF MODERN TECHNOLOGY, THE TANGLE SPRITE HAS PROBABLY BEEN AROUND AS LONG AS THERE HAVE BEEN THINGS THAT HE CAN TANGLE UP. THREAD, ROPE, GARDEN HOSES, HAIR, WIRES AND ELECTRICAL CORDS ARE HIS FAVOURITES. HE OPERATES AT NIGHT OR ANYTIME NO ONE IS LOOKING. SOMETIMES HE IS INVISIBLE AND CONTINUES TO TANGLE THINGS UP EVEN WHILE YOU'RE TRYING TO UNTANGLE THEM. IT IS NOT KNOWN IF A TANGLE SPRITE CAN UNTANGLE THINGS AS WELL AS HE TANGLES THEM UP, BUT EVEN IF HE CAN, HE IS CERTAINLY NOT INCLINED TO. A PRANKSTER AT HEART, HE IS NOT MALICIOUS IN HIS ACTS NOR DOES HE SEEK TO DO HARM.

Development

- Default Poser figures can be altered using the various parameter dials, which allow for a nearly infinite variety of combinations. Simply play around with the settings until you obtain the look you want; from the size and shape of the eyes to the thickness and muscularity of limbs, and the skin colour.
- Leaving backgrounds as a simple flat colour or as plain white puts all the focus on the figure.

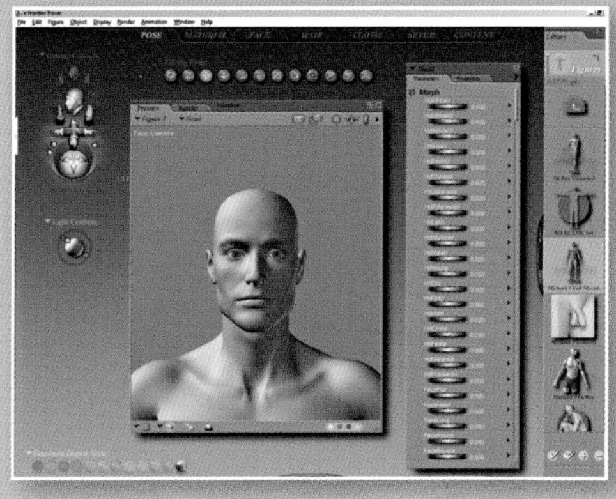

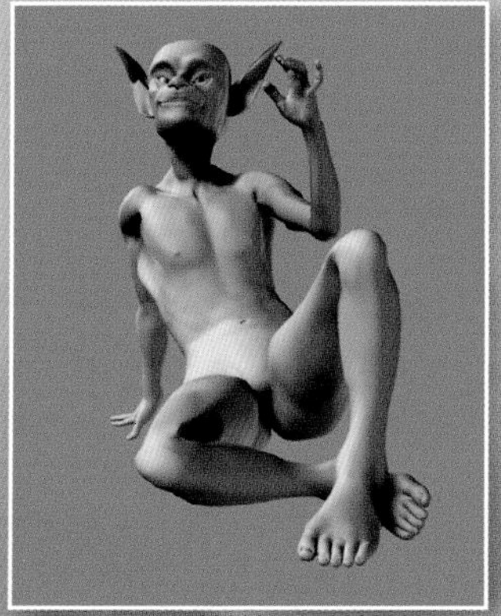

Media and Execution

- Poser, Photoshop
- No preliminary sketches were used on this image, as it was derived directly from the Poser model.
- The coiled and tangled rope was created using a Brush tool and simply painted on to the image in Photoshop.
- An embossing effect was used along with a drop shadow to give it an added dimension.

FURTHER STUDY
Gremlin, Steve Tiller (author)
Tangle Fairies.

ART BOB HOBBS

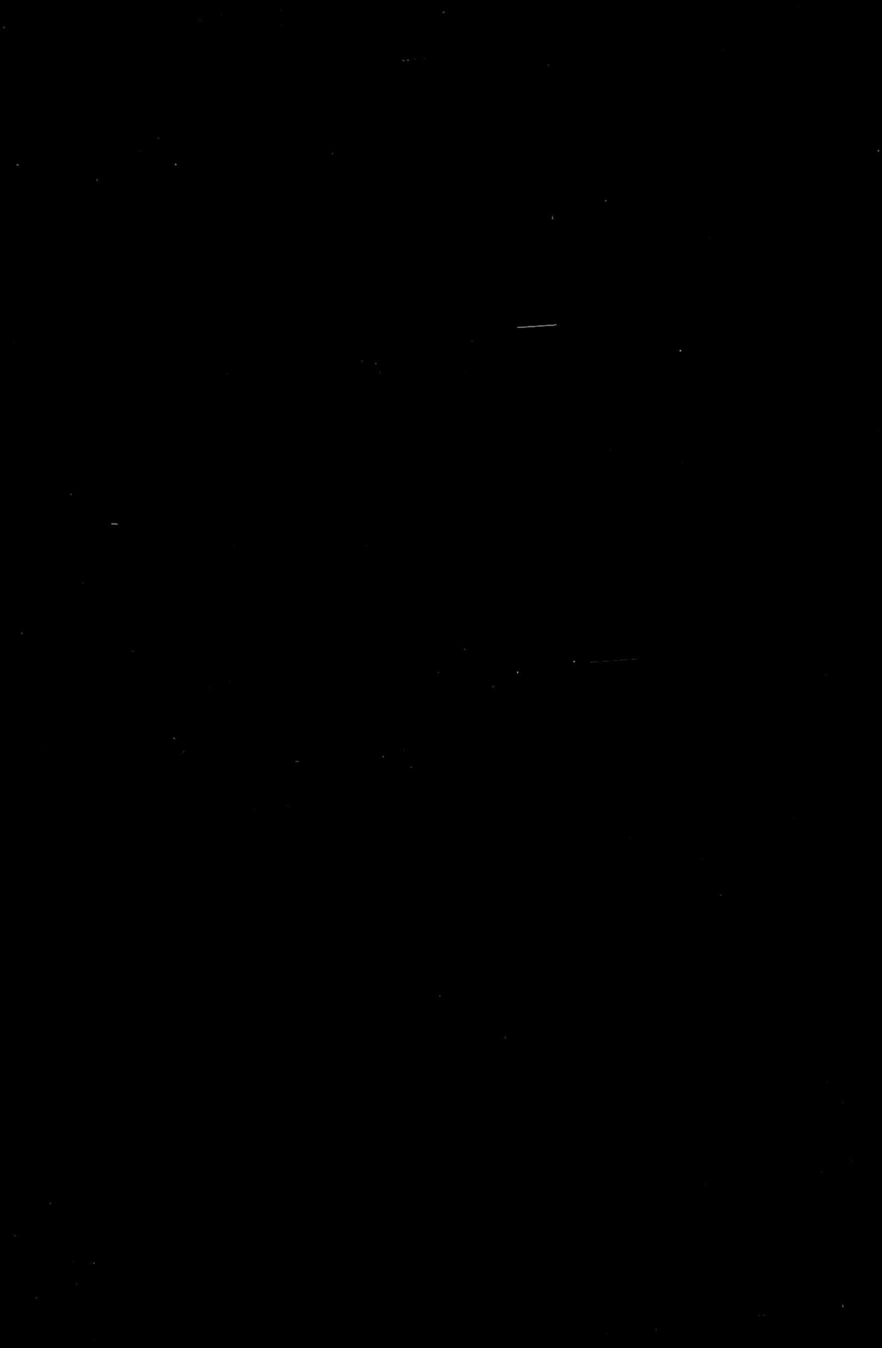

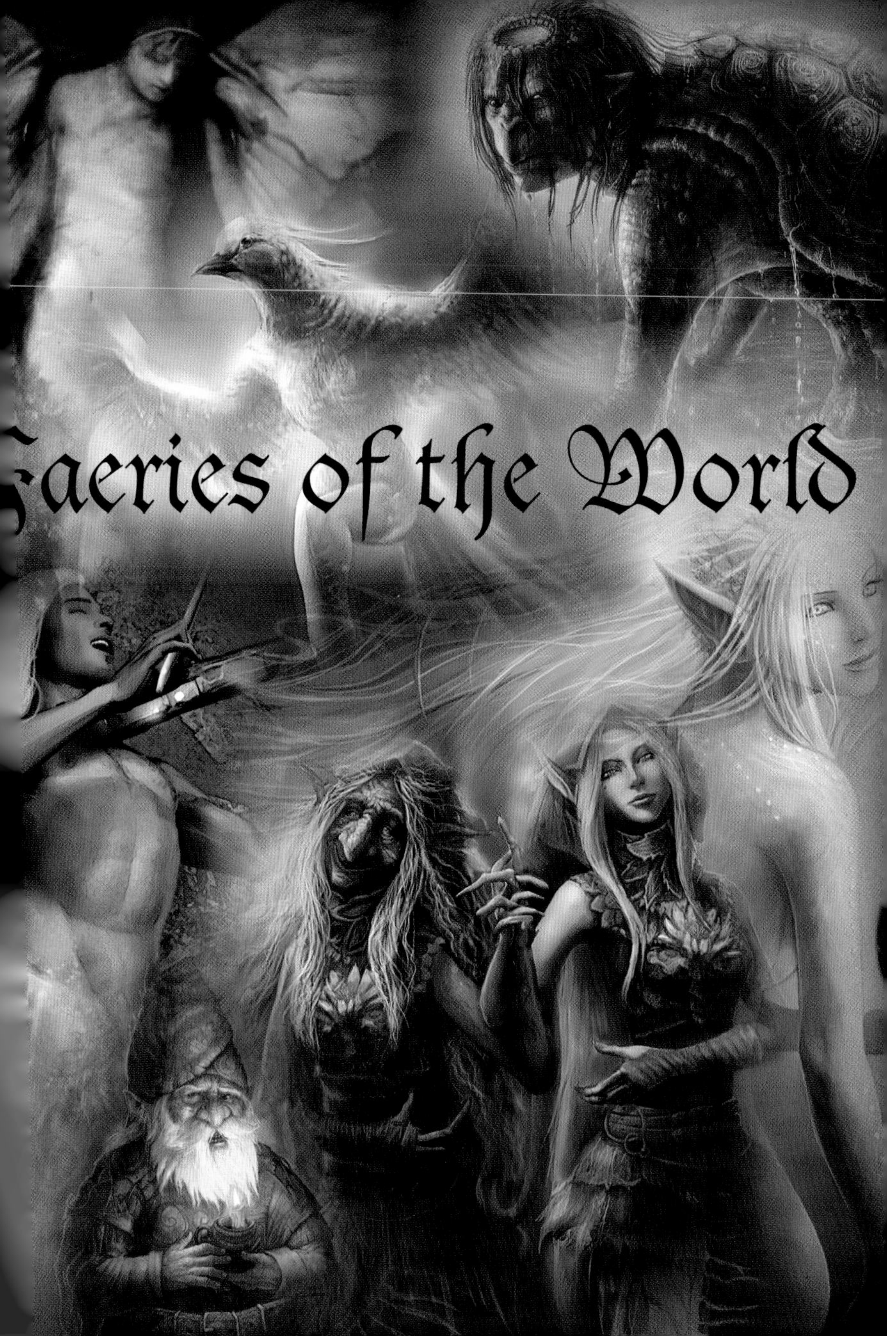
Faeries of the World

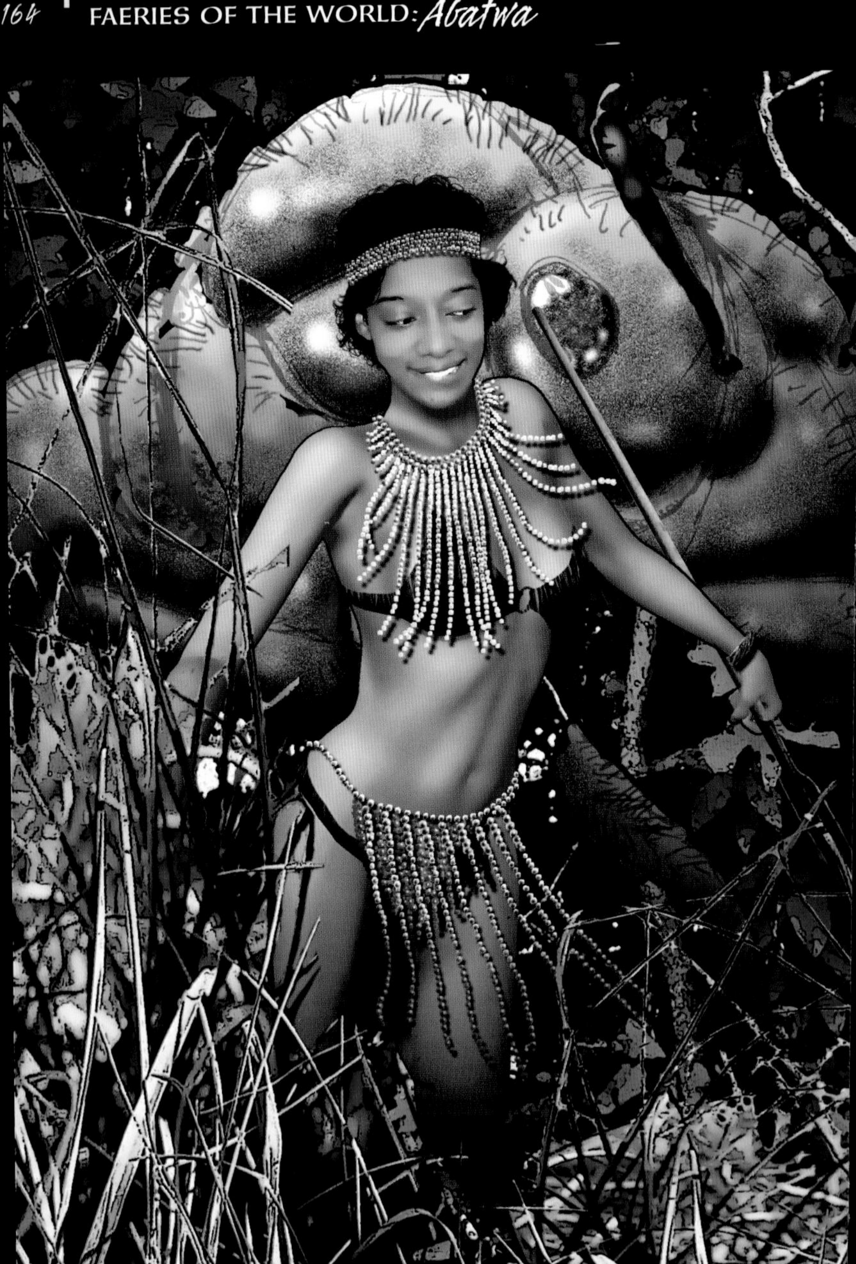

ABATWA

FOUND IN THE MYTHOLOGY OF THE ZULU OF SOUTH AFRICA, ABATWA ARE CONSIDERED TO BE THE SMALLEST CREATURES IN HUMAN FORM. THEY ARE SO SMALL THAT THEY ARE ABLE TO RIDE ON ANTS AND HIDE BEHIND BLADES OF GRASS. IN FACT, ABATWA LIVE IN WHAT APPEAR TO BE ANTHILLS, BUT IF YOU COULD LOOK INSIDE YOU WOULD SEE THAT THEIR UNDERGROUND HOMES GO DEEPER THAN ANY ANTHILL AND ARE FINELY DECORATED WITH MINIATURE PAINTINGS AND MOSAIC FLOORS. THOUGH TINY, ABATWA ARE FIERCE FIGHTERS AND HUNTERS AND CAN BRING DOWN PREY HUNDREDS OF TIMES LARGER THAN THEY ARE. IT IS SAID THAT ONLY VERY YOUNG CHILDREN, PREGNANT WOMEN AND MAGICIANS CAN SEE THEM – THEY AVOID CONTACT WITH ALL OTHER HUMANS.

Development

- Do plenty of background research by looking at as many photographic references as possible – in this case photos of Zulu village life, African landscape, grass and ants native to Africa.
- If you are using a model, choose one who has the right look to begin with to make your job easier, meaning less repainting is needed in Photoshop. Here, I wanted a cute and mischievous look, which this model was perfect for.

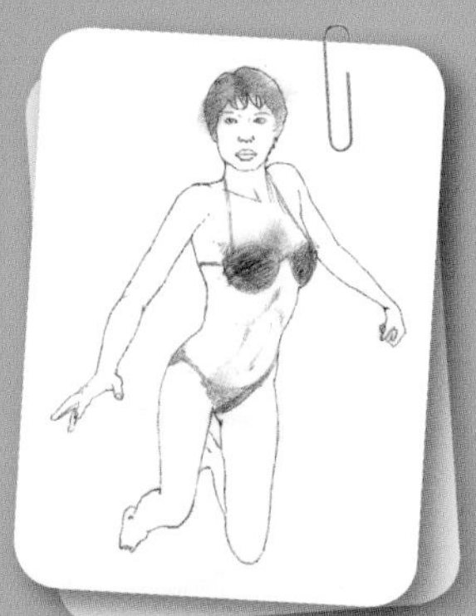

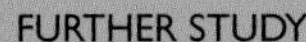

FURTHER STUDY
Zulu mythology, South Africa, African shamans.

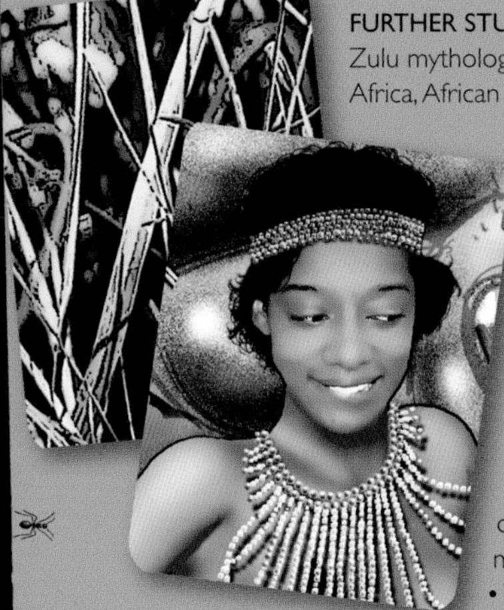

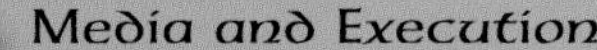

Media and Execution

- Pencil, photograph, Poser, Photoshop
- Rough pencil sketches were used to work out the basic composition. The face was taken from a photo of the model blended with a body created in Poser.
- The ant was rendered in pencil and scanned into Photoshop. Their colouring was done with the Airbrush then a Noise filter was used for texture.
- The grass and background foliage were based on photographs, scanned into Photoshop and manipulated with filters to give a watercolour effect,
- The clothing and beadwork were done by hand with the Paint tool.

ART BOB HOBBS
MODEL ANATAVIA BENSON

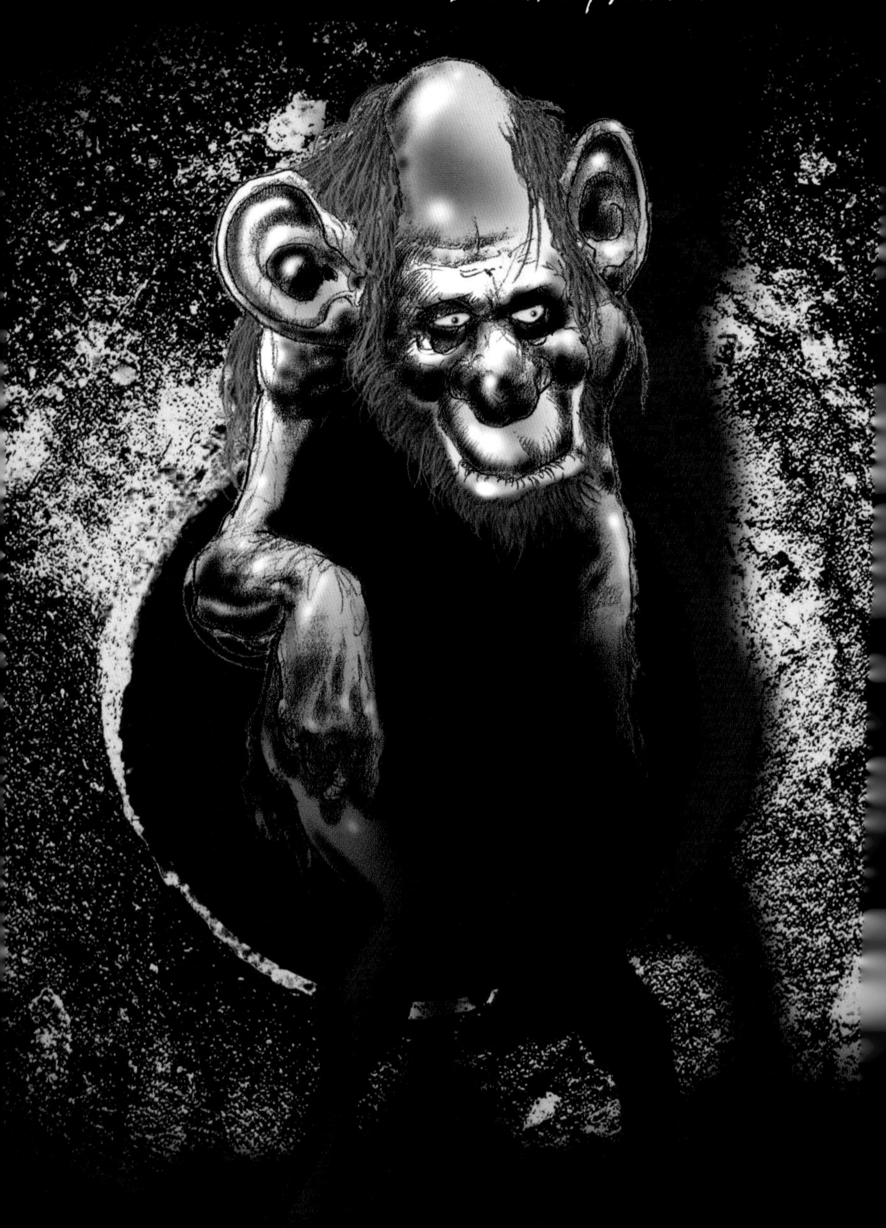

Bendith Y Mamau

THESE CREATURES BELONG TO THE UNSEELIE COURT. THEIR NAME MEANS 'MOTHER'S BLESSING' IN WELSH. A COMMON BELIEF IS THAT THEY ARE THE RESULT OF INTERBREEDING BETWEEN GOBLINS AND FAIRIES. BENDITH Y MAMAUS ARE PRONE TO KIDNAPPING HUMAN BABIES AND REPLACING THEM WITH THEIR OWN UGLY OFFSPRING KNOWN AS CRIMBILS. THEY DO NOT HARM THE CHILDREN THEY STEAL, BUT RAISE THEM AND TEACH THEM MUSIC AND SONG. WHEN THEY EVENTUALLY RELEASE THE CHILD, ITS MEMORIES ARE CLOUDY, SAVE FOR THE FAINT REMEMBRANCE OF SWEET MUSIC. THEY ARE REPUGNANT WITH STUNTED TWISTED LIMBS AND GREY SKIN. THEY HAVE LARGE BULBOUS NOSES, THICK STRAGGLY GINGER HAIR AND BIG EARS, BUT THEY HAVE FINE VOICES, SING BEAUTIFULLY AND PLAY WONDERFUL MUSIC.

Development

- Find inspiration in nature for your faerie creatures. Here a somewhat ape-like appearance and stance, bordering on Neanderthal, was used to depict the short, gnarled and repulsive Bendith Y Mamau.
- Look out for suitable background textures in clip art selections or take some digital photos to build up a collection on your computer.
- Keeping the image dark and dimly lit with a rough heavily textured background suggests a somewhat sinister, cave-dwelling creature.

Media and Execution

- Pencil, 3D textures, Photoshop
- The image was worked out in a series of sketches, becoming more refined with each one.
- The final pencil drawing was scanned and opened in Photoshop.
- A 3D background texture was imported and Photoshop tools and effects were used to finalize the colourization.

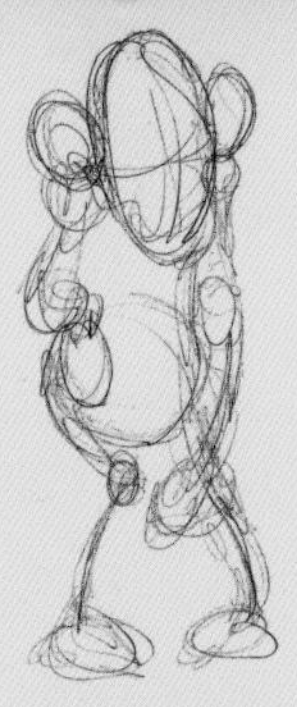

ART BOB HOBBS

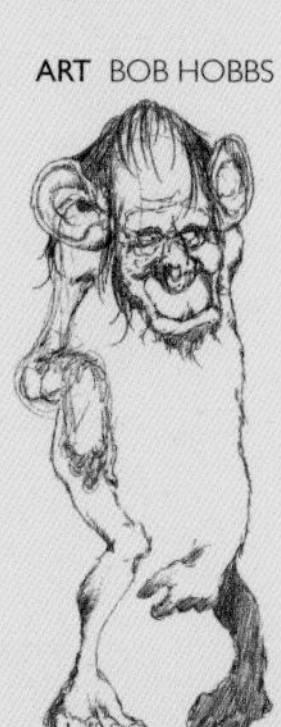

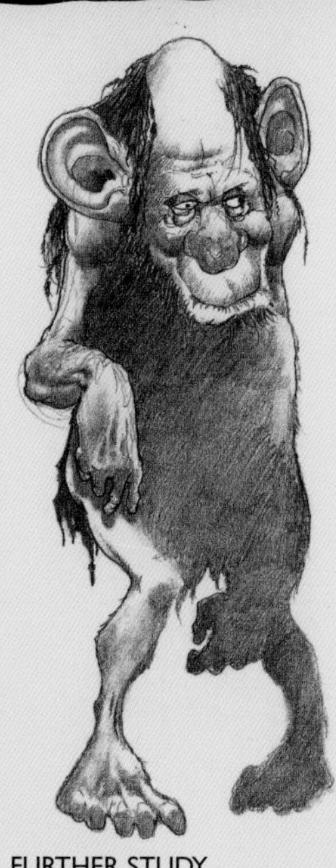

FURTHER STUDY
Welsh folklore, Unseelie Court, Crimbils, changelings.

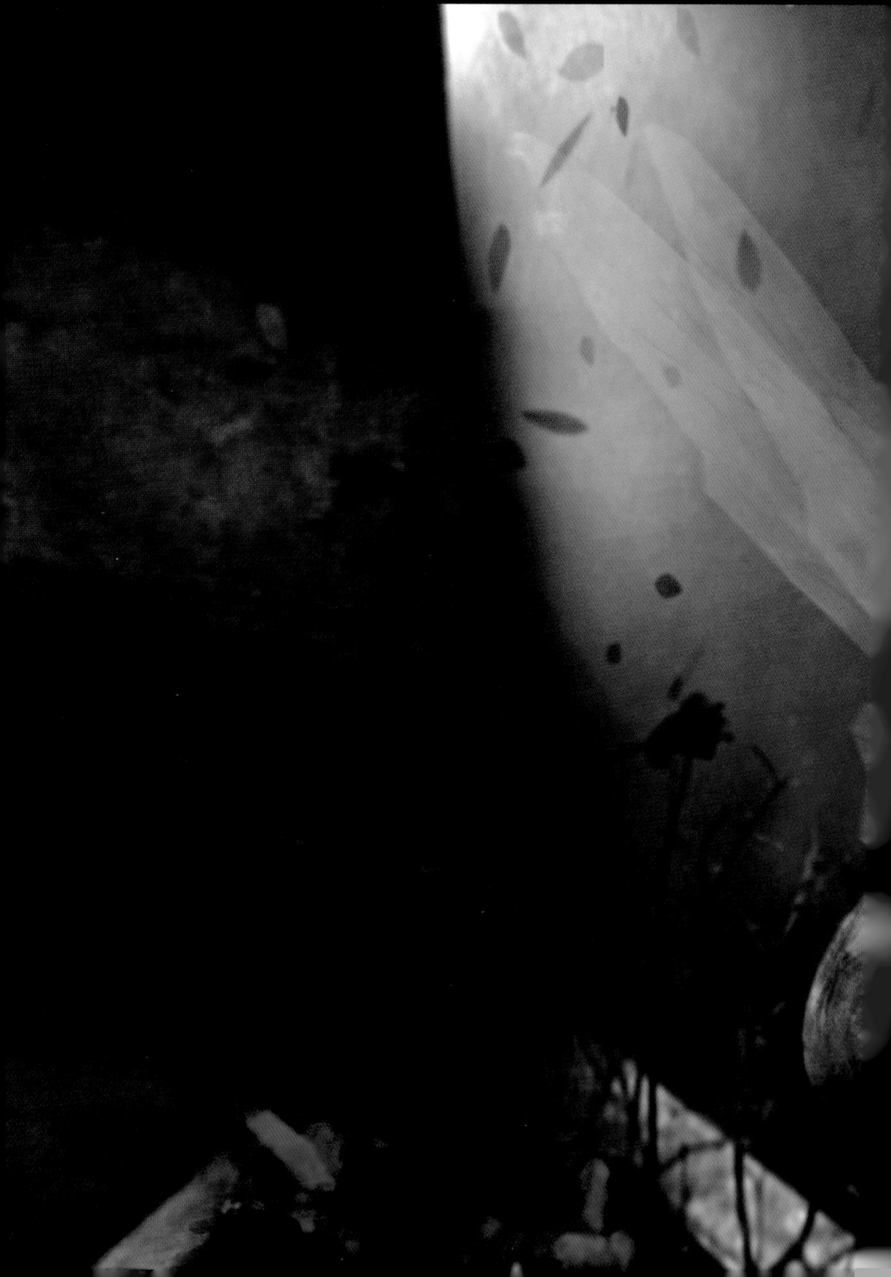

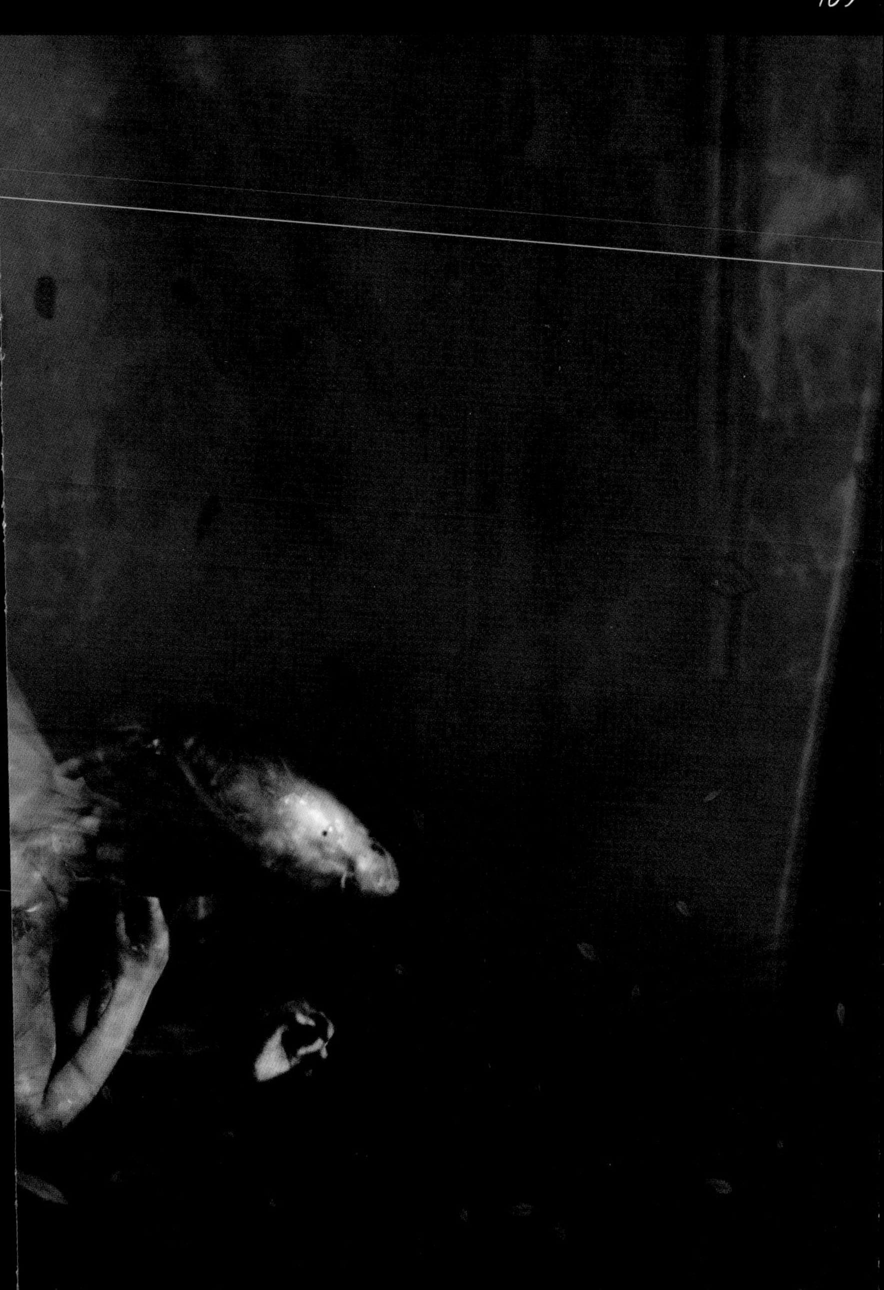

Bogle

THESE IRISH FAERIES ARE DANK, DIRTY CREATURES THAT LIVE IN PEAT BOGS AND MUD HOLES. THEY HAVE MANY OTHER NAMES INCLUDING BALLYBOGS, BOGGIES, BOGGANS, PEAT FAERIES, MUDBOGS AND BOG-A-BOOS. THEY ARE UGLY, COVERED IN GRIME, AND THOUGHT TO BE VERY STUPID, AS THEIR ONLY FORM OF COMMUNICATION IS THROUGH A SERIES OF GRUNTS, SLOBBERS AND GROANS. IRELAND'S DEPENDENCE ON PEAT FOR FUEL SPAWNED THE LEGEND OF THESE TINY SPIRITS WHO WERE ONCE THOUGHT OF AS GUARDIANS OF THE BOGS. IT HAS BEEN SUGGESTED THAT THE PRESERVED HUMAN REMAINS FOUND IN PEAT BOGS THROUGHOUT NORTHERN EUROPE ARE SIGNS OF RITUAL SACRIFICES MADE TO THE BOGLES. THEY ARE NOT KNOWN TO BE HARMFUL, BUT ARE FAIRLY UNPLEASANT TO BE AROUND.

Development

• Use a squatting pose to suggest a base creature and aim for an ugly yet somehow endearing face.

• A single strong downlight allows you to keep the majority of the image dark, yet still clearly pick out the faery crouching in the mud.

• Plants can be used to describe the scale. Here, we can discern that the faerie is tiny because of the plants to the left of him. Without these it would be difficult to know what size he is.

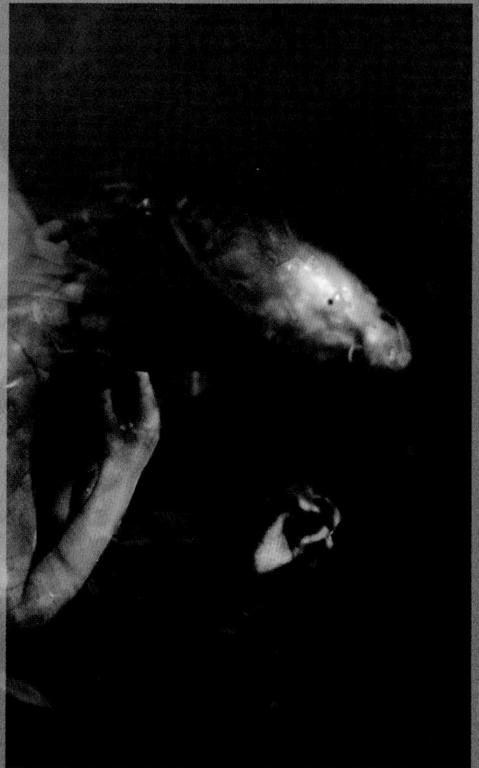

Media and Execution

• Photograph, Photoshop

• A model photograph was used for the crouching pose but was heavily over-painted in Photoshop.

• The head was painted to create a grotesque and hairy mask, and grimy textures were brought out in the body.

• Structural elements were painted on new layers with bright colouring.

• The strong light source was enhanced with the Brush tool set to Colour Dodge.

FURTHER STUDY

Ballybogs, Boggans, Gaelic folklore, Old Croghan Man (Iron Age bog body).

ART CHRISTOPHER SHY

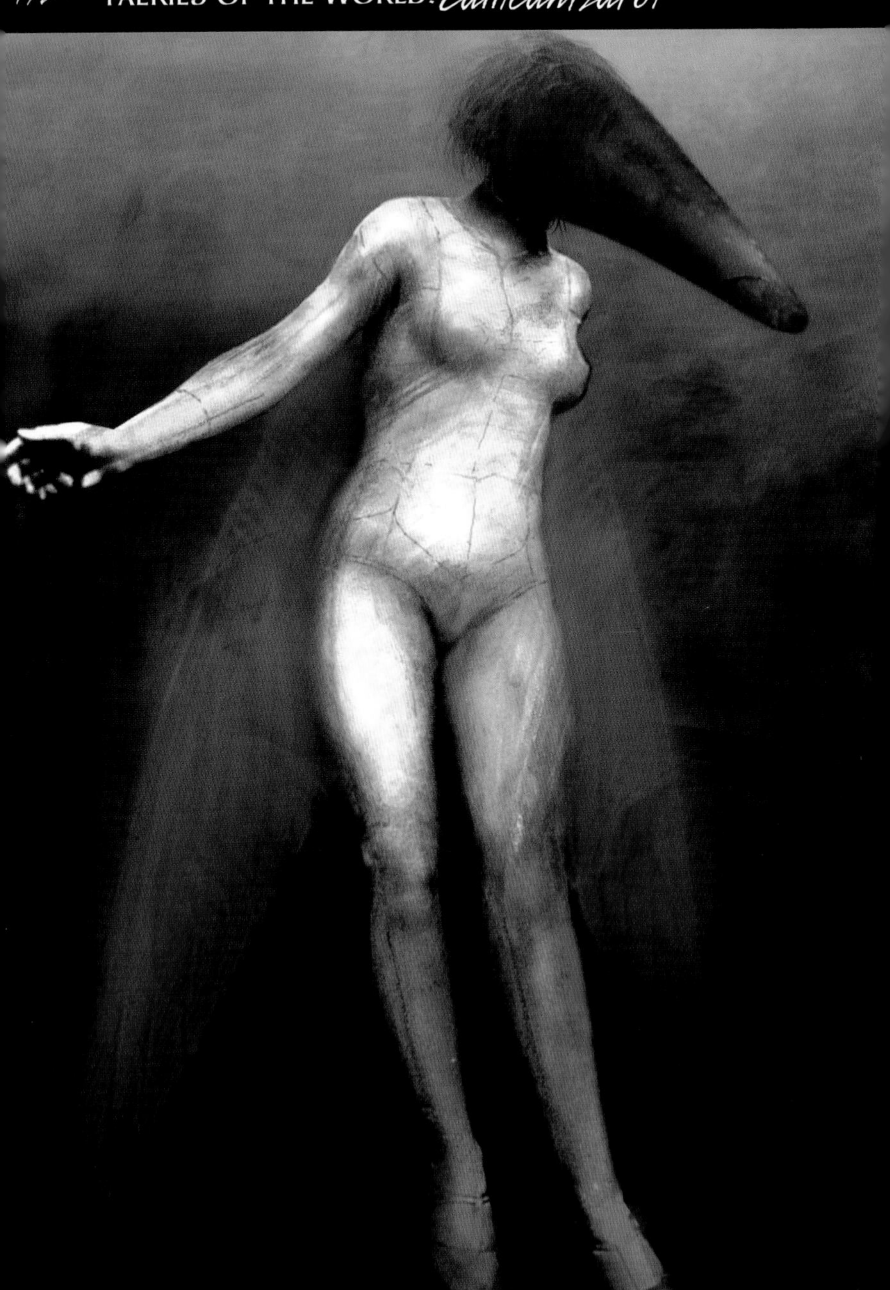

Callicantzaroi

THESE SEASONAL FAERIES ARE ONLY ENCOUNTERED DURING THE WINTER, PARTICULARLY AROUND THE YULETIDE FESTIVITIES IN GREECE, ITALY AND ALBANIA. THEY ARE SMALL, NAKED, TROOPING FAERIES THAT WEAR ELABORATE HEADGEAR AND RIDE ON CHICKENS. ACCOUNTS CITE THEM AS EITHER PARTIALLY OR TOTALLY BLIND, THOUGH THERE ARE NO KNOWN EXPLANATIONS AS TO WHY. THEY ARE FEARED, NOT ONLY FOR THEIR BIZARRE APPEARANCE, BUT ALSO FOR THEIR MALEVOLENT ACTIONS, WHICH INCLUDE DESTROYING PROPERTY AND STEALING THE SOULS OF NEWBORN BABIES. THE BURNING OF THE YULE LOG IS THOUGHT TO KEEP THEM AWAY, AS SMOKE IS ABHORRENT TO THEM AND THEIR SENSE OF SMELL IS HEIGHTENED BY THEIR BLINDNESS.

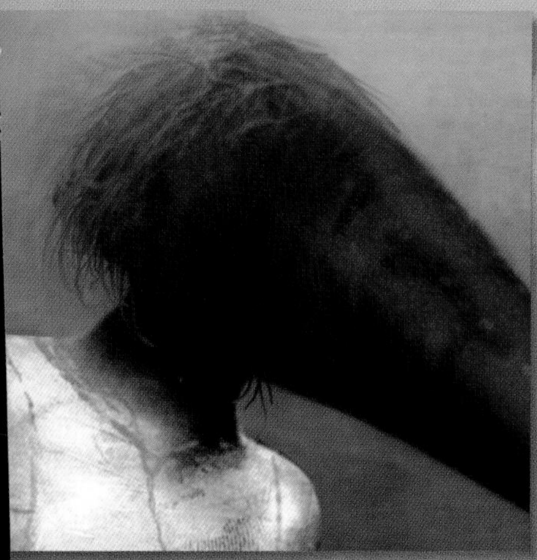

Development

- Create a sense of timelessness by toning your images with shades of brown and sepia.
- Explore different ideas for 'elaborate headgear' and play on the issue of their blindness. The intriguing cone shape used here turns an otherwise beautiful woman into a grotesque visionless monster.
- Try making the wings subtle and secondary to the figure by using a soft brush, barely defining their edges.

Media and Execution

- Photograph, Photoshop, acrylic paints
- The image started as a model photograph, which was opened in Photoshop and over-painted.
- A Gradient Fill was used to shade the background and then textured and blended.
- The image was printed out and touches of acrylic paint were added to bring out further texture in the brushstrokes.
- Curves dialog was used to tweak the contrast.

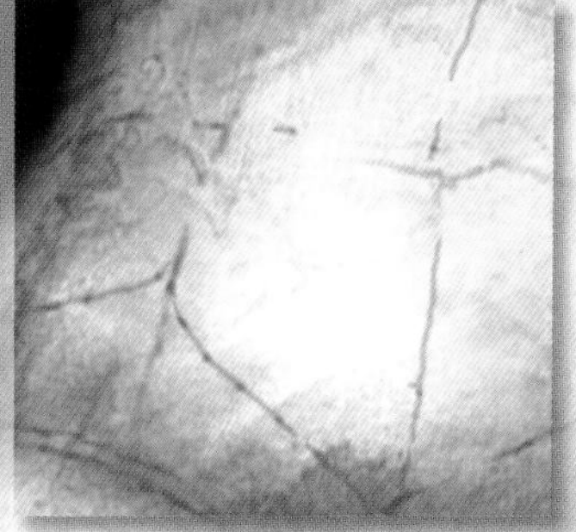

ART CHRISTOPHER SHY

FURTHER STUDY
Trooping faeries, Pagan deities, Greek folklore.

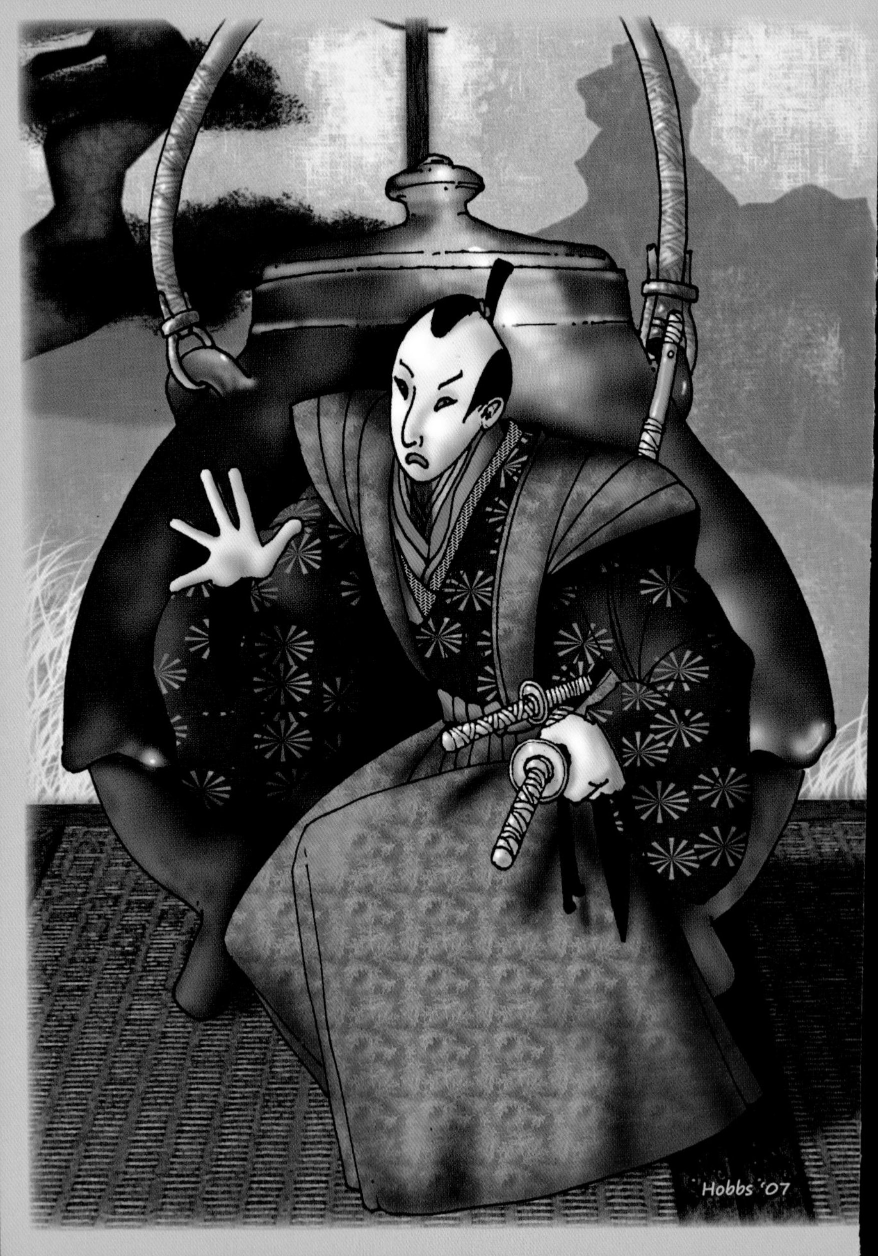
Hobbs '07

CHIN CHIN KOBAKAMA

THESE ELF-LIKE BEINGS HAVE THEIR ORIGINS IN JAPAN AND POSSIBLY CHINA. CHIN CHIN KOBAKAMA CAN BE EITHER MALE OR FEMALE AND BUT ARE OFTEN DEPICTED AS VERY TINY SPRIGHTLY BUT ELDERLY MEN DRESSED IN KAMISHIMOS, WHICH WERE WORN BY THE SAMURAI CLASS OF MEDIEVAL JAPAN. THEY ARE SIMILAR TO THE BROWNIES OF WESTERN FOLKLORE BUT THEIR MAIN INTEREST IS IN FLOORS AND RUGS. THEY MOVE INTO HUMAN HOMES AND CAN BE QUITE HELPFUL PROVIDED THEIR HOST KEEPS A CLEAN HOUSE. AS LONG AS YOU ARE NOT A SLOPPY HOUSEKEEPER AND PUT ENOUGH FOOD OUT FOR THEM, THEY WILL BE CONTENTED GUESTS.

Development

- Use reference books and websites to research the clothing worn by the Samurai warriors of feudal Japan.
- Martial arts books that cover Iaido, Kenjutsu or any of the arts that employ the Samurai sword or Katana will aid you in drawing the figure in the correct stance with the weapon.
- For the style of the artwork, look at old Japanese prints that feature figures in native clothing, such as the Kabuki theatre prints by artist Toshusai Sharaku.

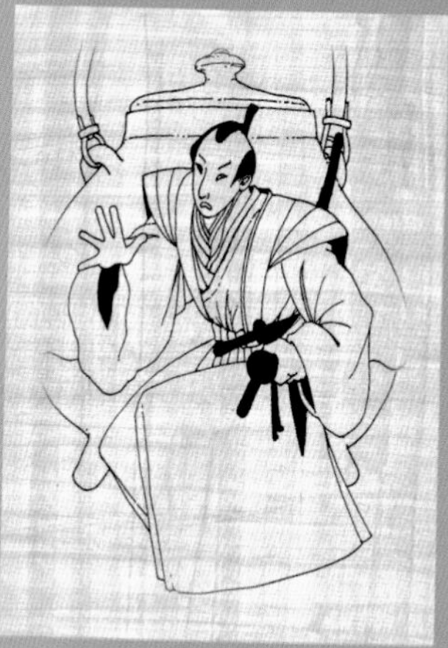

ART BOB HOBBS

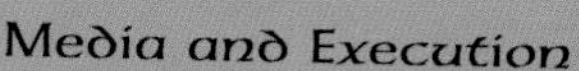

Media and Execution

- Pencil, pen and ink, stock textures, Photoshop
- Preliminary sketches were made in pencil, with the final sketch then rendered in pen and ink.
- The ink drawing was scanned into Photoshop, where the edges were cleaned up, the white background was deleted and the black lines were enhanced with the Levels dialog.
- The image was coloured using the various Paint tools, keeping the ink layer semi-transparent on top.
- Stock textures were used to create the background and floor mats.

FURTHER STUDY

Japanese folk tales, Brownie, Lafcadio Hearn (author) *Chin Chin Kobakama: The Fairies of the Floor Mats*

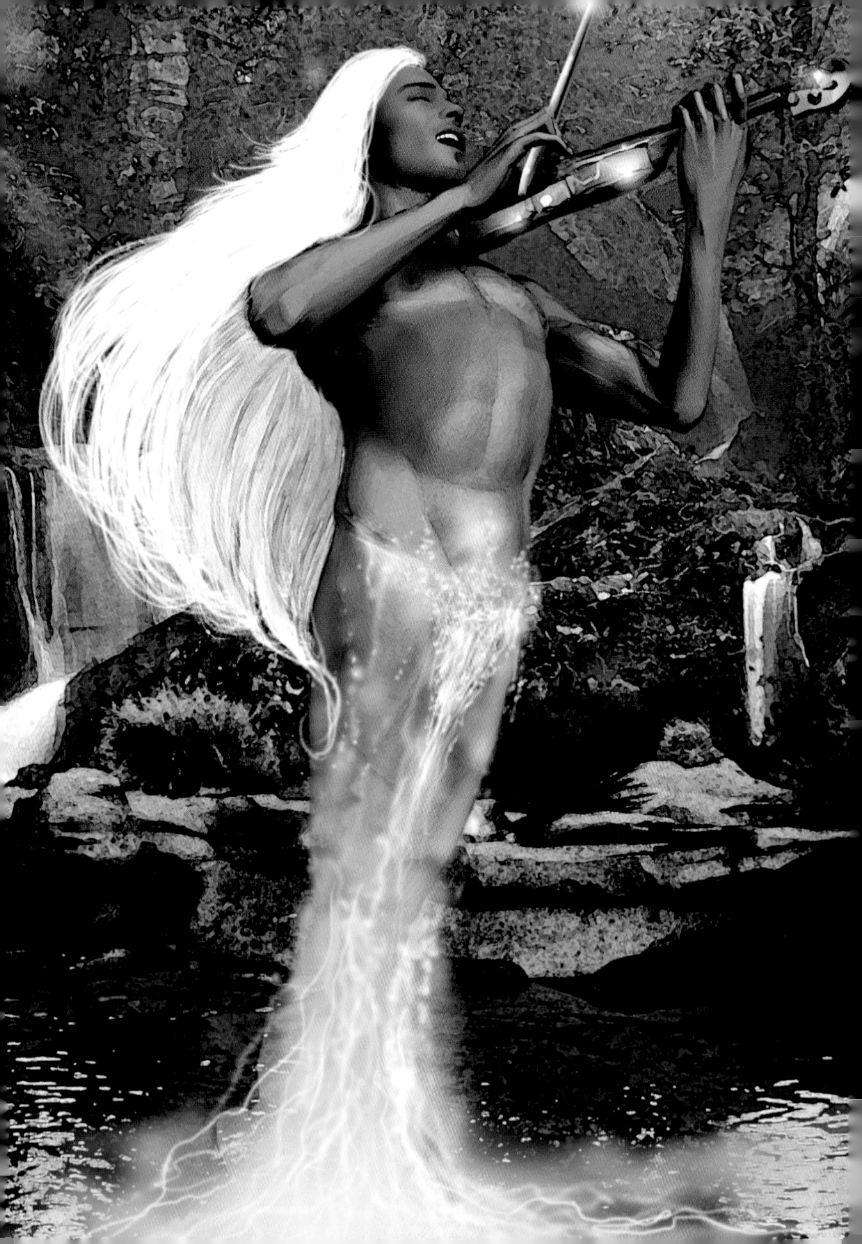

Fossegrim

THIS SCANDINAVIAN FAERIE IS ALSO KNOWN BY THE NAMES OF NACKEN, NOKKEN AND STOROMKARLEN. HE IS DEPICTED AS A VERY HANDSOME YOUNG MALE PLAYING AN ENCHANTED VIOLIN, WHOSE MUSIC LURES WOMEN AND CHILDREN TO LAKES AND STREAMS WHERE THEY ARE DROWNED. BUT THIS ISN'T ALWAYS THE CASE IN THE FOSSEGRIM LEGENDS; HE IS ALSO FABLED TO TEACH OTHERS HOW TO PLAY THE VIOLIN AS BEAUTIFULLY AS HE DOES. BY SOME ACCOUNTS, FOSSEGRIM ARE SMALLER THAN HUMANS BUT PERFECTLY FORMED EXCEPT FOR THEIR FEET, WHICH ARE MERELY VAPOUR. AMONG THEIR MAGICAL POWERS IS THE ABILITY TO SHAPE-SHIFT INTO VARIOUS FORMS INCLUDING TRANSFORMING FROM MALE TO FEMALE.

Development

- For an ethereal spirit look, try using long white hair, which is particularly effective on male characters (think Legolas in the *Lord of the Rings* films).
- Poser software allows you to create the figure, pose him, add the any props, such as the violin, and add the basic hair.

Media and Execution

- Poser, photographs, Photoshop
- The figure, violin and bow were created in Poser and rendered out to Photoshop.
- Several photos of landscape images were merged together with some cropping, erasing and airbrushing to create the background.
- The legs were erased and the swirling mist and foam were airbrushed in.
- The hair was painted in with a fine Airbrush in several layers to build up its volume.
- Final touches of highlights, blending and shading completed the image.

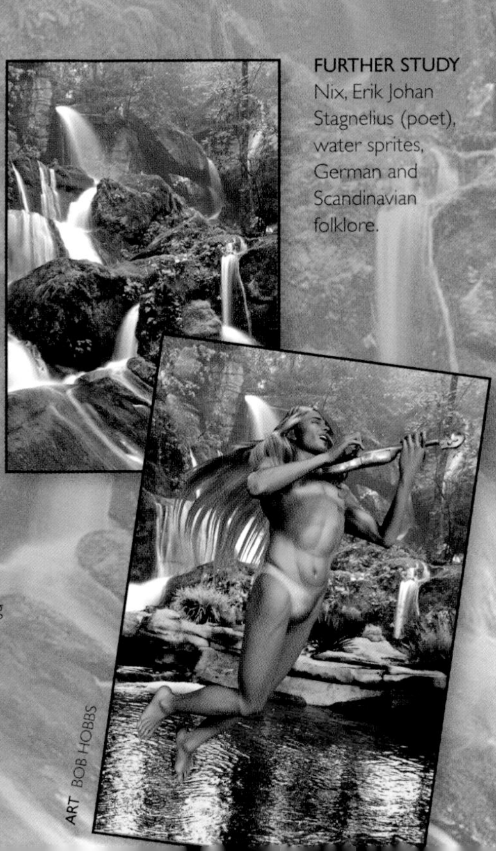

ART BOB HOBBS

FURTHER STUDY

Nix, Erik Johan Stagnelius (poet), water sprites, German and Scandinavian folklore.

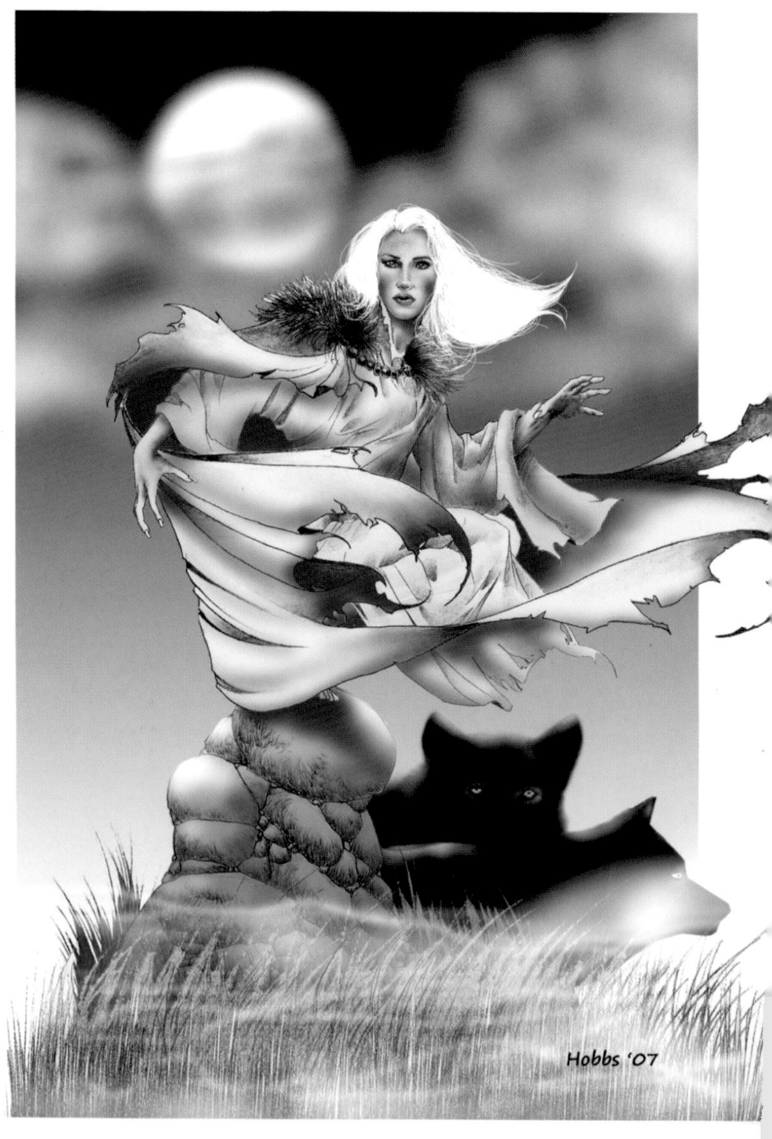
Hobbs '07

Frau Bercha

ALSO KNOWN AS PERCHTA, BERTHA OR PERCHT, FRAU BERCHTA IS A SOUTHERN GERMANIC PAGAN GODDESS, MISTRESS OF THE WILD HUNT AND PATRON OF WITCHES. HER NAME MEANS 'THE SHINING ONE'. IN ANCIENT HUNTING CULTURES SHE IS THE GUARDIAN OF ANIMALS AND NATURE. BERCHA CAN APPEAR IN ONE OF TWO FORMS: A BEAUTIFUL WOMAN DRESSED IN WHITE OR AS A HIDEOUS OLD HAG. 6 JANUARY, KNOWN AS TWELFTH NIGHT, WAS ONCE CELEBRATED AS HER FESTIVAL DAY. AS MISTRESS OF THE WILD HUNT, SHE LEADS HER GHOSTLY DOGS TO CHASE DOWN MORTALS TO THEIR DEATHS.

Development

- Two photographic references can be used for different parts of the image. Here, one photograph was used for the face and another for the body.
- Keeping the image fairly desaturated and lacking in colour conveys the feeling of a cold foggy winter's night on the moors.
- Use the ghostly silhouettes of wild dogs at her feet to give the image a touch of menace.

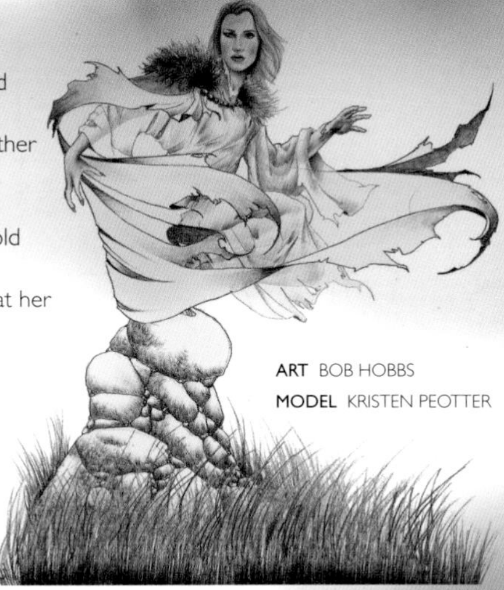

ART BOB HOBBS
MODEL KRISTEN PEOTTER

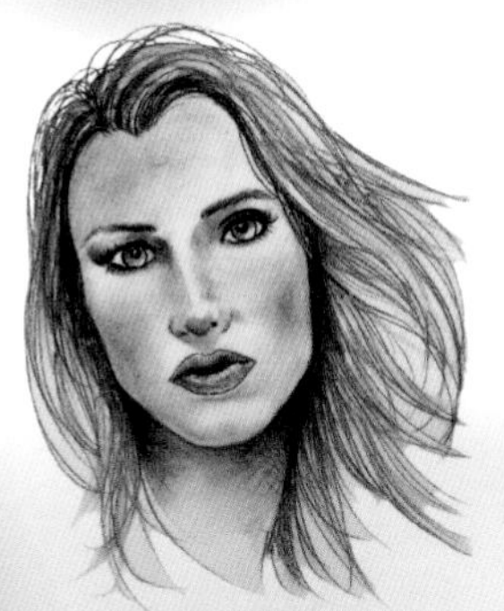

FURTHER STUDY
Germanic folklore, Holda, the Wild Hunt, Twelfth Night.

Media and Execution

- Photographs, pencil, Photoshop
- After rendering both the face and body reference photographs in pencil, these were scanned and merged together in Photoshop.
- The white background was removed and the image was colourized in layers, keeping the palette restricted to greys, white and black.
- Grass and hair were created with a fine Airbrush.
- Finally touches of highlights, mist and the graduated background were added.

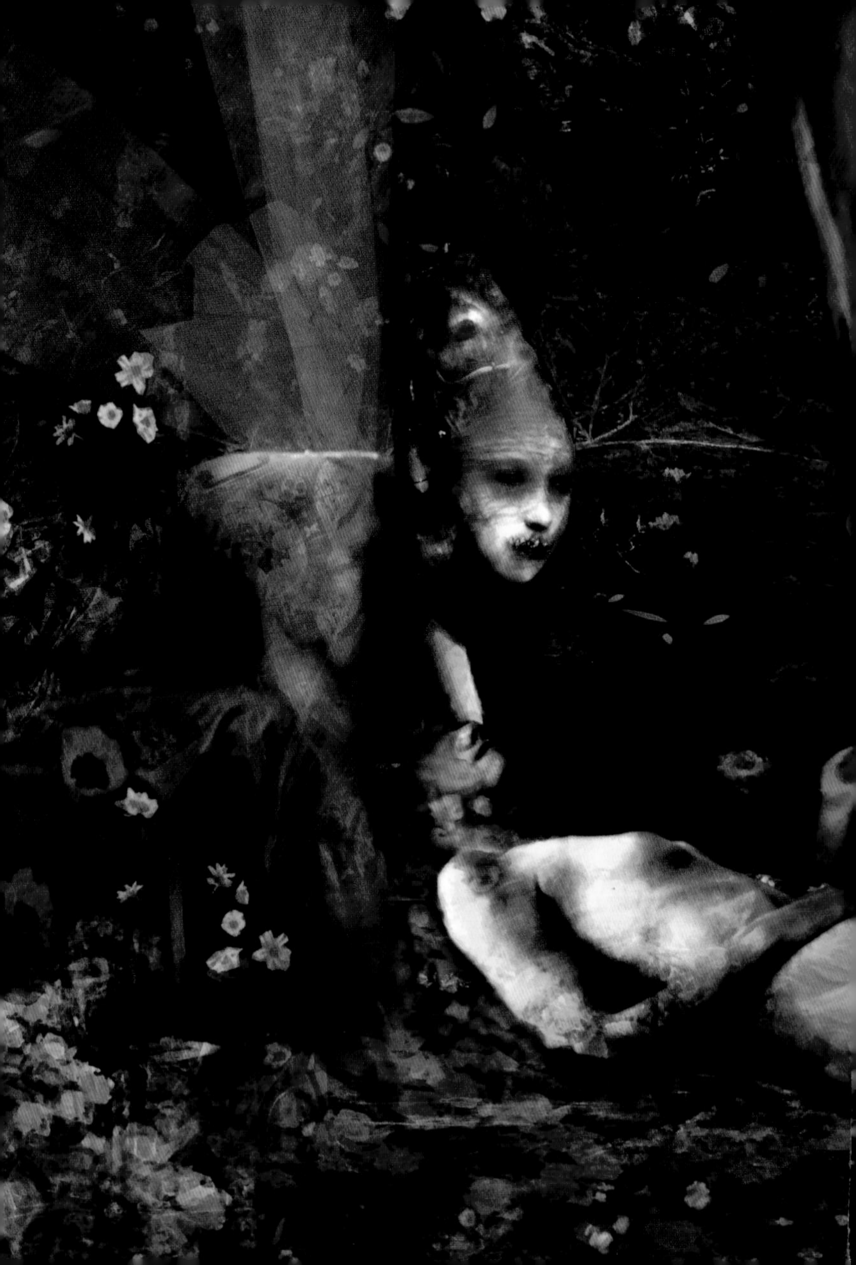

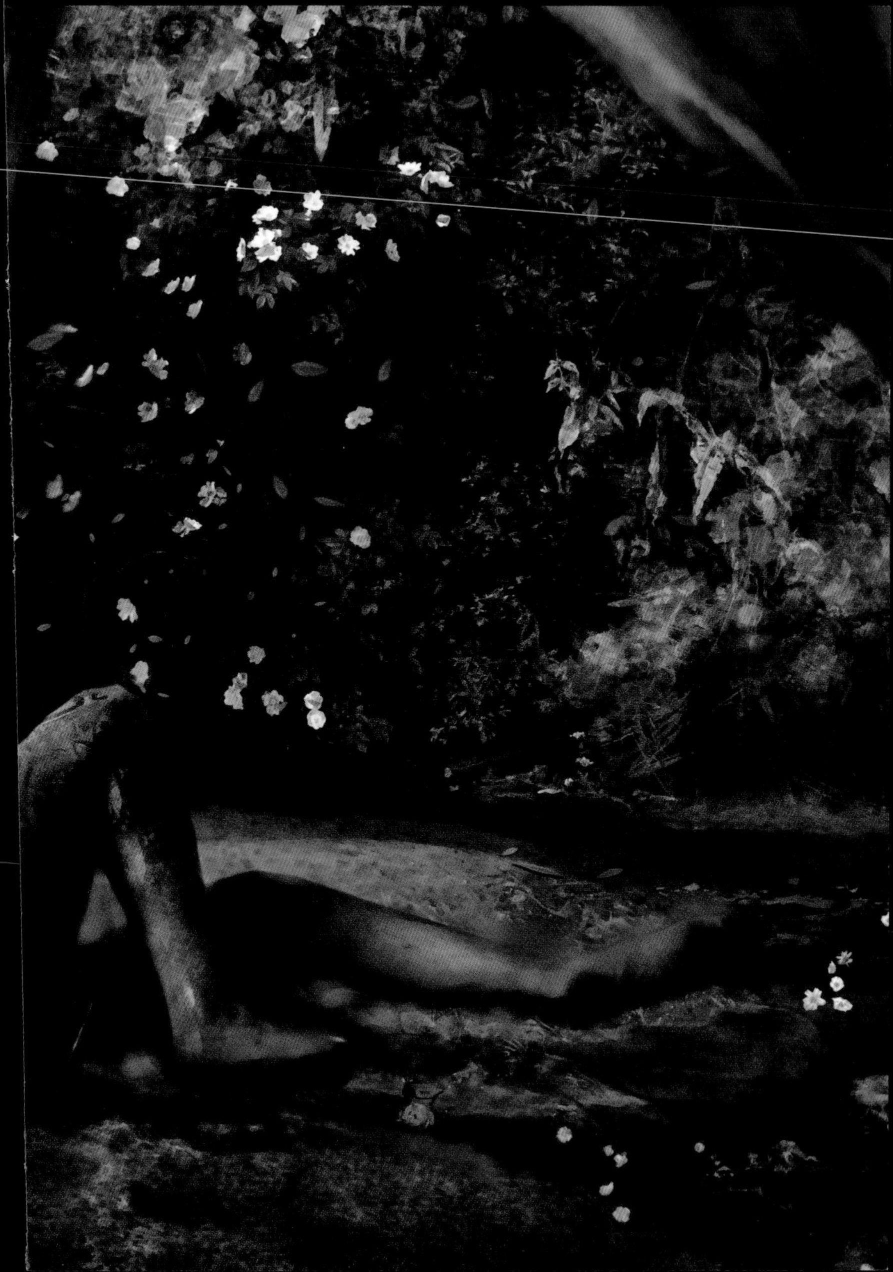

Fylgiar

IN ICELANDIC TRADITIONAL BELIEF, A BABY BORN WITH THE AMNIOTIC MEMBRANE OVER ITS HEAD IS THOUGHT TO BE SPECIAL, AND WILL GO THROUGH LIFE WITH A GUARDIAN SPIRIT, A FYLGIAR, TO WATCH OVER IT. THESE SPIRITS ARE USUALLY INVISIBLE AND ONLY MATERIALIZE TO WARN THEIR HUMAN COMPANIONS OF THEIR OWN IMMINENT DEATH. AT THAT TIME, THE NATURE OF THE FYLGIAR'S APPEARANCE WILL REVEAL THE MANNER OF THE PERSON'S DEATH: A BATTERED AND BRUISED FAERIE MEANS A VIOLENT AND PAINFUL DEATH, WHILE A RELAXED AND SERENE FORM DENOTES A CALM AND PAIN-FREE END. AFTER DEATH, THE FYLGIAR TRAVELS WITH THE HUMAN'S SOUL TO VALHALLAH WHERE IT WILL REMAIN UNTIL IT IS ASSURED THAT THEIR SOUL IS AT PEACE.

Development

- Study the legends and myths surrounding the faerie and make a list of the key things you want to include in your image.
- The only time a Fylgiar is visible is when their human ward is on the point of death, so you have little choice but to show this event in your image. However, this doesn't mean it has to be a grim portrayal, as this painting demonstrates.
- Make sure you relate the human and the spirit closely to each other, either by their physical proximity or using lighting, or both as here.

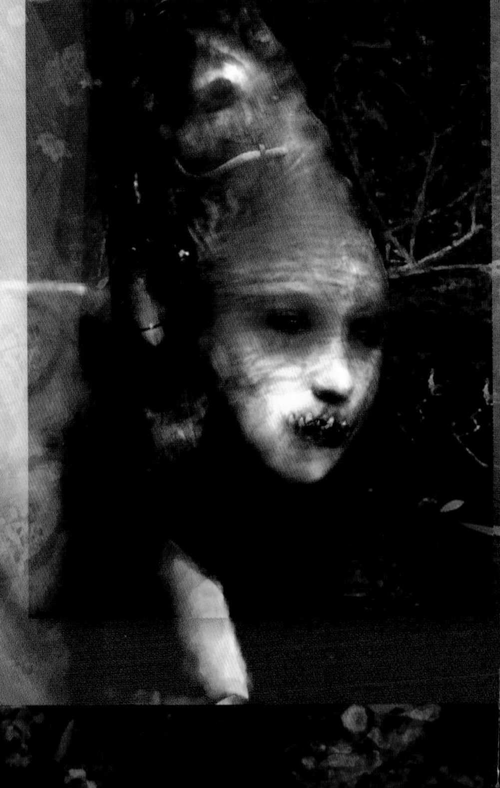

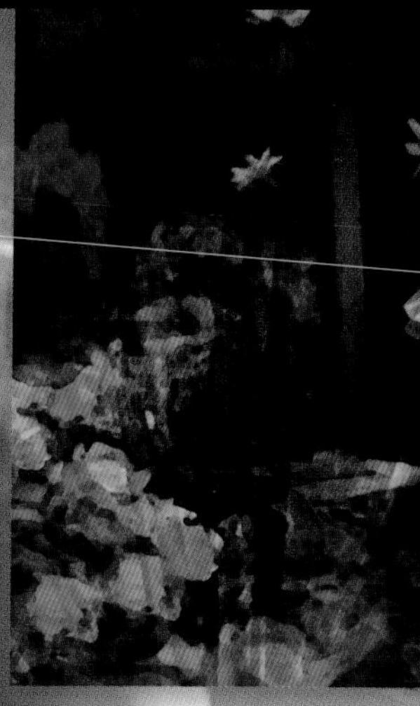

Media and Execution

- Pencil, Photoshop
- A rough pencil sketch was scanned and opened in Photoshop.
- The background was painted in loosely, with red predominating to create an edge of danger.
- Finally the dying figure and the spirit were placed on top of the background, with a golden shaft of light connecting the two.

FURTHER STUDY

Norse mythology, guardian angels, Valhallah, caulbearers.

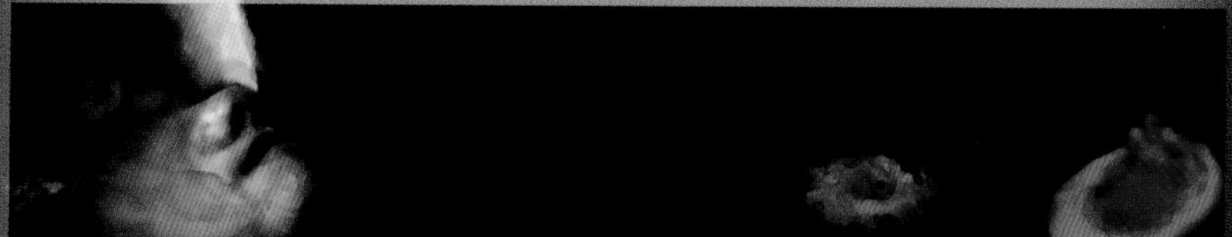

ART CHRISTOPHER SHY

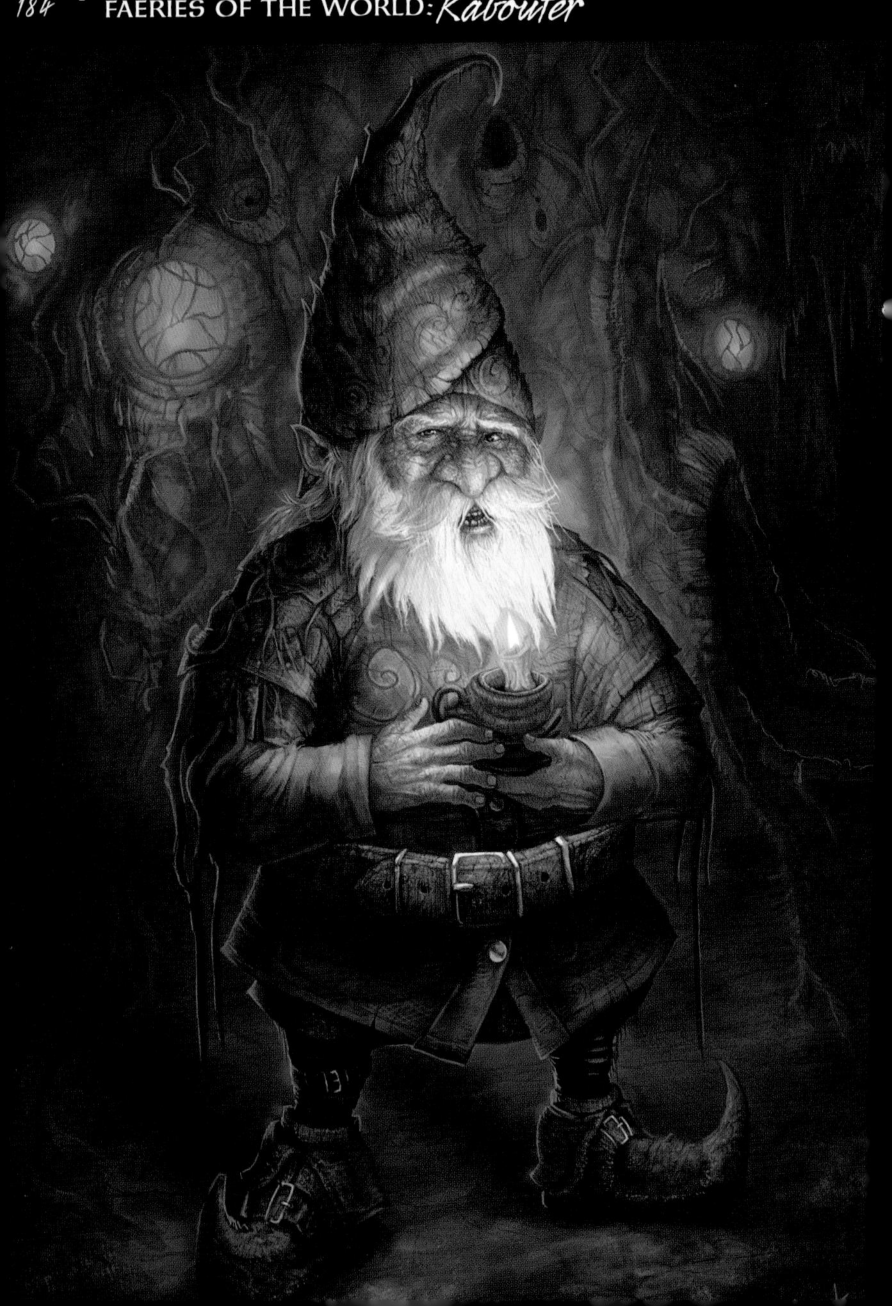

Kabouter

A KABOUTER IS A DUTCH GNOME, SMALL IN STATURE BUT A STRONG WORKER. LIVING IN SUBTERRANEAN KINGDOMS, THEY ARE KNOWN TO HAVE SKILL AT ENGINEERING, SMITHING AND CONSTRUCTION, AND ARE ALSO SAID TO GUARD BURIED TREASURE. THEY ARE EXTREMELY SHY AND AVOID CONTACT WITH HUMANS WHEREVER POSSIBLE. THESE EARTH-DWELLERS APPEAR IN THE FOLKLORE OF THE LOW COUNTRIES, WHERE IT IS CHRONICLED THAT THEY BUILT THE FIRST CARILLONS (BRONZE BELLS) OF THE NETHERLANDS. IN THE DUTCH FOLKTALE, *THE LEGEND OF THE WOODEN SHOES*, A KABOUTER TEACHES A MAN HOW TO MAKE CLOGS. MOST COMMON IN THEIR MALE FORM, THEY HAVE FULL, LONG BEARDS AND WEAR POINTED RED HATS.

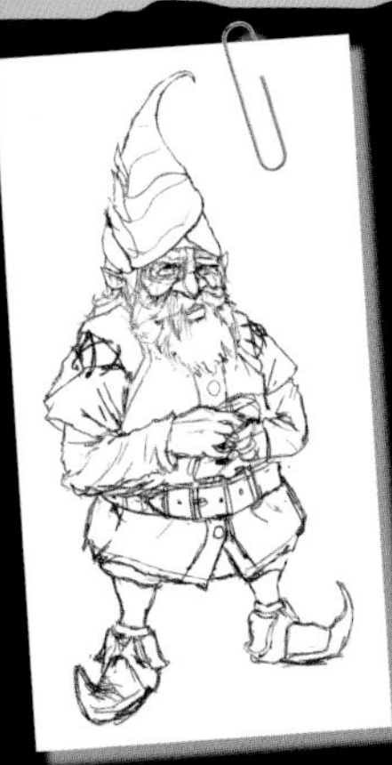

Development

- Kabouters live underground, which strongly influences their architecture and clothing designs.
- They have an 'earthiness' about them, which should be reflected in the colour palette used.
- Kabouters are benevolent, and don't have selfish or greed-inspiring goals. These characteristics need to come across through posture and facial expression.

FURTHER STUDY

Dutch folklore, gnomes, Kobold, William Elliot Griffis (author) *Dutch Fairy Tales for Young Folks*, Rien Poortvliet (illustrator) *Lives and Works of the Gnome*.

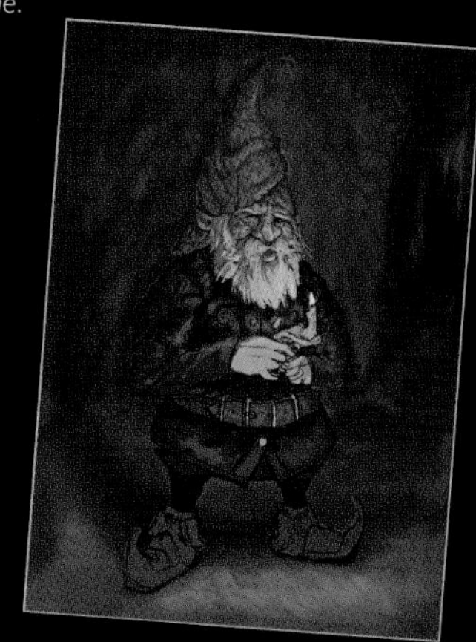

Media and Execution

- Photoshop
- The character began as simple sketch drawn in Photoshop with the default brush.
- The basic colours of the character and background were chosen, and then fleshed out with highlights and shadows.
- Proportions were fixed with the Liquify and Lasso tools, and the hands and candleholder were redrawn.
- Necessary details were added and filters were used to colour correct the image.

ART ARTEMIS KOLAKIS

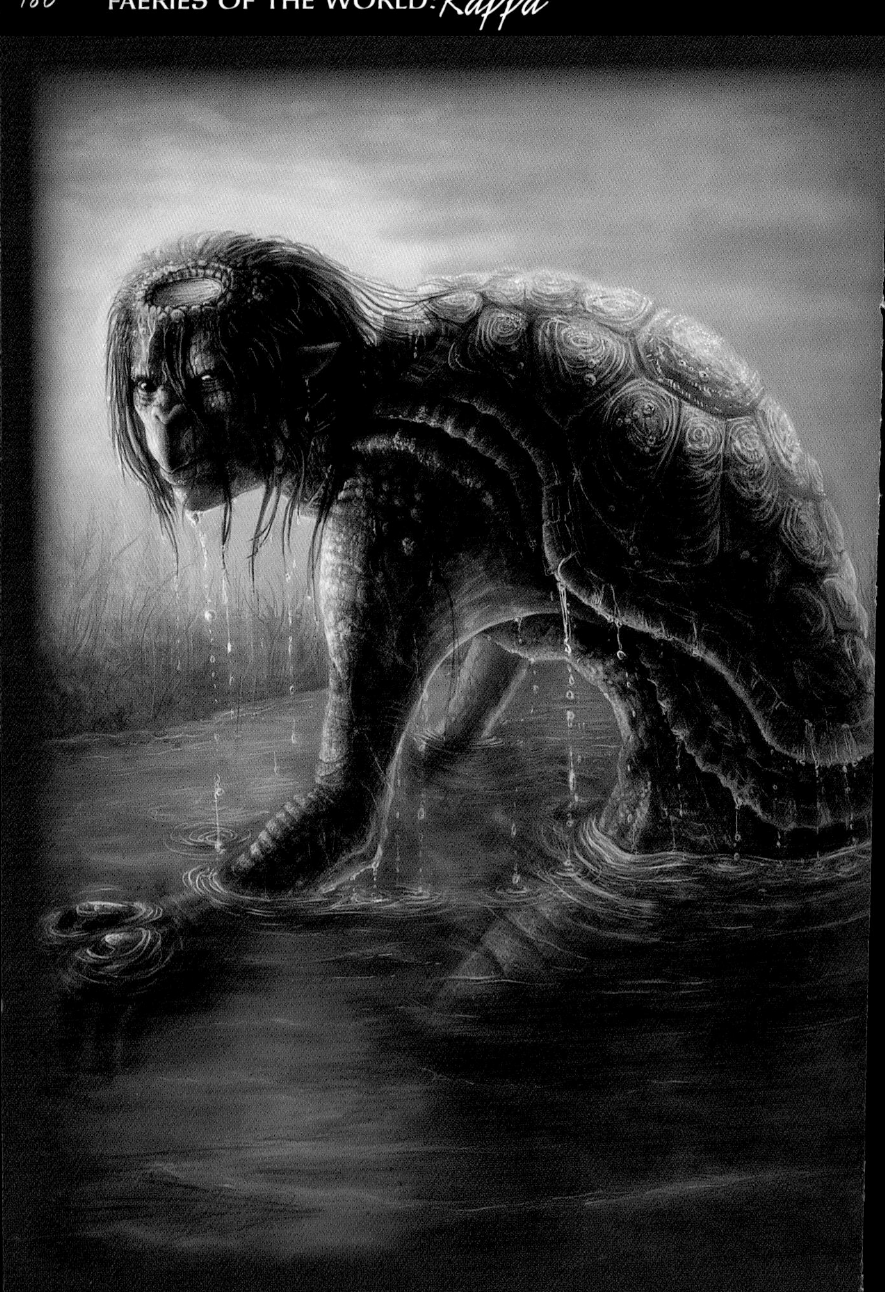

KAPPA

RIVER SPRITES FOUND IN JAPANESE FOLKLORE, KAPPAS ARE THE SIZE OF INFANTS AND HENCE ARE ALSO KNOWN AS RIVER CHILDREN. THEIR BODIES ARE MORE LIKE APES OR FROGS THAN HUMANS THOUGH. KAPPAS ARE USUALLY DEPICTED WITH BEAKS, SIMILAR TO EITHER A TORTOISE OR A DUCK, AND MOST PORTRAYALS SHOW THEM WITH THICK SHELLS AND SCALY SKIN. THEY HAVE LARGE DEPRESSIONS ON TOP OF THEIR HEADS FILLED WITH WATER, WHICH IS THE SOURCE OF THEIR POWER. IF THEY SPILL THIS WATER THEY BECOME EXTREMELY WEAK AND IMMOBILIZED – THEY MAY EVEN DIE. THEY ARE MASTERS OF KOPPO, A BONE BREAKING TECHNIQUE, AND TEND TO CHALLENGE HUMANS TO TEST THEIR SKILLS IN SHOGI OR SUMO-WRESTLING. KAPPAS ARE MISCHIEVOUS TROUBLEMAKERS WHO LIKE TO DISRUPT AND TRICK THE PEOPLE THEY COME ACROSS.

Development

- Mix human and animal forms in your faerie creatures – this Kappa blends human, turtle and ape-like qualities to produce a disturbing individual.
- Suggest weird and wonderful flaps of skin by showing light shining through them, such as the underarm flap here.

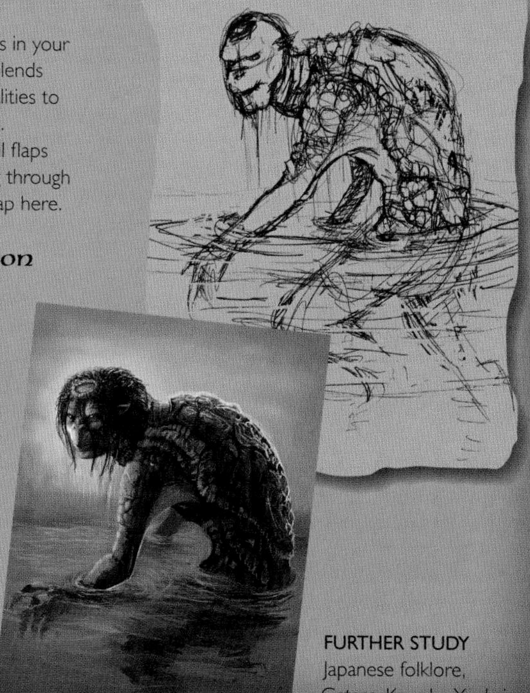

Media and Execution

- Pencil, Photoshop
- The Kappa was sketched out with pencil and then scanned and opened in Photoshop.
- Proportions were corrected with the Liquify filter.
- The colours and lighting scheme were added and then the whole image was colour corrected and prepared for print.

ART ARTEMIS KOLAKIS

FURTHER STUDY
Japanese folklore, Gataro, Kawako, Youkai.

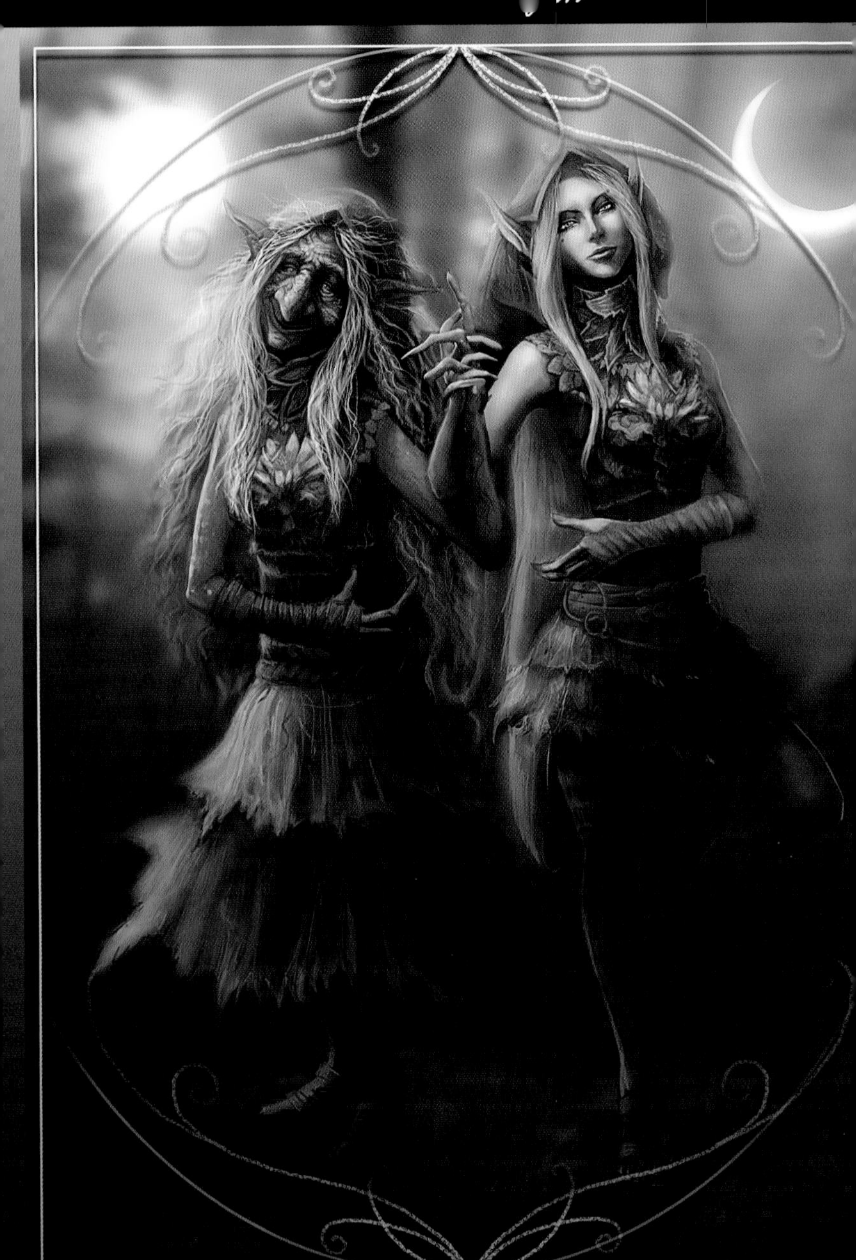

KORRIGAN

THESE COMPLEX SPIRITS FROM BRETON FOLKLORE CHANGE THEIR FORM DEPENDING ON THE TIME OF DAY. DURING THE DAYLIGHT HOURS THEY ARE REPULSIVE HAGS WHO ARE FOND OF STEALING HUMAN CHILDREN AND REPLACING THEM WITH CHANGELINGS, WHILE AT NIGHT THEY BECOME BEAUTIFUL NYMPHS WHO HAVE THE POWER TO MAKE ALL MORTAL MEN FALL IN LOVE WITH THEM. EVEN IN THEIR BEAUTIFUL FORM THEY ARE STILL SINISTER THOUGH, AND ANY MAN WHO DOES FIND HIMSELF AT THE MERCY OF A KORRIGAN WILL NOT SURVIVE LONG. AN OLD BRETON POEM DESCRIBES KORRIGANS DANCING AROUND FOUNTAINS BY THE LIGHT OF THE FULL MOON WITH FLOWERS IN THEIR HAIR. IN BOTH THEIR FORMS THEY CAN PREDICT THE FUTURE AND ARE ABLE TO MOVE AT LIGHTNING SPEED.

Development

- Use a collage-style image to represent the two forms of a Korrigan.
- Try working with another artist to get two different visions in the same piece.
- Include storytelling elements in your images, such as the sun and moon here.

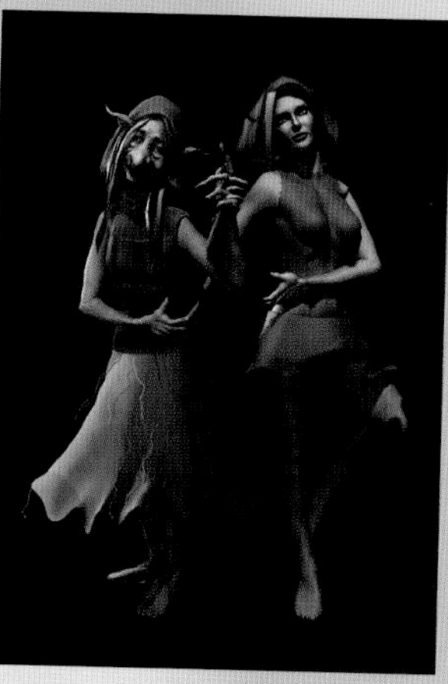

ART JULIANNA AND ARTEMIS KOLAKIS

FURTHER STUDY
Corrigan, folklore of Brittany, Morrigan Erik L'Homme (author) *Book of the Stars.*

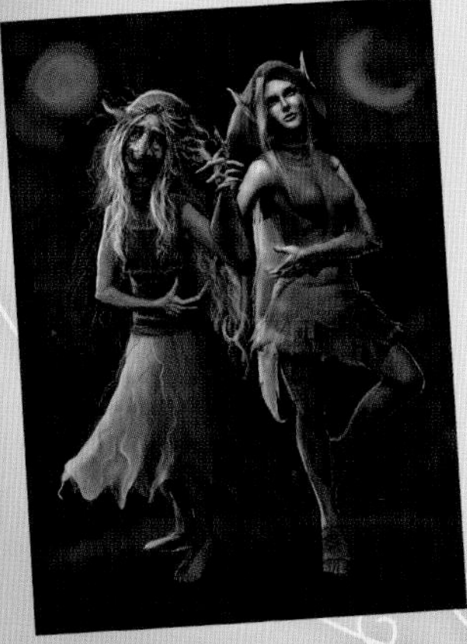

Media and Execution

- Softimage XSI, Photoshop
- Julianna created and posed two models in XSI.
- Artemis and Julianna then chose a figure each and began to paint over the characters in Photoshop.
- At the end of the process they swapped files and contributed a few details to the opposite side.
- The two files were merged, and the frame was added to finalize the image.

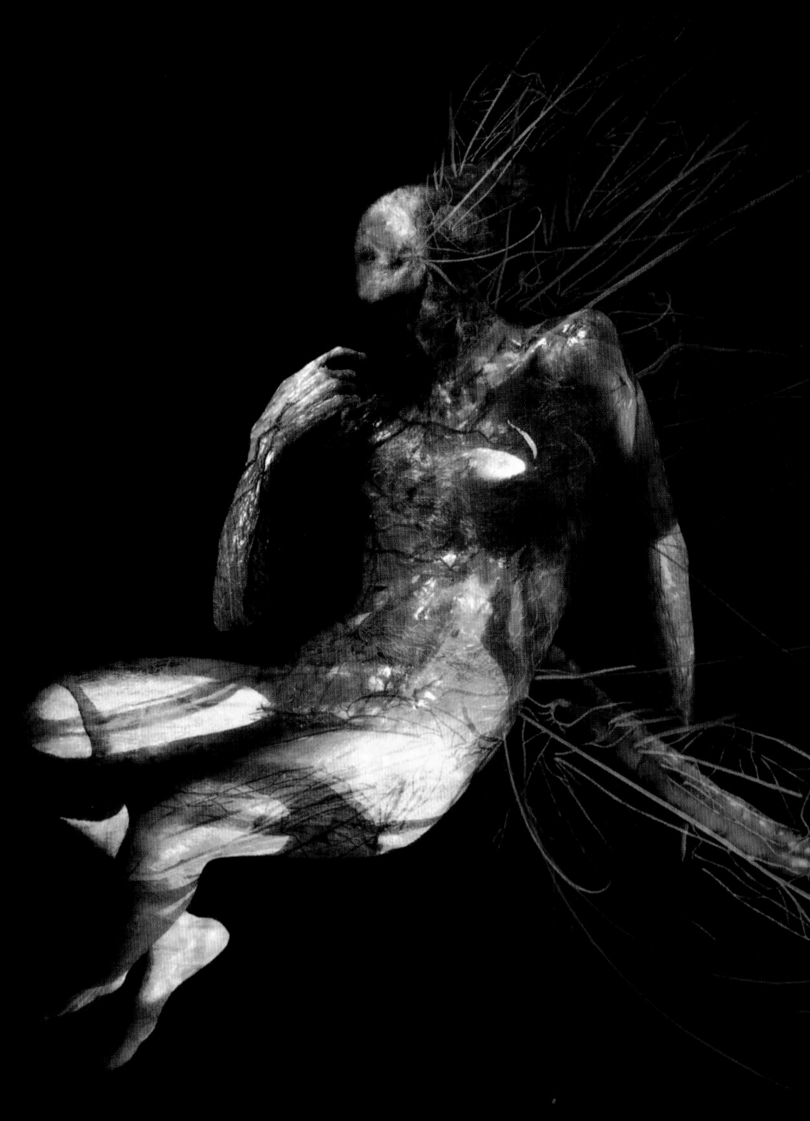

Lutin

THESE FRENCH SPIRITS ARE SHAPE-SHIFTERS EXTRAORDINAIRE, AND HAVE NEVER HELD A SINGLE FORM LONG ENOUGH FOR HUMANS TO CAPTURE AN ACCURATE LIKENESS OF THEM. THEY CAN TRANSFORM INTO ANY SHAPE – BOTH LIVING AND INANIMATE. AS WELL AS CHANGING THEIR SHAPE, THEIR DISPOSITION ALSO CHANGES IN AN INSTANT AND THEY CAN SWING FROM BENIGN TO DEVASTATING IN A FRACTION OF A SECOND. THEY MOVE FROM PLACE TO PLACE AT GREAT SPEED, AND ARE SOMETIMES MISTAKEN FOR FIREFLIES. THEY ARE REPULSED BY SALT, AND WILL GO OUT OF THEIR WAY TO AVOID IT. THEY MAKE THEIR HOMES IN A GREAT VARIETY OF PLACES, FROM HUMAN HOMES TO PONDS, LAKES AND STREAMS.

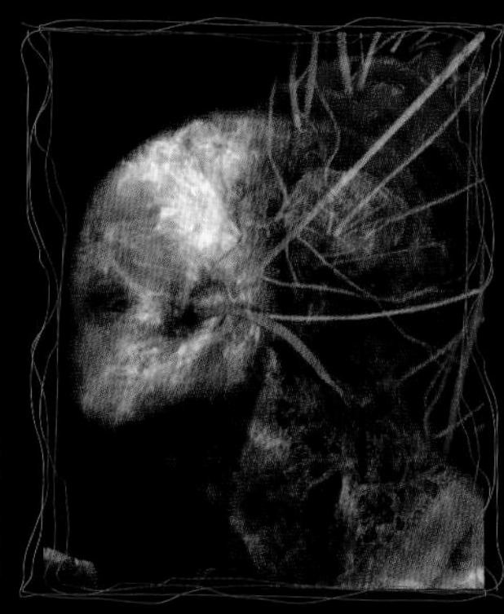

Development

- A somewhat confused drawing style conjures up the sense that this faerie does not stay in one form for very long, and is changing before your very eyes.
- Using a solid black background places all the emphasis on your faerie. If there is already a lot going on in the picture, avoid using a distracting backdrop.
- Experiment with Blending Modes in Photoshop to see the different effects they have when overlaying textures.

FURTHER STUDY

French folklore, Goblin, Nain Rouge, Marie Catherine d'Aulnoy (author) *Le Prince Lutin.*

Media and Execution

- Photograph, Photoshop
- A model photograph was used as the starting point, but was heavily over-painted to create a being very firmly in the fantasy realm. The legs were less retouched in terms of their shape, but strong lighting effects were added.
- The Smudge tool was used to distort the facial features and to create a very vague form.
- Textures were overlaid using various Blending Modes, and fine lines around the head and tail were drawn in with a hard-edged brush.

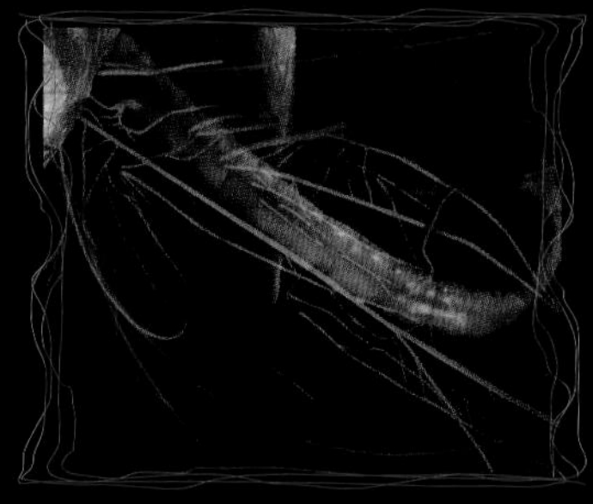

ART CHRISTOPHER SHY

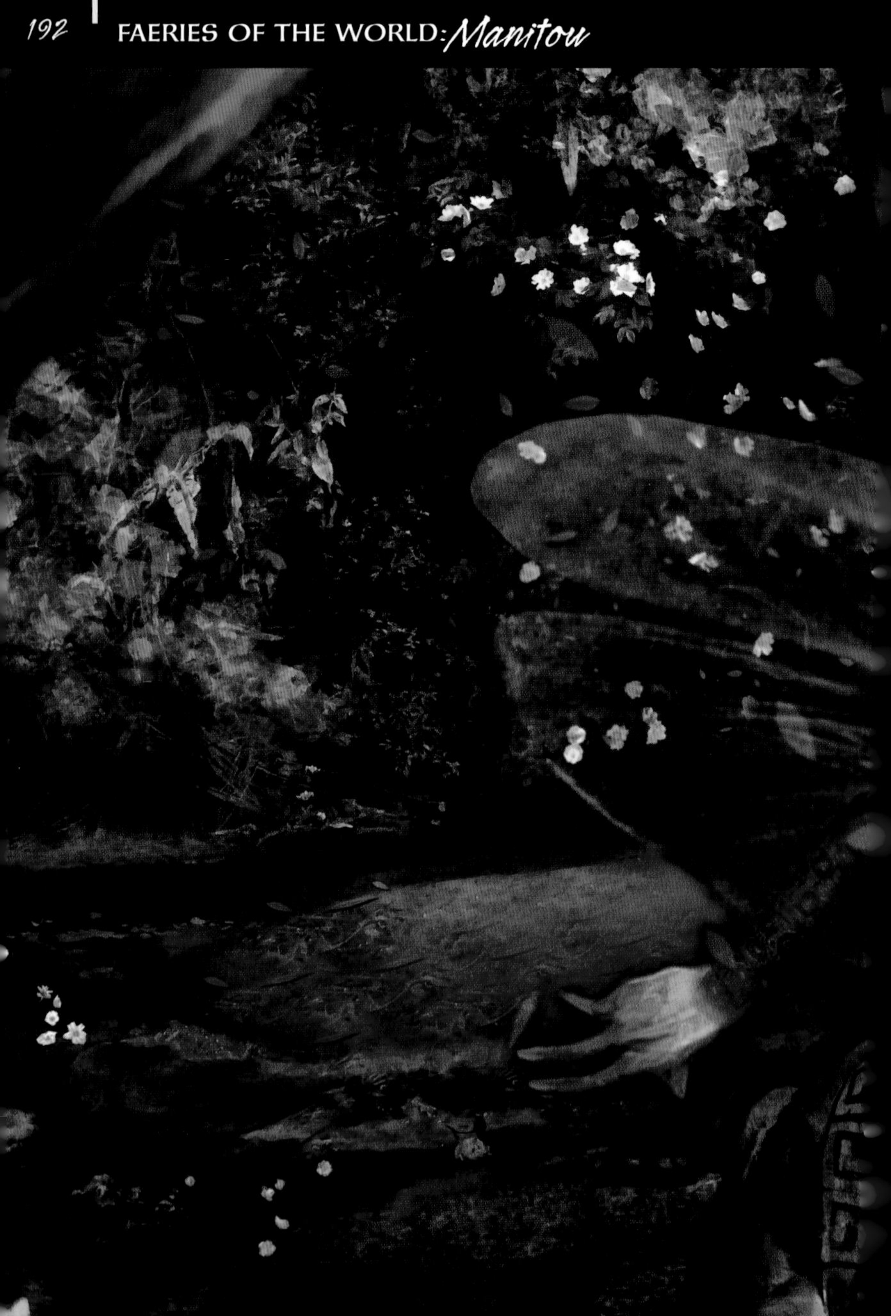

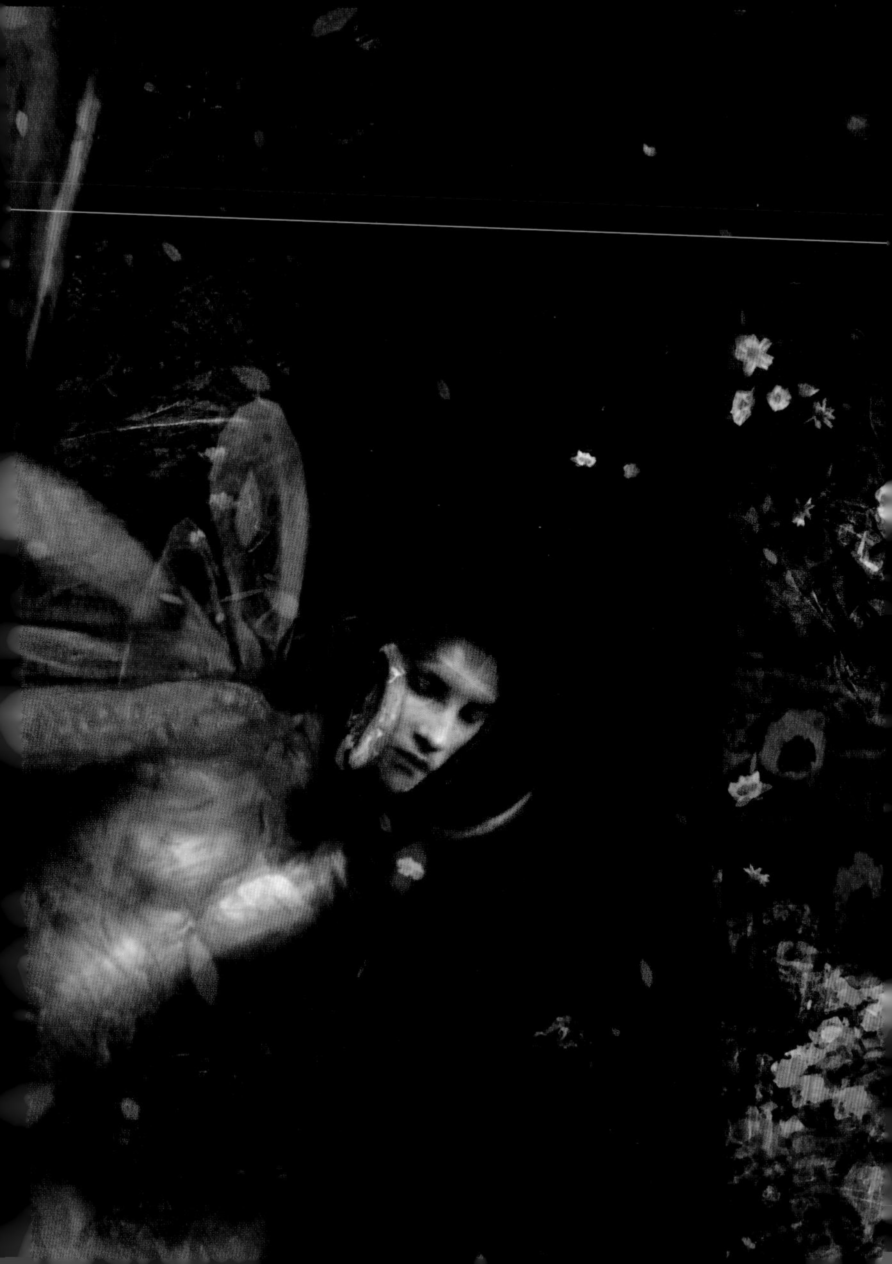

MANITOU

MYSTERIOUS SPIRITS FROM ALGONQUIAN (NATIVE AMERICAN) FOLKLORE, MANITOUS MAKE MAGIC BY DRUMMING AND ARE USUALLY DEPICTED WITH SETS OF ANTLERS OR HORNS. ACCORDING TO TRADITIONAL BELIEFS, EVERYTHING IN LIFE HAS ITS OWN MANITOU SPIRIT, BE IT ANIMAL, MINERAL OR VEGETABLE. THEY REPRESENT THE INTERCONNECTION AND BALANCE OF NATURE ITSELF, AND ARE TO BE SAFEGUARDED IN ORDER FOR THE NATURAL WORLD TO STAY IN HARMONY. ELABORATE SHAMANISTIC RITUAL CAN BE USED TO CONTACT THESE SPIRITS AND TO DRAW ON THEIR POWERS FOR CERTAIN TASKS. FOR EXAMPLE, PLANT MANITOUS CAN BE CONTACTED TO HELP WITH HEALING, AND CONNECTION WITH A BISON MANITOU WAS THOUGHT TO BRING SUCCESS IN THE HUNT.

Development

- Research Algonquian culture and customs to get a good understanding of the people and their folklore.
- Spend time looking at Native American art and textiles, and keep a sketchbook with any patterns that you find particularly appealing for use in your work, such as the design used here.
- Look at references of horned animals to understand their form and shape better. Don't necessarily choose the most obvious shapes, but look at various different kinds before settling on which to use in your image.
- As Manitous are so closely connected with nature, make sure your faerie blends in perfectly with its surroundings, but still stands out to the viewer.

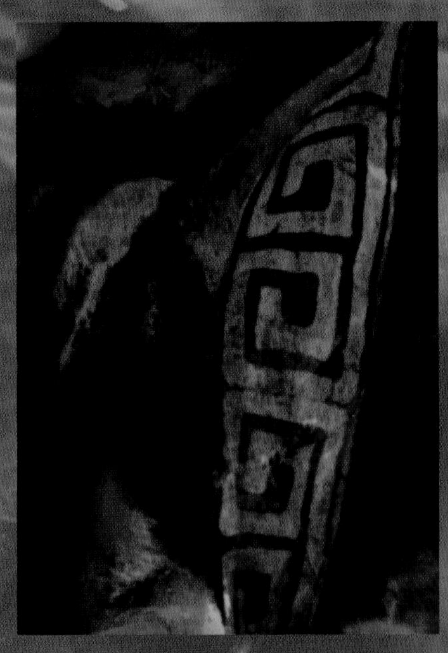

Media and Execution

- Photograph. Photoshop
- A model photograph was opened in Photoshop and heavily over-painted except for the face, which was kept fairly close to the original image but toned in an almost vintage photographic style.
- The wings were created on a separate layer, with careful manipulation of the Opacity in different areas to achieve this effect.
- A red light source was used on the left-hand side of the image to suggest a cave entrance.

FURTHER STUDY
Native American folklore and beliefs, shamanism.

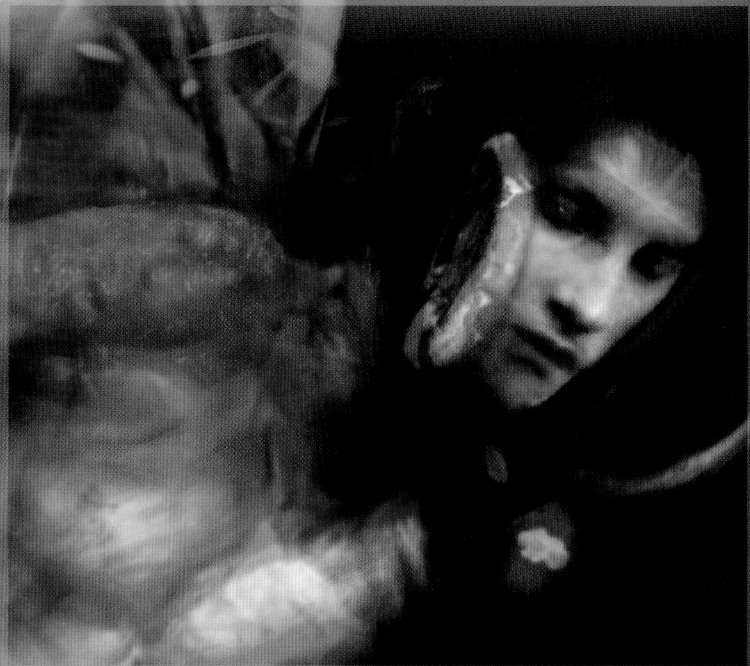

ART CHRISTOPHER SHY

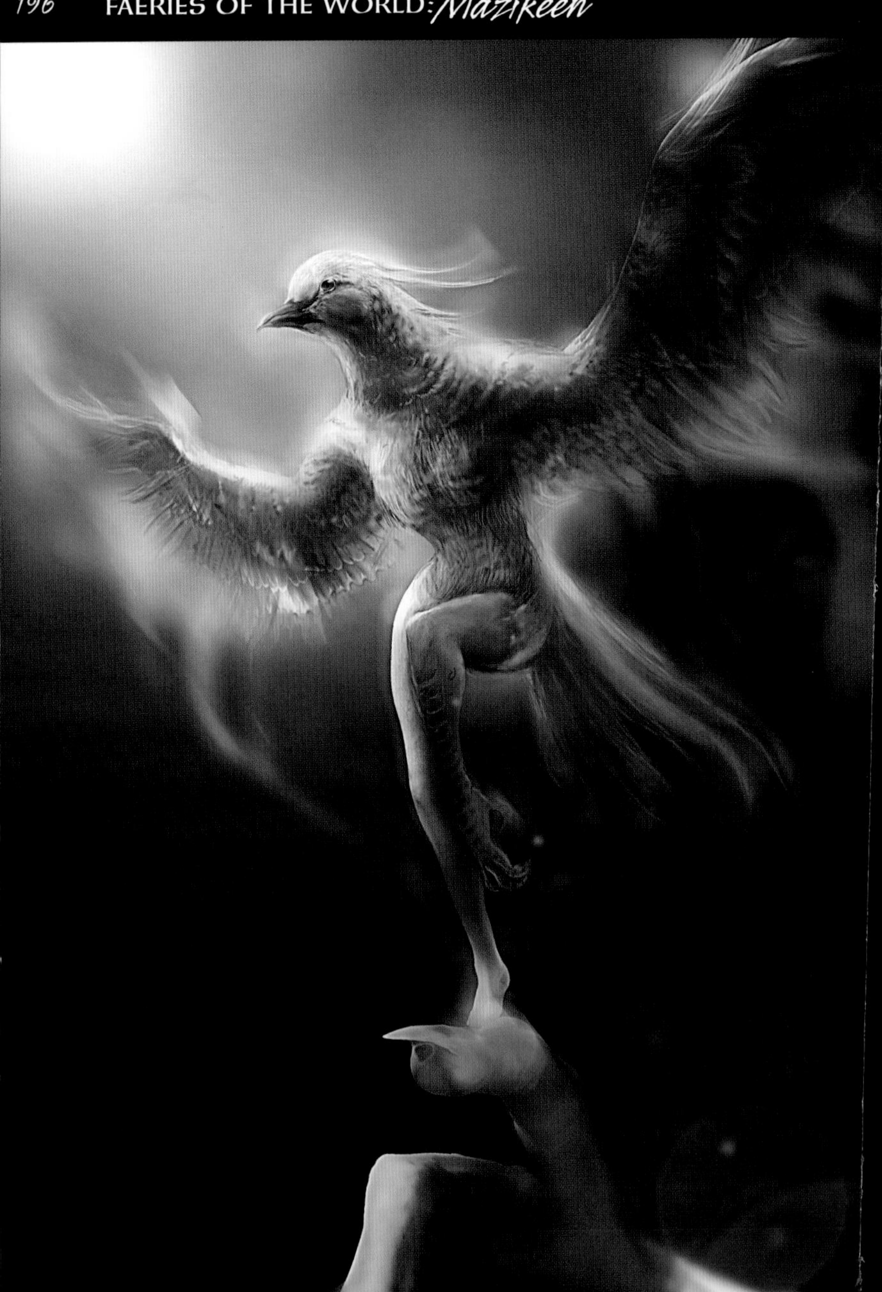

Mazikeen

THESE SHAPE-SHIFTING FAERIES ORIGINATE FROM ANCIENT HEBREW MYTHOLOGY, AS TINY WINGED CREATURES THAT CAN ASSUME ANY FORM THEY DESIRE. THEY ARE MALEVOLENT AND CAN CAUSE ALL MANNER OF TROUBLE RANGING FROM MINOR ANNOYANCES TO SERIOUS DANGERS. THERE IS AN OLD LEGEND THAT TELLS OF A WICKED MAN WHO HEARD A LOUD KNOCK ON HIS DOOR, BUT WHEN HE OPENED IT THERE WAS NOBODY THERE, JUST A DONKEY GRAZING UNDER A TREE. THE MAN MOUNTED THE DONKEY AND RODE IT AWAY, BUT AS HE DID THE DONKEY GREW LARGER AND LARGER UNTIL IT WAS AS TALL AS THE CHURCH STEEPLE, WHICH IS WHERE THE DONKEY LEFT HIM – PERCHED HIGH ON THE WEATHERCOCK. THE BEAST WAS A MISCHIEVOUS MAZIKEEN, TEACHING THE MAN A LESSON.

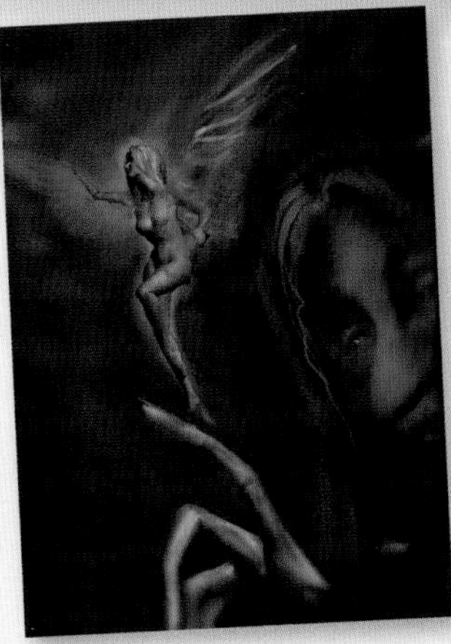

Development

- To portray a shape-shifting faerie, show it in mid transformation. Here a troll watches curiously to see what the Mazikeen will turn into as it tries to fly away.
- Use the Lens Flare filter in Photoshop to suggest a very bright light source and to add a sense of photorealism.

FURTHER STUDY
Hebrew mythology, Shedeem, Sheireem.

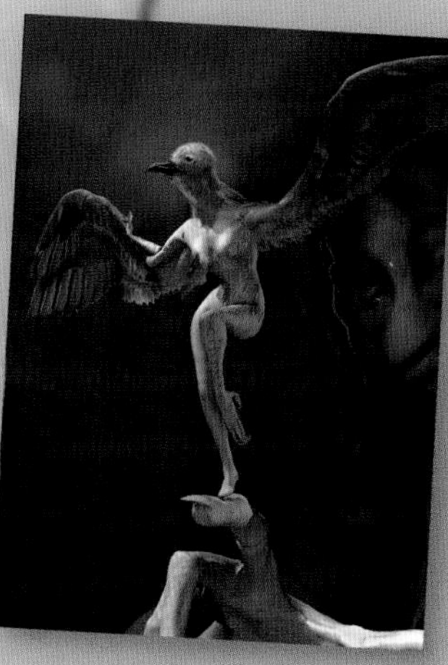

Media and Execution

- Softimage XSI, Photoshop
- The figure was modelled, posed, and rendered in XSI.
- It was then painted over in Photoshop.
- The Liquify filter was used to fix the body proportions.
- The light source was then added, and the highlights and details were painted in.
- The Lens Flare filter was used to create the characteristic circle shapes.

ART JULIANNA KOLAKIS

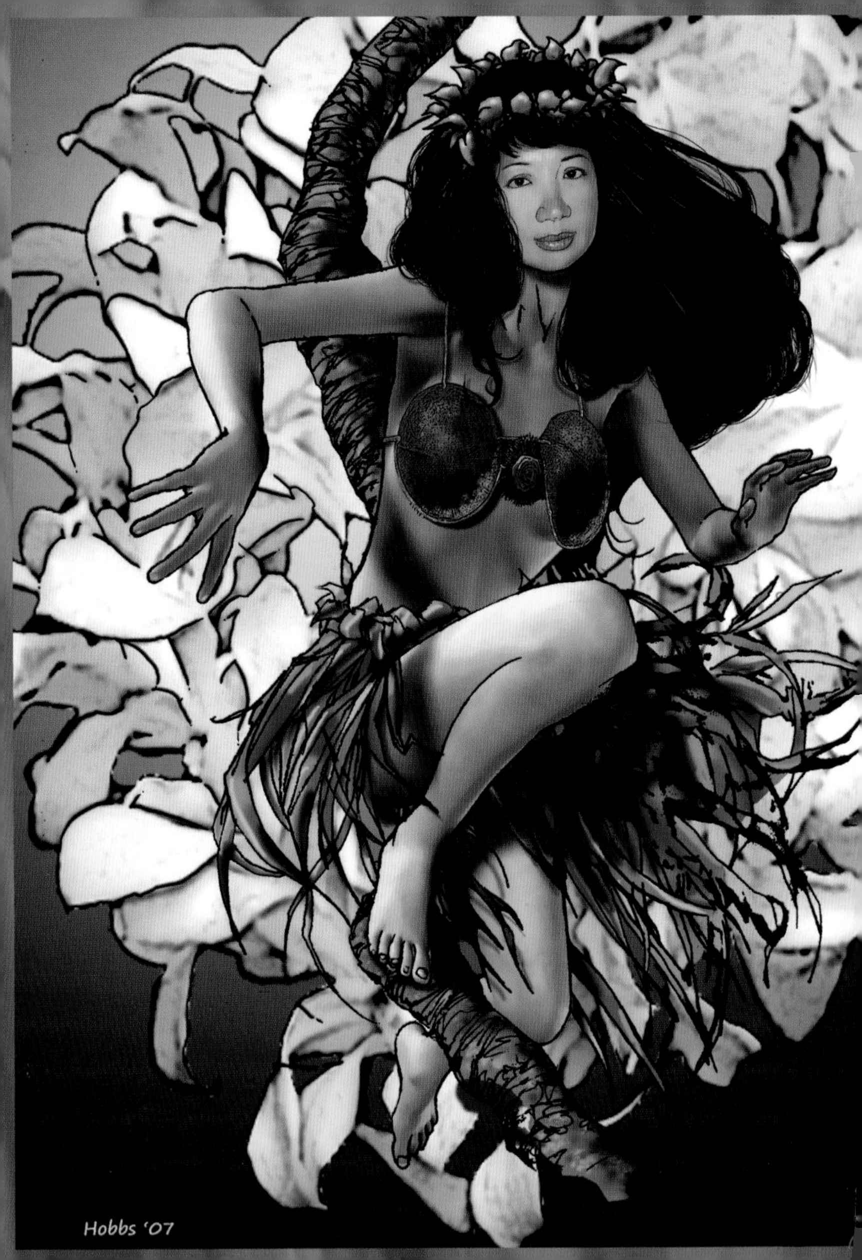
Hobbs '07

Menehune

ORIGINATING FROM THE ISLANDS OF POLYNESIA, PARTICULARLY HAWAII, MENEHUNES RANGE IN HEIGHT FROM ONLY 6IN TO 2FT (15-60CM), AND HAVE LONG STRAIGHT HAIR THAT FALLS TO THEIR KNEES. IN MANY WAYS THEY ARE SIMILAR TO NATIVE POLYNESIANS, ONLY SMALLER AND WITH MYSTICAL POWERS. MENEHUNES ROAM THE TROPICAL FORESTS AT NIGHT AND LOVE TO DANCE, SING, FISH AND PRACTICE ARCHERY AND CLIFF DIVING. THEIR LEGEND DATES BACK TO THE ISLAND'S FIRST INHABITANTS, WHO WHEN THEY ARRIVED FOUND DAMS, FISHPONDS AND TEMPLES, WHICH THEY ASSUMED WERE BUILT BY MENEHUNES. FEMALE MENEHUNES ARE SAID TO BE EXCEPTIONALLY BEAUTIFUL, AND SAILORS FROM OTHER LANDS WHO CAME TO THE ISLANDS WOULD OFTEN FALL IN LOVE WITH THEM.

Development

- When using a model, try to find someone whose origins roughly match those of your character.
- Use numerous references of Polynesian dress, Hawaiian hula dancers and orchids, which are common flowers in the Hawaiian Islands.

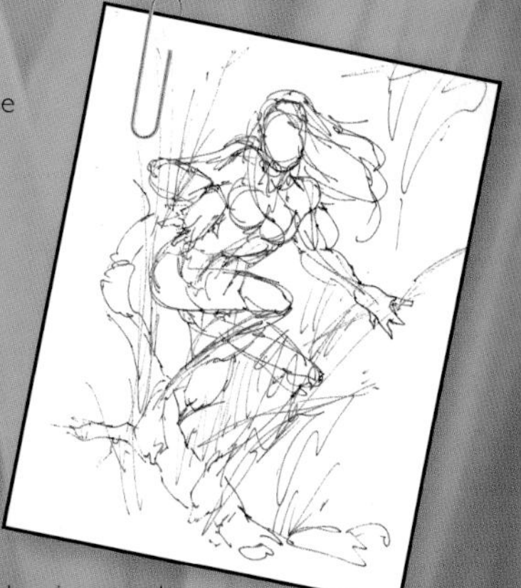

Media and Execution

- Photographs, pencil, pen and ink, Photoshop
- Preliminary sketches were made in pencil with the final sketch rendered in pen and ink.

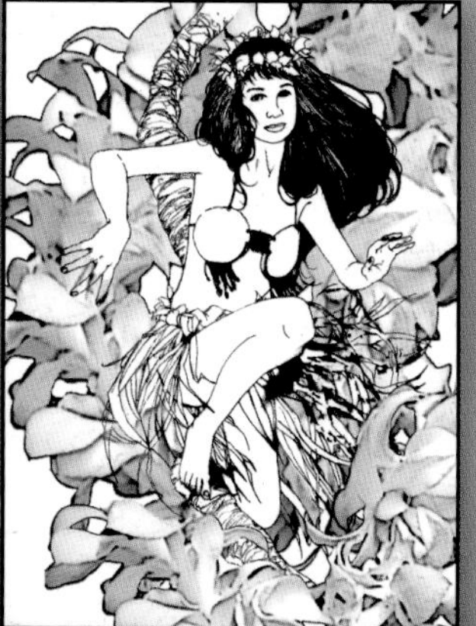

- The ink drawing was then scanned and opened in Photoshop.
- A photograph of orchid flowers was dropped into the background.
- Colouring was done in layers with flat colours placed first in layers below the ink layer followed by layers with tones and shading.
- Finally touches of highlights and the sunny background were added.

ART BOB HOBBS
MODEL CAROL GREEN

FURTHER STUDY
Hawaiian history, Polynesian folklore and mythology, Kahunas, Nawao.

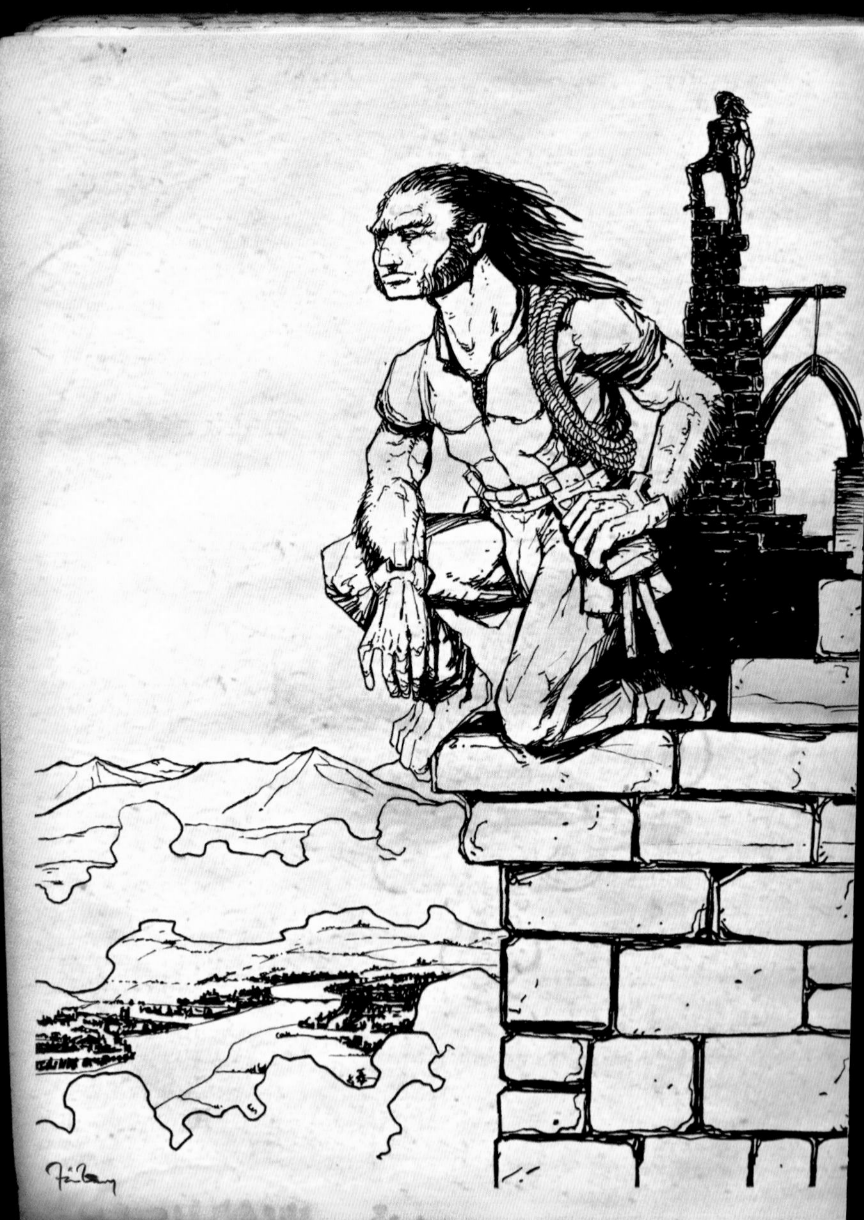

Pech

THESE SHORT, DWARF-LIKE CREATURES FROM SCOTLAND WERE RUMOURED TO HAVE BUILT GLASGOW CATHEDRAL IN THE 12TH CENTURY. PECHS WERE COMMON IN POPULAR FOLKLORE AND BARROWS AND MOUNDS WERE OFTEN CITED AS THEIR DWELLING PLACES, AS PROOF OF THEIR EXISTENCE. IT IS BELIEVED THAT THESE CREATURES MAY HAVE BEEN DISTORTED MEMORIES OF PICTS, EARLY INHABITANTS OF SCOTLAND WHO WERE ALSO SAID TO BE SHORT IN STATURE. THE IDEA THAT THEY BUILT GLASGOW CATHEDRAL COMES FROM THE FACT THAT, AFTER THE DARK AGES, LOCAL PEOPLE COULD NOT BELIEVE THAT MERE HUMANS COULD CONSTRUCT SUCH A MAGNIFICENT EDIFICE AND SO IT WAS SAID TO BE THE WORK OF THESE EXTRAORDINARY FAERIES.

Development

- The legend that the Pechs were great architects and builders gives rise to the idea that they are very strong but also intelligent. The final design shows a character that is clearly powerful but also has a noble stature.
- Try studies showing them as being more like medieval architects holding designs and wearing stonemasons' aprons (below right).
- The original design was considered too malevolent looking (below) and it was decided the figure should be heavier set and friendlier in appearance.

ART FINLAY COWAN

Media and Execution

- Pencil, technical ink pens, Photoshop
- The original pencil drawing was traced off on a light box using technical pens with a variety of nib widths.
- The final ink drawing was scanned and opened in Photoshop, where it was colourized slightly to make it more sepia toned.
- Finally, the artwork was layered over a scan of textured paper to give it an antique look.

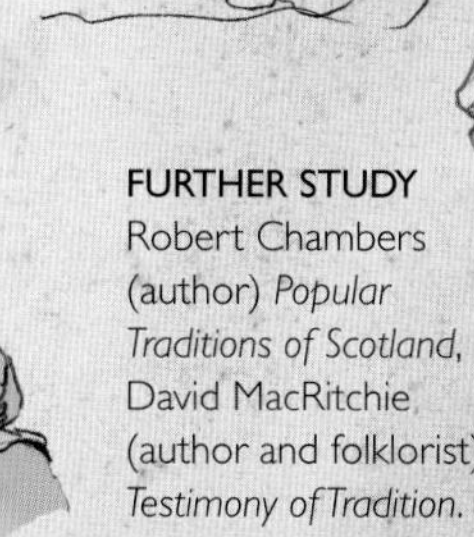

FURTHER STUDY
Robert Chambers (author) *Popular Traditions of Scotland*, David MacRitchie (author and folklorist) *Testimony of Tradition*.

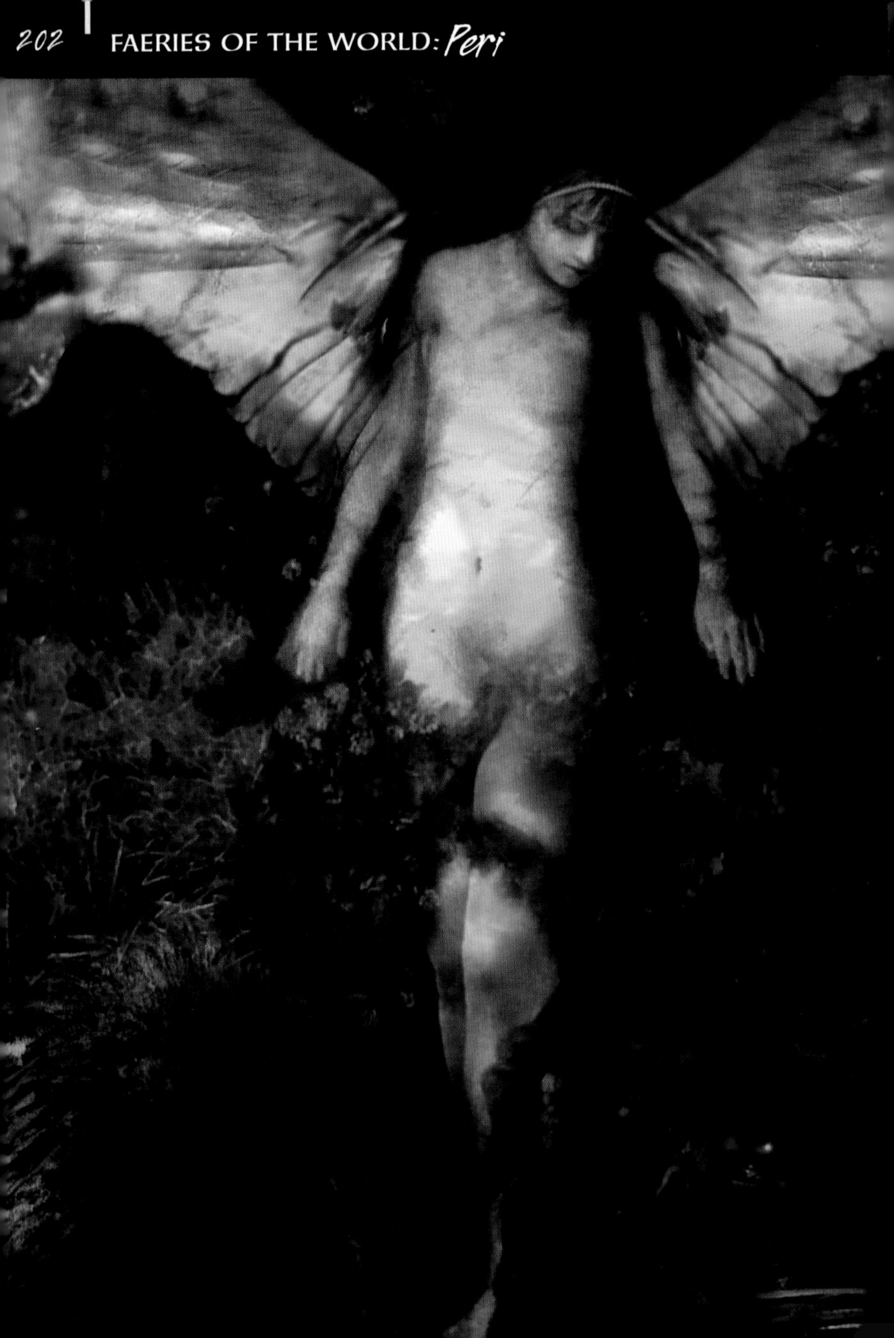

PERI

ACCORDING TO PERSIAN MYTHOLOGY, PERIS ARE A BEAUTIFUL RACE OF FAERIE-LIKE CREATURES DESCENDED FROM FALLEN ANGELS. THEY HAVE BEEN REFUSED ENTRY INTO PARADISE UNTIL THEY HAVE DONE THEIR PENANCE, AND THEREFORE FLY BETWEEN THE HEAVENS AND THE EARTH, OCCASIONALLY VISITING THE MORTAL REALM. WHILE VERY EARLY SOURCES CITE THEM AS EVIL, THEY ARE USUALLY THOUGHT OF AS BENEVOLENT AND TAKE THE FORM OF BEAUTIFUL WOMEN. PERIS UNDERWENT FIERCE PERSECUTION BY A CLASS OF WICKED SPIRITS KNOWN AS DIVS OR DEVS, WHO CRUELLY LOCKED THEM IN IRON CAGES. PERI-BANOU WAS THE NAME OF A BEAUTIFUL FAIRY IN *THE BOOK OF ONE THOUSAND AND ONE NIGHTS*.

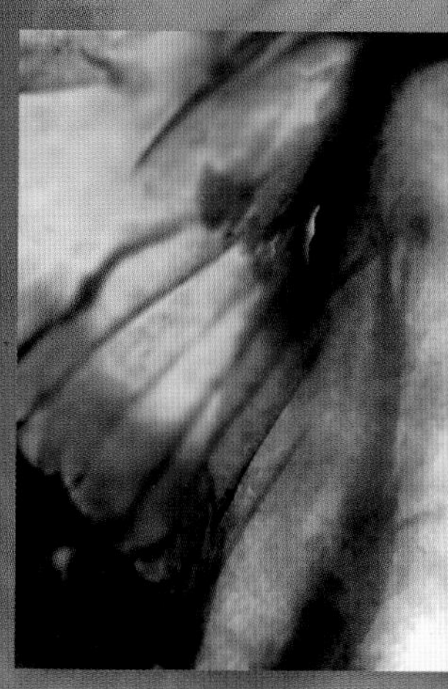

Development

- Grass and foliage can be difficult to paint from scratch so take digital photographs and then try out different filter effects to make them appear as though they are painted.
- Add mystery to your image by including less distinct elements that can only be seen on close inspection. Here, a shadowy wolf lurks in the lower left corner.
- Crop your images to maximize their impact. The wings of this Peri extend past the picture edges, but the closer crop makes for a more dramatic illustration.

Media and Execution

- Pencil, photographs, Photoshop
- The rough composition was sketched out in pencil and then scanned and opened in Photoshop.
- Various photographic elements were dropped in on new layers, including the grass and foliage and the wolf's face. These were then worked up and filtered to create a painterly look. The Opacity of the wolf layer was dropped right back to make it only barely visible.
- The Clone tool was used to paint the grass and foliage on to the figure.
- The image was desaturated and toned with a ghostly green hue.

FURTHER STUDY

The Book of One Thousand and One Nights, Gilbert & Sullivan's opera *Iolanthe*, Thomas Moore (poet) *Lalla-Rookh*.

ART CHRISTOPHER SHY

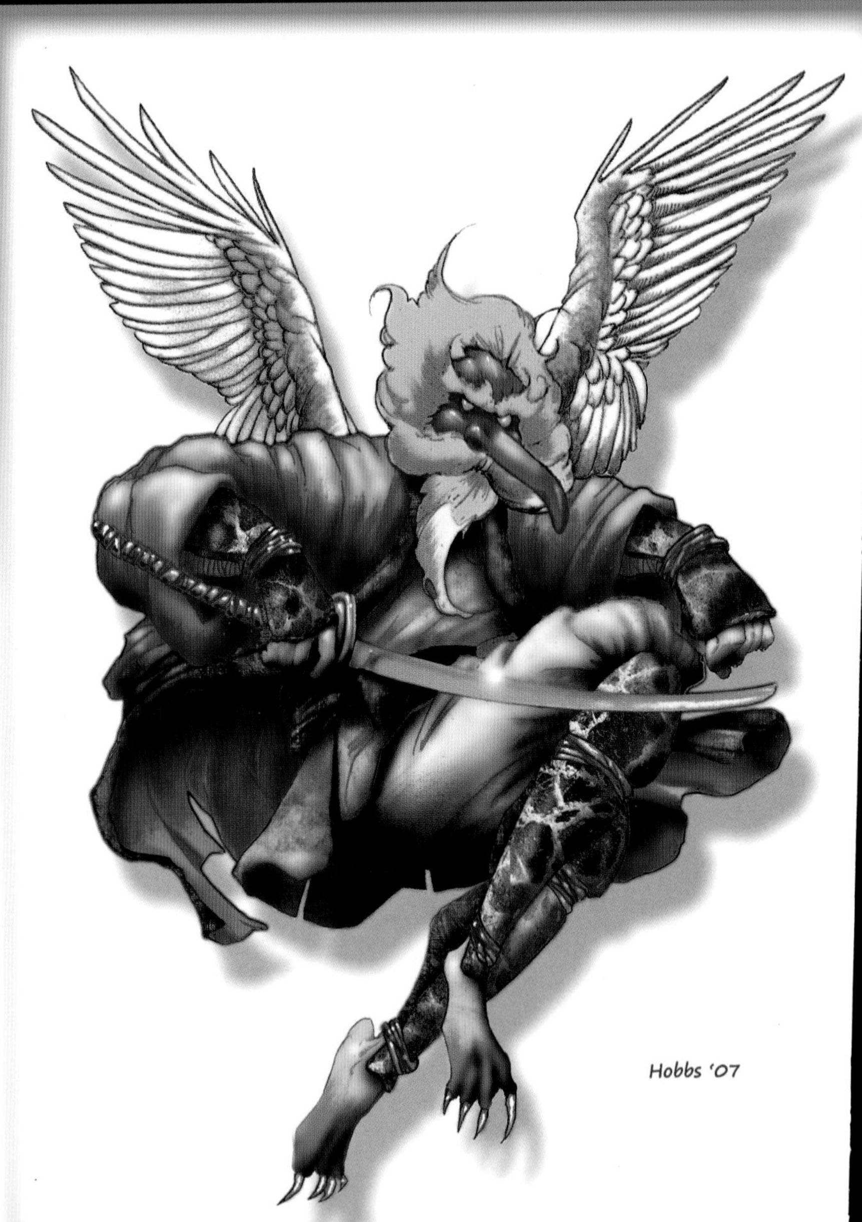
Hobbs '07

Tengu

THESE GOBLIN-LIKE CREATURES COME FROM THE MIST-SHROUDED FORESTS AND MOUNTAINS OF JAPAN AND APPEAR IN TRADITIONAL FOLKLORE, ART, THEATRE AND LITERATURE. THEY ARE DESCRIBED AS MALICIOUS SPIRITS THAT ENJOY CAUSING TROUBLE, KIDNAPPING CHILDREN AND TERRORIZING BUDDHIST PRIESTS. HOWEVER, THEY ARE SKILLED SWORDSMEN AND OFTEN TEACH THEIR SKILLS TO HUMANS. TENGUS HAVE SUPERNATURAL POWERS, AND APPEAR IN THE FORM OF A BIRD OF PREY MIXED WITH SOME HUMAN CHARACTERISTICS. THEY HAVE THE ABILITY TO SHAPE-SHIFT, TO SPEAK WITHOUT MOVING THEIR MOUTHS, TO APPEAR IN DREAMS AND TO MOVE INSTANTLY FROM PLACE TO PLACE WITH THEIR WINGS.

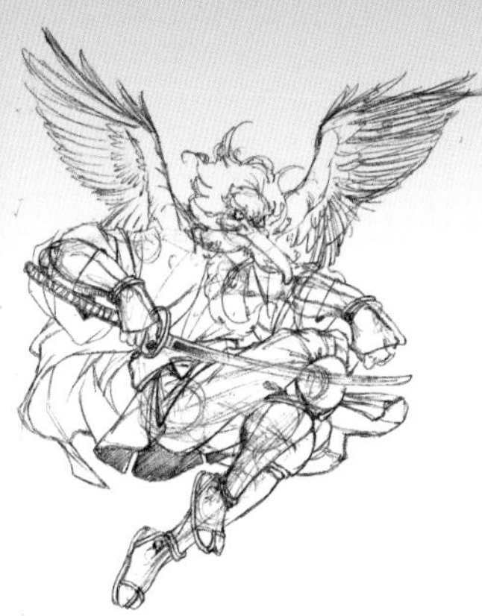

Development

- Use the Internet to research the background to legends, and find images to use as references, such as examples of ancient Japanese painting and sculpture.
- Where animal-like characteristics are needed, such as the beak-like nose, wings and clawed feet, use references along with your imagination to distort them into fantasy.
- Use colour to convey your message – the shade of the Tengu's face suggests aggression, which is further enhanced by his red robe.

Media and Execution

- Pencil, Photoshop
- The idea was roughed out in pencil, and a final pencil drawing was then scanned and opened in Photoshop.
- The image was colourized in translucent layers over the scanned pencil drawing.
- Tones were airbrushed in to build up the forms while some of the clothing elements were filled in with texture patterns from a personal textures library.
- Finally touches of highlights and a drop shadow were added to lift him off the page.

FURTHER STUDY
Japanese folktales, Yoshitsune, Karasu.

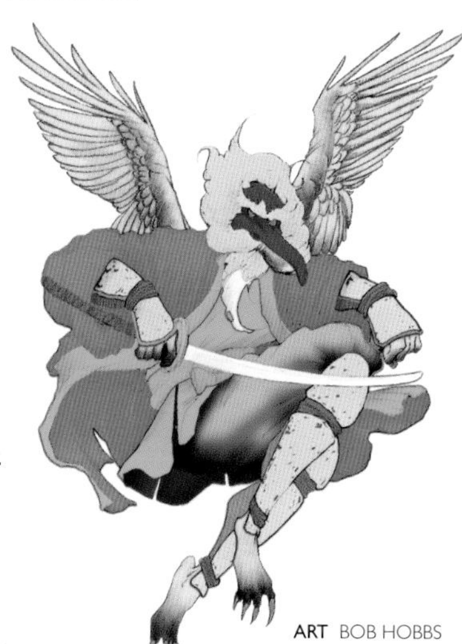

ART BOB HOBBS

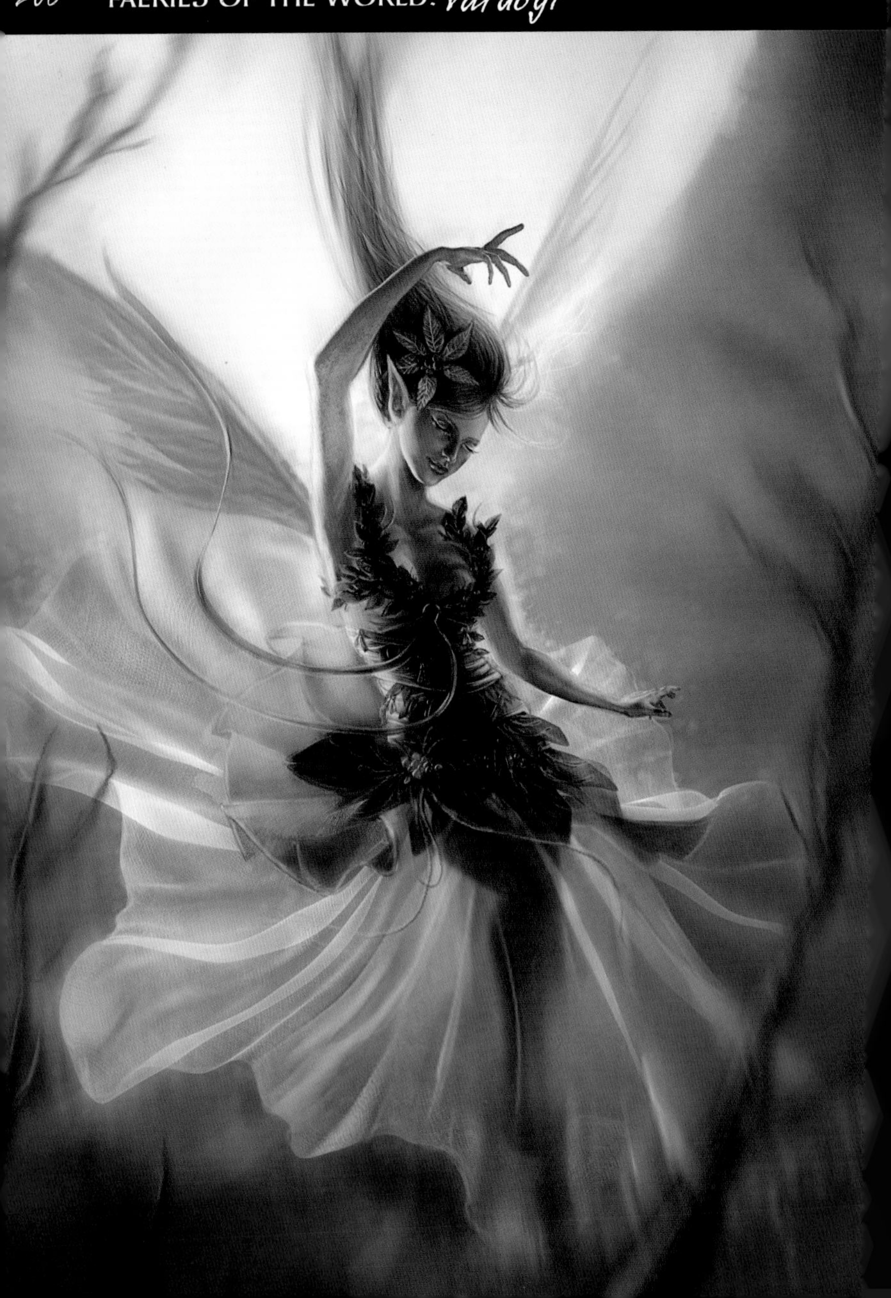

Vardogl

THESE TINY NOCTURNAL FAERIES APPEAR IN ICELANDIC FOLKLORE, AND ALSO IN NORWEGIAN LEGENDS WHERE THEY ARE KNOWN AS THUSSERS. THEY ARE PAINFULLY SHY AND AVOID HUMANS BUT ARE NOT AT ALL MALICIOUS. AT NIGHT THE WHOLE POPULATION OF VARDOGLS AWAKENS TO HONOUR THE MOON GODDESS WITH SONG AND DANCE. THEY ADORE TRADITIONAL SCANDINAVIAN FOLK MUSIC, AND PLAY THE FIDDLE EXCEPTIONALLY WELL. THEY ARE VERY COMMUNITY ORIENTED, AS SHOWN BY THEIR CELEBRATIONS, BUT WILL FLEE IF ANY HUMANS TRY TO JOIN IN.

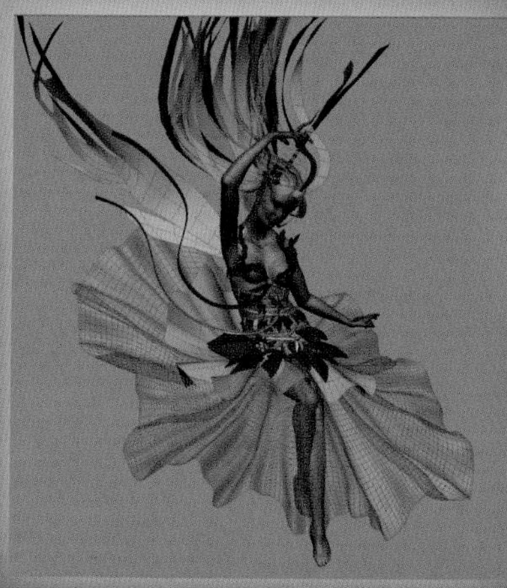

Development

- Apply blur to create a feeling of movement in your images. Here the faerie's hair and vaporous skirts really seem to be moving as she dances.
- Use a cool-toned colour scheme to evoke the feeling of being under moonlight. The blue shades used here also provide a suitably cold feel for this Icelandic spirit.

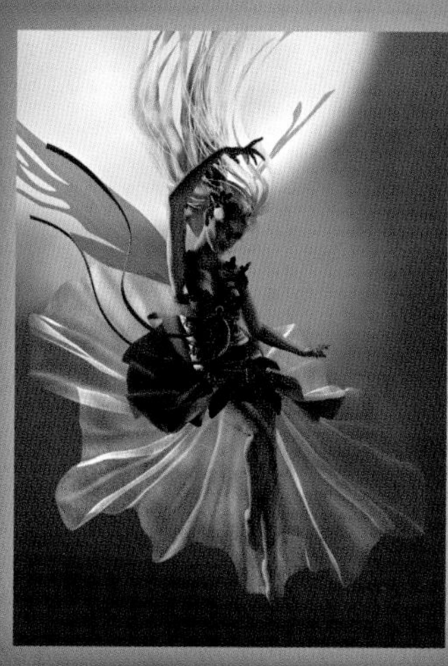

Media and Execution

- Softimage XSI, Mudbox, Photoshop
- The figure was modelled, posed and rendered as a 3D image.
- The background and figure were composited in Photoshop.
- Her proportions were fixed with the Liquify filter, then the image was painted and finally colour corrected.

FURTHER STUDY
Thussers, Scandinavian folklore, Folletti.

ART JULIANNA KOLAKIS

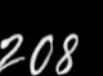

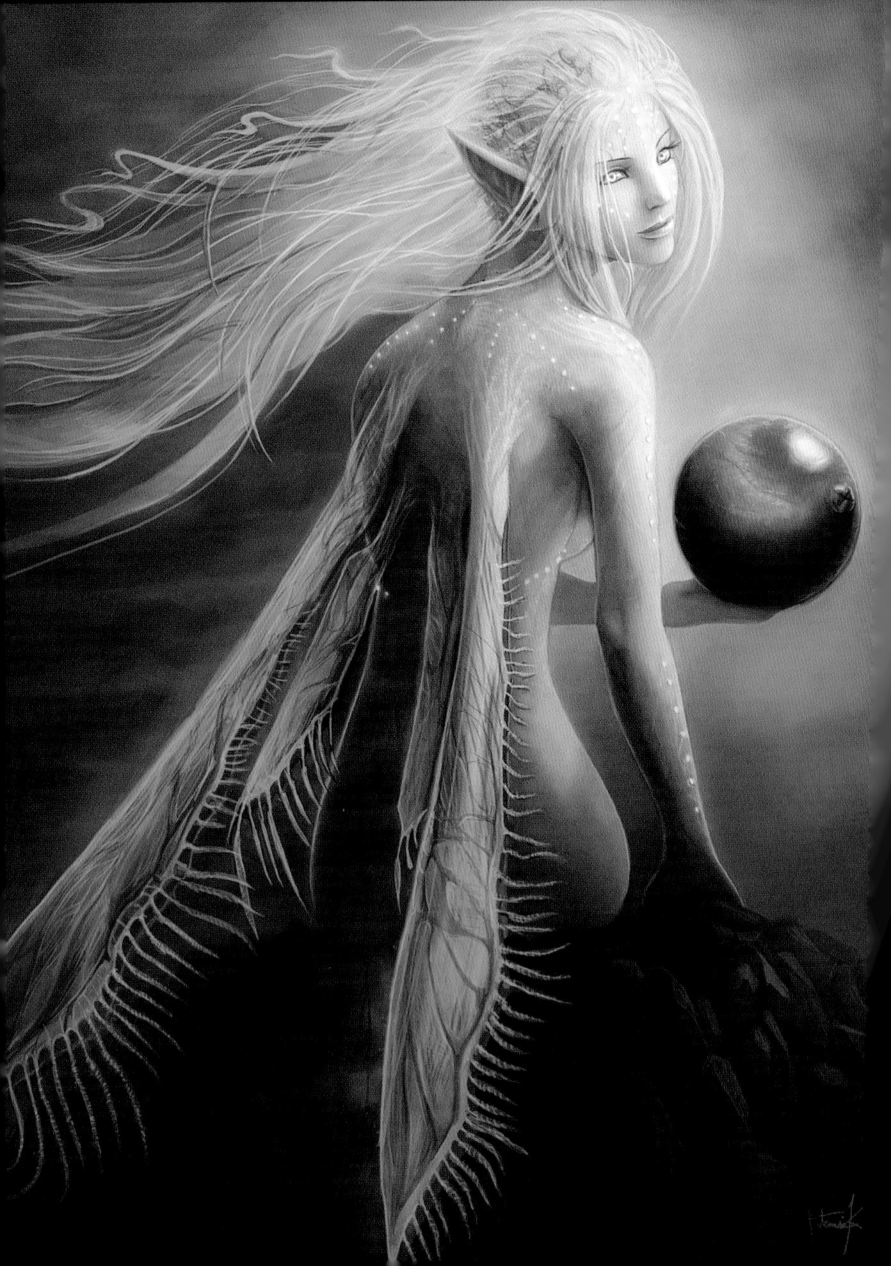

Venusleute

FOUND IN GERMANIC FOLKLORE, VENUSLEUTE – MEANING 'PEOPLE OF VENUS' – ARE EXTREMELY BEAUTIFUL AND TINY SPIRITS THAT LIVE IN THE ROCKS OF ZULOVA, IN THE SUMPERK COUNTY OF THE CZECH REPUBLIC. THESE STRANGE VENUTIAN FAERIES COOK, BATHE AND WASH THEIR CLOTHES IN BOWLS HOLLOWED OUT OF THE ROCKS. THEY ARE BENEVOLENT AND GIVE FOOD AND PROTECTION TO LOST CHILDREN. THEY HAVE THE ABILITY TO BECOME INVISIBLE, MADE POSSIBLE BY THE MAGICAL CAPS OF INVISIBILITY THAT THEY SOMETIMES WEAR.

Development

- Use all the tools at your disposal to capture a spirit's kindness and beauty, including colour palette, lighting scheme and facial expression.
- Use light and shadow to make spheres look truly three-dimensional rather than just flat circles.

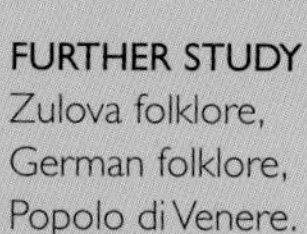

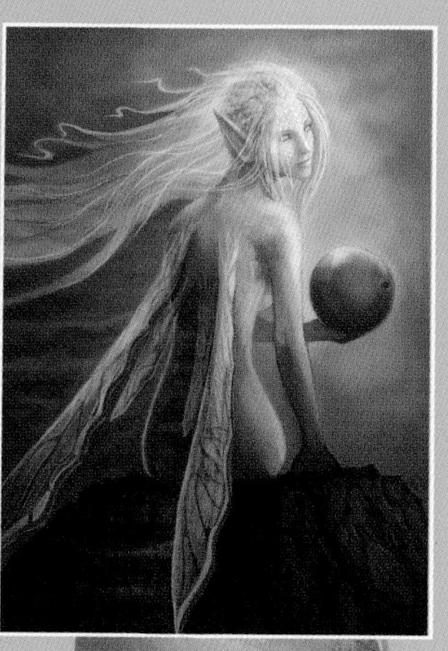

FURTHER STUDY
Zulova folklore,
German folklore,
Popolo di Venere.

Media and Execution

- Painter, Photoshop
- The composition was sketched out digitally in Painter software and then coloured.
- The image was dropped into Photoshop, where the proportions were fixed with the Lasso tool and Liquify filter.
- At the final stage, the image was colour corrected and prepared for print in Photoshop.

ART ARTEMIS KOLAKIS

Weiss Frau

THE CONCEPT OF THE 'WHITE WOMAN' APPEARS IN THE FOLKLORE OF MANY CULTURES WHERE SHE RANGES FROM BEING A BENEVOLENT GODDESS TO A MALICIOUS FIEND. IN GERMANY, SHE IS DESCRIBED AS AN ELF-LIKE CREATURE DESCENDED FROM THE NORSE LEGENDS OF THE WHITE ELVES, THE LJOSALFAR. THEY ARE OFTEN SEEN AS BEAUTIFUL FIGURES SITTING BY STREAMS COMBING THEIR BLONDE HAIR AND IN THIS SENSE THEY ARE RELATED TO THE SCANDINAVIAN KALLRADEN. THE WEISS FRAU IS ALSO SAID TO HAVE EVOLVED FROM ANCIENT BELIEFS IN NATURE SPIRITS, IN WHICH HER WHITE COLOURING REPRESENTS THE LIFE-GIVING POWERS OF SUNLIGHT. IN LATER STORIES SHE IS SAID TO BE A KIND, MATRONLY SPIRIT WHO PROTECTS CHILDREN WHILE THEY SLEEP.

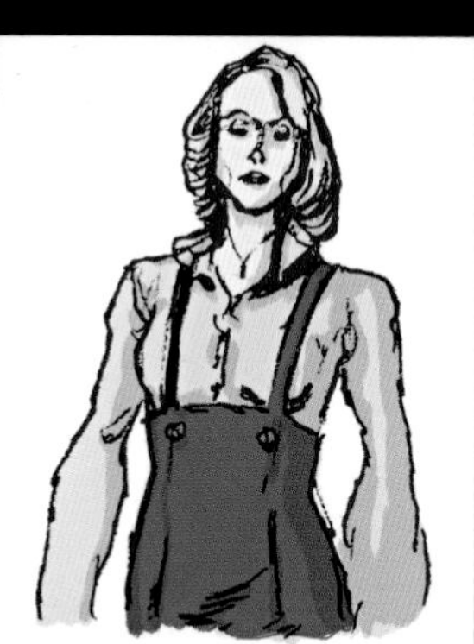

Development

- Emphasize the Germanic origin of the Weiss Frau by choosing a styling that was predominant in Germany during the 1920s and '30s.
- Consider the composition of the image carefully. Here the Weiss Frau is seen from beneath, as this is the angle at which a young child might see the spirit from its cot.
- Research the hairstyles that were popular in the 1930s, such as 'bangs' typical of the period, and the Chinese pageboy look.

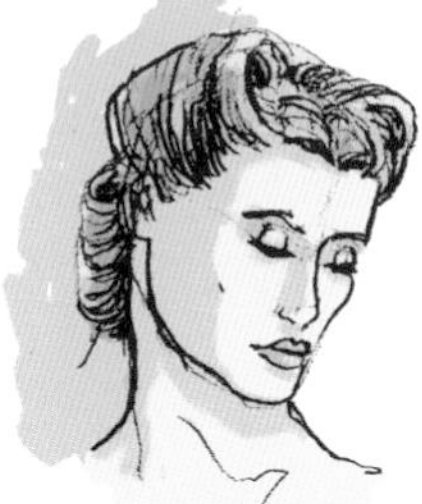

Media and Execution

- Photograph, pencil, Photoshop
- A large, rough brush was used in Photoshop to ensure an impressionistic result.
- The original image was in colour then reduced to black and white to create a more dramatic effect in keeping with the intended 'film noir' look.

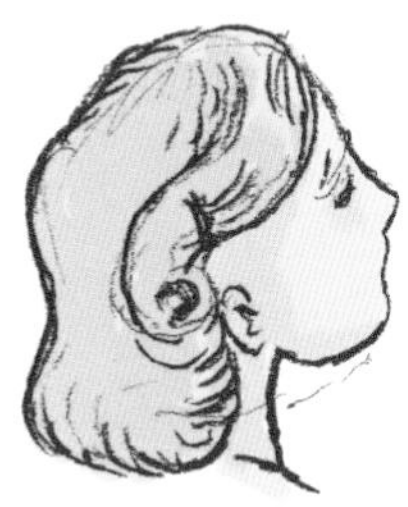

ART FINLAY COWAN
MODEL NICOLA GROVES

FURTHER STUDY
Frau Bercha, Witte Weiven, Dame Blanches, The White Goddess, Holda, White Lady, Midnight Beauty.

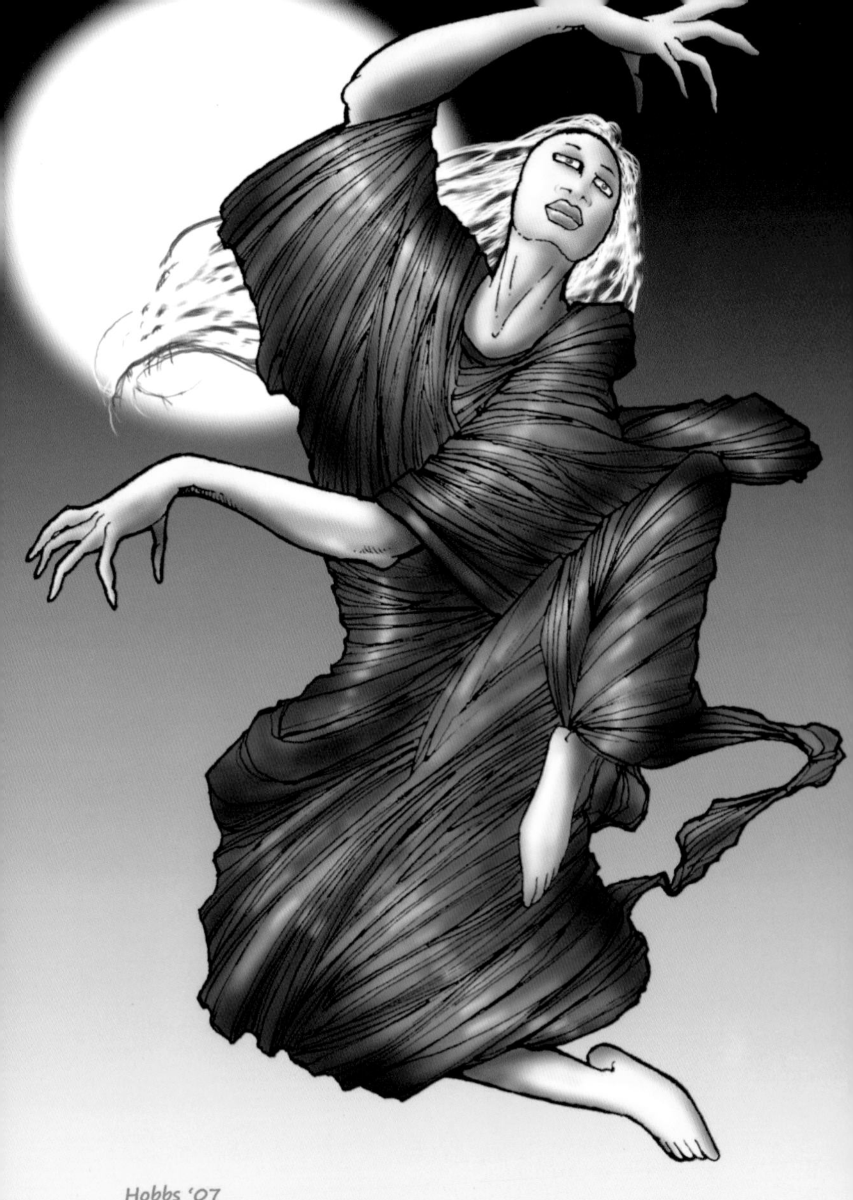
Hobbs '07

Yumbo

NATIVE TO THE FOLKLORE OF THE JOLOF PEOPLE ON GOREE ISLAND IN SENEGAL, WEST AFRICA, YUMBOES ARE SAID TO STAND ONLY ABOUT 2FT (60CM) TALL AND HAVE PEARLY WHITE SKIN WITH SILVER HAIR – A COMMON TRAIT AMONG SUPERNATURAL BEINGS IN AFRICAN MYTH. ANOTHER NAME FOR YUMBOES IS *BAKHNA RAKHNA*, WHICH MEANS 'THE GOOD PEOPLE'. THEY LIVE IN CAVES AND ENJOY FEASTING AND DANCING IN THE MOONLIGHT. THEY DRESS MUCH LIKE THE NATIVE INHABITANTS OF GOREE ISLAND WHEN THEY VENTURE INTO THE VILLAGES TO STEAL CORN FROM THE JOLOF HOUSEWIVES WHO HAVE BEEN POUNDING IT ALL DAY. DESPITE THIS TENDENCY TO STEAL FOOD, YUMBOES DO THEIR OWN FISHING AND OFTEN INVITE HUMANS TO THEIR FEASTS.

Development

- Research the country of origin of your faeries to get descriptions and photos of the people and their clothing.
- Here, a simple loose-fitting variation on the Pang was used. A Pang is an oblong cotton cloth worn by the Jolof people. Normally the Pang covers the whole figure with only the eyes and nose showing, but here it has been altered so you can see the figure's features more clearly.

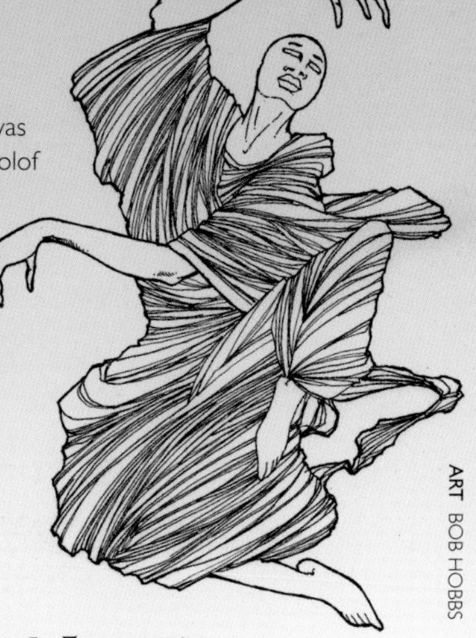

ART BOB HOBBS

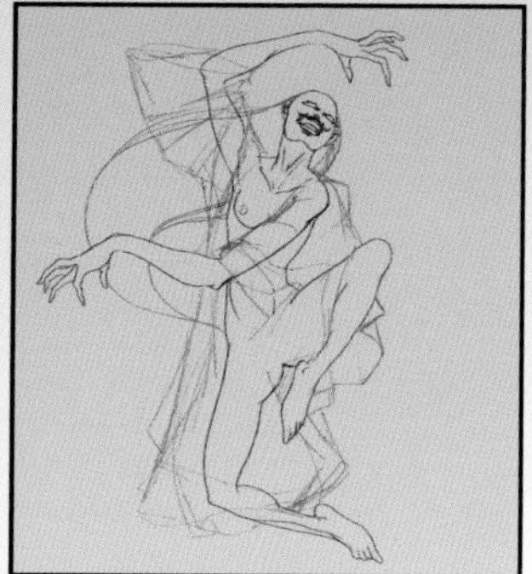

FURTHER STUDY

African folklore, The Jolof, Good Neighbours of Scotland.

Media and Execution

- Pencil, pen and ink, Photoshop
- A quick sketch was undertaken to develop basic stance of the figure, in this case a dancing pose.
- The sketch was refined, rendered in pen and ink then scanned and opened in Photoshop.
- Photoshop tools and effects were used to finalise the colourization.

Bob Hobbs

Bob Hobbs' credits include The Star Trek Concordance, Steve Jackson Games, *Amazing Stories* magazine, Wizards of the Coast and many more over the course of nearly 30 years as a fantasy artist. His work has graced the short stories of over 120 writers, including such well-known names as Ursula K. Le Guin, Larry Niven and Yves Maynard. Bob's work has been on display at the Atrium on Park Avenue in NYC, the RISD Museum and a number of science fiction conventions. Along with David & Charles, Bob is currently illustrating books for Xlibris, DragonPencil, Zumaya, Trafford and MidAmerica publishing houses. His original works are in many private collections including that of actor James Marsters, actress Debbie Rochon and The US House of Representatives.

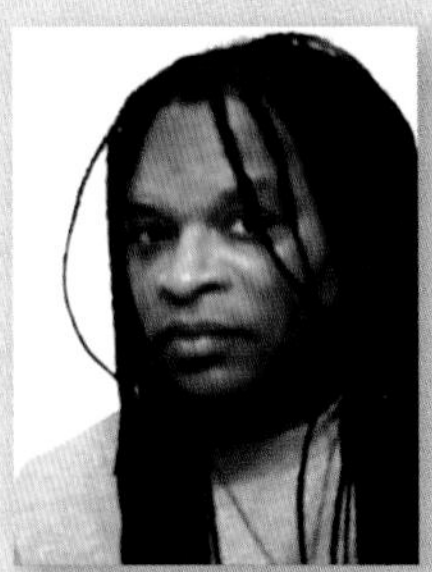

www.geocities.com/hobzart

Bob's thanks

Thanks to everyone at David & Charles Ltd, Finlay Cowan, all the contributing artists and all the lovely ladies who modelled for me. Special thanks to Ame, Freya and The Dark Goddess.

Finlay Cowan

Finlay Cowan is the author and illustrator of four practical art books on fantasy art and mythology published by David & Charles. He has worked as a storyboard artist in the film industry and with album sleeve designer Storm Thorgerson for many years on artwork for Pink Floyd, Muse and others.

He runs his own creative marketing consultancy, Endless Design, in London and lives in rural Italy. In his spare time he produces the *Subway Slim* graphic novels and performs with his band Night Porter.

www.finlaycowan.com
www.subwayslim.com
www.myspace.com/finlaycowan
www.myspace.com/subwayslim

Finlay's thanks

Special thanks to Bob Hobbs for the journey we have shared. Thanks to my models/muses Nicola Groves (Weiss Frau, Miss Underhill), Ida Olsen (Kallraden) and Chiara Giulianini (Syba). Finally, to all at D&C for keeping me off the streets.

Artemis Kolakis

Artemis Kolakis is a freelance concept artist living in Vancouver, Canada.

www.kolakisart.com

Artemis's thanks

Thanks to Diana and George and especially Julianna for this window of opportunity to contribute to such a great book, and to D&C for making it happen.

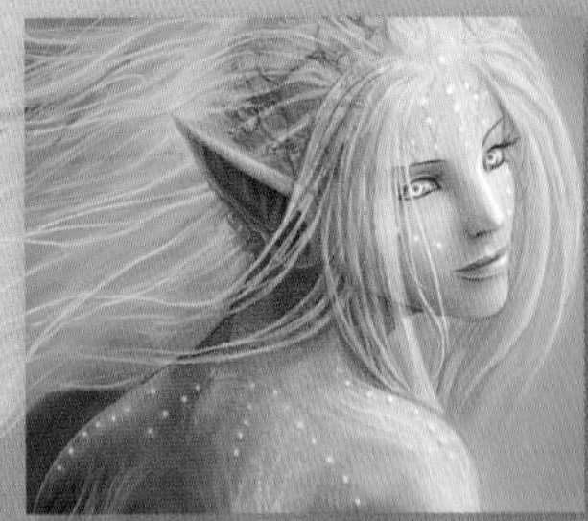

Julianna Kolakis

Julianna Kolakis began her career as a traditional painter, and later a digital painter. She now works in the entrainment industry as a freelance 3D modeller and concept artist.
www.kolakisart.com

Julianna's thanks

I want to thank my family and friends, most importantly my mom, Diana and my brother George for all their love and support. I'd like to thank Artemis for working together with me on this project. I also want to thank everyone at D&C as well as Bob Hobbs for this amazing opportunity.

RK Post

RK Post began his career freelancing for the fantasy gaming industry doing interior illustration for several major game companies. From 1996–2000 he worked in-house for Wizards of the Coast painting cover illustrations for games and novels. He is now a full-time freelance illustrator and 2D and 3D artist for a variety of clients including Gas Powered Games and Sony Online Entertainment.
www.rkpost.net
members.tripod.com/~rkpost

RK's thanks

Thanks to Bob Hobbs and to all the fans.

Christopher Shy

Christopher Shy founded Studio Ronin in 1994, and has illustrated over 1,000 books, as well as graphic novels such as *Silent Leaves*, *Ascend*, and *Good Apollo*. He has also produced work for Marvel comics and has designed stage sets. Recently, Studio Ronin and Christopher Shy completed work on the graphic novel *Pathfinder*, released by Dark Horse Comics, which was made into a film by Marcus Nispel. Studio Ronin handled design on the film in almost every aspect, from simple sword and helmet designs, to miniatures, and customs concepts, as well as the promotional materials.
www.studioronin.com

Chris's thanks

Thanks to the team at Studio Ronin, to Jerry Digby at Dotcommercial and to Bob Hobbs.

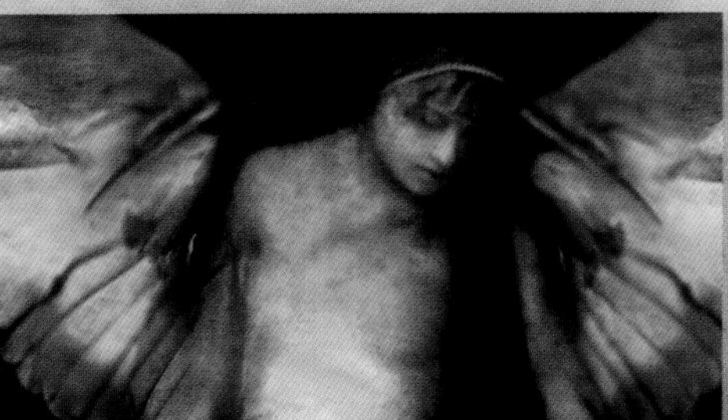

Alain Viesca

Alain Viesca is a professional fantasy artist, animator and storyteller who began his career as an anime artist, marketing his work primarily through fantasy conventions. He now shows his work at international art shows and galleries, sells prints and takes commissions. His home and studio are in Oklahoma City, USA.
www.AlainVArts.com

Alain's thanks

Thanks to Bob Hobbs, Freya Dangerfield and Ame Verso. Thanks also go to Gary Dominguez for assisting my 3D education and Anndrea for being patient and for the unending support.

INDEX

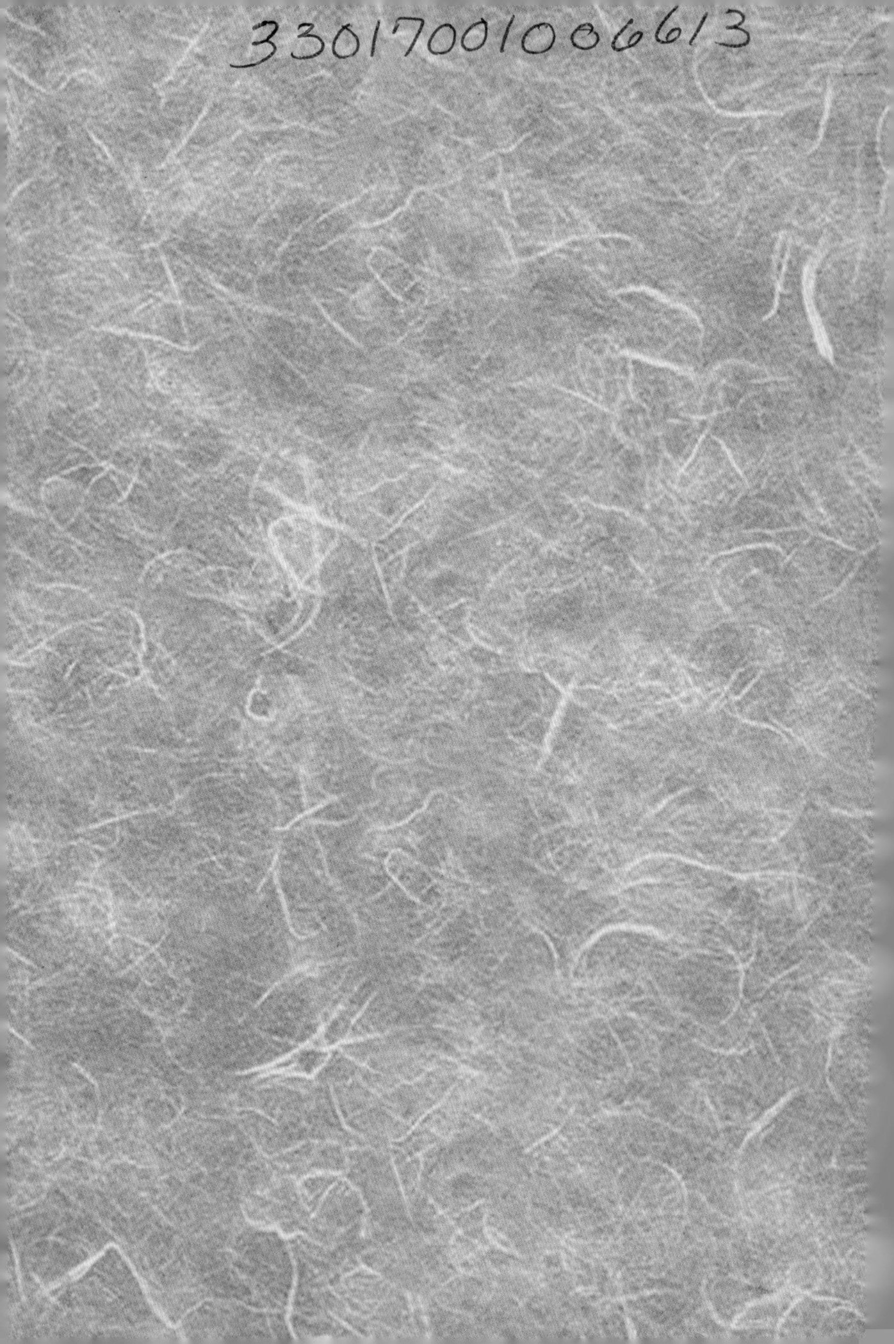